F. Fraser Darling.
1942

Johnson's England

DR. JOHNSON

by JOSEPH NOLLEKENS, R.A.

Lead cast of the original terra-cotta model, Victoria and Albert Museum

Johnson's England

An Account of the *Life & Manners* of his Age

Edited by

A. S. Turberville

Professor of Modern History in the University of Leeds

VOL. II

Clarendon Press Oxford

1933

OXFORD
UNIVERSITY PRESS
AMEN HOUSE, E.C. 4
London Edinburgh Glasgow
Leipzig New York Toronto
Melbourne Capetown Bombay
Calcutta Madras Shanghai
HUMPHREY MILFORD
PUBLISHER TO THE
UNIVERSITY

PRINTED IN GREAT BRITAIN

CONTENTS

VOLUME II

LIST OF ILLUSTRATIONS

VOLUME II

XV

TASTE

By OSBERT SITWELL *and* MARGARET BARTON

It is our happiness to live in the age when our hearts may hope for new advances towards perfection, assisted by the favour of a British King, of a monarch no less judicious to distinguish than powerful to reward; who knows the usefulness of that skill which delights the eye with beauty but not corrupts the manners by unlawful passions; and which has been hitherto learned in foreign countries for want of sufficient encouragement in our own.

Address to his Majesty of the Painters, Sculptors, and Architects, 1760.

I am persuaded that to be a virtuoso (so far as befits a gentleman) is a higher step towards the becoming a man of virtue and good sense than the being what in this age we call a scholar. For even rude nature itself in its primitive simplicity is a better guide to judgment than improved sophistry and pedantic learning. *Lord Shaftesbury* (1671–1731).

THE scene against which we discover the bulky figure of Dr. Johnson poised so delightfully and characteristically for a lifetime is one secure, placid, yet full of incident. A thousand different, and often contradictory, eddies of taste were at work under the general flow of time, shifting and dissolving its details and, like so many conjurors, substituting unexpectedly one form of chair and table for another, altering the rich landscape itself of England, creating, it may be, an elegant wilderness or a darkling tarn where had stood a brobdingnagian terrace or an Elizabethan walled garden, and replacing the gazebo at its angle with a turreted pavilion from China or a Gothic greenhouse. Even the stuffs and materials, the dresses of the women, had patterns blown upon them now from one quarter of the globe, now from another; China and ancient Greece, Hindustan, and Turkey, all contributed to the delicious confusion. None the less, the general effect that framed it in was staid and solid, though in various corners of our green land were to be detected strange exotics and anachronisms; pagodas and pineapples and palm trees, negro pages and stretches of water on which floated gondolas and black swans, pagan temples, mausoleums, artificial ruins, and carefully gaping grottoes, in which a well-remunerated anchorite conducted in public a life of celibacy and abnegation during half the year. But the actual architectural screen provided for the hearty movement of the performers was a sober, Palladian one.

Notwithstanding, as vigour gave way to grace, and grace to phantasy, it is possible, perhaps, to generalize and to say that the Doctor was born in a baroque age, lived through the rococo one, and died at the beginning of the romantic period; for though the two first-named movements did not, owing to the classical and yet protestant heart of our people, shape our architecture as elsewhere in Europe, they undoubtedly did affect everything else from furniture to morals.

Usually in any discussion of these systems—and recently there have been several—the meaning and derivation of the words themselves, so teasingly similar, is considered with gravity and expounded with learning; but to us the words 'baroque' and 'rococo' seem to have but little importance, being merely in their origin, like the description 'Gothic', terms of abuse invented for an ingenious and beautiful style of architecture by those out of sympathy with it. The labels in no way help toward a differentiation: yet no one with a sense of value can confuse the two: they are as easy to instance as difficult to define. . . . But various points can perhaps be stated, though with the certainty that every architect will condemn them; that baroque was often more of an ecclesiastical style than a domestic one, and that, therefore, for the building of churches it endured until much later than most people will admit; that baroque is a language of large buildings, and rococo of small ones; that cathedrals and palaces yet continued to be baroque while the pavilions in the gardens were rococo; that the aim of baroque is to impress and to stun the beholder, the aim of rococo to surprise him into delight; that the outside of a church may be baroque and its interior decoration be rococo; that baroque decoration is applied and rococo integral; that baroque has a quality of movement and painting, while rococo has grace and often quietness; that Blenheim Palace is one of the few baroque buildings in England, while the pavilions in the neighbourhood of Mrs. Thrale's house in Streatham and the grottoes on the river were rococo . . . and that the romantic which was to follow, though lacking a style, inherited many qualities of the two ages that had preceded it.

During the lifetime of Dr. Johnson, the arts were flowering with an insistence and robustness that in England had hitherto only been associated with poetry and the drama; but, as usual, it was the conviction of the best younger minds of the time, and the most aesthetically inclined, that though never before had taste and the arts it called forth been so pure and gracious, never, on the other hand, had they been so debased as in the previous generation; an opinion which, so far as it existed, the succeeding generation first reversed and then reciprocated. And indeed, as always in an age of intense national development, there were countless anomalies of taste: and very often the patron decried a particular new tendency of an art as ill-suited to the genius of the race, which was, on the other hand, within a few years to triumph precisely in that aspect of it.

Since King Charles I had paid the penalty of his connoisseurship royal patrons had been few; but with the first Hanoverian sovereign, beneath whose bewigged shadow the infant Doctor attained to the full speech of infancy, the darkness deepened. 'Under George I', wrote Horace Walpole, some half a century later, 'the arts sank to their lowest ebb'; yet, with George II, in whose martial reign Johnson reached his prime, it seemed to many observers that they fell lower still. Nevertheless, whatever may have been thought, it was not the arts themselves, but royal patronage, which had collapsed, and Pope in the opening lines of *The Dunciad* directs us to the truth when, invoking Dullness, 'the mighty mother', he thunders:

> You by whose care, in vain decried and curst,
> Still Dunce the second reigns like Dunce the first.

For it must be admitted that the first two Hanoverian kings, albeit they displayed that same love of music which for so long distinguished the Guelphs, were singularly obtuse in matters artistic and literary.

George II, our last soldier monarch, but prototype in his outlook of many subsequent military commanders, grew, it was said, really angry at the sight of a book: historically, he became no less exasperated at the glimpse of a drawing. Unfortunately Hogarth had chosen to dedicate to him his print, 'The March to Finchley'; and this satirical work was accordingly sent to St. James's Palace to obtain the royal sanction. The King examined it severely and demanded, 'Pray, who is this Hogarth?'... 'A Painter, Your Majesty.'...

'I hate bainting and boetry,' replied the enlightened Prince, 'neither the one nor the other ever did any good. Does the fellow mean to laugh at my Guards?'... 'The picture, an'it please Your Majesty, must undoubtedly be considered a burlesque.'... 'What!' he shouted, 'a bainter burlesque a soldier! He deserves to be picketed for his insolence! Take his trumpery out of my sight!' Mortified at this reception of his work, Hogarth erased the inscription to the hero of Dettingen and dedicated the print instead to the King of Prussia.

Perhaps, then, it was as well that the patronage of art no longer lay solely with the monarchy. Just as the political power had been gradually wrested from the hands of the kings during the seventeenth century, so had the power, or obligation, of patronage—which so often accompanies it—been assumed by the English nobility and the wealthy families from which this was so continually recruited. But though by the time Johnson was born patronage was aristocratic, yet it still bore the imprint of dead kings.

Whether owing to some unconjectured and innate vanity in the English character, or merely to a puritan distrust of art except in its more concrete expressions, portraiture had ever, historically, been the manifestation of it which, since the Reformation, the English patron had favoured. To saints, angels, and martyrs, pagan deities and mythological heroes, he paid but little attention: his own face, and those of his numerous progeny, were all that he considered necessary, in the way of beauty, to perpetuate for the applause of an astonished posterity. This tendency had been further encouraged by the generous patronage accorded to Vandyke by Charles I. Thus portraiture had become established as the one English manifestation of pictorial art and long remained its chief duty and only remunerative branch. Indeed from the day of Vandyke onward, money, much money, and not a little fame, could be earned by the painter who adopted it as his whole profession.

Under Kneller and Hudson, the quality of the goods—for such they had become—began to show a deterioration. Portraits by Kneller bore little resemblance to any particular sitter, though they all of them betrayed a somewhat indefinite likeness to a type, the idealized English lady and gentleman of the period. Their predominant note, therefore, was one of vague flattery. Richardson's *Theory of Painting* gives us an example of how far it could be carried by the artist, when he relates how the Duke of Hamilton called on the artist one day, to see the picture, lest there was some need of alteration before it was delivered to him.

The Duke looked a great while at it, said nothing: serious—went to the glass and looked at himself, returned to the picture; went back to the glass—rather out of humour. Sir Godfrey was uneasy, piqued—asked with some warmth if His Grace disliked the picture. 'Zounds,' said he, 'when I look in the glass I am a poltroon, when I look there I am a man of quality.' And then took out his pocket book, and presented him with a bank bill. 'No, my Lord,' said Sir Godfrey, 'By God, I will not receive more than one for the same picture; you have overpaid it already!'[1]

This sentiment of the Duke was modest but, as a rule, the painter was absolutely compelled to flatter, for vanity was characteristic of the age, as perhaps of every epoch of vigour and expansion; and the personal conceit of the sitter was only equalled by the technical conceit of the artist. Thus Jervas—who gave lessons in painting to Pope—on finishing a copy of a Titian, glanced complacently from one to the other and then observed, 'Poor little Tit! How he would stare!'

But though a painter might read such merit into his own work, any objective symptom of it would have speedily been discouraged by his clients; for more was not required of art than to be a pleasant and impersonal commodity. In no way was it considered as an individual expression. Further, if the work of any artist was easy to identify, because of its style, content, or technique, this was counted a defect. In consequence, Hogarth was despised and the pictures of Gainsborough had fewer supporters than those of Sir Joshua Reynolds among contemporary critics, because of the 'affected style of their handling', or, in other words, by reason of their greater originality and loveliness.

The reason of that superiority which we now see in the portraits by Gainsborough over those of all other artists of his period, is undoubtedly to be sought in the fact that he employed no assistants, like Hogarth before him, but unlike Sir Joshua; who, notwithstanding, is so delightful a portraitist

[1] Jonathan Richardson, *Works* (1773), p. 114 *n*.

that he almost reconciles us to a method of wholesale production, for which, if moderately and wisely indulged, there may be a certain warrant. Further, this healthy spirit of co-operation was not by any means limited to portraiture, but was present in every form of pictorial art; Lambert never painted the figures in his landscapes, nor Hayman the background to his conversation-pieces; Canaletto frequently painted the buildings which show through Zuccarelli's feathery trees; and a specialist always travelled with Tiepolo, to evoke for him the architectural splendours among which stroll his dwarfs, greyhounds, and plumed figures.

Hogarth was perhaps the only English painter of this period whose talent and accomplishment were in no manner dependent on such props. Yet himself as a portrait-painter never really attained to favour: nor need this astonish us, for, as we have suggested, the gentry of the eighteenth century expected above all to be flattered. Not theirs was the 'Paint me with all my warts' attitude characteristic of periods both earlier and later; the wise portrait-painter understood his obligation. Thus, when Sir Joshua was an unknown young man in Rome, he executed a few caricature groups,[1] spirited and grotesque, but, we are told, he soon abandoned this medium of his own accord, 'since it must corrupt his taste as a portrait painter, whose duty it becomes to aim at discovering the perfections only of those whom he is to represent'[2]. This being, from the point of view of the patron, the correct posture for the artist to adopt, it is little marvel, then, that sitters to Hogarth were often enraged when they contemplated his lively versions of their appearance. Indeed, sometimes they refused to pay him for such vile libels, as they naturally conceived them to be. In consequence we discover this great artist, the father of English painting, and a man of the strongest and most national character, obliged to address to one of his unwise clients, a nobleman, the following intimidating letter:

Mr. Hogarth's dutiful respects to Lord . . . . Finding that he does not mean to have the picture which was drawn for him, he is informed

[1] Now in the Dublin Gallery. They are somewhat in the style of Thomas Patch, who worked in Florence, and were undoubtedly influenced as well by the once famous and now neglected Ghezzi, who has left many memorials of his art in Rome.

[2] Northcote, *Life of Reynolds* (1813–15), vol. i, p. 46.

TAIL-PIECE TO THE CATALOGUE OF THE SOCIETY OF ARTISTS, 1761

Engraved by W. Hogarth

again of Mr. Hogarth's necessity for the money. If, therefore, his lordship does not send for it, in three days it will be disposed of, with the addition of a tail, and some other little appendages, to Mr. Hare, the wild beast man; Mr. Hogarth having given that gentleman a conditional promise of it for an exhibition on his lordship's refusal.

The sum was paid.

To a later age, however, it remains surprising that Hogarth's other paintings were no more appreciated than his portraits. In illustration of this we may mention that the famous set of six pictures, known as 'Marriage à la Mode',[1] was sold in 1750 for only 120 guineas, from which 24 guineas must be deducted for the cost of their frames. The experts failed him. Fuseli called his drawings 'the chronicle of scandal and the history-book of the vulgar', while Walpole dismisses him as a painter who possessed 'slender merit'. . . . Perhaps, unknown to themselves, the wide popularity of his engravings, which must at that time have made them seem hackneyed, prejudiced the aesthetic judgement of the *cognoscenti*. 'The whole nation', wrote the Abbé Le Blanc, 'has been infected (by them) as one of the most happy productions of the age. I have not seen a house of note without these moral prints.' And Dr. Johnson must continually have faced them in other houses which he visited, as well as in that of Mrs. Thrale, where 'amongst the numerous prints pasted on the walls of the dining-room . . . was Hogarth's "Midnight Conversation"'.

And here, after considering the ironic and satiric side of his genius, which, since it interpreted a side of the English character, was to be perpetuated and carried on for a century and a half, though in water-colour and charcoal rather than in oils, by Rowlandson, and a host of lesser but yet distinguished artists, such as Bunbury, Gillray, and the Cruikshanks, we may pause to note how difficult it is to decide where patronage hinders, where aids, the arts. Some of its best results are accidental. Thus if, as we have seen, the English patron had always, in the beginning influenced by religious principle or prejudice, and subsequently by the tradition it had inaugurated, favoured portraiture at the expense of every other form of art, and had imposed it as the sole means of livelihood upon the artist, the effects of his predilection were unforeseen: since finally it caused to flourish

[1] Now in the Tate Gallery.

the intensely patron-free arts of caricature and landscape. Caricature, and the kindred art of ironical drawing, was a defiant, if often subconscious reply to the patron, as though the artist were to shout back to him, 'Well, if you want your blessed likeness, here it is. . . . If you really want people to know what your family looks like, and the sort of life it leads, here goes!': while the origin of English landscape-painting is to be traced, we apprehend, to another secret and more precious rebellion; this time on the part of the lyrical soul of the artist, to which was denied any official opportunity of expression. Portraiture constituted, as it were, the journalism of painting, enabled the painter to support himself if he were fortunate; but the true artist could not live by earning money alone and the covert poetry in which he indulged, not merely for his own amusement, but to replenish the wells of his own inner existence and in this manner to save his soul alive, was the interpretation of landscape. Yet few patrons ever for a moment considered the buying of such a canvas—so that for long it remained a clandestine pleasure, almost a vice: to such an extent that, after his death, Gainsborough's house was found stacked with unpurchased landscapes.

The reason that they had remained unsold, although the world acknowledged Gainsborough to be a great master, was the convention, the truth of which the patrons had guaranteed for themselves through the manner of their patronage, that the English painter could only achieve distinction in portraiture; a convention which it took time to break down. Naturally, such a view of English art was sedulously encouraged abroad, where in time it was exploited by a whole series of writers, including Du Bos, Montesquieu, and Winckelmann, who among them actually succeeded in inventing a theory to account for this presumed inferiority; that our climate was inimical to every manifestation of art except portraiture, and that therefore nothing else of any pictorial virtue could ever proceed from this country. Foreign artists, or more often the dealers, reaped the benefit: for the English were becoming rich, and, beyond having their likeness registered by a 'face-painter' at home, they spent their money largely on Italian and Dutch pictures, though, for the most part, these were old masters. They preferred their painter dead; but if alive he must not be an Englishman. Gradually, toward the end of the eighteenth century, this attitude improved, but even as late as 1766 the following incident occurred to sum it up. West had executed a historical composition, which, as being the first English effort of its kind, had aroused exceptional interest. So much was it talked of, that noblemen who, for one reason or another, could not themselves go to inspect it, asked permission for it to be brought to their houses. The artist's servants earned £30 in tips for showing it, yet not a single visitor so much as inquired its price. At last one rich and enthusiastic admirer was asked outright why, if he liked the work so much, he did not purchase it? 'What could I do, if I had it?' he replied. 'You surely would not have me hang up a modern English picture in my house unless it was a portrait?'[1]

There was, of course, besides the face-painters proper, a whole tribe of journeymen painters, who spent the year riding all over the land, from country-house to country-house, and country-town to country-town, offering their services to those of the gentry who were too poor, or too conservative, to spend any part of the year in London. These artists were, in fact, tradesmen; and most of them were shocking daubers, though sometimes the monotony of their work is redeemed for us by an astonishing naivety.

And then, too, there were numerous artists who devoted their lives to portraying those animals in which the squires delighted: dogs and horses. They also rode from house to house, but their superiority over the journeyman painter of human beings is nearly always very marked; and in this direction, indeed, we produced the finest and most famous painters of their kind in Europe. But for the most part those artists living during the first half of the century who were not employed in the actual portrait industry or in that other system of manufacture, the copying of old masters—which we discuss shortly—were forced to earn their bread in more humble allied trades. Sometimes they worked as draughtsmen to the booksellers and, in consequence of the talent they showed, an increase of magnificence, as well as an improvement in the quality of the drawings, was continually discernible in illustrated books throughout the

[1] In after years West was appointed historical painter to King George III and found many patrons. Far harder was the case of Richard Wilson, who died in penury.

century.[1] And one of the best of these, an exquisite piece of rococo work, with a strong Gothic influence, is an edition of Gray's poems illustrated by Bentley and published in 1753. Here a full-page engraving shows us an Eton College Chapel where naked nymphs and mermaids leap like fish from the waters of the Thames flowing beside it, while, again, a very fine drawing of a cat peering into a bowl of goldfish illustrates that ode the unmanly tenderness of which earned for him Dr. Johnson's censure.

Other artists were engaged in painting scenery for the theatres. Loutherbourg, who came to England in 1771, earned 500 pounds per annum from Drury Lane, and Lambert ruled over the stage world at Covent Garden.[2]

Further, in the London of that epoch, as in the Moscow and Constantinople of yesterday, every inn or place of business displayed over its door a board, which indicated more or less plainly to the eyes of all those who could not read the nature of the trade pursued within; and many a proud and promising young artist, who at the moment could not find a patron, was obliged for a time to adopt the painting of these signs as his profession, while others there were who passed their lives in it. 'Our streets', wrote Addison, in 1711, 'are filled with Blue Boars, Black Swans and Red Lions not to mention Flying Pigs and Hogs in Armour, with many other creatures more extraordinary than any in the deserts of Africa.'[3] This fabulous colony of the upper air attracted much attention, and continued to do so until nearly the end of Dr. Johnson's lifetime, although its existence flouted a law passed for paving the streets and removing 'the signs and other obstructions.' ... One famous sign, hanging outside a public house in Drury Lane, was of so striking a nature that every day crowds of country-people could be seen assembled there, vacantly staring at it for hours. It consisted of a full-length picture of Shakespeare and was suspended in an elaborate carved and gilded frame from some rich ironwork.[4]

[1] Between the years 1724 and 1731 appeared Rapin's *History of England*, with engravings by Vertue; the success of which volumes inspired Hogarth to publish his prints.

[2] See *infra*, pp. 185–6.

[3] *Spectator*, vol. i, No. 28.

[4] This sign was taken down in 1775, when the Act was passed, and could be seen thereafter in the window of a pawnbroker's shop in Lower Grosvenor Street, where it remained until it rotted away.

THE CAT AND THE GOLDFISHES

From the engraving by R. Bentley

Another technical application of their medium, out of which artists could contrive a living, lay in the painting of coaches. And indeed no artist need have considered this derogatory to his talent or calling, for many of the best decorative painters of the period were engaged in it. Throughout the eighteenth century, coaches, ever influenced in their shape and style by the current aesthetic theory of the decade, were of an unparalleled if varying beauty; but those of the first half of the century were of a more architectural order, while those of the second half relied more on painting for their effect.

To-day the sole example with which we are familiar in this country is the state coach of the Royal Family; a wonderful cage of gold and glass, dragging behind it a load of deities and mythological creatures, Neptunes and mermaids, as well as liveried footmen, and with its panels finely painted by Cipriani. But, in the time of which we are writing, there existed thousands of coaches of an almost equal grandeur, and it is impossible to exaggerate the loveliness added to everyday life by the spectacle of them.

There were, then, several if somewhat irregular ways, in addition to portraiture, by which the artist, if he were willing, could earn an income. Moreover, as the century advanced, commissions for decorative work became more numerous. Money was plentiful, and patronage was extending. All over Britain the country gentlemen were rebuilding their homes, abandoning Gothic towers on hill-tops and creating for themselves damp but commodious mansions in the valleys.

And the interiors of these were at least becoming less uncomfortable, if much more crowded. In the first decades of the century a room was not treated as a background for pictures, but was allowed instead to achieve an architectural dignity and unity. The walls of drawing-room or great parlour were panelled, or hung with tapestries, velvets, and embroideries. Only paintings of a superficially decorative quality, classified as furniture-pieces and specially executed to fill the spaces over door or chimney, were admitted. (These usually were the concoctions of inferior artists, who had been more than willing to run up a view of a temple or two among green trees, a lawn and a broken statue, for forty or fifty shillings.) Painted ceilings, too, were in demand, but these translated heavens, full of tumbling, or, as it might be, shivering deities, must be conjured up by the hand of a foreign, if possible an Italian, artist, for such imaginings were beyond the English mind: while, with the growing passion for antique sculpture, *grisaille* was sometimes required of the artist as well; and in this the French painters excelled. Thus, once again, the foreigner scored, since comparatively high prices were paid for this kind of decorative work.[1] Even then, of course, the dining-room was hung with family portraits; but otherwise it was held that pictures should, together with antiques, now purchased in increasing numbers, and with those other enigmatic objects termed 'curios', be placed in the gallery.

Thus in the middle decades of the eighteenth century, when pictures began to spread over the walls of drawing-room and boudoir, it was natural enough that they should be still selected on the same old principle; be bought not for their own sakes, but for their effect in a room. And this, no doubt, is what Richardson intended to signify, when he made the much-quoted remark that 'many are accustomed to look at pictures as though at a piece of rich hangings'. Those which did not please at first sight, or required a closer examination, were regarded as being more suited to the 'Curio Cabinet' than to the walls of a living-room. They were, in fact, chosen primarily for their decorative appeal, and perhaps it was the presence of this quality in the works of Carlo Dolci, Guido Reni, and the Caracci which caused them to be so eagerly sought after. Notwithstanding, this would never have been admitted, for the practice, as so often, was in direct opposition to the aesthetic theory of the time.

So great had been the inflow of old and foreign pictures, that in 1737, long before it had reached its greatest dimensions, a writer in the *London Magazine* in whose language people thought they could detect—we fancy without much injustice—something of the simple patriotism and vigour of Hogarth, declared: 'The picture-jobbers from abroad are always ready to raise a great cry in the prints whenever they think their craft is in danger; and indeed it is their interest to depreciate every English work, as hurtful to their

[1] Clermont, for example, an obscure French artist, received £500 for painting a staircase.

trade, of continually importing shiploads of dead Christs, Holy Families, Madonnas, and other dismal dark subjects . . . on which they scrawl the terrible cramp names of some Italian masters.'[1] Certainly the rule still held good that the painter (like the poet of to-day) was better dead; but, if alive, must be a foreigner—more than that, a foreigner residing and working abroad. Even Canaletto is stated by some writers—though their information was probably erroneous—to have prospered to a greater extent in Venice than when he came to reside in London, in spite of his three ducal patrons, Beaufort, Northumberland, and Richmond; while Vershovis, an exquisite worker in ivory, was, according to Horace Walpole, so much patronized by the English visitors to Rome that he decided to live in England; where he starved. . . . If, then, the artist had the misfortune to be at the same time English and alive, and had no wish to paint portraits, nor to engage himself in painting signs or the panels of coaches, he must occupy himself with buying, restoring and, still more, copying the works of the dead: such was the duty of the living. No artist, however gifted, was deemed to be above such employment; while if he was unfortunate enough never to achieve distinction, he could spend an embittered lifetime, still hoping; comforting himself, even though he was now too old for any original effort, with the reflection that copying was the recognized training for that creative work which one day he intended to attempt in circumstances of peace and plenty.

A copy of a picture fulfilled two chief purposes. To the simple art-lover, it was equivalent to the photograph of to-day, a reminder of beauty glimpsed; to the boaster, to him proud of possessions, it shone like a false jewel; for some owners seemed indifferent whether their pictures were original or not, so long as they presented to the uninitiated the illusion of a costly collection. In illustration of this, we have the surprise of a traveller in England, who, writing in 1763, leaves us an account of Lord Tilney's splendid house at Wanstead; where a most imposing gallery of old masters proved on closer examination to be, one and all, obvious and badly executed reproductions.

Sometimes again, the owner himself was ignorant and believed in the indisputable authenticity of his property;

[1] *London Magazine*, July 1737, p. 385.

resenting any doubt of it, and appearing, indeed, to regard it almost in the same light as he would have viewed an insinuation against the virtue of his wife. Of this type, Richardson, the painter, tells us: 'Some years since, a very honest gentleman (a rough man) came to me, and amongst other discourse with abundance of civility invited me to his house. "I have a picture of Rubens, it is a rare good one. There is little Howard t'other day came to see it and says it is a copy. G— d— him, if any one says that picture is a copy, I'll break his head."'[1]

Many collectors were veritably deceived, more especially if a semblance of age had deliberately been imparted to a picture. And though the faking of pictures was no new practice,[2] nevertheless the eighteenth century constituted in the forging of pictures, as in so many other directions, a golden age. In the early part of the next century, after the French Revolution and Napoleonic wars—by which time copying had, for the moment, ceased—many famous foreign continental collections came into the market. These were composed of genuine old masters, and since the English were then able, as were the Americans a century later, to secure, by reason of their superior wealth, the largest number of them and the best,[3] a glance at these new arrivals in consequence often sadly disillusioned many a stay-at-home owner of an 'old master' acquired during the previous century.

But if even copies of old paintings were easily swallowed up, still more anxious were our ancestors to own antique statuary. The origin of this craving, we think, as of the desire to possess pictures, can be traced to the gradual growth of the Grand Tour as the customary 'finishing-off' school for young men of quality. The last years of the seventeenth century had seen it firmly established, and probably Lord Burlington, who is stated 'to have spent several years in Italy before he attained his majority', was the precursor of it. He, with his love of the arts and talent for their sponsoring, was necessarily an exception: for most young peers on their tour seem to have absorbed little from their new environment.

[1] Jonathan Richardson, *Works*, p. 315.

[2] According to Sanderson, it existed in the time of Charles II, when the painter Lanière used to 'temper his colours with soot, and roll them up till they cracked and contracted an air of antiquity'. *Graphice* (1658), p. 16.

[3] See footnote, p. 29, note 1.

Some fifty years later we find that true connoisseur, Sir Joshua, much astonished by the attitude of the English in Rome. 'Instead of examining the beauties of the works of fame, and why they are esteemed, they only enquire the subject of a picture, and the name of the painter, the history of a statue, and where it is found, and write that down. Some Englishmen, while I was in the Vatican, came there and spent above six hours in writing down whatever the antiquary dictated to them. They scarcely ever looked at the paintings the whole time.'[1] Again, so fast entangled in the English mind was the sense of antiquity with a love of the fine arts, that Barry relates how the first Duke of Northumberland of the second creation—a man, incidentally, of taste and chief patron of Canaletto—told him, 'as a matter he could not account for, that he had once proposed to Mr. Hussey an employment which he thought would be perfectly agreeable; which was to make drawings, *large as the originals*;[2] of all the celebrated antique statues; that he would build a gallery to place them in; but that Mr. Hussey[3] refused.'

For the full comprehension, then, of our national taste throughout the eighteenth century, the classical predilection and preoccupation of the English mind, together with the accompanying conservative prejudice in favour of the oldest, among all ordinary members of the educated classes, cannot be over-stressed. So remote is this attitude from that of the modern man, that to him it must seem a mania; but in reality it was a last northern manifestation, albeit a sterile one, of the Renaissance spirit. Even when, after the Peace of Aix-la-Chapelle in 1748, money gradually fertilized the taste of a new leisured class, this partiality persisted and, moreover, thereby attained a wilder range; for it was the English education, whether pursued at public school or grammar

[1] C. R. Leslie and T. Taylor, *Life and Times of Sir Joshua Reynolds*, 2 vols. (1865), vol. i, p. 51.

[2] The italics are ours.

[3] Giles Hussey (1710–88) pronounced that 'every human face is in harmony with itself', and is now chiefly remembered for the discovery to which this formulation of his views led him; that the drawing of the human form should be corrected by the musical scale, and that, after the keynote had been obtained, the proportions of the face should be determined by it. He was much distressed by the jealousy plainly demonstrated by his fellow artists when they heard of his discovery.

Nevertheless he was immensely admired by Barry who said: 'The perfections that were possible to him but a few artists can conceive', and placed a portrait of Hussey behind that of Phidias, in his 'Elysium' at the Society of Arts. (James Barry, *Works* (1809), vol. ii, p. 566.)

school, which inspired both patron and artist with their perpetual tendency to 'go classic'. Antiquity, rather than beauty, remained the criterion, when applied to the arts.

In the 'thirties, the collecting of antiques—by which was chiefly signified statuary—had already been fashionable: by 1750 it had grown into an obsession and all over Italy English patronage had become a by-word for lavishness and want of discrimination. A regular trade in ancient objects had by then developed in Rome and the English artists who flocked thither to learn drawing, as now, more usually, they attend the studios of Paris, were obliged to earn their living less by painting than by acting as agents in the buying, restoring, and often total fabrication of antiques, just as their brothers at home were similarly forced to spend their time in the copying of old masters; a process which in both instances no doubt prevented a large number of them from pursuing careers so unsuited to their lack of talent.

Of this body of young artists exiled in Rome, Nollekens in his youth was a prominent member.[1]

> I got all the first and best of my money [he confessed in after years] by putting antiques together. Hamilton and I, and Jenkins, generally used to go shares in what we bought. And as I had to match the pieces as well as I could, and clean 'em, I had the best part of the profits. . . . Jenkins followed the trade of supplying the foreign visitors with intaglios and cameos made by his own people that he kept in a part of the ruins of the Coliseum fitted up for 'em to work in slyly by themselves. . . . Bless your heart! He sold 'em as fast as they made 'em.

From the first discoveries until the early years of the nineteenth century,[2] restoration was regarded as a matter of course; but never does the reconstitution of antiques appear to have been more empirical than in the days of which we are writing. During the seventeenth century, when Roman soil was still producing its yearly crops of statues, the Popes and Cardinals who reaped them, the Barberini, Borghesi, and Giustiniani, would never for a moment have deigned to exhibit in their galleries any but the most perfect specimens: so that badly mutilated statues, and all broken fragments,

[1] J. T. Smith, *Nollekens and his Times* (2 vols., 1828), vol. i, p. 251.

[2] Until, in fact, owing to the intervention of Canova, the 'Elgin' marbles were spared the final indignity of being arranged and renewed according to the current nineteenth-century conception of how they ought to look.

marble hips and hands and noses, had been at once discarded, consigned to cellar or rubbish-heap, or buried in mounds in the garden, where in time they were crowned with thickets of ilex and bay. Now, however, these neglected spots were ransacked by the jackals of the ancient world, who subsequently freely, and even fancifully, restored their finds; and then sold them for large sums to our ancestors.

Notwithstanding, it is hard to blame them for so doing. 'The English Virtuosi,' we read, 'have no value for statues without heads; Lord Tavistock would not give a guinea for the finest torso ever discovered.'[1] But in time the demand for antique statuary, or at least statuary which produced the appearance of being antique, became so great that the buyers became less fastidious: so much so that Cunningham, in his life of Nollekens, tells us of a loose head of Minerva in Rome, which 'even an Englishman would not purchase'. Nollekens, however, bought it, and then for 50 guineas the trunk of the same, or another, goddess; and having united the two, he sold it—or them—for 1,000 guineas. Such practices at least in no way injured works of art in good condition; were as nothing compared to the deliberate splitting up and rearrangement of a whole and perfect group. 'At Rome,' wrote an eye-witness, 'you may often see broken statues made into busts or heads. I myself have looked on while statues were sawn in half and attached to marble slabs as reliefs or conversely while figures in good condition were sawn off a relief and a principal figure thus frequently made of a subordinate one.'[2] There was nothing, in fact, which the English would not buy. The people of Rome used to say, 'Were our amphitheatre portable, the English would carry it off'. And though they failed in any translation of the Colosseum, they did, to a limited extent, succeed in carrying off the Forum; for in numberless English country houses are to be seen round tables of varying size, their tops consisting of many multicoloured squares of different marbles, chipped and hacked off pillars and portals, and then brought home, tastefully polished and laid flat, and enclosed by a circle of solid bronze to keep the bits together.

Nevertheless, though the English Virtuosi may have had no use for statues without heads, busts were popular.

[1] Dallaway in Nichols's *Illustr. Lit. Hist.* (1817), vol. iii, p. 728.

[2] Canova, *Discorso sopra gli antichi*, p. xli.

Originally, at the beginning of the eighteenth century, they had been considered, as were pictures, from an architectural point of view; as an aid and embellishment to a fine house. In example, Sir Robert Walpole ordered for Houghton busts by the dozen; and, doubtless, the same wholesale commissions issued from many country houses, old as well as new. But slowly familiarized with the profiles of the ancient world, after this fashion as much as by the Grand Tour, people began to like them for their own sake, and then to see in them a possible medium for modern portraiture; until, by the fifth decade of the century, English sculptors, who had hitherto found their only secure employment in executing monuments on tombs, whether effigied or allegorical, were kept very busy modelling portrait busts. And by the time Nollekens returned from Rome, with the prestige behind him of a ten years' residence in that great centre of the arts, he easily obtained orders, and soon became celebrated as an exponent of this medium. 'The taste,' says *The London Tradesman* in 1747, 'for busts and figures prevails much of late years and in some measure interferes with portrait painting. The nobility now affect to have their busts done that way, rather than sit for their pictures, and the fashion is to have their apartments adorned with bronzes and figures in plaster and wax.'[1] Moreover, a dead peer competed with a quick for the attention of the sculptor; since not content with the portraits and busts of him already accumulated during his lifetime, it was the custom for the nearest relative, the moment the great man had breathed his last, to send for a sculptor to take a cast of his face.

Having thus in a general sense reviewed the taste of the patrons during the first half of Dr. Johnson's lifetime, how it was formed, and how revealed in the sort of the collections they made, it is, perhaps, fitting that, before we approach the subject of the gradual improvement in the level of taste manifested during the reign of George II and chiefly wrought by the growing popularity of the Grand Tour as an institution, we should dwell on the treasures amassed, and the real connoisseurship exhibited, by one of the great English amateurs—for England could, even at this time, boast a few of the most notable collectors in the world.

[1] W. T. Whitley, *Artists and their Friends in England, 1700–1799* (1928), vol. i, p. 87.

THE MARQUIS OF TAVISTOCK

After the painting by Sir Joshua Reynolds

Of these, the most exceptional and individual, and yet in some ways the most typical, was Dr. Mead (1673–1754). Not only was his collection unrivalled both in its dimensions and quality, but, in this most rare, he was a generous patron of the living as well as of the dead. His house was the first to be thrown open to students of art, and a number of scholars and artists were kept continually in his employ. His friend, Dr. Maty, wrote of him: 'No foreigner of any learning, taste or even curiosity, ever came to England without being introduced to Dr. Mead; as it would have been a matter of reproach to have returned without seeing him. On these occasions his table was always open, where, what seldom happens, the magnificence of Princes was united with the pleasure of Philosophers.' And for once it seems as though this funebrial eulogy was deserved. He had received the honour of exchanging presents with Louis XV; and King Charles III of Naples, a great lover of the arts, had invited him to his palace so that he might show him his own treasures; but more interesting than these royal compliments is the fact that when in 1719 Watteau, already wasted with consumption, visited England in order to consult him, he was at once commissioned by Dr. Mead to paint two pictures, 'A Pastoral Conversation' and 'Italian Comedians';[1] while, moreover, because of the prevailing and exclusive taste for portraiture in this country at the time, these were the only ones this great artist painted during his stay in England.

Although it must be kept in mind that this was no casual display of taste, but both the life-work and life-recreation of a patron of genius and a man, in other directions, of marked ability, it is interesting to reflect on so noble a collection, and to deduce what we can from the presence and absence of certain objects. It resembled other galleries formed at this period in its scope, which was extremely heterogeneous; for though possessed of a genuinely aesthetic outlook, Dr. Mead had doubtless inherited the traditional point of view of the English connoisseur, and perhaps feeling it his duty, and at the same time inspired by the scientific spirit which should accompany his profession, had amassed objects

[1] At the dispersal of Dr. Mead's collection after his death these were sold by auction. But though this took place in 1754, thirty-three years after the death of the great artist, and albeit high prices were already being paid for his work on the Continent, they fell for only £42 and £52 10*s*. respectively to Alderman Beckford, father of the author of *Vathek*.

of curiosity as much as of beauty. Thus, besides books, drawings, prints, and statuary, it contained fossils, Egyptian mummies, and animals preserved in spirits. As for the pictures, the catalogue of the sale enumerates:

45 portraits by Holbein, Titian, Rubens, Rembrandt, Hals, Ramsay, Richardson, Kneller, and others;

23 landscapes and sea pieces by Claude, G. Poussin, Rembrandt, Breughel, Salvator Rosa, Vandeveldt and others;

13 architectural and ruin pictures by Canaletto, Pannini and N. Poussin.

14 Dutch still-lives and animal pictures.

55 Historical pictures by Julio Romano, Veronese, the Caracci, Rubens, Solimena, Vandyck, Watteau, Bourdon, Guercino, Teniers, N. Poussin, Borgognone, Barrochio, Palma Vecchio, Gerard Dou, G. Poussin, Rembrandt and Carlo Maratti.

Among the remaining pictures were five copies, and some sketches by Raphael.

The pictures realized altogether just over £3,400. The highest sum given for any one item was £183, paid for a Carlo Maratti, Sir Joshua's favourite painter. Works by Holbein, Rubens, and Claude came next in price, and brought in over £100 each.

Readers will at once notice that no primitives are mentioned in the account of the sale. To the eighteenth century the dawn of painting was the Renaissance. No artist earlier than Raphael was admired, because the kingdom of art was entirely limited to the pictures produced since his birth, and to the works of Romans and Greeks, though not of the archaic Greeks. Nothing else existed in it.... Then, again, there is no representative of the Spanish schools of any period; but this was because for many years to come the student was obliged, if he wished to see a single Spanish picture, to visit Spain. The work of the great Spanish artists was the property of the Crown, or else belonged to rich convents and grandees. Moreover, exportation was prohibited under severe penalties.

But Dr. Mead was not alone in his display of real taste and knowledge. Whatever its absurdities, the Grand Tour was, year by year, educating the patrons, and, through them, benefiting the arts. English painting was beginning to blossom at last.

In 1734, between forty and fifty young men, lately returned from their travels—all of them peers or the sons of peers—formed themselves into a body, which was named the Dilettanti Society; founded in part for convivial purposes, in part for the encouragement of the arts. Richardson's widely-read essay[1] had done much to stimulate their interest in painting which, he urged, since it resembled in many of its aspects history, poetry, philosophy, and theology, was essentially the study of a gentleman. Moreover, the young gentlemen were strongly advised to buy objects of beauty and antiquity as a sound financial investment.

The early meetings of the Dilettanti Society were conducted in flippant mood, and in ceremony and ritual was their particular joy. The President sported a scarlet toga, the tailoring of which was supervised by the official painter to the Society, and the Master of the Ceremonies was decked out in a long robe of crimson taffeta—'full pleated with a rich Hungarian cap and a long Spanish Toledo', while in this instance his position further entitled him to wear this costume at masquerades. The Secretary, incidentally, dressed as Machiavelli. . . . Once a week the Society met, for its members to dine together and drink—more, perhaps, than was good for them—to 'Grecian Taste and Roman Spirit'. And it may be significant when we remember how little pleasure George II took in the arts, that though they toasted 'Viva La Virtù', it was not until fifty years later that they drank the health of the King.[2] For the rest, the Society provided young men who showed promise in painting, sculpture, or architecture with the means of going to Italy to pursue their studies, and, on their return, with commissions which ensured them both a living and a guarantee that their work would become known; and, despite apparent frivolity, the names of most of the great connoisseurs and patrons are found included in the list of its members. Not, indeed, until some generations later were solemnity and intelligence regarded as identical virtues. The reign of the doctors and the professors, the theorists, critics, and earnest-minded was still to come, and without doubt these untoiling butterflies accomplished more for English art than all the labouring

[1] *An Essay on the Whole Art of Criticism in relation to Painting* (1719). In 1722 the Richardsons' guide-book to the art treasures in Europe was the first to be published and satisfied a much-felt want. In the 'sixties it was still, according to Winckelmann, the best work on the subject.

[2] In 1789; a symbol of the outburst of loyalty, when George III recovered from his first attack of insanity and resumed his royal function.

stage-elephants of the next century, because a lot of money, judiciously spent, and not a great amount of advice, is ever that which the artist needs.

Thus the Grand Tour played a part that it is impossible to exaggerate in forming the taste, even of those who stayed at home. Due to it, equally, were the current classic obsession and the waves of rebellion against it which lay just under the surface. Two unfortunate events occurred abroad, which aided the impetus of the antique; the new finds at Herculaneum and the discovery, through the stupid fall of a peasant, of Pompeii. Alas! these things, interesting in themselves, were to influence art everywhere in the most deplorable fashion, and were finally responsible for the extinction of the Italian tradition in Europe. The connoisseurs went Pompeii-mad; though one good effect of the more thorough acquaintance with the ancient world which resulted therefrom was a growing preference for objects which were Greek in workmanship. Taste moved eastward and Athens, though in those days very distant, became the goal of pilgrimage.

Lord Charlemont had been almost the first connoisseur to discriminate between Greek and Roman art. In 1749 he had travelled to Greece, accompanied by Richard Dalton in the capacity of draughtsman. On his return, he published the first engravings of the Parthenon and the Erechtheion. These pioneers were followed by 'Athenian' Stuart and Revett, who devoted four years to measuring and drawing the famous ruins of Athens. The *Antiquities of Athens*, issued in 1762, earned so great a success that two years later, when the Dilettanti Society found itself with money in hand, Lord Charlemont, who was a member, suggested and organized a further expedition to Smyrna, with Dr. Chandler in charge and Revett as draughtsman, and the *Ionian Antiquities* which ensued was quickly established as one of the most important publications of the century. Nor was Lord Charlemont's connexion with books entirely antiquarian, for when they appeared in 1756 the exquisite designs of Piranesi, fruit of the same mania for the antique, although in his case they owe so much more to a sombre and fantastic imagination than to scholarship, were dedicated to the same noble lord.

Howbeit each fresh discovery, though it aided knowledge

and bred discernment, became a burden to the artist of the day. No statue, no bronze, no vase could be unearthed, except it inspired the critics and commentators with a new set of rules for the living creators to follow. Many such systems had made their appearance since Du Fresnoy's didactic poem was published at the end of the seventeenth century, and Richardson's *Theory of Painting*, issued in 1715, was, in fact, but a development of the ideas therein contained. Nevertheless it became the standard work on the subject during the first half of the century and remained so for many years afterward. Several of Reynolds's *Discourses* are based on it, and we need only compare the quotations on page 27 with the following from Richardson to detect Sir Joshua's indebtedness.

A painter of this class (historical) must possess all the good qualities requisite to a historian. . . . He must moreover know the forms of the arms, the habits, customs, buildings, etc. of the age and country in which the thing was transacted more exactly than the other needs to know them. And as his business is not to write the history of a few years or of one age, or country, but of all ages, and all nations as occasion offers, and he must have a proportionable fund of ancient and modern learning of all kinds. . . . He must . . . have the talents requisite to a good poet: the rules for the conduct of a picture being much the same as those to be observed in writing a poem. . . . He must be furnished with a vast stock of poetical as well as historical learning. Besides all this it is absolutely necessary to a history-painter that he understand anatomy, osteology, geometry, perspective, architecture and many other sciences which the historian or poet has no occasion to know. . . .[1]

A painter should read the best writers such as Homer, Milton, Virgil, Spenser, Thucydides, Livy, Plutarch, etc., but chiefly the Holy Scripture. . . . He should also frequent the brightest company and avoid the rest.[2]

None of the apocalyptic systems hitherto presented had so far ever borne perceptible results or in any way affected the artist—except that Richardson's treatise on painting had fired Reynolds as a boy with the ambition to become an artist and had also been responsible, many years after he had read it, for the remark of Dr. Johnson to the effect that he had been surprised how much could be found to say on the subject. Now, however, unless he paid heed in turn to all the

[1] Richardson, *Works* (1773), pp. 10–11.
[2] Ibid., pp. 109–10.

doctrines thus formulated, and which, though all tending in the same direction, constantly superseded one another, it was generally recognized that there was no health or virtue in him. The imagination of art lovers and students of history, more than that, of the whole reading public, had been stirred by the recent discoveries, so that, bolstered up by the prestige attaching to these, the essays of Winckelmann, from their first publication in 1756, at once exercised an influence on more creative minds. It was not that he proclaimed anything fresh—but that he said it louder and more often, until it appeared to be the vehicle of a new and authoritative conception.

'Let no man,' he thundered, 'who has not formed his taste upon antiquity take it into his head to act the connoisseur of beauty: his ideas must be a parcel of whimseys.' Thus old theories were constantly revived, as well as new ones founded. The close relationship which the ancients had discerned between poetry and painting was now again as clear as the Greek dawn. The brush, like the pen, must instruct and improve; and Homer once more became the sole and final court of appeal in all aesthetic disputes. Modern pictures were admired only in so far as it was supposed the Greeks would have admired them; for Winckelmann had written, 'Imitation of the Ancients is the shortest way to perfection in the fine arts', and the best painters were necessarily those who most resembled them. Thus Raphael and Michelangelo were reverenced nigh as much as the sculptors of Athens; while Andrea del Sarto, Correggio, Julio Romano, Guido Reni, Carlo Dolci, the Caracci, and the two Poussins, were awarded second-class honours. (There was Rubens, too, who proved a great source of inspiration, though his exuberance caused misgivings.)

As for the relics of that ideal if delusive world which the connoisseurs now imagined for themselves, the Laocoon still held its own, even against the advancing army of pygmies from Pompeii and Herculaneum. Ever since, when found near the Sette Sale in Rome, it had writhed once more into daylight in 1506, this had evoked the most fervent admiration. As is their way, artists read into these marble figures more than existed in them. Michelangelo had designated the group 'a marvel of art', and Bernini had perceived in the stiffness of the thighs the effect of the serpent's poison, beginning its

CHARLES TOWNELEY IN HIS LIBRARY

From the engraving by W. H. Worthington after the painting by J. Zoffany

deadly work. Now, perhaps because of the labour that had gone to the making of such an immense marble machine, it took precedence over every other object, was recognized as the supreme example of a 'silent poem', and received the inevitable, if muddled, title of the 'Homer of Art'. Naturally the egregious Winckelmann, a scholar with little understanding or feeling for art, who with the narrow arrogance of his type had contrived to usurp the throne of aesthetics, wrote pages of rhapsody on the emotions it aroused in him; while the world at large stressed its literary and intellectual qualities and ignored its possession—or lack—of plastic ones.

It seemed as though Greece had now triumphantly taken, not only Rome, but all modern Europe captive. Its influence upon the everyday life of the time was prodigious, deepening until it permeated every manifestation of it from houses, and even stables, to furniture and jewellery. Ornament became progressively less exuberant; vigour gave way to etiolation; and there was a continual effort to achieve Hellenic purity. Even those lovely baroque coaches we have described, though in England they bumped and rolled along for another decade or so, had soon to shed their allegories, their gilded suites of deities, satyrs, and mermaids, and were forced to rely on the beauty of a shell-like form, aided by a little judicious floral decoration. Already when he visited Paris in 1765, Horace Walpole found that they were very simply painted, and that everything was *à la grecque*. 'We English are living upon their old gods and goddesses,' he wrote, 'I roll about in a chariot decorated with cupids, and look like the grandfather of Adonis.'[1] . . . Now the art of the seventeenth century, and even of the early part of the eighteenth, was beyond the pale. Winckelmann termed it gaudy, meretricious, and corrupt. The only qualities which the age could see in Borromini and Bernini were insipidity and blustering extravagance. Vanbrugh, too, was abhorred for deviating from the Grecian laws of architecture, and until Reynolds, who was never in doubt as to the merits of a beautiful object when he saw one, however much he might stumble over the aesthetic roots of its beauty, said a courageous word on behalf of the 'painter-like' quality of his building—a thing he was the first critic to comprehend—

[1] Walpole, *Letters* (ed. Toynbee), vol. vi, p. 302.

Blenheim and Castle Howard were treated as fit merely for derision.

The Greeks, in fact, were acknowledged to be incapable of error, and it was only in the interpretation of details that the critics differed. And this interpretation was happily varied. A work of art represented, they admitted, an idea in the mind and was no mere imitation of nature. Yet, to make the argument convincing, some compromise had to be sought for between truth and ideal beauty.... Again, the growing distaste for mannerism was leading inevitably up to a fresh victory for realism; but not for a moment was this suspected. Indeed, the Dutch painters were hated for their slavish imitation of nature, a thing utterly contemned, and many stories were current among the enlightened to prove how free from this vice had been the great artists, how independent, for example, of their models. Thus Richardson bequeaths us the following moral tale:

> A Bolognese nobleman, a great patron of Guercino's, was induced by this last to endeavour to get out of Guido what woman was the model he made use of for his fine and gracious airs and heads.... 'For God's sake, Signor Guido,' ⟨he said to the painter,⟩ 'what astonishing beauty of a girl do you hug up to yourself that supplies you with such divine airs?' 'I will show you,' said Guido, ... so he called his colour grinder, a great greasy fellow with a brutal look like the devil and bade him sit down...; and then, taking his chalk, drew a Magdalen after him exactly in the same view and attitude and same lights and shadows but handsome as an angel.[1]

It was, perhaps, influenced by such a story and in emulation of Guido that Nollekens, when commissioned by Townley to restore the arms of Venus, had employed J. T. Smith as the model; for the doctrines had at last begun to take effect. Hitherto, as we have suggested, painters and sculptors had followed their own light, and even now the instinct of decoration—'purer ornament' was demanded by the high priests, and decoration was to be sacrificed as leading only to decadence and deformity—was not so easily to be uprooted. Sir Joshua, for instance, who dealt in aesthetic theories with more abandon than any of his contemporaries, and placarded rule after rule for other artists to follow, himself in reality continued to paint for his own pleasure, and to gratify his eyes rather than to exercise his intellect. Indeed he could

[1] Jonathan Richardson, *Works*, pp. 95–6.

do little else, for as we shall see, the theories he formulated were so multitudinous that many of them were antagonistic; but he held them all, and, albeit the least pedantic of painters, he had persuaded himself that art was altogether an intellectual affair. 'It is the same taste,' he wrote, 'which relishes a demonstration in geometry that is pleased with the resemblance of a picture to an original and touched with the harmony of music.'[1] . . . He actually ventured so far as to say that 'the value and rank of every art is in proportion to the mental labour employed in it, or the mental pleasure produced by it'.[2] . . . 'A mind enriched by an assemblage of all the treasures of ancient and modern art will be more elevated and fruitful in resources, in proportion to the number of ideas which have been carefully collected and thoroughly digested.' And, again, that 'excellence is never granted to a man but as the reward of labour'. . . . On this point it may be that he was but following Dr. Johnson, who had already pronounced, in very much the same vein, upon the value of knowledge to a poet; who would in consequence be able (he tells us in *Rasselas*) to pack his verse with 'remote allusions and unexpected instruction'. Sir Joshua and the artists akin to him, and of his generation, were too busily occupied in painting and theorizing to allow either occupation to be frustrated by the other; but alas for them and for us, the new generation of artists were beginning, consciously and conscientiously, to practise the maxims laid down for them by the critics, and the attitude, as we have exemplified it, of Sir Joshua, the painter of pleasure, was to culminate a century later in that brutal puritan doctrine, the Apotheosis of Work.

Sculpture, however, rather than painting, for the most part engrossed the attention of the *cognoscenti* (so that pictures by promising young classical enthusiasts were in accordance often executed to resemble as much as possible bas-reliefs). Purity and severity were the fashion, and as soon as Winckelmann had declared a static pose to be an essential ingredient of Hellenic serenity, the fluttering braggadocio movement imparted to solid marble by the seventeenth-century taste ceased, and in its stead reigned the peace and stillness of death. It was, perhaps, natural that this

[1] Reynolds, *Discourses* (1887), p. 104.
[2] Ibid., p. 39.

concentration of interest on sculpture should lead to such an emphasis of the human form as debarred all else from being treated. Draperies were discarded, and the growing passion for nudity threatened to conquer the very realms of portraiture. On pedestals princes were exhibited nude in their market-places—though not in England: and even the emaciated shape of Voltaire, more suitable to the brush of a Hogarth than to any Greek chisel, rose up stark naked in white marble. This last experiment, however, was not considered successful, and henceforth togas were more than ever firmly established as the mode for famous men.

Nevertheless, toga or no toga, statues came to be regarded simply as petrified or fossilized men and women: and a thorough knowledge of anatomy was deemed as indispensable to the artist as to the surgeon. The training of both was equally scientific and, to the layman, gruesome. 'Notwithstanding your natural repugnance to the handling of corpses,' wrote Burke to his protégé, Barry, 'you ought to make the knife go with the pencil, and study the anatomy in real, and, if you can, in frequent dissections.'

There can be little doubt that Barry followed this advice, for he was excessively painstaking, if not very talented. But he possesses for us an interest altogether independent of merit, in that, according to most of the theories of the day, he should have developed into the perfect master. He lived in an absolute whirl and frenzy of admiration for the antique, and his seriousness of temperament earned him the title of the Ethical Painter. To one critic, at least, he was all that an artist should be, for of his pictures Dr. Johnson pronounced: 'Whatever the hand may have done, the mind has done its part. There is a grasp of mind there which you will find nowhere else.' . . . As for the man himself, there was a refreshing discrepancy between his views on the functions of art and the voice in which he expressed them; for his ideas were pure and lofty in the extreme, but his language was appallingly coarse and blasphemous. On Christian meekness, he was especially eloquent; for it, particularly enthusiastic; but he cursed volubly during his discourse. Nor did this humility, which he so extolled, extend altogether to his opinion of his own pictures in the Adelphi; since he wrote of them: 'For public interest and ethical utility of subject, for the castigated purity of Grecian design, for beauty, grace, vigorous effect and execution, (they stand) successfully in the view and neighbourhood even of the so justly celebrated Orleans Collection.'[1]

The truth is that Barry was born a poor painter, and remained one, in spite of the encouragement and advice lavished on him at the very time that rebels against all these theories—rebels whose names would one day be justly famous —were being neglected and frequently allowed to starve in their garrets. Yet, in spite of the loud trumpetings, the inspired denunciations of the classical doctrinaires, there were those—and they had existed since the early part of the century—who perceived that there was in the world not a little beauty that the Greeks had never exploited . . . and already, in the purity of some Greek gallery on a very quiet evening, there could be heard, far away, a curious rolling murmur, as it might be of thunder or massed drums, over the horizon: for the great Romantic Movement, of which the Revolution and Napoleon, Shelley and Byron and Beethoven, and the new Houses of Parliament, are merely so many different manifestations, was on the way. Nothing could resist it . . . but as yet the eighteenth-century romantics were almost inarticulate, their achievements slight.

Hogarth had been almost the first Englishman to express dissatisfaction with the theories of his day. But it is not easy to deduce much from his *Analysis of Beauty*, beyond noting that in his championship of the wavy line, he was, in fact, protesting against the religion of symmetry. . . . And Sir Joshua (Sir Joshua of all people!) wrote that 'The art of *seeing* Nature is the greatest object of painting, and the point to which all our studies are directed.'[2] It was this slow development of a new point of view which was shortly to discredit an entirely intellectual theory of art. And nothing could be more characteristic of our period than that Reynolds and Walpole, so different and yet both typical of

[1] This superb collection was on view in London. It had been formed by the Regent (Philip of Orleans, nephew of Louis XIV). In 1792, the Duke of Bridgewater, Earl Gower, and the Earl of Carlisle bought the whole collection for £43,000. They selected for their own keeping ninety-six of the best pictures, which formed the nucleus of three famous galleries, at Stafford House, Bridgwater House, and Castle Howard, and sold the remaining pictures in England for £41,000.

[2] It is not without interest that at the end of the seventeenth century, Du Fresnoy had written: 'The principal part of painting is to *know* what is most beautiful in Nature and most proper to that art.'

it, can each of them be quoted in support of the two opposing views; for they, together with all their other sensitive and imaginative contemporaries, were composed of a mass of conflicting tendencies. Moreover, not only the painters, but the patrons, too, had started to see Nature with new eyes; for the Romantic Movement, indeed, is in its origin as much rooted in landscape, as the Classical in temples.

It must always remain uncertain at what period modern man began to admire his surroundings. . . . Certainly no artistic expression of it is to be discovered in England until the eighteenth century; and it seems, again, as if the Grand Tour had not only originated fashions, encouraged morbid absurdities, and led to a wider patronage of the arts, but, by accident, had cleared the path to a new understanding and comprehension of the beauties of Nature. For though the northern traveller could remain unaware of statues and pictures, however much he was in their neighbourhood, with the obstinate insensibility of an Addison, it was difficult for him, as he drove through Switzerland on his way to Italy, to ignore altogether the white peaks and torrents and valleys and forests, and green, snake-like glaciers. All these claimed his attention with an almost blatant insistence. One of the earliest Englishmen, as it were, to notice the Alps appears to have been John Dennis, who crossed them in 1688 and records that 'I experienced a delightful horrour, a terrible joy, and at the same time that I was definitely pleased, I trembled'. . . . And these sensations soon became a common experience, for underlying the sober, classical taste of the English, had always existed, one of the manifold contradictions in our national character, a romantic northern strain, to which such things made an especial appeal, and the growing enthusiasm of the English amateur for Claude, the Poussins, and, above all, for Salvator, was instinctive and whole-hearted. Salvator Rosa began to influence the traveller through the stories of his wild and romantic career, a liberty-loving poet who dwelt among brigands, no less than through his pictures, which revealed a new grandeur and magnificence in Nature, a new and heroic despair in man. Soon every traveller to Rome and Naples, though he journeyed thither still to view the fragments of the ancient world, looked out on the landscape from his swaying chariot with eyes borrowed from this great painter, seeing wave and wood and torrent, monstrous cloud and wind-blown tree, rocky pinnacles and water flowing over dark green tresses, with that sombre Neapolitan vision which is the complement of blue seas and mandolines. Everywhere on the way a likeness to his pictures was rapturously observed, and thus scenery was focused by the observer in a manner quite new. Gray and Walpole were pioneers in the art of seeing Nature as a series of potential pictures; and it is not without significance that the word 'picturesque'[1] is found used for the first time in its full modern sense in a letter written in 1740 by Gray from Rome; whither he was accompanied by Walpole. And let us listen, too, to a description of a drive, which Walpole wrote to Richard West:

> But the road, West, the road! winding round a prodigious mountain, and surrounded with others, all shagged with hanging woods, obscured with pines or lost in clouds! Below, a torrent breaking through cliffs, and tumbling through fragments of rocks! Sheets of cascades forcing their silver speed down channelled precipices, and hasting into the roughened river at the bottom! Now and then, an old foot-bridge, with a broken rail, a leaning cross, a cottage, or the ruin of a hermitage.[2]

This new sensibility was to bear fruit in many directions, in art, literature, and in the construction of gardens.

With the coming of this novel interest in landscape, the Roman pastoral poets were re-read, from a fresh angle; and the Classicists cleverly compromised by detecting a resemblance between Theocritus and Virgil on the one hand and the landscape painters of the previous century on the other; a likeness which authorized in the classic enthusiast, too, a certain degree of approbation of the works of Claude, Salvator Rosa and the Poussins. This was not, they held, incompatible with the Greek view of art and its purpose; for the scenes were idealized, so appealing more to the poet than to him whom Dr. Johnson sternly precipitated into crystal for us with the words 'a mere lover of naked nature'; while, in addition, these painters had fortunately added to them, if somewhat perfunctorily, human figures, and this gave employment to the mind. Inevitably, however, the theorists in the end consulted Homer, and noting, as they chose to think, an absence of visual description in his language, finally posted landscape as an inferior form of art, in the same

[1] It is not in Dr. Johnson's *Dictionary*.
[2] Walpole, *Letters*, vol. i, p. 38.

category as 'animals, fruit, or any other still-life or pieces of drollery'. Thus the two factions were not to be reconciled, the cleavage between them deepening with the years. Barry, loyal to the last to intellect and pure reason, expressed himself, as was to be foreseen, with some vehemence on the subject of 'inconsequential things, portraits of dogs, landscapes, etc.; things, which—the mind, which is the soul of art, having no concern in them—have hitherto served to disgrace us over all Europe'. But, despite all he could say, Poussin and Claude and Salvator were eagerly bought at enormous prices, and nature was viewed entirely through their eyes.

It is easy to understand that the temporary and qualified praise conceded even by the classicists to these painters, and the enthusiasm felt for them by their adherents, would not and could not extend to the Dutch seventeenth-century masters, for northern scenery was not 'picturesque' and the common-sense country of Ruysdael and Hobbema, with its windmills, dykes, and broad meadows could never have sheltered a vine-crowned Bacchus or the slightly impersonal race of nymphs, naiads, and demigods who were then, pictorially, the rage; but how is it, we wonder, that their charity did not extend to the several living English landscapists whom these same Italian classic scenes, and their painters, inspired?

> As our poets warm their imaginations with sunny hills, [we find Walpole writing,] or sigh after grottoes and cooling breezes, our painters draw rocks and precipices and castellated mountains, because Virgil gasped for breath at Naples, and Salvator wandered amidst Alps and Apennines. Our ever-verdant lawns, rich vales, fields and haycocks and hop grounds are neglected as homely and familiar objects.[1]

This, of course, however well phrased, is only half untrue. Gainsborough was hard at work on his landscapes, and soon the Norwich School would be beginning. . . . But at least it might have been expected that, with critics of less originality than Walpole, the other painters to whom it applied would have found favour. Of these Richard Wilson was the most talented; but contemporary triumph was won by men with now forgotten names.

The *cognoscenti* must be excused for their neglect of Wilson.

[1] Walpole, *Anecdotes of Painting* (ed. Wornum), vol. ii, p. 333.

They had talked themselves into a state of sheer and utter muddle. The Classicists had won, as it were, within the home: the Romantics had triumphed outside, in the open air. There was no need, happily, to be Greek in the garden, and there, at least, it was permitted to be moody, to indulge in the most wild and extravagant dreams. Irregularity of appearance was inherent in the conception of the picturesque; and, moreover, a studied untidiness was felt to be a relief from the rectangular trimness of the house. . . . More and more, the art of the garden came to be regarded, not as an art in itself, but as a domain of painting. 'All gardening,' Pope had pronounced, 'is landscape painting'; and even Vanbrugh, when consulted as to the laying out of the garden at Blenheim, had answered, 'Send for a landscape painter'. Now Walpole included an essay on gardening among his *Anecdotes of Painting*. And, when gardening ceased to be looked on as a branch of painting, even then it was not treated as a thing by itself, but became incorporated in sculpture, because, with the advent of 'Capability' Brown, the actual country was turned into merely so much clay, to be modelled at will, with no attention paid to natural contours. Every house, people said, should have a landscape made to it from a drawing previously sketched at the window of the saloon.

Meanwhile, in all directions the formal gardens, those lovely great machines of stone and water, were being overthrown and battered down, their sites converted into ingenious life-size models for the landscape painter. Bastions, stone terraces, and rusticated grottoes, robust avenues and basins edged with wavering white plumes, statues placed in pairs and lines, endless flights of shallow steps, thunderous cascades, crunching gravel and sculptured evergreens, gave way to simpering velvet slopes, serpentine and tinkling streams, winding paths, groves of delicate young trees, and bridges that must either be Chinese or Gothic. So that the scene should still more nearly resemble a painting, artificial ruins, representing a Greek temple, or bits of one, were artfully disposed in the dip of a valley, or upon an inappropriate knoll.

A piece of Palladian architecture [wrote Gilpin] may be elegant in the last degree. . . . But if we introduce it in a picture it immediately becomes a formal object and ceases to please. Should we wish to give it picturesque beauty, we must use the mallet . . . we must beat down one half of it, deface the other and throw the mutilated members around in heaps. In short, from a smooth building we must turn it into a rough ruin.[1]

. . . It is not every man who can build a house that can execute a ruin. To give a stone its mouldering appearance—to make the widening chink run naturally through all the joints—to mutilate the ornaments; to peel the facing from the internal structure.[2]

Fortunately for the owners of estates, it was not always necessary to build artificial ruins, the construction of which was not less expensive than that of a house you could live in. No, Henry VIII and Cromwell had both adorned our country with a plentiful supply of genuine and economical ones, hitherto unnoticed. These now were venerated as objects of picturesque beauty. In some cases, indeed, it was held that monarch and Lord Protector had not been thorough enough; these were judged by the eye of the connoisseur to be insufficiently ruined, deficient in decay, and, as at Roche Abbey, 'Capability' Brown, or some one of his sort, was summoned, to shatter a last window or break, where it should be broken, a perfect capital. Lawns were rolled out and trees planted to increase the romantic aspect, until after a final pounding and battery, the workmen departed, and at last the deer lay in dappled clouds by the roofless cloister and the crumbling arch.

Gradually, as the country gentleman contemplated the view, he became more interested in and appreciative of these relics, began to turn away from Greece, as the ideal world, toward the more dim and mysterious epoch of the Middle Ages; and now when there was an insufficient supply of the real article, Gothic temples, rather than classical ones, began to be built, despite the manifest absurdity of their conception. This transference of allegiance is, of course, reflected in the correspondence and writings of Horace Walpole, for we find preserved in them the reflection of every eddy of fashion and shifting of taste. Yet he always collected objects because he thought them beautiful or for their romantic associations, never for their archaeological value. 'A Gothic Church or convent fills one with romantic dreams', he confesses; but this was on account of their newly perceived

[1] W. Gilpin, *Essays* (1792), p. 7.

[2] Ibid., *Observations . . . made in the year 1772* (1808), vol. i, page 73.

aesthetic merit, and not from a love of archaeology. 'I abhor all Saxon doings, and whatever does not exhibit some taste, grace or elegance, or some ability in the artists.'[1] . . .

The Gothic, perhaps, had strengthened an inclination long repressed and regretted, though always innate, in the English character, a taste for the grotesque and fantastic. And this found its chief expression in caricature and Chinoiserie. Chinese pavilions and pagodas soon became as much part of the prospect from an English house as Gothic tracery, though often, too, they were hidden away, so as to produce a pleasant element of surprise, behind a weeping willow or the arch of a bridge. From the earliest years of the eighteenth century, China possessed an indescribable fascination for Europe. And this resulted in the Chinoiserie style; which in England was the nearest approach to rococo, giving birth to the most decorative and delightful objects, wall-papers and mirrors, beds and tables of an altogether remote and fabulous elegance.

The habit of tea-drinking had become fashionable in the reign of Queen Anne (and, as all admirers of Dr. Johnson are aware, was very firmly established in his day), and, to further it, oriental porcelain had been imported by the East India Company. With the painted cups and saucers came other ceramics, as well as embroidery and lacquer-work. The vogue for these led to their being imitated by English craftsmen, for the rich decoration of the Chinese, and their alleged love of irregularity, appealed, in their lighter moments, to the rebels against 'pure taste.' Imagination was further stimulated by the letters, published at intervals, of French Jesuit missionaries in China; and in 1743 had appeared in an English translation an account of the pleasure gardens of the Summer Palace, by one of these priests, Attiret, who was painter to Ch'ien-Lung. This had aroused the greatest interest, helping to strengthen the reaction against the formal garden.

Yet, after this description of a pleasure domain which evoked numberless others in Europe, inspired by it yet strangely different from it, how curious to reflect that, as Mr. Sacheverell Sitwell has pointed out in a recent book,[2] the Emperor had been engaged in creating for his own

[1] Walpole, *Letters*, vol. x, p. 313.
[2] Sacheverell Sitwell, *Spanish Baroque Art* (1931).

enjoyment, not a Chinoiserie, but its opposite, a phantasia on western themes; so that when in England the owners of estates were designing new gardens in, as they thought, a Chinese manner, they were but distorting once more an already distorted reflection of their own ideas, focused through the eyes of the Son of Heaven. Moreover, the embellishment of their creations was, of necessity, entrusted to men who had never visited China, and the designs for summer-house and tea-house, ornamental waters and bridges of wood or stone were, perforce, adapted from oriental plates and lacquer screens; and such similarity as exists between gardens of East and West was certainly never enough to justify the French in characterizing landscape-gardening—which, so Gray said, is the only art we can call our own—as '*le goût Anglo-Chinois*'.

The Chinese obsession, though less enduring and more pleasing than the great classic obsession, and never leading to so many comic results, had its amusing aspects. Thus Sir William Temple announced in an authoritative way, that the Chinese employed a special word, 'Sharawadgi', to indicate the beauty of studied irregularity. The word entered on an immediate popularity, which endured as long as the fashion whence it had sprung. 'I am almost as fond of Sharawaggi (*sic*) or Chinese want of symmetry in buildings as in grounds or gardens,' wrote Walpole in 1750.... But in the end it appeared that there never was such a word, nor one remotely like it.

Meanwhile house and garden would affect Chinoiserie and Gothic, the styles alternating, for Sharawadgi was read equally into both of them. It was all very well for Walpole to write, 'Whenever you come to England you will be pleased with the liberty of taste into which we are struck and of which you can have no idea'; but not every visitor found this to his liking. 'Angeloni', alias John Shebbeare, writing in 1755, has left us the following account of the havoc wrought by Chinese idolatry:

> The simple and sublime have lost all influence, almost everywhere, all is Chinese or Gothic. Every chair in an apartment, the frames of glasses, and tables must be Chinese: the walls covered with Chinese paper fill'd with figures which resemble nothing of God's creation, and which a prudent nation would prohibit for the sake of pregnant women. . . . Nay, so excessive is the love of Chinese architecture

become, that at present foxhunters would be sorry to break a leg in pursuing their sport in leaping any gate that was not made in the eastern taste of little bits of wood standing in all directions.

The gothic, too, has its advocates; you see a hundred houses built with porches in that taste, such as are belonging to many chapels; not to mention that rooms are stuccoed in this taste, with all the minute unmeaning carvings, which are found in the most Gothic chapels of a thousand years standing.[1]

So the streams of taste circled round and sidled down a thousand different channels, yet were all related in their source, even when they appeared to flow from opposite directions. Vigour and invention mark every branch of thought and design, and in painting a very evident improvement makes itself felt throughout. Already, by the time George III[2] ascended the throne, the English were no longer the worst painters in Europe—though no one seemed to notice the change. Probably they were the best, for the last glowing and flickering of the Venetian fires was dying down, and the most delightful of the French eighteenth-century pictures were already painted. . . . Who was there in Europe to be matched against Gainsborough, not only as a landscapist, but as a painter of fine and pompous portraits; who against Stubbs, that English primitive, with hounds and horses as his angels? . . . Yet, however great our painters, the English taste remained loyal to portraiture; and most pictures were either family groups, conversation pieces, single figures, or portraits of animals for country gentlemen.

The initial year of George III's reign witnessed also the end of private patronage; in the sense that the Society of Artists inaugurated the first of its annual exhibitions, and by means of them, painters, though they continued to benefit by the friendship of influential persons, were no longer entirely dependent on it for a living.

Yet the influence of these exhibitions was not altogether to the good, for, as Sir Joshua pointed out, the wish to please every one which they fostered exposed the artist to a very

[1] John Shebbeare, *B. Angeloni, Letters on the English Nation* (1755), vol. ii, p. 261.

[2] George III did his best to encourage the arts and fancied himself both as collector and patron, but he was not too discriminating. Politics entered into his pictorial taste, so that the Whig Sir Joshua was only awarded a commission as the result of his insisting on it as a condition of his retaining the presidency of the Royal Academy.

real peril. Nevertheless, through the institution of them, the merit of Gainsborough, Reynolds, and other great English painters became more widely recognized, and so, finding they could no longer compete, foreign artists at last abandoned England, thereby affording our own masters an opportunity of proving what they could achieve. Then, in 1768, the Royal Academy was founded—with Sir Joshua as President and Dr. Johnson as Professor of Ancient Literature—to merge all private academies and societies into one official body; and, if the influence it wielded was, as now, never very extensive, its exhibitions were, as now, very crowded.

It may be that one sign of the vigour of eighteenth-century England is to be discovered in the vehemence with which it followed the novelty of the moment, the pitch to which it carried a craze. Once the public had tasted the joys of an exhibition, it became insatiable in that direction. 'The rage to see these exhibitions,' Horace Walpole tells us, writing in 1779, 'is so great that sometimes one cannot pass through the streets where they are. But it is incredible what sums are raised by mere exhibitions of anything; a new fashion and to enter at which you pay a shilling or half a crown.' Not only, indeed, were people willing to pay their shillings, but there was even a widespread inclination to buy pictures. 'Since the arts have found protection from the throne, the taste for virtù has become universal; persons of all ranks and degrees set up for connoisseurs, and even the lowest people tell familiarly of Hannibal Scratchi, Paul Varnish, and Raphael Angelo.'[1] Tradesmen, who, in the phrase of Thackeray, were rising into manly opulence, regarded the ownership of a picture as a patent of gentility, while the Macaronis poured out their money almost as freely at the auction-rooms as on the gaming-tables. A perfect orgy of spending ensued and the prices of works of art rose every day higher, until works of the Italian masters of the sixteenth and seventeenth centuries soared to sums of four figures. . . . Alas! the Revolt of America marks the end of this delicious extravagance. Its effect on the picture-market was instantaneous; and three years later, the splendid collection at Houghton, which even seventy years before, when works were cheap, had cost Sir Robert Walpole a hundred thousand pounds, was, to the distress and chagrin of Horace Walpole,

[1] *Fugitive Miscellany*, 1775.

sold by his nephew to the Empress Catherine of Russia for thirty thousand.

In 1756, Burke had published his essay on the Sublime and the Beautiful; which for the rest of the century supplied to the connoisseurs an acceptable explanation of the two qualities they found in art. He had been the first to comprehend that aesthetic emotion was not a matter entirely of the intellect, but of the nerves and senses also; and, in his axiom that 'a clear idea is another word for a little idea', he nearly, if negatively, approached a definition of romanticism. Beauty, he laid it down, was that quality which causes quiet satisfaction and is founded on pleasure; involving smallness of scale, bright and clear colours, delicacy and smoothness. Thus a landscape by Claude, or a picture by Raphael or Carlo Dolci, and the majority of Greek (or what at that time passed for Greek) statues, the Venus de Medici and the Apollo Belvidere, were all imbued with this quality. But the Sublime, on the other hand, inspired awe and terror, and, with pain as its basis, was profoundly disturbing to the emotions. Dark and gloomy colours, vagueness and vastness of size and conception, rugged lines, and all that could induce 'delightful horror, which is the most genuine effect and truest test of the Sublime', were immanent in those things laying claim to this higher distinction. 'All works of great labour, expense and magnificence are sublime . . . and all buildings of very great dimensions or objects of very great richness and splendour . . . for in contemplating them the mind applies the ideas of the greatness of exertion necessary to produce such works, to the works themselves; and therefore feels them to be grand and sublime.'[1]

The Laocoon, the works of Salvator, both contained ingredients of the Sublime. But in literature was it to find fullest expression. From 1760 to 1763, the Ossianic poems were in process of appearing, and the immense and widespread influence of these vulgar and counterfeit productions must ever remain one of the most mysterious incidents in the whole, perverse history of Taste. Even their so strict adherence to Burke's rules for the Sublime might surely have

[1] The idea that a work great in size must perforce be great in manner and conception died very slowly. But Burke himself perceived the fallacy underlying his argument when he saw the pictures of his protégé, Barry, in the Adelphi.

aroused misgivings as to their authenticity. Ghosts, giants, storms, red-rolling eyes, and nightmarish torrents of blood are all provided in suspicious plenty, in order to furnish the reader with the needful and exquisite basis of pain. 'I saw a ghost on the darkening air. His stride extended from hill to hill.' Beauty was outdistanced and the Sublime was leading, winning on every side. Soon it would rise to new heights and sink to fresh depths in the towers and caverns of Fonthill Abbey, and advance by means of a myriad intimidating shadows from a past that had never existed. Poets would once again write ballads, and, in their spare time, drink out of skulls. The hypothetical vices of the Middle Ages would become the fashion: 'The flimsy giantry of Ossian has introduced mountainous horrors. The exhibitions at Somerset House are crowded with Brobdingnag ghosts'; so wrote Walpole in 1784. Common sense, indeed, was dead, and in that same year died Dr. Johnson, its curiously picturesque and comforting embodiment.

BIBLIOGRAPHY. (*a*) JAMES BARRY, *Works* (2 vols, 1809); *An Inquiry into the obstructions to the acquisition of the Arts in England* (1775); *A Letter to the Dilettanti* (1798). EDMUND BURKE, *Essay on the Sublime and Beautiful* (1756). ALLAN CUNNINGHAM, *Lives of British Painters, Sculptors and Architects* (6 vols., 1829–33). JAMES DALLAWAY, *Anecdotes of the Arts in England* (1800). EDWARD EDWARDS, *Anecdotes of Painters* (1808). The Rev. W. GILPIN, *Essays* (1792); *Observations . . . made in the year 1772* (2 vols., 1808). WILLIAM HOGARTH, *The Analysis of Beauty* (1753). J. LE BLANC, *Letters on the English and French Nations* (1747). WILLIAM MASON, *Works* (4 vols., 1811). Dr. MATY, *The Life of Dr. Richard Mead* (1755). JAMES NORTHCOTE, *Life of Sir Joshua Reynolds* (2 vols., 1813–15). R. PAYNE KNIGHT, *An Analytical Inquiry into the Principles of Taste* (1805). Sir UVEDALE PRICE, *Essays on the Picturesque* (1794). Sir JOSHUA REYNOLDS, *Discourses* (ed. Zimmern, 1887). JONATHAN RICHARDSON, *Works* (1773). JOHN SHEBBEARE, *B. Angeloni, Letters on the English Nation* (1755). J. T. SMITH, *Nollekens and his Times* (2 vols., 1828). HORACE WALPOLE, *Letters* (ed. Toynbee, 19 vols., 1903–25); *Anecdotes of Painting* (ed. R. Wornum, 3 vols., 1888). J. J. WINCKELMANN, *Reflections on the Painting and Sculpture of the Greeks* (1756).

(*b*) Sir LIONEL CUST, *History of the Society of the Dillettanti* (1914). CHRISTOPHER HUSSEY, *The Picturesque* (1927). A. MICHAELIS, *Ancient Marbles in Great Britain* (1882). JOHN PYE, *Patronage of British Art* (1845). C. R. LESLIE and T. TAYLOR, *Life and Times of Sir Joshua Reynolds* (2 vols. 1865). G. F. WAAGEN, *Works of Art and Artists in England* (1838).

XVI

PAINTING AND ENGRAVING

Edited by ANDREW SHIRLEY

It is in Painting as in Life; what is greatest is not always best. I should grieve to see *Reynolds* transfer to Heroes and to Goddesses, to empty splendor and to airy fiction, that art which is now employed in diffusing friendship, in reviving tenderness, in quickening the affection of the absent, and continuing the presence of the dead.—*The Idler* (24 Feb. 1759).

Painting, Sir, can illustrate, but cannot inform.—*Life of Johnson* (1784).

ACHIEVEMENT and change mark this period of painting, which is commonly associated with the foundation of the Royal Academy and with the careers of Reynolds and Gainsborough. Yet it is not possible to regard these, or indeed any two artists as the determining factor of the century's art. It is true that in his painting Reynolds expresses most fully the accepted stylistic ambitions of his time, just as in the *Discourses* he clothed them in words. But he was not the first painter of importance to make the tour of Italy, the source of the new ambitions. Equally must it be remembered that Gainsborough's art proceeds from a totally different stimulus, that his inspiration fed the succeeding generation rather than his own. Towards the end of the time there are mutterings of new doctrines in landscape. Furthermore, the resources of watercolour and engraving are enlarged by discovery to give the artist freer play. In fact this period, though so often called the golden age of our painting, lacks the static quality suggested by that phrase.

What is remarkable is that for the first time in history the body of English artists united for a common purpose and so achieved what was to them and to their public the outstanding event of their time—the foundation of the Royal Academy. But this in itself was no more responsible for the resurrection of English art than the Royal Society's charter was responsible for the birth of Newton. Socially, indeed, the Academy raised the artist's status and enlarged the scope of his appeal and practice: artistically it widened, even if it stereotyped, his education. But the mere recognition of forty artists as the leaders of their profession contains no new creative principle; and though this centralized authority facilitated the flow of ideas, we must look outside it for the source of the ideas themselves.

Between 1715 and 1722 Jonathan Richardson had published his four books,[1] and these soon became to every nobleman on the Grand Tour the guide-book and gospel of art. Inspired by them the artists found new gods in the Italian painters, and Reynolds went to Italy to learn for himself the secrets of Raphael and Michelangelo. The new doctrine and the manner of its presentation by the aestheticians evoked a fervour for 'great art', for compositions of dramatic scenes, called history paintings, culled from the poets or from history. In the seventeenth and early eighteenth century the decorative allegories on walls and ceilings had principally been painted by foreigners. But the Englishman, now aiming at something nobler than decorative effect, found confronting him obstacles of perilous draughtsmanship new to his experience. It was realized that to conquer them regular instruction in drawing was necessary; and from the struggle to achieve this the Academy in part proceeds.

The change in aesthetics was accompanied by a further reaction in technique, stimulated by experience gained from Italian journeys. A pioneer of new methods was Allan Ramsay, afterwards a Court painter of distinction, who studied on the spot the works of Luti and the contemporary Roman School. His innovations struck the older painters with horror. George Vertue, the first historian of the English School, protests: 'Certain it is that hitherto the manner he paints in is neither like the valuable manner of Dahl, Kneller, Lilly, Riley, Dobson, Vandyck, Rubens, or Titian—it is rather lickt than pencilled'.[2]

The names in the list are significant, for they give the artistic descent of the old English School as it was in 1740. The tradition of Vandyck had stood for fine draughtsmanship with the brush ('pencilling') and colour, in which Venetian secrets had their part. But the performance of its latest exponent, Kneller (d. 1723), whose success and conceit dominated our painting for forty years, had quite eclipsed the source. So strong and unquestioned was the authority of his

[1] *An Essay on the Theory of Painting* (1715); *An Essay on the whole Art of Criticism in Relation to Painting* (1719); *An Argument in behalf of the Science of a Connoisseur* (1719); *An Account of the Statues and Bas-reliefs, Drawings and Pictures in Italy, France, etc., with Remarks* (1722).

[2] Vertue, *MS. Notebooks in the British Museum.*

Names from left to right:

George Vertue
Hans Hysing
Michael Dahl
— Thomas
James Gibbs
Joseph Goupy
Matthew Robinson
Charles Bridgeman
Bernard Baron
John Wootton
J. M. Rysbrack
Gawen Hamilton
William Kent

A CLUB OF ARTISTS, 1735

From the painting by Gawen Hamilton in the National Portrait Gallery

name that in 1752 John Ellys, the King's painter, could say to young Reynolds, fresh from Italy, 'Ah, Reynolds, this will never answer. You don't paint in the least degree in the manner of Kneller!' adding in petulant explanation, 'Shakespeare in poetry and Kneller in painting, damme!' [1]

Such was the spent tradition from which the new generation swung away. When Reynolds went to Italy, Raphael and Michelangelo were his first masters; but though his great critical powers compelled him to acknowledge their superiority, his intellectual bias, an outstanding quality with him as a man rather than as an artist, led him also to appreciate the eclectic painters of Bologna. Through them he advanced to the study of Venetian colour, which remained a passion with him all his life. He was for ever—and at times to the detriment of his work—experimenting with pigments: he would even buy an old master and completely rub it away to learn how the paint and glazes had been laid on. To assimilate such varied ingredients required a powerful individuality; but out of them he formed a massive and homogeneous style in portraiture, though his imaginative pieces do not always carry the same conviction. Spurred on by his success and teaching, his contemporaries tried to digest the same food. The level of their portraiture is far higher than in the early part of the century; but they broke down more completely, and fell into patchiness, when handling more ambitious themes.

This general advance in technical excellence was achieved in the face of many obstacles, not only of tradition but of patronage. In 1740 Kneller's authority obsessed the artists' minds. Some fresh ideas might have been expected from the many foreign painters who came here, but they were only the traditional raiders on English patronage; they made their money while the market was good, viewed with profound distrust and jealousy by the native artists until they left with loaded saddle-bags. Meanwhile the fashion was moribund which tricked out saloons and staircases in painted mythology, and the field for the history-painter was by so much narrowed. Landscape was barely tolerated except in its relation to horsemen or houses. There was indeed plenty of business for the portrait painters; but they reiterated their statements in the idiom of 1700. This is hardly surprising, once

[1] Northcote, *Life of Reynolds* (1813–15), vol. i, p. 54.

their mediocrity is forgiven, since they laboured under every disadvantage. There were in London plenty of pictures of the finest quality by old masters. Frederick, Prince of Wales, was adding intelligently to the royal collections; and there were eminent private collectors too. But only one of them, Dr. Mead, Watteau's patron and physician, went so far as to let students copy pictures in his possession: in general such galleries were closed to the professional public. So late as 1800 we hear complaints against fees, equivalent to a guinea to-day, extorted by housekeepers and janitors at Wilton. Experience was not to be afforded at this rate. Nor did the auction rooms give them greater opportunity, for only the well-dressed were admitted to an important sale. An artist could reckon on no materials for study excepting such collections of drawings by old masters or prints as he could form himself. Architects flourished; they were enabled to travel abroad and humble themselves before Palladio's shrine; theirs was a fashionable art. But no such intelligent patronage came the painters' way. Sir Robert Walpole rewarded John Ellys[1] for his help in forming the Houghton collection with the Keepership of the King's Beasts at the Tower.

A portrait painter was often called, and without offence, a 'face-painter', and the phrase had this much truth in it, that few of them did, and some could not, paint more than the face. 'At a distance one would take a dozen of their portraits to be twelve copies of the same original. Some have their heads turned to the left, some to the right; that is all the difference, excepting only the countenance or likeness, they have the same neck, the same arms, the same colouring, the same attitude.'[2] This orthodoxy of pose was achieved by the drapery-painters rather than the artists themselves. The hallowed example of Vandyck, Lely, and Kneller, who had employed their own assistants for accessories, by now had licensed an arrangement by which several artists employed the same drapery-painter. It is hard to credit the share taken in the manufacture of portraits by these painters' ghosts. Hamlet Winstanley, pupil of Kneller and master of Stubbs, having to paint a family group in Lancashire, sketched the heads of his

[1] The success of Ellys's career is a tribute to the importance of ministerial support at a time when an artist's politics could still affect appointments.

[2] Abbé le Blanc, quoted by W. T. Whitley, *Artists and their Friends in England, 1700–99* (1928), vol. i, p. 54.

sitters on the spot, and sent them up to Vanaken, the drapery-painter in London, who fixed them in position on the canvas, and then painted the rest of the picture. So vital to success was Vanaken's help considered, that the principal native painters threatened to withdraw their work from him if he assisted Van Loo, their French rival. Hogarth was not far out when he caricatured Vanaken's funeral with all the eminent portrait painters attending as desperate mourners. And official recognition of such skill lasted till the election of Peter Toms, better known as Reynolds's drapery-man than for his theatrical scenes, as foundation member of the Academy.

Three painters of varying eminence stood aside from this common practice. Hogarth and Joseph Highmore, of whom we shall hear again, have other claims to distinction. But it is more surprising to find John Ellys writing to a sitter in 1751:

I should get my pictures done sooner if I did not do every part of them myself, for I may tell you as a friend (for I am not dealing with you as a painter) I never liked the picture in my life which was of two hands on one cloth; for the drapery painter always makes the drapery more conspicuous than the head, so in reality it is a picture of drapery with a head put to it as a background.

The truth is that even those who enjoyed the most flattering patronage were scantily trained, but the public seemed content with such talent as the painter could display unaided.

There was little opportunity for instruction and regular study in 1740, and it is hard to determine what a pupil learnt from his master. His most profitable experience came no doubt from making copies of the great man's work; he might thus learn at least to lay paint on canvas and to colour, even if in drawing the blind led the blind. Beyond this his multifarious duties left him little time for enterprise. Reynolds required Marchi, his first assistant, to do anything from painting or arranging draperies to posing as a model; and as Northcote states elsewhere, his advice to pupils was verbal rather than practical. Yet here was a man pre-eminently interested in artistic education. There remained a drawing academy in St. Martin's Lane, a relic from the early years of the century resurrected by Hogarth. Of this pathetically important institution *The London Tradesman* writes in 1747:

Painting. The present State of this art in Britain does not afford sufficient education to a painter. We have but one Academy meanly supported by the private subscriptions of the students, in all this great metropolis. There they have but two figures, a man and a woman, and consequently there can be but little experience gathered. The subscribers to this lame Academy pay two guineas a season which goes to the expense of the room and lights. The subscribers in their turn set the figure, that is place the man and woman in such attitude in the middle of the room as suits their fancy. He who sets the figure chooses what seat he likes and all the rest take their places according as they stand in the list and then proceed to drawing, every man according to his prospect of the figure.

Here, it is true, there was nothing that could be called regular instruction: it was a drawing club rather than an academy. But Reynolds, after his return from Italy, Hogarth, Hayman, and other leaders attended; and drawing at their side, learners picked up what they could. And there was this added virtue that it kept alive the ideal of a drawing school, and formed a meeting ground where artists could elaborate projects for realizing this and kindred schemes.

The weakness of native draughtsmen in the early part of the century had lost them the most lucrative and important commissions outside portraiture. These had gone principally to foreigners; but we can see from a list of eminent painters in 1748 that their numbers had diminished considerably since George I's time. The list runs:

Austin, Browne, Barratt, Blakey, Crank, Dandridge, Eccard, Ellys, Fry, Gainsborough, Goupy, Goodwin, Green, Grilsieir, de Groit, Hayman, Hogarth, Hoar, Hymore, Hudson, Jenkins, Knapton, Lambert, Lens, Mathias, Monamie, Murry, Penny, Pine, Pond, Ramsey, Reynolds, Scot, Seymour, Shackleton, Soldy, Somers, Spencer, Smith, Toms, the two Vanhakens, Van Blake, Van Diest, Vanderbank, Vandergucht, Verelst, Wills, Wotton, Worsdale, Wood, Wilks, Wilson, Wollaston, Zink.[1]

Of the foreigners, easily the most important is Christian Frederick Zincke, the German enameller. George II, a patron at least of portraiture—perhaps he did not regard it as 'bainting'—was eager to engross the whole of Zincke's activity, though he had a more distinguished clientele than any contemporary. Vertue records how

Zincke often at Court draws the pictures of the Royal family—having drawn the Prince of Wales and the three Princes— the young

[1] *Universal Magazine*, Nov. 1748.

THE LIFE SCHOOL AT HOGARTH'S ACADEMY IN ST. MARTIN'S LANE

From the painting by W. Hogarth

children—the King and Queen have sat to him. The Queen advised him to be sure to make the King's portrait young—not above twenty-five—and the King commended his work and admonished him not to make the Queen's portrait above twenty-eight. The King was so well satisfied that he was pleased to say he took more pleasure in sitting to him than he did to any other painters, for that his works were beautiful and like. He bespoke many copies of his picture and at the same time before the Queen (being present) he said 'I should like that you employ all your time in pictures for me, I will take them all'.[1]

The majority of the English names are extremely obscure; but the rising and the falling stars are nicely balanced, and it is interesting to see Reynolds and Gainsborough so early included. Of the older generation Hudson, Reynolds's master, who had the biggest practice in portraits, Hogarth, and Highmore stand out. Hogarth, the greatest satirist in English painting, exercised little technical influence on his time. His broad style, evolved with conscious irreverence for the old masters, was considered rough and unfinished; nor did his arrogance or readiness to caricature his rivals in their works and in their persons help to popularize his methods, brilliantly suited though they were to their purpose. Among the public, too, he had as a painter the narrowest circle of admirers. His portraits were too honest, too distinct from the common type, to be commissioned without risk. Even his great series of satires, engravings of which sold in thousands, failed to please in paint: the 'Marriage à la Mode' was even raffled. Of Highmore it is sufficient praise to say that till recent years many of his works have passed as Hogarth's. An able portraitist, an illustrator of more than common power, with a nice gift for the figure, though lacking Hogarth's ability to fill his subject with relevant detail, he has solid merit.

Hogarth has an historical importance that rivals his standing as an artist. Through engravings from his work he reached an enormous public and prepared them to welcome narrative pictures and in particular the conversation piece that was to become so typical of the period. In its essence this is a blend of the seventeenth-century family group and the genre picture. The idea of portraiture, that is to say, is necessary; but the relation of figures to their setting is also important. There is an instructive criticism by a contemporary of Zoffany's

[1] Vertue, *MS. Notebooks in the British Museum.*

painting of the famous scene in *The Farmer's Return*, where Garrick, as the farmer back from town, tells the story of the Cock Lane Ghost. 'This painter absolutely transports us in imagination back again to the theatre. We see our favourite Garrick, and we see his wife and children—in terror and amazement.'[1] Here the localization of the episode and the convincing likeness are the source of the painter's success with the observer. But the subject could equally well be a family taking tea in the drawing-room or a collation *en plein air*; an assembly of artists or a musical party. The convention had a wide vogue, and among its interpreters were Hayman, Devis, Highmore, and Copley. But in the hands of the greater painters, Hogarth, Gainsborough, and Zoffany, the figures that justified the commission take a secondary place in the picture.

It is singular that Hogarth, the man whose gift it was to alienate his fellow artists by arrogant originality or personal satire, while he derided potential patrons as obsessed with the old masters, should have influenced English artists towards corporate action. No one was less suited by temperament or declared faith to lead the movement which ended with the foundation of the Royal Academy; yet inadvertently he took the first step towards it.

In 1739 the Foundling Hospital was opened and in the following year Hogarth presented his portrait of Captain Coram, 'the Old Gent who proposed and projected first . . . and is thought to be very well'. Other artists followed his example and in 1746 the benefactors were elected Governors of the Hospital where they held an annual dinner. From pictures by Ramsay, Wilson, Hayman, Highmore, and Gainsborough—to name only a few—a very respectable gallery of modern art was formed. It became fashionable to visit it; a collection of contemporary paintings was thus for the first time discussed; and by thus insensibly preparing the public for the idea of annual exhibitions, the artists were solving one of their major problems.

For if it was hard for an artist to see any pictures of quality in London, it was almost harder for him to exhibit his own or by any other means to make his name known. There were indeed dealers in old masters, fakes, and modern paintings;

[1] W. T. Whitley, *Artists and their Friends in England, 1700–99*, vol. i, p. 180.

THE CONVERSATION PIECE: A FISHING PARTY

From the painting by W. Hogarth in the Dulwich College Picture Gallery

but they were dangerous aids. Too often a painter who had accepted an advance against a possible sale would find himself obliged to work off the debt by copying. It was safer to persuade a friendly tradesman or tavern keeper to hang up the pictures in his shop or parlour. Of course potential patrons were admitted to the studio; but any regular attempt on public favour by a private exhibition was almost unknown. A rare instance is Highmore's announcement in the *London Evening Post*, 1744.

Mr. Highmore proposes to publish by subscription twelve prints by the best French engravers after his own paintings, representing the most remarkable adventures of Pamela; in which he has endeavoured to comprehend her whole story as well as to preserve a connection between the several pictures, which follow each other as parts successive and dependent, so as to complete the subject. This is more distinctly illustrated in the account attached to the proposals, wherein all the twelve pictures are described and their respective connections shown. All the pictures being now completed and to be seen at Mr. Highmore's house, the Two Lyons, Lincoln's Inn Fields.

Unless he paid for an advertisement in the Press or was advanced to some official appointment, an artist could hope in 1740 for no notice from the newspapers: and the surest means to publicity that remained to him was the engraved portrait. A foreign observer touched the truth on the artists' side when he wrote: 'The painter's name appears under the plate . . . it is a public acknowledgement of his existence, which might be otherwise obscure, and he does not expect more of it than that.'[1]

The ambition to achieve some status for the arts had been fermenting for some years. At St. Martin's Lane and at the Turk's Head, Gerrard Street, more than one scheme had been formulated. In 1753, an academy of twenty-one had been proposed—thirteen painters, three sculptors, one chaser, two engravers, and two architects—with adequate professorships attached. Without financial backing the idea was necessarily chimerical, and the artists meeting at the Turk's Head refused their assent and subscriptions to what they probably regarded as the proposal of a caucus. So Hayman, Newton, and the other moving spirits reverted from the artists to the public in their appeal for funds. Again, professorships were to be provided and competent instruction of young artists was to

[1] Rouquet, *L'État des Arts en Angleterre* (1758), p. 127.

assure the progress of the generation. Connexion with the Crown, if only nominal, was a further aspiration. The Dilettanti Society was prepared to negotiate and to provide funds for the artists. But it soon appeared that the professionals were less ready to allow the gentlemen a share in the administration than they were to take their money. And once more the business fell flat.

At last, in 1759, the artists, at their annual dinner at the Foundlings, agreed upon a plan for an exhibition and also solved the problem of housing it. Their first approach succeeded; the Society for the Encouragement of Arts, Manufacture, and Commerce agreed to lend their room; and the period of the exhibition was fixed for April 21 to May 8, 1760. A better choice could hardly have been made. They acquired the aegis of a polite society; and the great room in the Strand, opposite Beaufort Buildings, was large enough and well lit—a rare combination then. The artists hoped to establish a charitable fund for their fellows whose 'age and infirmities or other lawful hindrances prevent them from being any longer candidates for fame'. The Society refused to allow an entrance fee, though the sale of catalogues at sixpence realized a profit of over £100. And the artists were so far emboldened by their first public success that on George III's accession they delivered an address to him which was composed by Johnson.

The artists applied to the Society for the use of their room in 1761, but met with fresh difficulties. Once more a charge for admission was vetoed, and a rider equally unpalatable was added, that the Society's committee should select and hang the exhibition. This was too much patronage. The previous year the walls had been seeded with productions, often immature, that had won the Society's premium; and an uninstructed public had taken them, being prize-winners, for the cream of British art. When it is remembered that these were separately classified for sons and daughters of peers, young gentlemen and young ladies, and thirdly for art students, the professionals will be excused for refusing to show again in supposed competition with such company.

So the Society's proposal was declined, and the artists, distinguishing themselves as The Society of Artists, found a room for £40 for the month in Spring Gardens, Charing Cross, and here they continued to exhibit for several years. Its shabbiness—it was an auction room over a china warehouse —was no deterrent to visitors; and £650 were the net proceeds in 1761. The only entrance fee was a shilling for the catalogue which served as a season-ticket. Hogarth drew the caustic tailpiece—a monkey, richly dressed as a connoisseur, watering withered trees symbolizing the old masters.

Meanwhile a less distinguished residue continued faithful to the Society of Arts in the Strand and next year enrolled themselves as The Free Society of Artists of Great Britain. Their story can be briefly told. After a few years the patron Society's arrogance evicted from the committee of management all the artists, who thereupon seceded and held their own exhibitions in Maiden Lane, Covent Garden. There they prospered well enough, and their receipts, though small, were adequately managed for their charities. But in 1768, with miscalculating ambition, they built a gallery next to Cumberland House, Pall Mall; and their first show there coincided with the first year of the Royal Academy. Between 1769 and 1773 receipts fell from £189 to £81. Their gallery was sold, and after 1779 they ceased to exhibit. However admirable might be the intentions of the Free Society, it lacked the talent and the patronage necessary for success. Romney was the only painter of mark to be even a fitful contributor, and his name alone was not sufficient counterpoise to the Society of Artists or the Academy.

The Society of Artists, however, grew from strength to strength. It included the greatest painters of the day and had the biggest membership at a time when quantity mattered. In 1765 it was incorporated by royal charter, and by 1767 the receipts touched the gay figure of £1,145. Naturally, perhaps, the administration fell into the hands of a committee which arrogated to itself the powers of electing president and secretary, of filling any vacancy in its own ranks, and of managing the exhibitions. Such oligarchy bred discontent, and a crisis arose when members demanded under the charter that a proportion of the directors should retire each year. They won their case by reference to the Attorney-General's opinion, and at the election of 1768 sixteen of the twenty-four directors were not returned. The remaining eight handed in their resignations to the newly elected president, Joshua Kirby, formerly a coach-painter.

Thus in appearance the members of the Society of Artists

had won a clear victory. But in fact the ablest and most influential part of the Society followed the ex-directors. West and Chambers acted for them and apprised the King of these dissensions. Then with two others they formed a committee to draft a constitution, based largely on the project of 1753. This the King received and sanctioned, and on December 10, 1768, the Royal Academy of London came into being with Joshua Reynolds as president. On January 2, 1769, he delivered the first of his fifteen discourses.

The 'Instrument', as the constitution was called, owed much to experience. The council was varied by yearly election, only the president, secretary, and keeper, being permanent officials. The posts of treasurer and librarian were in the King's gift, and through the former he controlled the expenditure, to which he contributed freely in the first years. The hanging committees were chosen at first by lot from the Council. 'They had no pay. Mrs. Malyn [housekeeper] prepared the dinner in the little passage room between the 2 rooms at the Royal Academy, Pallmall—roasting the principal joint on a string. Once while each Committee continued it was customary to invite Sir Joshua Reynolds and Sir William Chambers to dinner, on which day Mrs. Newton, the Secretarys wife prepared a pye she was famous for making, of veal & Ham in a large dish.'[1]

While the constitution was thus far democratic in the relations of officers to members, as regards the outside world it was most exclusive. There had been virtually no limit to the membership of the Free Society or of the Society of Artists. But the Academy was to have no more than forty members,[2] with twenty associates. Moreover, it refused to acknowledge the existence of any kindred authority in art. No member might exhibit with any other society; and the effect of this was naturally that every aspirant to public distinction exhibited at the Academy, the only road to title. For instance,

[1] J. Farington, *Diary*, vol. i, p. 277.

[2] The original members were Reynolds (president), Newton (secretary), Chambers (treasurer), G. M. Moser (keeper), Penny (professor of painting), Thomas Sandby (professor of architecture), Wale (professor of perspective), Cotes, West, Baker, Chamberlin, Gwynn, Gainsborough, Cipriani, Meyer, Paul Sandby, Catton, Hone, Bartolozzi, Tyler, N. Dance, Wilson, Toms, Kauffmann, Yeo, Mary Moser, Wilton, Barrett, Carlini, Hayman, Serres, Richards, Zuccarelli. G. Dance, W. Hoare, and Zoffany were nominated by the King in 1769 and by 1773 membership had been completed by the election of Cosway, Burch, Nollekens, and Barry.

in 1783 there were 233 non-members who exhibited and only thirty-three members. But the field of recognition was narrowed. While the first project embraced, besides the major arts, chasing, engraving, and seal cutting, of these only engraving was accepted in 1770, and that only partially. It was not till 1881 that it was possible for an engraver to attain the full rank of Academician.

To the student the Academy was certainly a blessing. The ambition to study in Italy was uppermost in every young artist's mind; and now a travelling scholarship enabled the winner to work for a year in Rome without expense. At home the drawing school was the object of care and expenditure which was backed by the King's generosity. Most of the casts from St. Martin's Lane had already been secured; and £90 was paid for a lay figure, while the Society of Artists could only afford £20. The most eminent anatomist of the day, Dr. William Hunter, lectured as professor to the students. There were minute regulations for the conduct of the life class. Four men of different types were retained as models at 5*s.* a week, with a 1*s.* extra for each sitting. The women models, disapproved of by the morality of the day, were paid half a guinea for a sitting of two or three hours. But the Society could only offer 7*s.* 6*d.*, though their accounts also include such occasional items as 'Liquor for the Woman Model 4*s.*'

A different Academician set the figure each month; and there was a rule that no person under twenty should draw from the female model unless he was married. Further it was enacted that no one, 'The Royal Family excepted, is admitted into the academy during the time the female model is sitting.' This propriety may be compared with the public outcry against the nude casts in a room adjoining the Great Gallery at Somerset House. They were 'the terror of every decent woman'; a correspondent to another paper declared that many women rather than pass them by had sacrificed the pleasure of seeing the best pictures; 'has decency entirely left the direction of the institution or has the unblushing countenance of a P[eters] laughed you out of the sense of delicacy?'

The Academy was established first at an auction-room in Pall Mall, nearly opposite the site of the present Carlton Hotel; and its principal qualification was that it had top light. Here artists remained till 1780 when new rooms were opened for them in Somerset House, rebuilt for George III, by their treasurer, Chambers. There was the great exhibition gallery, reached through the offensive 'plaister academy', apartments and offices for the keeper and secretary, and the Council Room in which hung Reynolds's portraits of the King and Queen. On May 1

the exhibition of the artists at the Royal Academy was opened in the new buildings, Somerset Place, where a noble suite of rooms has been adapted for that purpose. The grand room is at the top which receives a fine refracted light from the arched side-windows above. The rooms beneath are appropriated for drawings, models, statues, busts, &c. At the end of one are the portraits of their Majesties by Sir Joshua Reynolds, which, if it were not likely to be deemed high treason against the prince of painters, we should be apt to criticize pretty freely. The *tout ensemble* of the present exhibition is allowed on all hands to do infinite honour to the British arts and certainly contains many pictures that will prove lasting monuments of the real genius of the several artists.

The concourse of the people of fashion who attended the opening of the Royal Academy exhibition yesterday was incredible; the carriages filled the whole wide space from the New Church to Exeter Change. It is computed that the door-keepers did not take less than £500 for the admission of the numerous visitants of all ranks.

This figure must be one of the *Morning Post's* hyperboles, for the whole season only brought £3,069 in receipts. But from this time onwards the Academy existed without financial support from the King.

This fanfare opening marks the final victory of the Academy. The Free Society was no more. The Society of Artists, too, had decayed since 1769, when it was strong in its following and in funds. Joshua Kirby, its president, never recovered from the King's acceptance of the Academy project; and James Paine, the architect, active and capable, succeeded him. Undeterred by the example of the Free Society, biased perhaps by its president's profession, it now built a gallery near the Lyceum. But the debt contracted in this venture ruined its finances, and after holding only one exhibition there in 1773 the members were obliged to sell it. This loss of prestige they never made up, and in two of the next six years no shows were held. The Academy's clause against exhibiting with rival bodies had made inroads on the membership.

THE ANTIQUE SCHOOL OF THE ROYAL ACADEMY AT SOMERSET HOUSE

From the painting by J. Zoffany

Zoffany, Wright of Derby, Valentine Green, and Cosway in turn deserted: George Stubbs, almost their last painter of distinction, accepted associate rank in 1780, and this symbolized defeat. In 1791 they showed for the last time at Spring Gardens, their place of origin.

The generation of 1740 had thus accomplished great changes in their thirty years. Where there had been the one lame academy described by the *London Tradesman*, there were in 1770 four drawing schools, of which three were gratuitous. The ideal of a charitable fund was realized, and the artist secured from the imminence of degradation. At the other end of the scale he was uplifted by positive connexion with the Crown. The Society of Artists had a charter. The Academy was Royal and its diplomas were signed by the King. George III may have wanted the refined judgement of 'poor Fred', his father, but he backed the Academy to the extent of £5,000, and the example of his patronage of modern art spread to others.

An artist had been to the outer world an unpractical, unplaceable tradesman—face-painters, coach-painters, and house-painters had alike belonged to the Painter-Stainers Company. By 1770 he had become some one to be admitted to the drawing-room at a large reception. Undoubtedly Reynolds's social success had some part in this recognition, but it takes more than one man's personality to account for the rapid advance from the artists' simple dinners at the Foundlings to the Academy banquets when noble, and even royal, guests were present. The Academy's art, rather than the Academicians themselves, at once took its place in polite life. By 1770 it had become unfashionable to visit their rivals; 'at least 'tis unfashionable to say you have been to any other; but while Elmer excells so in dead game, still life, and droll portraits and Stubbs in animals and trees, I must own I've pleasure in seeing their performances, though not exhibited at the Royal Academy'.[1]

At the same time, whether as cause or effect, the newspapers began to take art seriously and to report the exhibitions, until by Johnson's death such reviews were stock-in-trade. The first exhibition of 1760 is noticed in only one journal, the *Imperial Magazine*; and such gaps are not uncommon. For instance, the opening of the Royal Academy's first exhibition

[1] *Diaries of Mrs. Philip Lybbe Powys* (1899), p. 122.

in 1769 attracted no more than one brief note without criticism, apart from the *Gazetteer's* record that 'on Wednesday (April 28) was opened for the first time the exhibition of the Royal Academy in Pall Mall to a very crowded and brilliant rout of persons of the first position'. But the illuminations at the Academy for the King's birthday a few weeks later are described at length.

On the other hand, the rival exhibitions of 1761 stirred partisanship. A correspondent in *The Public Advertiser* claims to see in the newspaper reports an attempt to 'puff off the Turk's Head artists'; another, with Hogarth's tailpiece in mind, implies that the scheme was designed to push the claims of living artists against old masters. In course of time the newspapers came to adopt their protégés, whom they championed in Ruskin's manner by attacking every one else. It was in 1774 that Reynolds first met serious criticism on a charge that his colours fled. The following year Nathaniel Hone, R.A., brazenly submitted to the Academy 'The Conjurer', a caricature of Reynolds's style in general and of his 'Ugolino' in particular. Naturally it was rejected; but Hone showed it himself, and a spate of more or less scurrilous verses descended on the President. Those by the Rev. Henry Bate, Gainsborough's protagonist, are worth quoting:[1]

> What 's Raphael, Guido, and the rest?
> Poor dogs, Sir Joshua, at the best!
> If no idea bright
> They lose—without Hone's demi-devil
> Like Bow-Street runner—most uncivil—
> Bringing the theft to light!
>
> Such rude detections are not clever,
> But ridicule can't live for ever!
> 'Tis well, 'your colours fly';
> For though the models ne'er decay,
> Yet will the *copies* fade away,
> And with them satire die.

The paucity of early notices is probably due to the dearth of journalists competent to write them, and what appeared may have been often the work of amateurs. With Bate's editorship of the *Morning Post*, art criticism becomes a

[1] William T. Whitley, *An Eighteenth Century Art Chronicler, Sir Henry Bate Dudley, Bart.* Walpole Society, vol. xiii, p. 56.

THE ROYAL ACADEMY OF ARTS, 1772

From the engraving by R. Earlom after the painting by J. Zoffany

regular feature of journalism, and notes were even included on the progress of pictures still in the artist's studio. The following critiques of Reynolds and of Gainsborough appeared from Bate's pen in the same year; and we may suppose them evidence of what interested the educated public in a picture. Of Reynolds's group, the Marlborough Family, he writes:

The composition abounds with every absurdity, and as to the plagiarisms they are really capital. The Corregiesque character in some, the Carlo Maratti in others, with those negative characters which the painter has given to the remaining part of the group, added to the servile character of the draperies of Vandyck, and others again in the manner of Rembrandt, make it the worst of all oil Olios that ever was exhibited, although meant as a very capital performance.

The complexions of the figures too are most cadaverously insulted. It is well known that the two principals were always troubled with the gripes, but nevertheless it was cruel of Sir Joshua to physic them to that unmerciful degree to bring them down to the deadly tone of his palette.[1]

Of Gainsborough, however, he writes:

He has been reproached with negligence in finishing, but if his pieces be viewed at a proper distance, which, as it is manifestly his design, is the only just way of estimating their merit, this imputation will appear totally without foundation. . . . No. 119 is a most inimitable performance—the cows in this piece seem to have a force that detach them from the canvas. No. 120. Only to be exceeded by the preceding.[2]

Bate's acid strictures on Reynolds were partly inspired by the Academy's insult to Gainsborough in rejecting his 'Duchess of Cumberland' in 1772. We need not concern ourselves with the rights and wrongs of the quarrel and reconciliation that followed, nor of the final breach. The importance of the episode lies only in the result—that Gainsborough showed no more with the Academy after 1783. Instead he kept his works permanently on view at Schomberg House, and Bate wrote frequent notices of them in his new paper, the *Morning Herald*, where he devoted regular space, 'the Painter's Mirror', to art-criticism. Journalism, it was proved, could support a painter against established authority.

Of the important artists in the period, Romney alone

[1] William T. Whitley, *An Eighteenth Century Art Chronicler, Sir Henry Bate Dudley, Bart.* Walpole Society, vol. xiii, p. 34. [2] Ibid., p. 35.

attracted little attention from the critics. He seldom showed in public, and then with the Free Society which had fallen into disrepute. But he had a certain following among the younger generation, and a fine connexion. Reynolds's income was, of course, princely; his price for a head rose from 5 guineas in 1753 to 25 in 1760, and two years later Johnson states he was making £6,000 a year. In 1786 Gainsborough was charging 40 guineas for a head, 80 for a half-length, 160 for a full-length portrait. Romney's professional income in the same year was 3,504 guineas; and seeing that he had no public position, this was a considerable achievement.

With the interest of the papers and a variety of galleries now at his command, the artist ceased to be 'generally speaking the property of picture dealers' by whom he had been 'held in somewhat the same kind of vassalage and dependance that many authors are by booksellers in this day'. He could risk with an increased chance of a sale something more than a commissioned picture. Mural painting on a grand scale was out of fashion. However, there was, as has been said, a compensating demand for narrative pictures. Thus far the popularity of history-painting is related to that of the conversation piece; and painter and public were the more disposed to prefer the former's merit, when the high priests were descanting on Grandeur, Ideal Beauty, and High Art.

Perhaps this popularity would not have come so soon but for the vogue of the illustrated book. From mere portraits of kings and statesmen ambitious publishers advanced to commission battle-pieces, coronations, and treaties to embellish the page. Naturally they turned for designs to the mural decorators and scene painters, as artists of trained imagination; and for Hogarth's generation such work spanned the gap between the fashion for painted walls and the exhibitions. Hayman's name was established in 1740 and he commanded a high price: while Samuel Wale, also an original academician, was paid half a guinea each for drawings, Hayman could get two. But the age of successful prints from a single picture does not come in till the exhibitions. Woollett's engraving from Wilson's 'Niobe', for instance, which brought the publisher £2,000, was issued in 1761; his 'Death of Wolfe', after West, dated 1776, made £15,000 in fourteen years. Such figures prepare us for the astounding triumph of Copley's 'Death of Chatham', which he showed at his gallery in 1781.

REGULUS

From the painting by Benjamin West in Kensington Palace. By gracious permission of His Majesty the King

Over 20,000 people paid their shilling to gaze at it in reverent silence: and the Academy receipts fell that year by almost £1,000. Hayman's paintings for Vauxhall Gardens had made some stir in 1756; but it would have been incredible in that day that such crowds should pay to see them.

History-paintings were in the ascendant and fired popular enthusiasm; the scale at least on which such works were designed was impressive. The principal hero was the American painter, Benjamin West, afterwards Reynolds's successor as President of the Academy. Out of a slender, theatrical talent for composition he built up a vast reputation. Drummond, Archbishop of York, tried to raise a fund of £3,000 to enable him to abandon portraiture, but failing in this, introduced him to the King. George became his patron and commissioned vast canvasses of heroes and paladins to dignify Windsor. In 1770 Walpole says that he 'gets three hundred pounds for a piece not too large to hang over a chimney'.[1]

Appreciations of his art are astounding. Even Reynolds, generally a capable, common-sense critic, could bow his head before the 'Regulus' and say, 'Mr. West, you have conquered'. Less instructed minds went further. 'He goes on painting like a Raphael and really outdoes everything one could have expected'.[2] 'As an artist he will stand in the front rank. His name will be classed with those of Michael Angelo and Raphael but he possessed little in common with either. As the former has been compared with Homer and the latter to Virgil, in Shakespeare we shall perhaps find the best likeness to the genius of Mr. West.'[3] By this fantastic selection of comparisons the wholly literary quality of the history-painting school is revealed. Nor was this conception of painting confined to the public; it existed in the minds of the artists themselves.

A quotation illustrative of this may be taken from a description given, as was common in exhibition catalogues and the like, by the painter of his own work. The Society of Arts had intended to adorn their great room with paintings of English history or 'relative to the institution and views of the Society' by ten Academicians. But when the negotiations

[1] *Letters* (ed. Toynbee), vol. vii, p. 379.

[2] W. T. Whitley, *Artists and their Friends in England, 1700–99*, vol. i, p. 262.

[3] Ibid., p. 262.

broke down, the whole was entrusted to one of them, James Barry. At last in 1783 the series, the grandest project[1] in this vein of the generation, was completed and Barry writes of it:

In this series of six pictures or subjects useful and agreeable in themselves, I have endeavoured to give them some such connection as might serve to illustrate one great maxim on moral truth; viz. that the obtaining of happiness, as well individual as public, depends upon cultivating the human faculties. We begin with man in a savage state, full of inconvenience, imperfection and misery; and we follow him through several gradations of culture and happiness, which, after a probationary state here, are finally attended with beatitude or misery. The first is the story of Orpheus; the second a Harvest-home, or Thanksgiving; the third the Victors at Olympia; the fourth Navigation or the Triumph of the Thames; the fifth the Distribution of Praemiums in the Society of Arts, etc.; and the sixth Elysium, or the State of final Retribution. Three of these subjects are poetical, the others historical.

How far the artist could stray from the essentials of his art, is shown by part of William Hodges's description of his 'Effects of Peace'. 'The two dogs in the front of the picture point out the beneficence of the landlord, by the care his tenant has taken of them in the recess of the hunting season'.[2]

Landscape, apart from topography, never won recognition in the same degree. The appreciation of it grew slowly, and in 1829 Lawrence could still congratulate Constable on being elected academician against a history-painter. It was not landscape at the Foundlings that excited praise, though it was as thoroughly represented there as history-painting or portraiture. Vertue records only one landscape by Gainsborough and neglects Wilson entirely. A rare appreciation, this time in verse, shows the elementary state of criticism.

Hayman by scenes our senses can control
And with creative power charm the soul.
His easy pencil flows with sure command
And nature starts obedient to his hand.
We hear the tinkling rill, we view the trees
Cast dusky shade and wave in gentle breeze.[3]

[1] The other great design was the decoration of St. Paul's with sacred pictures; but the plan was vetoed by Dr. Terrick, Bishop of London, lest it should be regarded as 'an artful intrusion of popery'.

[2] Edwards, *Anecdotes*, p. 249. His comment may be added, that the landlord appears nowhere in the picture.

[3] From an anonymous poem, *c.* 1750.

Yet some good work was produced at this time, though often in disguised forms. Wootton, for instance, was thought of as an animal painter; yet his charm lies as often in the country scene as in the horse or hound that provoked the commission. Richard Wilson, to us a most brilliant and luminous painter, failed signally with the public[1] after his return from Italy, and the place to which his talents entitled him was usurped by the banal George Barrett.

Wilson's lack of success is the more striking, since his art, though it transcends that of all competitors in the same manner, reflects the current rules of composition. A poem by the Rev. William Gilpin, brother of the painter, tells us how landscapes should be constructed and demonstrates the formality in arrangement necessary for success. It is dedicated to William Locke of Norbury who had been Wilson's companion in Italy. After marking the importance of studying from nature and of choosing objects suited to the scene, he proceeds to Disposition.

> With equal vigour DISPOSITION claims
> Thy close attention. Would'st thou learn its laws,
> Examine Nature, when combined with art,
> Or simple; mark how various are her forms,
> Mountains enormous, rugged rocks, clear lakes,
> Castles, and bridges, aqueducts and fanes.
> Of these observe, how some, united please;
> While others, ill-combined, disgust the eye.
> That principle which rules these various parts,
> And harmonising *all*, produces *one*,
> Is Disposition. By its plastic pow'r
> These rough materials, which Design selects,
> Are nicely balanc'd.[2]

The poem contains an excellent recipe for the choice of the sky best suited to your subject—'light mists full oft give mountain-views an added dignity'; but a more informative passage concerns the power of contrast.

> The lake's contracted bounds
> By contrast varied, elegantly flow:
> Th' unwieldy mountain sinks; here, to remove
> Offensive parallels, the hill deprest
> Is lifted, there the heavy beech expung'd

[1] His works were rarely mentioned by reviewers, and his death passed unrecorded by a single newspaper.

[2] Rev. W. Gilpin, *Landscape Painting*, lines 133–45.

Gives place to airy pines; if two bare knolls
Rise to the right and left, a castle here,
And there a wood, diversify their forms.
Thrice happy he, who always can indulge
This feast of fancy; who, replete
With rich ideas, can arrange their charms
As his own genius prompts, and plan and paint
A novel whole. But tasteless wealth oft claims
The *faithful portrait*, and will fix the scene
Where Nature's lines run falsely, or refuse
To harmonise. Artist, if thus employ'd,
I pity thy mischance.[1]

Such are the stage-properties recommended for the successful pursuit of landscape-painting. The scenery may not be wholly English; but the implied moral is that, if one is to study Nature, one had better study her in Italy. Nor is it surprising that the only painter mentioned throughout is Claude. Mr. William Jackson of Exeter records Reynolds's opinion that Claude was the Raphael of landscape, but also that Gainsborough thought his pencilling insipid. Gainsborough indeed escaped the Italian bias of his contemporaries. By native instinct he founded himself (for he was probably untaught) upon the old English tradition of landscape, which had its roots in the Netherlands. He enriched its realist if generalized view of the countryside by his gifts for effects of light and colour. An Italian painter wrote in 1777: 'His large landscape ['The Watering Place'] is inimitable. It revives the colouring of Rubens in that line. The scene is grand, the effect of light is striking, the cattle very natural. But what shall I say of the pencilling? I really do not know; it is so new, so original that I cannot find words to convey my idea of it.'[2] Rubens had indeed a profound effect upon him both in landscape and portrait; copies from him are among Gainsborough's earliest works; and it is significant that his only visit to the Continent was to Flanders.

The powers of his genius were inevitably recognized: he was accepted as Reynolds's rival in portrait, and sold more landscapes than is commonly supposed. But his influence in landscape was on the future rather than the present. His observant love for the quieter passages of country life introduced a fresh range of interests and sentiments: Constable

[1] Rev. W. Gilpin, *Landscape Painting*, lines 268–84.
[2] W. T. Whitley, *Artists and their Friends in England, 1700–99*, vol. i, p. 323.

THE ROMANTIC LANDSCAPE

From a painting in the Dulwich College Picture Gallery, English School

and the painters of the Norwich School were later to draw inspiration from these themes. One cannot imagine that Gilpin with his grandiloquent outlook really approved Reynolds's purchase of Gainsborough's painting, 'Girl with Pigs'. But with the next generation Gainsborough's art and that of Dutch and Flemish painters who influenced it carried increasing weight, and finally usurped the throne of the authorities designated by Reynolds.

As with history-painting, however, it was again the print-sellers who gave a real impetus to appreciation. In 1741 John Boydell began to publish engravings from his sketches in or about London, which brought him such success that the series at length embraced England and Wales. Though of the poorest quality, they hit the public fancy; and there was at once a market for engraved portraits of noble seats and ruins. The engraved landscape for the majority replaced the grandee's Canaletto or Walpole's Samuel Scott. Boydell's views had their more capable imitators, and a number of volumes, important for their illustrations, were published—Hearne and Byrne's *Antiquities*, Watt's *Views of Gentlemen's Seats*, or Middiman's *Views*. Their success, which was considerable, may be interpreted with the appreciation of Canaletto's style. For landscape, even if the British public of that day did not care much for it, could at least be understood as a form of portraiture.

In labours for volumes such as these the English water-colour school took shape, and able men like Hearne, M. A. Rooker, and Dayes employed their talents. Later Turner and Girtin were to graduate in the same university. Antiquaries in search of ruins and gentlemen in search of the picturesque were accompanied by their own draughtsmen, who used water-colour as the natural open-air medium. But even the greatest artists—J. R. Cozens, Gainsborough, and Paul Sandby—were hampered by severe limitations of palette and equipment. Paints, for instance, were only prepared in liquid form, till the brothers Reeves, founders of the present firm, invented cakes in 1781. Even so the more brilliant colours were unknown to water-colour at this time, and it was hard to avoid a cold effect. The greater variety obtained in the next generation is as much due to the colourmen as to the artists.

The rise of the colourmen is a special feature of the

eighteenth century. The earliest of them was a servant of Kneller's; and we know of another, Powel, established by 1734. By the middle of the century the trade was well recognized. In 1746 Mrs. Elizabeth Emmerton 'at the Bell over against Arundel Street in the Strand' advertised that her colours were ground in horsemills 'of which there is not the like in England', and that a horsemill could be seen at work in her shop. If large quantities were required colours were sold in jars; otherwise they were 'tied up in bits of bladder of about the bigness of a walnut', and bladders continued in use till the middle of the nineteenth century. Reynolds, who would pay any price for pure colours, dealt with at least three firms—Charles Sandys of long Acre, John Middleton of St. Martin's Lane, and Poole of High Holborn. We may guess from this that the fading of colours was due to experiment rather than to the use of poor pigment.

The whole trade that served the arts centred round the drawing school in St. Martin's Lane. Here lived also the frame-makers, like the brothers Gosset, employed by Hogarth, Gainsborough, and Hoare of Bath. There was Simon Henniken, too, almost the only maker in London of 'laymen', or lay figures for drapery, which usually were obtained from Paris. Chippendale sometimes accepted commissions to design frames, and we know of one 'very rich and most elegant' executed for the full length of the Duke of Northumberland by Pine, presented to the Middlesex Hospital in 1767.

Whereas St. Martin's Lane had bounded the artists' colony on the west in 1740, by 1784 it was the eastern margin. Adrian Maskens, who framed Barry's vast pictures for the Society of Arts, lived in Compton Street, Soho. The still surviving firm of Newman, who supplied colours, among others, to Wilson and Cosway, opened in Gerrard Street. But in Vertue's day it had been 'a credit' for artists to live in Covent Garden. Ellys, Hudson, Ramsay, and Zincke were all established there in the shadow of Kneller. Some painters of reputation, who had a specialized clientele, lived outside this circle. Highmore, who from his upbringing had a good legal connexion, was in Lincoln's Inn Fields: so was Dandridge with his city patrons. Mrs. Grace, who died worth £20,000 earned in portraits, lived in Shorter's Court, Throgmorton Street, to be near her clients. However, with the rest of Society the artists moved westwards. Wootton led the field by building a house in Cavendish Square; by the time Romney took over Cotes's house there, the neighbourhood was the height of fashion. Reynolds lived first at 5 Great Newport Street, where the early portraits of Johnson were painted. His studio was probably in the garden at the back, for the house now contains no room suitable for the purpose. Hogarth had been for some time established in Leicester Fields, when Reynolds moved in opposite—a better neighbourhood, but 'become as it were a depository for old stores, broken flags, rubbish and dirt'. Gainsborough took Schomberg House, Pall Mall, in 1774: and a few, ahead of their time, were in Bloomsbury. But generally speaking, Soho had become the artists' parish in the 'seventies and 'eighties.

Of Johnson's relation with painters there is either very much or very little to say. With Hayman he was well enough acquainted and was intimate with Ramsay and Barry. Reynolds was one of his greatest friends, and with him he might have met the more important artists of the day. Through him he was appointed Honorary Professor of Ancient History to the Academy. But almost the only official record of him is that he presented to the library on behalf of his friend, Levett, the *Institute of the Danish Academy*. He used to visit the exhibitions, but we may doubt if he looked much at the walls. When Thrale suggested that it was business that had prevented Sir Joshua from reading *Taxation No Tyranny*, Johnson offered another explanation: 'I never look at his pictures, so he wont read my writings.' At the banquets, however, he loved to attend, and by 1783 he writes in a proprietary vein: 'On Saturday I dined as usual at the opening of the Exhibition. Our company was splendid, whether more or less numerous than at any former time I know not. Our tables seem always full. . . . Poor Lowe met with some discouragement but I interposed for him and prevailed.' There is no satisfactory explanation of his support of this singularly poor artist, Mauritius Lowe. His picture, 'The Deluge', here alluded to, was at first rejected by the hanging committee, but by Johnson's appeal reinstated. Northcote says it was 'execrable beyond belief', Johnson, that it was 'noble and probable'.

Johnson's lack of interest in painting requires more explanation than his short sight. In spite of unrivalled opportunities for informing himself, he understood next to nothing of the business. That he could assist Reynolds with the *Discourses* is a token of his gift as a preface writer. Only its connexion with humanity could warm his enthusiasm. His preface to the catalogue of the 1762 exhibition was inspired by its charitable motives; he was interested by the idea of acquiring the Houghton collection for the nation as it would keep both the pictures and the money in the country. But in his emphatic preference of portraits above allegories he speaks for the general public of all ages. One may guess that painting offended the utilitarian element in his morality. He deplored it once as staring in men's faces, 'very indelicate in a female',[1] and again, as 'a waste of time, of that time which can never return'.

The popularity of engravings has been frequently mentioned in this chapter as stimulating a general interest in painting. It is now time to abandon the eighteenth-century attitude of considering prints only in relation to pictures, and to review what the engravers would have called their own achievements. The success of the illustrated books was echoed in the magazines, where plates enlivened pages of the fashionable archaeology. Printshops were the galleries of the ordinary citizen and there he could purchase for a few shillings the portrait of a topical character. Thomas Bowles and Philip Overton were leading publishers of the portrait print; but the trade had its pirates, too, like Robert Sayer, whose hacks turned out cheap versions of better work: from their large number we can guess the demand. Owing to its popularity in these forms engraving came to be recognized as a first-rate means of publicity. This was the ripe age of the London Tradesman's Card, of which the function lay somewhere between the card in its modern sense and a handbill. Rare examples from a great number of plates that have survived the clearances of generations suggest a very large output in this kind. Even outstanding artists—Hogarth, Bartolozzi, Vivares, to name a few only—were content to produce graceful designs for such ephemeral purposes.

Thus occupation increased, but not the engraver's prosperity. In theory, and too often in practice, he remained the

[1] Speaking of Angelica Kauffmann. Nevertheless Johnson sat to Frances Reynolds ten times, and for three hours at a time.

THE EXHIBITION OF THE ROYAL ACADEMY, 1787

From an engraving after the painting by Johann Heinrich Ramberg

printseller's hack. It is significant that the forms of contemporary engraving highest in esteem—line and mezzotint—were those which lent themselves most to the translation of painting. It was the same with collectors, to whom Rembrandt, for instance, was of small account. We must not yet look for original work from the engravers, since the public did not expect it of them.

There is no doubt that English engraving in all its forms reached its nadir in 1740. George Vertue was the official head of the native line-engravers. He was a prolific engraver of portrait-heads and one of the most renowned for book illustration. But his method, though painstaking, was stereotyped, even though he had more technical resources than his contemporaries. For important and imaginative enterprises French engravers were called in. Highmore advertising the illustrations to *Pamela* mentioned the engagement of Frenchmen in commendation of the project. Insular Hogarth would have preferred English work to foreign talent; but in the same year, 1744, he states in the announcement of the 'Marriage à la Mode', that six French artists have been engaged. Gravelot is to us the most important of these, since for some time he was resident in England and inspired the younger generation with the ambition to study in France.

However, by the end of the period the tale is reversed. Two great Englishmen were to challenge the respect of the Continent, Woollett and Strange. Both had studied abroad and came back with a well-developed technical apparatus. They were as able as Le Bas—a more important personage in English engraving than his abler French contemporaries—to produce a warm general tone and clear shadows. They had mastered the technique of founding an engraving on etching, and had furthered it. Moreover, they contributed draughtsmanship superior to anything seen in England within memory. Strange's official recognition was delayed by the Jacobite escapades of his youth, but, ultimately, he reached through West's support a knighthood. His prints and Woollett's were not only appreciated in England. They were widely copied in France and Germany; and a large part of the great sums made by them came from abroad. Woollett's prints after West won him the newly created post of Historical Engraver to His Majesty. But it was his engraving from Wilson that first distinguished him; and as a translator of landscape he was far ahead of such able men as Vivares or Major.

Very much the same story holds good of mezzotint. The fine skill of John Smith's work after Kneller had flagged to an insipid formula in the hands of the younger Faber. But the revival of the art is due more to the calibre of the artists working in the medium than, as in line engraving, to external circumstance. Mezzotint did not profit from the illustrated book trade to which it was unsuited. The bloom of a fine impression would rub off on the opposite page; and the plates needed too much reworking for a big edition. One does not find mezzotint used for illustration till steel was substituted for the copper plate early in the nineteenth century.

But from the 'sixties the demand for mezzotint portraits increased. Undoubtedly Reynolds's style was particularly suited to this form of translation. But it was also stimulated by the fine quality of McArdell's imaginative work and by the greater technical resources of his successors, Valentine Green, the Watsons, and J. R. Smith. The style became famous on the Continent as *la manière anglaise*. Walker went to St. Petersburg as engraver to Catherine the Great. And while our line engravers were studying in Paris, Haid and Jacobé, the leaders of the Viennese School, came for instruction to England.

Meanwhile a variety of new methods allied to etching came into use. Aquatint had been practised for some years abroad before it was introduced here. We need not discuss the uncertainty of the tradition which alleges that Charles Greville bought the secret from Le Prince and taught it to the water-colour painter, Paul Sandby. Sandby's *Views in Aquatinta from drawings in South Wales* (1775) are the earliest essays in the manner published in England. It was, however, quickly taken up by others, its kinship of effect with water-colour bringing it popularity. The work done at the end of our period was not on the whole important, but by the 'nineties the original publications of Malton, Daniel, and Turner were being issued, and in the new century Ackerman, the publisher, controlled a number of fine reproductive craftsmen like Stadler, Havell, and Lewis.

Stipple, a newly discovered technique, from its first practice enjoyed great favour, and being founded on etching, the plates lasted well enough to be used for books. The great vogue of the stipple illustration is, properly speaking, outside our period; but the forerunners of a long series—Harrison's *Novelists' Magazine* and Bell's *British Poets*—were issued before Johnson's death. It was the ideal method for reproducing the soft drawings of Cipriani or Kauffmann; and Bartolozzi had a special intuition for interpreting their style. He came to England in 1764 at the suggestion of that miscellaneous character, Richard Dalton, librarian, printseller, and antiquary, and from his etchings after Guercino's drawings rapidly made a name. His success in stipple was unchallenged; he made a fortune, though he lived considerably beyond his income. The Englishman, W. W. Ryland, was as early in the practice of stipple. He had studied in Paris, where he may have met François or Demarteau, the originators of the crayon manner, of which stipple is an extension. He took part in Charles Roger's publication of *Prints in imitation of Drawings*, 1778, and some plates in the crayon manner are among them, executed soon after his return. As an artist in stipple he takes equal rank with Bartolozzi; and though he never attained academic honours he was appointed engraver to George III. But his skill with the copper plate proved his undoing—he was hanged for forging bank-notes in 1783, as had been foretold by his prospective pupil, William Blake.

These new experiments and the methods of Woollett and Strange had made etching familiar to a greater number of engravers than ever before. Yet, as with water-colour, the period is one of planting rather than fruition: and very little was produced that we should now call original work. Though landscape painters were trying their hand at soft-ground etching, few others practised etching unalloyed. Thomas Worlidge produced some plates in imitation of Rembrandt; but these were regarded as curiosities. It remained for the caricaturists, Rowlandson and Gilray, one of the earliest of the Academy students, to reassert the power of the art. For the rest, professional engravers were too fast in the publisher's grip to have time for any but commercial work. However, it is worth remembering that Blake began his career as an original engraver with the *Morning or Glad Day* in 1780. He had been through the mill of conventional apprenticeship with Basire and could produce fine hack-work with the best of them. But his restoration of line-engraving to the status of the original art belongs really to the nineteenth century.

The great engravers from the first exhibited their work with the other artists, and some were even thought worth a notice in the papers. But the formation of the Academy had a most adverse effect on them. It was a curious position. The public knew quite well that fine work was being done by living engravers. An instructed critic like Reynolds could say of McArdell that he 'got everything but the colour'. Connoisseurs collected prints not only, like Granger, for historical interest, but for their aesthetic value. Yet at first engravers were denied the Academy entirely, though in 1770 the law was repealed and they were admitted to associate rank.

Strange in his pamphlet says that their exclusion was due to personal hostility to himself. 'At length, the more effectually to prevent every chance, that I might have, of partaking the honours they were sharing, it was proposed that nothing less than a total exclusion of engravers should take place.'[1] But the second reason he gives on the Academy's behalf is probably the juster. 'They therefore said,—that engravers were men of no genius,—servile copiers,—and consequently not fit to instruct in a royal academy . . . I shall, indeed, so far agree with the royal academicians, that engravers in general are not qualified to instruct in an academy, no more than portrait painters, landscape painters, miniature painters, coach painters, &c., of which this academy is chiefly composed.'[2]

It is easy to understand the painter's attitude. An engraver's ordinary relation with him was that of an employed copyist with inevitable short-comings. And the idea would be emphasized each time a painter turned over his collection of prints, from which he studied the compositions of old masters as we should now from photographs. The method of treatment pursued by Gilpin in his book on prints (1768) probably represented a fairly common state of mind. Engraving is there considered purely in terms of painting. Mezzotint is praised because it approaches that art most nearly. But no attempt is made to estimate the peculiar

[1] Strange, *Inquiry into the Rise of the Royal Academy* (1775), p. 112.
[2] Ibid., p. 118.

qualities of engraving, to say what it could do rather than what it could not do.

Such advocacy after the event as Strange's was not calculated to benefit the engraver's cause, especially as his jealousy of Bartolozzi—elected to the Academy as a painter—was notorious. It is true that a number of the engravers exhibited with the Academy from the start, while there were still other societies open to them. But the Academy's attitude undoubtedly split the profession. Woollett, Strange, and later Sharp refused all connexion with it; they were strong enough in their royal appointments to stand out. Strange may be unfair in hinting that Major, the first engraver to fall to the A.R.A., was influenced as a man with a family by its financial advantages. But it is significant that some time elapsed before the six associateships reserved for engravers were filled. The grievance was a real one and lasted with spasmodic eruptions for a hundred years.

BIBLIOGRAPHY.—ANON., *Conduct of the Royal Academicians* (1771). Sir W. ARMSTRONG, *Sir Joshua Reynolds* (1900). JOHN BROWNLOW, *Memoranda, or Chronicles of the Foundling Hospital* (1847). ALLAN CUNNINGHAM, *Lives of British Painters, Sculptors, and Architects* (6 vols., 1829–33). AUSTIN DOBSON, *William Hogarth* (1879). Miss A. EARLAND, *John Opie and his Circle* (1911). E. EDWARDS, *Anecdotes of Painters* (1808). JULIA FRANKAU, *John Raphael Smith* (1902). F. GALT, *Life of Benjamin West* (2 vols., 1820). Rev. W. GILPIN, *Essay on Prints* (1768); *Essays*; *Poem on Landscape Painting* (1791). ALGERNON GRAVES, *Royal Academy of Arts* (3 vols., 1906); *Society of Artists of Great Britain* (1907). ALGERNON GRAVES and W. V. CRONIN, *A History of the Works of Sir Joshua Reynolds* (4 vols., 1899–1901). A. M. HIND, *Short History of Engraving and Etching* (1903). JOHN IRELAND, *Hogarth Illustrated* (1798). JAMES NORTHCOTE, *Life of Sir Joshua Reynolds* (2 vols., 1813–15). JOHN PYE, *Patronage of British Art* (1845). SAMUEL REDGRAVE, *Dictionary of Artists of the English School* (1874). Sir J. REYNOLDS, *Discourses* (ed. Zimmern, 1887). J. J. ROGERS, *John Opie* (1878). L. ROGET, *Old Watercolour Society* (2 vols., 1891). Royal Academy of Arts. *Minutes, Papers of the Incorporated Society of Artists of Great Britain.* Royal Society of Arts, *Minutes.* C. E. RUSSELL, *English Mezzotint Portraits* (2 vols., 1926). WILLIAM SANDBY, *History of the Royal Academy of Arts* (2 vols., 1862). J. CHALONER SMITH, *British Mezzotinto Portraits* (4 vols., 1878–84). J. T. SMITH, *Life and Times of Joseph Nollekens* (2 vols., 1928). GEORGE STEEVENS and JOHN NICHOLS, *Genuine Works of William Hogarth* (1808). Sir R. STRANGE, *Inquiry into the Rise and Establishment of the Royal Academy* (1775). GEORGE VERTUE, *MS. Notebooks in the British Museum.* HORACE WALPOLE, *Anecdotes of Painting* (3 vols., Wornum's edn., 1888); *Letters* (19 vols., Toynbee's edn., 1903–25). H. WARD and W. ROBERTS, *George Romney* (2 vols., 1904). W. T. WHITLEY, *Thomas Gainsborough* (1915); *Artists and their Friends in England, 1700–1799* (2 vols., 1928). *Gilbert Stuart* (Harvard University Press, 1932). Dr. G. C. WILLIAMSON, *Life and Works of Ozias Humphry* (1918); LADY VICTORIA MANNERS and Dr. WILLIAMSON, *John Zoffany* (1920).

XVII

SCULPTURE

By KATHARINE A. ESDAILE

Painting consumes labour not disproportionate to its effect; but a fellow will hack half a year at a block of marble to make something in stone that hardly resembles a man. The value of statuary is owing to its difficulty. You would not value the finest head cut upon a carrot.—*Life of Johnson* (19 March 1776).

UNTIL the reign of George I, the terms sculptor and mason were virtually synonymous. A few sculptors were not masons, i.e. members of the Masons' Company who had gone through the routine of apprenticeship and afterwards taken out their freedom; but every mason was a sculptor, and in many instances the monuments they erected were more important than their buildings. It is as sculptors that men like Nicholas Stone, Joshua Marshall, and William Stanton excel. That the first worked at Windsor, Holyrood, and Kirby, that the second built Temple Bar and St. Mary Aldermanbury, and the third Belton, is interesting enough; but their real distinction lies in their monuments, even up to 1720 by far the most important field open to the sculptor. Throughout the seventeenth century foreigners like Le Sueur, Fanelli, and Cibber were indeed employed by the Court, but not to the exclusion of the English masons, who could count the highest nobles, as well as country squires and merchants, among their patrons. When Francis Bird returned to England in 1698 after years of training in Brussels and as Le Gros's assistant in Rome, he found it of great professional assistance to have married a mason's daughter,[1] and among Bird's patrons were the Duke of Newcastle and the Earls of Oxford and Huntingdon.[2]

The accession of George I, the least artistic of our sovereigns, saw the advent of a group of foreign sculptors who, though they spent their lives in England and looked on themselves as Englishmen, were destined to change the history of English sculpture. 'As to sculpture, that has of late years made

[1] B.M. Add. MSS. 23076, 50.

[2] Lord Oxford's receipt for Dr. Grabe's monument is at Welbeck, as the late Mr. R. G. Goulding told me; the work is, like the Newcastle monument, in Westminster Abbey, the Huntingdon tomb in St. James's, Piccadilly.

greater advances than painting in many and rare works of several hands' [margin] 'Rysbrack, Schemak^{r}. Rubillac.' This, Vertue's verdict, expressed the views of his own time.[1] These men were not masons; but their work became fashionable. The commissions for monuments and for the portrait busts, now beginning to be a normal form of domestic decoration, went to them; and the masons proper fell back on the architectural work which was once only a small part of their activities.

The record of one man's life will illustrate the point. When Edward Stanton, the third of a notable family of sculptors settled in Holborn since the reign of Charles I, took over his father William's studio shortly after 1700, he received a long series of commissions for works in his father's manner, with life-sized effigies or stately portrait busts. After 1716 his monuments lessen in size; the portraits disappear; and though his work is always distinguished in execution, his opportunities are few and relatively unimportant.[2] He took a fellow mason, Christopher Horsnaile, into partnership,[3] and the pair executed a mantelpiece at Ditchley[4] and numerous monuments of a decorative type; but Stanton died, and it was as a mason in the modern sense that his partner contracted for portions of the Mansion House.

The disappearance of alabaster from the sculptor's repertory of materials is another symptom of the new order. Under the Tudors its use was universal, except where local stone was preferred, though foreign marbles may appear in the settings; under the early Stuarts the native alabaster and white marble imported from Italy and the Low Countries are almost equally popular; under Charles II it is only the masons, not foreign-born sculptors like Cibber or Gibbons, who continue to use alabaster for effigies, and that by no means always;[5] and after 1700 it has virtually gone out.[6]

[1] B.M. Add. MSS. 23076, 50a.

[2] See 'The Stantons of Holborn', in *Archaeol. Journal*, 1930.

[3] I only know of one independent work by him, a fine bust at Haverfordwest; but others may well exist.

[4] I have to thank the late Viscount Dillon for this information. Other decorative works by the partners probably exist, but I have not come across them.

[5] Bird's father-in-law aforesaid 'had great dealings in Italy for marbles'. B.M. Add. MSS. 23076, 32a.

[6] The latest alabaster effigies which I have seen are Edward Stanton's to the Lucy family (1704/5) at Christ Church, Brecon.

The polished marbles and weeping loves of Pope's *Elegy on an Unfortunate Young Lady*, like the storied urn and animated bust of Gray, were not from English quarries.

Yet another factor in this cleavage between the sculptor and the mason was the increasing employment of fashionable architects as designers of monuments. Inigo Jones had designed Chapman's in St. Giles-in-the-Fields, out of personal friendship, and the same cause may have led Wren to draw out that of Dr. Dillen in St. Peter's in the East, Oxford;[1] but Gibbs published a large number of his designs without a word of Rysbrack and Scheemaker, who carried them out; Kent designed many more, including three of the most conspicuous in Westminster Abbey;[2] Leoni designed Rysbrack's Pulteney in the Abbey Cloisters and lesser works elsewhere; and Robert Adam's designs were modelled and carved, and sometimes re-drawn, by Rysbrack and Van Gelder. Masons such as James Rose, Robert Crutcher, Thomas Stainer, and the elder Taylor, who actually signs himself *Civis Londinensis*, were executing large and important works between 1707 and 1730; early in the reign of George II they disappear. Vertue does not mention them, though he was out to collect all he could about the art they practised; and though he casually alludes to '— Stanton now living', he did not even trouble to ascertain the Christian name of the author of some of the most remarkable monuments erected in his youth. Witness the history of the pediment of the Mansion House. By 1744 it was, in Vertue's words, 'ready for carving', and the Committee applied to various artists for ideas. Scheemaker, Roubiliac, and Gravelot were foreigners; Cheere, another competitor, was Scheemaker's pupil; the elder Taylor, *Civis Londinensis*, had a promising son just back from Italy; the Committee 'voted 8 in 10 for the son of a Citizen and their Country man'; and the world pronounced the mason's victory a job.[3]

The eldest of the new-comers was Peter Schaemaekers,

[1] The drawing is in the Soane Museum. Wren's design for the Westminster urn containing the bones of the Princes in the Tower was done at the request of Charles II, and the work executed by Joshua Marshall; no other works of the class are attributed to him.

[2] Those of Newton (erected 1731), Stanhope (1734), and Shakespeare (1741).

[3] A full account of the incident will be found in my *Life and Works of L. F. Roubiliac* (1928), p. 59. The 'promising son' was Sir Robert Taylor, founder of the Taylorian Institution, Oxford.

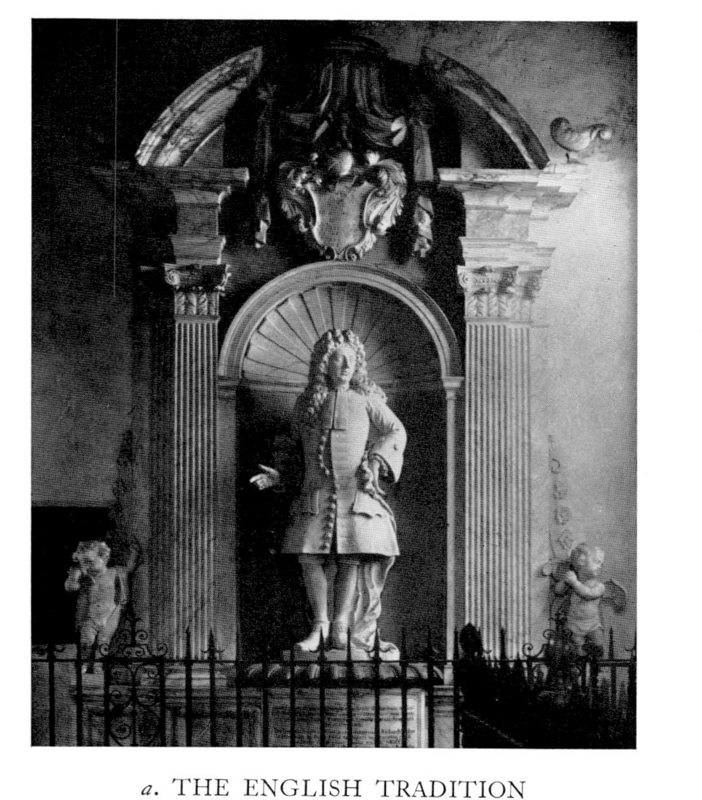

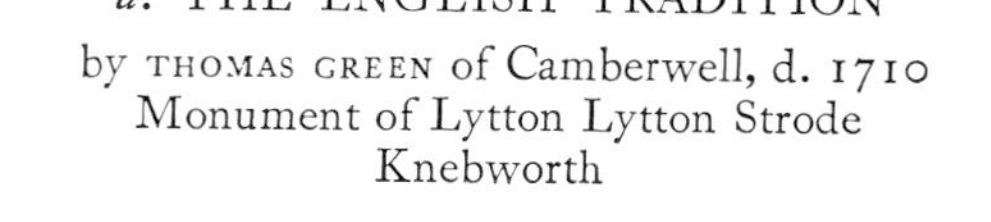

a. THE ENGLISH TRADITION

by THOMAS GREEN of Camberwell, d. 1710
Monument of Lytton Lytton Strode
Knebworth

b. THE HIGH ROMAN FASHION

Monument of Louis, First Earl of Rockingham, at Rockingham, by PETER SCHEEMAKER and LAURENT DELVAUX, 1729

Scheemakers, or Scheemaker (1690–1771)[1]—his name grows steadily more English—the son of an Antwerp sculptor. Born in 1690, he came to England with his friend Laurent Delvaux to work in the studio of their fellow-countryman Plumier, and on his early death they made their name by carrying out from his models the monument of Sheffield, Duke of Buckingham, in Westminster Abbey. After a brief time under Francis Bird, both went to Rome, whence Scheemaker returned with '18 or 20 moddeld . . . some so soft and fleshy', said Vertue, 'others a fine spirit and true antique taste—I am persuaded no master heretofore hath brought so many compleat works in that perfection of their own studios into England'. A born trainer of men, he taught practically every notable sculptor of the age, from Nollekens, who carried his manner into the nineteenth century, to Banks, who headed the counter-revolution against his style known as Neo-Hellenism, whereas his greater rival John Michael Rysbrack (1693–1770) had fewer disciples, and those of less importance.[2] The son of an Antwerp painter, he came to England in October 1720, and Vertue, who began by 'much admiring' his work, soon went on to say that 'everybody can distinguish' his superiority over his rival Scheemaker, while Walpole pronounced him 'the best sculptor that has appeared in these islands since le Sueur'. Like his rival, he did an enormous mass of decorative sculpture in addition to monuments and portraits, and in the most important art book published in Dr. Johnson's lifetime, Charles Rogers's *Prints in Imitation of Drawings* (1775), we are told that, 'When Sculpture had made the most despicable and disagreeable appearance among us in the reigns of Queen Anne and King George I, Mr. Rysbrack again presented her to us with all the charms of beauty and elegance'. That solitary genius Louis François Roubiliac (1705?–62), the son of a Lyonese banker, left the profitable decorative sculpture of the day alone, took but three pupils in all at the end of his life, and died a bankrupt, ruined by spending more money on his works than he received for them. 'The Pheidias of his day', 'the great Mr. Roubiliac', such were the verdicts of Chesterfield and Shelburne.

[1] These are not the dates in the *D.N.B.* One is Vertue's, the other is based on a Sale Catalogue of 1771, when Scheemaker was living at Isleworth.

[2] One, Vanderhagen, settled in Shrewsbury about 1758, and the surrounding country is full of modest works in his master's manner.

In what did the innovations of these great men consist? Primarily, in the introduction of a pyramidal style in place of the vertical or horizontal lines of early works. This type of composition, starting in Italy, is found all over Europe by the end of the seventeenth century, but its earliest examples in England would appear to be Bird's bust of Shadwell in the Abbey and the colossal work at Stamford signed by Pierre Monnot of Besançon and finished and erected by his assistant William Palmer.[1] This important monument of 1704 represents the third Earl of Exeter and his wife in Roman dress, recumbent on a sarcophagus, and attended by colossal figures of Wisdom and Justice; and so powerful was the example that by 1740 there were numerous specimens of this type of composition in Westminster Abbey alone. The symbolism after all was familiar: it was the composition, the deliberate copying of Roman art, that was new, and we must devote a paragraph to its analysis.

In Elizabethan and Jacobean England the 'star-ypointing pyramid', that classical emblem of eternity, was to be found on countless monuments, but only as a decorative adjunct, alone, or grouped by way of contrast with such symbols of mortality as Time, Death, or a child blowing bubbles, or else placed at the corners of the main design. Eternity then, an old idea made more emphatic, is the main theme of the pyramidal monument of Johnson's day; and the Roman dress which often went with it was itself a symbol of immortality.[2] The sarcophagus had begun to replace the altar tomb over a century before Johnson was born; by the reign of Anne it had become almost universal, and the habit of adorning it with reliefs—the storied urns of Gray—had begun. But the English instinct for portraiture was not to be baffled; hence the combination of vigorous portraits, bareheaded *à la romaine*, or in the wig of the stately daily life of the time, with Roman dress; the nightcap, however, almost always goes with contemporary costume, the loose gown worn with it at home offering suitable drapery. The old temple-like structure which formed the setting, though used here and there by Rysbrack with good effect, is more conspicuous in

[1] This statement is based on Palmer's mention of the work to Le Neve as his own. Palmer's foreign training is visible in every line of his original works, especially in the Hon. Margaret Watson at Rockingham.

[2] See my *English Monumental Sculpture since the Renaissance* (1927), chap. iv.

the dwindling output of such masons as were still employed on monumental sculpture;[1] but the resolute realism of the portrait head was common to both schools.

'Portraits', wrote Hogarth, 'always have been, and always will be, popular in England', and portraits were rigidly insisted on. Eton, Vertue tells us, lent the famous portrait of Henry VI in 1719 to assist Bird in making the bronze statue there; Rysbrack was entrusted with making a death-mask of Sir Isaac Newton in 1727, which Roubiliac used for the famous statue at Trinity,[2] as he had portraits and descriptions supplied him for the statue of Sir John Cass in 1738;[3] and such examples might be multiplied even from the sixteenth century.

Johnson's own opinion confirms Hogarth's view, and the nation at large would assuredly have supported him when he said, 'I had rather see the portrait of a dog that I know, than all the allegorical paintings they can shew me in the world':[4] the allegories which he elsewhere defines as 'one of the most pleasing vehicles of instruction' were literary, not artistic. The demand for portraits was inexhaustible, and the bust, which, during the seventeenth century, had been almost confined to the royal family and the high nobility, was rapidly coming into favour after 1720. Bushnell's bust of Talman and Gibbons's of himself, both before 1700, are but the beginnings of a movement in which country parsons, town clerks, surveyors, painters, architects were as eager as the nobility to be commemorated, and to have their wives commemorated, by Rysbrack and Roubiliac.

'Sculpture in England', wrote Hogarth's friend J. B. Rouquet in 1755, 'has hitherto been almost wholly funerary; it has only recently been used for other purposes', for busts, that is, and decorative sculpture. Campbell's *Vitruvius Britannicus*, Walpole's *Aedes Walpolianae*, are eloquent of the new field offered by the great house. The citizen followed suit with his shepherd and shepherdess, his Pluto and his Proserpine, from the leaden figure factory started by John Nost of Mechlin about 1690 and taken over by Sir Henry

[1] There is a good example with figures in contemporary dress so late as 1744 at East Ham, another of 1727, by James Fisher of Camberwell, at Marholme near Peterborough.

[2] See *Roubiliac's Work at Trinity College, Cambridge* (1924), p. x.

[3] *Life and Works of L. F. Roubiliac*, pp. 92–3.

[4] Quoted by Birkbeck Hill from Johnson's *Works* (1787), vol. xi, p. 208.

Cheere, one of Scheemaker's most distinguished pupils and for a time his partner; Robert Lloyd's mischievous lines are perhaps not too familiar for quotation:

> And now from Hyde Park Corner come
> The gods of Athens and of Rome;
> Here squabby Cupids take their places
> With Venus and the clumsy Graces;
> Apollo there, with aim so clever,
> Stretches his leaden bow for ever.

Noblemen of taste such as Lords Burlington and Cobham, the Duke of Chandos and Lord Tilney, made of Chiswick and Stowe, Canons and Wanstead, and of their pleasure grounds, museums of contemporary sculpture,[1] as they adorned niches and doorways and chimney-pieces indoors with elaborate carving. If a statue were wanted, the artist might produce a copy after the Antique, but he was more likely to present his own conception of a mythological subject or to re-create the features of the great men of the past. The antiquarian spirit had developed during the peaceful years of Walpole's rule; the statues of Alfred the Great at Stourhead, of William III at Bristol, Hull, and Petworth, alike bear witness to the fact. Hence the erection of monuments in Westminster Abbey to Shakespeare, Milton, Ben Jonson, Samuel Butler in the first half of the eighteenth century; to Shakespeare on the Boydell Gallery, to Milton at St. Giles's, Cripplegate, in the second. The Universities again began to think of their great men; but Rysbrack's Wren at Queen's, his Alfred at Oriel, and Roubiliac's Chichele at All Souls are thrown into the shade by Christ Church, which acquired a regular gallery of her great men culminating in Rysbrack's colossal Locke of 1756. Trinity College, Cambridge, did even better when benefactors presented the first statue of Newton and the marvellous series of busts in the Library;[2] and at Trinity College, Dublin, Van Ost's Dr. Delany rivals Roubiliac's Swift as the gem of the collection in its Library.

It is difficult to give any exact account of the cost of sculpture during the period under review. Our knowledge depends upon a few documents and allusions referring to the

[1] Nor is an interest in the art confined to them: the lists of collections in Dodsley's *London* (6 vols., 1761) are eloquent of its existence among the professional men of the 1750's who would previously have confined themselves to pictures.

[2] See *Roubiliac's Work at Trinity College, Cambridge.*

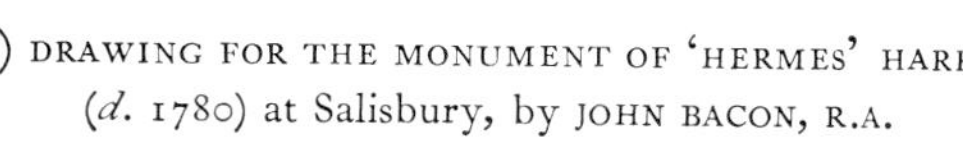

(*a*) DRAWING FOR THE MONUMENT OF 'HERMES' HARRIS
(*d*. 1780) at Salisbury, by JOHN BACON, R.A.

(*b*) MONUMENT OF SIR ISAAC NEWTON
In Westminster Abbey, by JOHN MICHAEL RYSBRACK

more distinguished men, and must therefore be regarded as top-prices; and it looks as though the foreign-trained sculptor commanded more than the English mason of perhaps equal merit. Thus in 1708 Grinling Gibbons received £322 18*s.* 4*d.* for the justly abused monument of Sir Clowdisley Shovell,[1] whereas, only nine years before, William Stanton had only £253 13*s.* 4*d.* for five life-sized effigies at Mitton, Yorks.;[2] but Gibbons was working for Queen Anne herself, which may have made a difference. For the monument of Dr. Grabe (d. 1711), seated on his own sarcophagus, Bird received £50 from Lord Oxford,[3] and Vertue records that though Gibbs received £100 for each of the allegorical statues on Prior's monument, he gave Rysbrack, who carved them, only £35 apiece.[4] The same sculptor charged 35 guineas for a marble bust, 'near ten guineas' more than his rival Scheemaker,[5] and in 1744 Roubiliac asked 10 guineas for Mr. Bedford's 'Busto in clay', promising 'for 30 guineas more to do the same in Marble'.[6] Four years later that improvident sculptor, as his friend Wilton told Farington long afterwards, lost £300 over his colossal masterpiece, the Argyll monument in Westminster Abbey, for which he charged the Duchess £1,400; when we remember that Bacon received £6,000 for the Chatham monument some thirty years later the sum seems small indeed.

Nollekens charged £100 for a first sketch of a monument,[7] and this figure prepares us in some degree for the colossal sums wasted in St. Paul's.[8] But for our period it is safe to say that the price of sculpture was absurdly low in relation to that of painting, if we consider the relative cost of labour, materials, transport, and fixing, for the last of which the unwary sculptor was often made responsible. It was not every one who, like Nollekens, found a gold-mine by executing endless replicas of popular portraits; or, like Bacon, would fall back on stereotyped emblems such as 'our old friend, the pelican', no matter who or what the subject was.[8]

[1] *Times Literary Supplement,* June 7, 1928; Bird was blameless in the matter.

[2] Whittaker's *Whalley,* p. 492.

[3] Receipt at Welbeck communicated by the late R. C. Goulding.

[4] B.M. Add. MSS. 23076, f. 14.

[5] B.M. Add. MSS. 23079, f. 27.

[6] Document in the possession of the writer.

[7] J. T. Smith, *Life and Times of Joseph Nollekens* (1828), vol. i, p. 50. For the prices paid to the 'Peninsular' School of Sculptors see G. L. Smyth's *Monuments and Genii of Westminster Abbey* (1829), *passim.*

[8] Cf. Allan Cunningham's *Life of Bacon* (1830), p. 243.

There was a genuine public interest in sculpture in the reign of George II. The newspapers are full of epigrams upon the subject, of notes on promised or newly-completed monuments or portraits, of suggestions that the public would do well to see such and such a work while it was still in the sculptor's studio. As early as 1709, Thoresby's *Ducatus Leodiensis* tells us, 'many of the Nobility and Gentry of London' visited the statue of Queen Anne which Andrew Carpenter, or more properly speaking, André Carpentier, had been commissioned to execute for the Moot Hall at Leeds.[1] The fire of journalistic epigrams proves that Vertue was not the only visitor to sculptors' studios in the 1720's, '30's, and '40's; and in 1733 Queen Caroline herself went to Rysbrack's to see the equestrian William III already mentioned. She inspected his other works, and her remark that James I looked like a hangman[2] caused the old Catholic Vertue to growl out that, considering how she came to the throne, such sentences were unbecoming. Nor was this her only act of patronage. She sat to the sculptor for the busts at Windsor and Hertford House; she induced the King to sit; and ordered that set of portraits of Newton, Locke, Boyle, Clarke, and Wollaston for her Grotto at Richmond[3] which gave rise to Swift's bitter epigram,

> Lewis the living poet fed,
> And raised the scientific head;
> Our noble Queen, to save her meat,
> Exalts those heads that cannot eat.[4]

But such patronage was a symptom rather than a cause. The contemporary literature of the Handel statue at Vauxhall (1738), for instance, is enormous, and the erection of the Duke of Argyll's monument in Westminster Abbey, like that of Duncan Forbes's statue at Edinburgh, gave rise to pages upon pages of controversy in the magazines both in England and Scotland. It is not surprising therefore to find a merchant prince, Sir Richard Hoare, erecting a temple at Stourhead for Rysbrack's Hercules, where that sculptor's Nymph of the Grot still reclines above the sources of the Stour, with Pope's

[1] It is now in the Museum and Art Gallery, Leeds.

[2] *Fi, il me semble a une boureau* [*sic*], B.M. Add. MSS. 23076, f. 45.

[3] Afterwards at Windsor, where their origin had been forgotten. They are now at Kensington Palace. The bust of Clarke is by Guelfi.

[4] For another and courtlier epigram on the same subject, see Swift's Poems.

(*a*) BUST FROM THE MONUMENT OF DANIEL LOCK
At Trinity College, Cambridge,
by LOUIS FRANÇOIS ROUBILIAC

(*b*) MODEL FOR THE HEAD OF THE STATUE OF SIR HANS SLOANE
In the Apothecaries' Garden, Chelsea,
by JOHN MICHAEL RYSBRACK

THE PORTRAIT BUST

lines cut upon the marble rim of the brimming pool beneath her; or Lord Burlington adorning Chiswick House with decorative sculpture from the same chisel; or the Ansons of Shugborough commissioning for their garden 'a beautiful monument, the work of Mr. Schemacher, the scene laid in Arcadia'—a reproduction in stone of Poussin's famous picture of the shepherds at their comrade's tomb—as well as 'the *choragic* monument of *Lysicrates*, the octagon tower of *Andronicus Cyrrhestes*, and the Arch of *Adrian* at *Athens*, embellished with naval trophies in honour of Lord *Anson*'.[1]

There was a new demand both for portrait busts of great men to be placed in private libraries as well as public, and for smaller decorative figures, terracottas or casts of terracottas, indicative of the owner's taste. Hence the astonishing number of commemorative portraits of poets and philosophers, architects and statesmen, which are mentioned in Vertue's note-books, occur in sculptors' sale catalogues, and exist in the untouched houses of the period—the acquisitions collected not of noble patrons only but of scholars like Dr. Delany and Shenstone.[2]

We must also remember the extraordinary popularity of the monuments in Westminster Abbey which for centuries had been one of the sights of London for the country cousin. Shakespeare's 'gilded monuments of princes' is probably coloured by memories of Henry VII's Chapel, of which an eighteenth-century critic said they would be better 'if shown alive and in action'.[3] Donne talks contemptuously of the verger's patter which Sir Roger de Coverley took so seriously a century later, and Addison and Goldsmith have immortalized their own emotions in the place. Weever's *Funeral Monuments* of 1631 speaks of the crowds who daily visited the tombs; Chamberlayne's *Angliæ Notitia* describes the monuments in the seventeenth century; and during the eighteenth century Newbery's *Guide* was always having to be reissued to include the newest works. The most popular

[1] Pennant's *Tour from Chester to London* (1790).

[2] It was only the King and one or two great nobles who had collected Fanelli's small decorative bronzes in the previous century, but the sale of sets of casts of small works for 7 guineas is recorded more than once by Vertue, and even later in the century Carlini and other sculptors advertise casts of their new groups for sale at high prices, 5 and 6 guineas each; Delany's purchases of portraits are recorded in his wife's Autobiography; Shenstone's *Letters* disclose a demand even for statuettes of Chaucer.

[3] Ralph's *Public Buildings of London* (ed. 1783).

tomb of all, that of Queen Elizabeth, was erected by James I, who was also responsible for those of his own family; Queen Anne had put up Shovell's monument at her own expense; those of three Admirals, the first of many so erected, were voted by Parliament in 1740;[1] and from that time onwards, though only one monument in the Abbey was erected by a sovereign,[2] the nation was busy commemorating its great men, the elder Pitt himself moving that Wolfe's cenotaph should be put up at the public expense. Victory and Westminster Abbey were the lot of many Englishmen in that great age of conquest and expansion, and Londoners of an antiquarian turn of mind were constantly dropping in to see the latest monument or, like Nollekens, to scold the vergers for taking so little care of the works of art under their charge. One and all, however, admired the modern monuments—not those which we are trained to venerate, for the old Gothic tombs, we are told, merely encumber the church;[3] there is no more curious proof of the change of taste due to the Gothic Revival and the Oxford Movement than a comparison of the terms used by Newbery's *Guide* and by Dean Stanley of the same works.

Nor was this interest in sculpture confined to town. New monuments were perpetually appearing in our country churches, and when the whole population went to church, the whole population was familiar with them. The excitements of Elizabethan days, when a huge work was brought to a remote village by barge and ox-cart,[4] accompanied by a party of men from the sculptor's studio to supervise their erection and spend several weeks in the place, were over, it is true, since such work was in the eighteenth century entrusted to ignorant local masons;[5] but all the same they were something new to look at.

It may be well to give a couple of examples of the criticism of the time, taken not from Vertue's Note-books but from periodicals. No antiquary can be taken as representative of his age in the sense in which the journalist, who must hit

[1] B.M. Add. MSS. 23079, 38b.

[2] That of Major André by Van Gelder after Adam, erected by George III.

[3] Ralph's *Public Buildings of London*.

[4] Cf. the accounts for the Bottesford monuments of 1593 and at Belvoir, *Art Journal*, 1903. The Sussex monument at Boreham occupied twelve ox-carts. J. T. Smith's lament as to the local mason is in *Nollekens*, vol. i, p. 230.

[5] J. T. Smith, *Nollekens*, vol. i, pp. 229–30.

MONUMENT OF THE SECOND DUCHESS OF MONTAGU
at Warkton, Northants, by LOUIS FRANÇOIS ROUBILIAC
THE DRAMATIC MONUMENT

the taste of his contemporaries or fail, is representative; and our third quotation is a supreme instance of the attitude of the serious Christian towards the art of his time and country. Pope and Gray, as we have seen, allude to the weeping cherubs, portrait busts, and storied urns, sarcophagi, that is, sculptured in relief with episodes relating to the dead; but the contents of the periodical and the diary cannot be suspect as literary ornaments or antiquarian jottings, and are therefore the more valuable as evidence.

The whole sixteenth number of the revived *Spectator* of 1753 is devoted to eulogizing Roubiliac's monument to the Duchess of Montagu, then 'to be seen in St. MARTIN'S Lane'. The reader is assured that, whatever may be said of the greatness of France and Italy, we, too, 'have one excellent sculptor', and this is the proof:

> Had the task of commemorating her been attempted by a man of mean talents, he would have placed the Dutchess in her robes all alive upon her own tombstone, looking at a poor snivelling boy wiping his eyes with a white handkerchief, and weeping for her death; or perhaps surrounded by a group of cherubims and seraphims that continually do cry.
>
> Another of better abilities would have placed the Graces in affliction round her tomb and bewailing her death, and herself alive at her own funeral; and excepting this last thought the former part had not been amiss, and yet it is vastly inferior to the present design . . . in which the sculptor I am speaking of has conceived the happiest thought imaginable, he has made even the fates themselves under the figures of three beautiful women to convey this idea.

Pope's weeping loves are therefore out of date, the tricks of 'a man of mean talents'; a good sculptor would, it is assumed, give us allegorical figures bewailing the Duchess's death, and the thought 'had not been amiss'; but it takes the 'magic hands' of the genius whom the *Connoisseur* would reveal—the phrase is used in a later paragraph—to create such a work as this or its companion monument, already at Warkton and 'equally perfect', in which 'charity under a female form, assisted by her children, was fixing the medallion of the Duke on the temple of fame, and the Dutchess beholding it from below'. 'These monuments', the writer concludes, 'shall be wept over when the Duke and Dutchess shall be forgotten, if it is in the power of time to obliterate the memory of his Grace's charities and her beauty.' The dramatic monument has come to its own; incident, not commemoration, is now the keynote of the tomb of high distinction.

Two years later it is another story. 'Our pious forefathers', wrote Bonnell Thornton in the *Connoisseur* in 1755, 'were content with exhibiting to us the usual emblems of death, the hour-glass, the skull, and the cross-marrow-bones; but these are not sufficient for our present more refined age. The Three Fatal Sisters, mentioned in the Heathen Mythology, must be introduced, spinning, drawing, and cutting the thread of life.' The moralizings of a young man about town in search of something to write about are not to be taken too seriously, but that there were critics who felt the Heathen Mythology an outrage on the symbolism of Our Pious Forefathers is obvious, or he would not have written thus.

Our third extract reveals the attitude towards art taken up by the chief religious figure of the age. On March 16, 1764, Wesley writes in his *Journal*: 'I once more took a serious walk through the tombs in Westminster Abbey. What heaps of unmeaning stone and marble! But there was one tomb which showed common sense; that beautiful figure of Mr. Nightingale endeavouring to screen his lovely wife from Death. Here indeed the marble seems to speak, and the statues appear only not alive.' And again, on March 25, 1771: 'I showed a friend coming out of the country, the tombs in Westminster Abbey. The two with which I still think none of the others to be compared are that of Mrs. Lady Elizabeth Nightingale, and that of the Admiral [General Hargrave] rising out of his tomb at the resurrection.'

Here again is the sense that drama is of the essence of a monument, only it is what he regards as Christian drama, illustrating the fear of death, the hope of resurrection, that wins Wesley's praise. There is no more curious contrast in literature than the verdicts of the eighteenth and nineteenth centuries upon these very works; but if we are to be fair to the sculpture of Johnson's age it is Wesley's verdict, not Ruskin's or Dean Stanley's, that we must accept. To the men of the Oxford Movement skull and crossbones were crude and repellent, allegorical figures pompous and pagan, and Roubiliac's work false in sentiment and theatrical in appeal; Ruskin even coined the word Roubiliacism to connote all that in art he most detested. Such things were part of the latitudinarianism of the age they hated; had they known many of the tombs in Belgium, France, and Italy, they would have found monuments more startling still in countries far from latitudinarian. It was not a matter of religion but of period, and it is in a Catholic church, not in a Protestant, that an archbishop's hat is hung upon the Cross beside him.[1] As for the *Connoisseur*, urns and cherubs, skulls and crossbones, had been consecrated for Englishmen by centuries of love and reverence: it was reserved for the Methodist Bacon to reintroduce the Cross into monumental sculpture,[2] though it is Flaxman, who avowed his aim of Christianizing his art, who generally gets the credit.

There is on record no more prosaic mind than that of Johnson's friend Joseph Nollekens, R.A., yet even Nollekens was forced to be dramatic. We have only to look at his monument to Mrs. Thrale's uncle, Sir Thomas Salusbury, at Offley (was Dr. Johnson, who sat to the sculptor that year, responsible for the commission?), or at his enemy Banks's Halliday monument at Halesowen, to see how strong the compulsion was on artists of opposite types. Nollekens, who had spent some years in Rome after his apprenticeship to his Rome-loving master Scheemaker, and filled note-book after note-book with sketches after the Antique, had a romantic subject. How does he treat it? Sir Thomas in his youth was attached to an heiress whose guardians forbade the marriage; after long estrangement she met him one day under the boughs of a spreading oak and renewed their troth, and in the end they married. Here is Nollekens's version of the story. Against a dark pyramid behind rises the oak tree, cut by a most unfortunate sarcophagus; before it, fashioned on bas-reliefs of the Roman marriage, stand Sir Thomas and his wife, he towering above her and holding out a wreath, she veiled and bending, the modest image of a Roman bride.

[1] Fayd'herbe's monument of Mathias van den Hove (erected 1665) at Malines.

[2] There is a solitary exception to this rule, Crutcher's figure of Religion holding a Cross on Stainer's monument to Dr. Turner (d. 1713) at Stow-nine-Churches. Rysbrack never introduced such things into his monuments, though he was a devout Catholic, and his drawings exhibited between 1759 and 1770 are largely religious in character; but Roubiliac did a statue of Religion, now lost, for Gopsall Park.

In his life, as in his art, Nollekens was a Roman of the Romans; and the dreamy Banks, whose sympathies were all Hellenic, was sometimes forced to be dramatic. Major Halliday, owner, after Shenstone, of the Leasowes, was boating one day with his wife on the lake there, a few months before Johnson died, when her pet dog fell into the water; a powerful swimmer, he plunged after it at once, was seized with cramp, and sank before her eyes; and this is Banks's version of the story.

The gates of death are shut: above them stands the spirit of the dead, veiling his face lest he should see his young wife's anguish; parted from him by the image of his own grave she kneels and weeps, her shag-dog at her feet. Each sculptor has a story to tell, each tells it in his own way; and that way is dramatic not static.

It was during Dr. Johnson's lifetime that the organization of English art training took place. He was two years old when Kneller formed his abortive Academy; he was working for Cave when Thornhill's succeeding Academy was, with its casts and other properties, in 1735 merged in the really dignified St. Martin's Lane Academy which Hogarth has pictured for us, with Roubiliac as Professor of Sculpture.

This institution was in its turn to give place to the completer organization of the Royal Academy; but whereas the previous schemes had placed painting and sculpture on equal terms, only three sculptors were nominated as foundation members of the academy and there was no professorship of sculpture till 1810. The first Keeper, Carlini, was, it is true, a sculptor; but his main function was to keep order; it was always Reynolds, and never Carlini, who delivered the annual Discourse; and among Reynolds's Discourses one only is allotted to sculpture as against fourteen to painting. The importance of study abroad, recognized by English sculptors of the seventeenth century and widely practised in the eighteenth, was, however reaffirmed; and it was a sculptor, Thomas Banks, who was the first to benefit by a Travelling Studentship in 1771.

It was not professional incompetence, assuredly, that called for a Royal Academy, as the demand for English work abroad will show. An elegant statue of that universally beloved Governor of Barbados, Henry Grenville, was put up

MONUMENT OF LADY ELIZABETH NIGHTINGALE
in Westminster Abbey, by LOUIS FRANÇOIS ROUBILIAC
THE DRAMATIC MONUMENT

in the Town Hall there in 1756;[1] English sculptors were working for Jamaican patrons over twenty years before that;[2] and Rodney, Wellesley, and Cornwallis were afterwards the subject of notable works at Spanish Town, Bombay, and Calcutta. Members of the Merchant Venturers, servants of the East India Company, were commemorated by English sculptors in Eastern churches and forgotten cemeteries; and when the Emperor of Morocco required sculptors, it was to George III that he wrote in 1766 to send him 'ten workmen in marble, all clever in their profession'.[3] Yet within ten years a decline in the art was perceptible, and this must be accounted for.

First, no doubt, we must place the increasing habit of confining the sculptor's part to the model, sometimes even only to the design, the execution being left to his assistants. In Elizabethan and Stuart days the sculptor did all the important portions of a work himself; in the immense list of Stone's works only three effigies are recorded as carved by his underlings. Stanton's output half a century later was still larger, and though he too entrusted the execution of a few effigies to other hands,[4] the bulk of them were his own work, as the execution proves. In the next century Rysbrack certainly finished most of his portraits himself, and the contrast between the mechanical character of those which he did not and the exquisite surfaces of his own carving is obvious enough; finally, we have it on record that Roubiliac was horrified to find one of his three pupils daring to put a chisel to one of his busts.

But Roubiliac's friend Joseph Wilton, R.A., who took on two of those pupils as assistants after his death, had no conscience at all. He designed the Wolfe monument in Westminster Abbey, but we have the authority of Nat Smith, one of those assistants, for saying that he never put a tool to it, and his decorative sculptures at Somerset House were modelled as well as carved from his designs.[5] John

[1] J. T. Smith, *Nollekens*, vol. ii, p. 51.

[2] See F. C. Cundall (*The Art Journal*, 1907), 'English Sculpture in Jamaica'.

[3] Quoted from the original at the Record Office.

[4] Thus the execution of two of the three effigies at Hurst, Berks., and Courteenhall, are quite unworthy of the excellent designs or of the chisel which twenty years later could produce such splendid works as the Lord Coventry at Elmley Castle or the Shirburne monuments at Mitton; the reason can only be that suggested in the text.

[5] J. T. Smith, *Nollekens*, vol. ii, pp. 107, 110.

Bacon, R.A., carried the decline still further, innocently by inventing a superior pointing instrument for his own use which made it easier for a modeller to delegate the carving to a subordinate, and guiltily by stereotyping such commonplaces as the drooping female figure for use on all occasions, whether warrior, statesman, or young girl were to be commemorated. It is a thousand pities that, when Sir Charles Grandison came 'to inter the venerable remains of his father', Bacon was still an apprentice in a Lambeth pottery, since more than any English sculptor of his century he turned out the very type of monument on which Sir Charles had set his heart, 'elegant, but not sumptuous, with a modest inscription that shall be rather a matter of instruction to the living, than a panegyric on the departed'. Bacon's works and aims could not be better defined, but it is odd that the Academy's first Gold Medallist should have been a potter's boy whose determination to be a sculptor arose from the sight of the sculptors' models being turned into terracotta in his master's kilns; Nollekens, who though the older man, outlived Bacon four and twenty years, was far more the typical Academician. Trained under Scheemaker, a student for seven years in Rome, he sent more works to the Academy than any sculptor on record, but, alas, though he modelled his own work, the carving was all done by sweated assistants. He carried his master's manner into the nineteenth century; his monument to Mrs. Coke (d. 1803) at Holkham, for instance, though the spirit of the age had led to the substitution of a figure of Religion for a Virtue, is purely pyramidal, as much an echo of Scheemaker as his compositions with medallion portraits which abound from Somerset to Denbighshire, and his busts—weaker echoes of Scheemaker's high Roman manner—which may be numbered by hundreds. The work of the man who carved every notability of his long day from Johnson and Garrick to the Duke of Wellington and Castlereagh, and is besides the subject of one of the most curious biographies in literature, can never lose its interest; but even his unscrupulous use of the sculptor's 'ghost' did less harm to art than the precepts of Dr. Johnson's far greater friend Sir Joshua Reynolds, the first President of the Royal Academy.

For the institution to the establishment of which the great

artists of the previous age had looked forward as to an Age of Gold came into being at a most unfortunate moment. We have already seen that the English artists who went to Italy before the reign of George III studied the Antique and the Renaissance with equal zest. Stone's records of his own studies, Vertue's of Scheemaker's models, the contents of existing Sale Catalogues such as those of Francis Bird and Nollekens prove it; and the collections of terracottas of all sorts and periods which men like Nollekens and Hudson acquired are further evidence of the catholicity of taste thus inculcated. But in 1754 the discoveries at Herculaneum had sent the world back to Greece, and the publication of Winckelmann's *History of Ancient Art* ten years later marked an epoch in the history of Europe. It was not the historian's fault that most of the statues on which he based his conclusions were commercial copies of earlier works, often wrongly restored, for the crime of wholesale restoration had not yet been realized; but the fact, like the belief in the original character of inferior copies, vitiated his conclusions because his imperfect material inspired the belief that Greek art generalized, and avoided individuality as much as possible. Hence the fatal doctrine of the Ideal and Typical spread over Europe, one of its most conspicuous converts being Sir Joshua Reynolds; consequently, when the first Academy students, who had had no Professor of Sculpture to direct them, were sent to Rome in 1771, they were instructed to concentrate upon the Glorious Antique; and when the President gave his students his one Discourse upon their art, it proved to contain a furious attack upon the moderns in general and the School of Bernini in particular. His attitude was the more unfortunate that when, with great public spirit, the young Duke of Richmond had built and fitted up the gallery of casts already alluded to for the use of all who could produce a reference, the collection included works by Michael Angelo and other masters of the Renaissance, so that something of the breadth of training obtainable in Rome was available to London students; but the Gallery was soon closed owing to the behaviour of some of the young men, and at the Royal Academy all save the Antique was *taboo*, the whole modern development of sculpture anathema. We cannot blame the students whom Reynolds addressed for following out his precepts. The use of modern dress in sculpture was, they were told, 'the prostitution of a noble art'; the 'imaginary improvements' of the moderns in the representation of action and perspective were destructive of sculpture; generalized forms in repose are alone permissible. When such doctrine was preached from the Presidential chair, what could the student do but carry it into practice?

Two young men listened with conviction, Thomas Banks, R.A. (1735–1803), and John Flaxman, R.A. (1755–1828), and it was the fruit of Reynolds's teaching which filled St. Paul's with monuments and enabled the younger Prince Hoare to boast in 1803 that 'competition with the fine forms and beautiful outlines of the ancient statues has banished the vitiated outlines of Puget's and Bernini's School, and our Exhibitions have afforded examples of a finer and correct style'. That style had only begun to appear when Johnson died, but a study of the Royal Academy Catalogues will show that the urge to classical subjects grew stronger in his lifetime, and Johnson himself was to be one of its most conspicuous victims.

For Neo-Hellenism, unlike its Neo-Roman predecessor, does not use the idiom of the other arts of its time. Whereas painting, poetry, and sculpture alike treated a sovereign of the age of Pope as Caesar, neither poet, painter, nor sculptor dreamt of treating George III as Pericles. Under the early Georges, whatever the costume, the head, whether represented with short hair, wig, or nightcap, was a portrait as realistic as a realistic age could make it; whereas a sculptor who executed portraits, as Banks executed those of Warren Hastings and Horne Tooke, 'while meditating upon Plutarch's heroes', was not likely to put his subject first. To compare Roubiliac's Colley Cibber or Daniel Lock with Banks's Warren Hastings at the India Office is to perceive the difference between an art which aims at facts and one which is based wholly upon theory. Westminster Abbey and St. Paul's will illustrate the contrast, and the Abbey sculpture is by no means the best of its class: it is as true of Rysbrack and Scheemaker as of Roubiliac, that 'it is his misfortune that his best performances are buried in the country'.[1]

Dr. Johnson himself was brought into contact with at

[1] *The Spectator*, 1753, see p. 83.

(*a*) MONUMENT OF MARY, THIRD DUCHESS OF MONTAGU (*d.* 1775)
at Warkton, Northants, by VAN GELDER after ROBERT ADAM

(*b*) THE DEATH OF ELOISA
Royal Academy, 1786
MONUMENT OF MRS. PETRIE at Lewisham, by THOMAS BANKS, R.A.

THE FRUITS OF WINCKELMANN AND REYNOLDS

least four sculptors, Roubiliac, who wanted him to write an epitaph; Nollekens, whom he probably met at the house of his old friend Saunders Welch, the father of Mrs. Nollekens, who, the Doctor declared, 'would have been mine, had not little Joe stepped in'; Bacon, who executed Johnson's bust at Pembroke and the posthumous statue in St. Paul's; and Wilton, about whose tablet to Mrs. Salusbury at Streatham he corresponded with Mrs. Thrale. All we know of the interview with Roubiliac is a vivid vignette of the attic in Gough Square, to which the courtly Sir Joshua had brought his friend the sculptor, and the instructions given to the excitable Frenchman to keep to the point, with 'no more of this rhodomontade'. Of Wilton and Bacon there are no personal touches whatsoever in Johnsonian records, but of Nollekens we hear a good deal. There is Johnson's annoyance with him for giving him no wig,[1] and his verdict that 'though a man may for convenience wear a cap in his own chamber, he ought not [in a bust] to look as if he had taken physic', a view with which we may compare Vertue's remark that 'no wig, ruff hair debases the idea of a fine gentleman'.[2]

One of the most striking comments on the new movement is the statue of Dr. Johnson in St. Paul's. Bacon, an admirable portrait sculptor, wished to represent him as he was in life; Reynolds, the most powerful member of the Memorial Committee, insisted on classical costume and on the bare head which Johnson himself had disapproved in Nollekens's bust.[3] The statue therefore is a failure. It has been taken for that of St. Paul, with Howard and his symbolic keys opposite for St. Peter; it has suggested to one of the best Johnson scholars of to-day 'a retired gladiator, meditating upon a wasted life';[4] and it stands as the outward and visible sign of the doctrines by which one of Johnson's dearest friends finally destroyed the continuity of tradition which had hitherto made English sculpture, whether

[1] Nollekens actually gave him the short crisp locks of Reynolds's model, White the paviour; see J. T. Smith's *Nollekens* throughout this section, though he knows nothing of the Offley monument (p. 85).

[2] Compare this verdict, B.M. Add. MSS. 23079, 34 b, with an opinion of 1717, when Dr. Clarke wrote to Dr. Charlett that a peruke would have rendered Bird's statue of Gibbs 'detestable'. Poole, *Oxford Portraits* (1922–5), vol. ii, pp. 6–7.

[3] Tradition told me by Bacon's great-granddaughter.

[4] John Bailey, *Johnson and his Circle* (1913), p. 1.

executed by masons or by immigrants, a great and living portrait art.

BIBLIOGRAPHY.—A large proportion of the statements in this chapter are founded on personal observation alone. The following works have been consulted:

F. C. CUNDALL, 'English Sculpture in Jamaica,' in *The Art Journal* (1907). ALLAN CUNNINGHAM, *Lives of British Painters, Sculptors, and Architects* (7 vols., 1829–33). K. A. ESDAILE, *Roubiliac's Work at Trinity College, Cambridge* (1924); *English Monumental Sculpture since the Renaissance* (1927); *Life and Works of L. F. Roubiliac* (1928); 'The Stantons of Holborn' (*Archaeological Journal*, 1930). W. HOGARTH, *Notes of My Life* (1833). ROBERT LLOYD, *Poems* (1762). THOMAS PENNANT, *Tour from Chester to London* (1790). MRS. R. L. POOLE, *Oxford Portraits* (3 vols., 1922–5). S. REDGRAVE, *Dictionary of Artists of the English School* (1874). J. B. ROUQUET, *L'État des Arts en Angleterre* (1755). W. L. SPIERS, *Notebooks of Nicholas Stone* (Walpole Society, vol. vii, 1918). J. T. SMITH, *Life and Times of Joseph Nollekens* (2 vols., 1828). G. L. SMYTH, *Monuments and Genii of Westminster Abbey* (1829). THIEME-BEKKER, Allgemeines Kunstler-Lexicon (6 vols., 1878).

XVIII

ARCHITECTURE AND THE GARDEN

By GEOFFREY WEBB

Whether to plant a walk in undulating curves, and to place a bench at every turn where there is an object to catch the view; to make water run where it will be heard, and to stagnate where it will be seen; to leave intervals where the eye will be pleased, and to thicken the plantation where there is something to be hidden, demands any great powers of mind, I will not enquire: perhaps a sullen and surly speculator may think such performances rather the sport than the business of human reason. But it must be at least confessed that to embellish the form of nature is an innocent amusement, and some praise must be allowed by the most supercilious observer to him who does best what such multitudes are contending to do well.—*Life of Shenstone.*

ARCHITECTURE

IN the coach going to Oxford in the spring of 1776 'Johnson expressed his disapprobation of ornamental architecture, such as magnificent columns supporting a portico, or expensive pilasters supporting merely their own capitals, "because it consumes labour disproportionate to its utility". For the same reason he satirized statuary. "Painting (said he) consumes labour not disproportionate to its effect: but a fellow will hack half a year at a block of marble to make something in stone that hardly resembles a man. The value of statuary is owing to its difficulty. You would not value the finest head cut upon a carrot."' Boswell did not agree, and Gwynn, the architect, their companion on the journey and 'a fine lively rattling fellow' replied: 'What, Sir, will you allow no value in architecture or in statuary? Why should we allow it then in writing? Why do you take the trouble to give us so many fine allusions, and bright images and elegant phrases? You might convey all your instruction without these ornaments.' Johnson smiled with complacency, but said: 'Why, Sir, all these ornaments are useful, because they obtain an easier reception for truth; but a building is not at all more convenient for being decorated with superfluous carved works.' The discussion did not end here, and it seems to have been a most enjoyable journey, for Boswell remembers it with pleasure a year later in a letter to Johnson.[1]

This extreme utilitarian view of architecture is no doubt

[1] Dated July 28, 1777.

a considerable exaggeration of the great man's opinion, assumed for the benefit of that fine lively rattling fellow, Gwynn, who was well known as the author of a *Discourse on Public Magnificence*; but it has been chosen as an opening to this chapter partly because it is one of Johnson's longest recorded utterances on the subject and more especially because it truly reflects an aspect of the eighteenth-century attitude to architecture which is often ignored in the accounts of its romantic admirers. These are all too ready to recall the elegance and refinements of the façades, the rational splendour of the great seats, and to hold up to admiration the orderly yet elastic view of art which could give discipline to streets and squares and yet allow of so much variety in individual monuments. The less spectacular forces which went to the moulding of eighteenth-century architecture are more apt to be forgotten; yet they have a very important share in the responsibility for these qualities we so much admire. For the speculative builders and their middle-class clients, though they accepted as much of the classical discipline as was useful to them, had not the same sense of romantic conviction about the authority of Roman and Palladian examples as the Italian travelled grandees and their fashionable architects, and though that filtering down of fashions in art from one social stratum to another, which is so familiar to us from Tottenham Court Road, obtained then as now, the sense that 'pilasters and what the orders required' were expensive disproportionately to the effect gained was undoubtedly an important force making for the relative abandonment of these classical trimmings in the latter part of the century. Robert Adam's tendency to seek variety of composition in the arrangement of comparatively plain masses cannot be attributed to this feeling in any considerable measure: there were other and better-known forces at work among the Grand Tourists themselves; but it certainly contributed powerfully to popularize his ideas. And it is the work of the speculative builders in London and their even humbler fellows in the country districts that gives the tone to the whole eighteenth-century architectural scene.

It is fitting to begin with London, partly because that was Johnson's *milieu* in a very special sense, and partly because in London many of the forces affecting eighteenth-century vernacular architecture can be seen in close juxtaposition, and their interactions be observed more closely. Moreover, fashions first appear in London and spread from there to the provinces at varying speeds, so that London practice becomes a standard for the whole country. In trying to picture Johnson's London—and the same applies to his England generally—we have first of all to think back into position an immense amount of the débris of former centuries. Quite apart from buildings of importance that have been lost since his time, as Old Somerset House, which Johnson himself saw replaced, or Northumberland House, gone within living memory, or the Holbein Gate in Whitehall, which makes such a picturesque feature in Canaletto's well-known picture, there was a mass of early work patched and remodelled, surviving wherever fire or replacement due to appreciation of site values permitted. In the City and Westminster much of this would be fairly recent, but included a great deal of late seventeenth-century building, noticeable for its high-pitched roofs and elaborately enriched eaves-cornices of white painted wood. But in districts, which are now considered definitely urban and were then outside the operations of the City or Westminster building regulations, was a medley of all the regional building traditions of the home counties. Most remarkable of these were the timber-frame building types, the weather boarded, and the plastered. On both sides of the lower Thames at Limehouse and at Rotherhithe good examples of the weather-boarded architecture can be found surviving to this day as public houses. They are especially common in Essex where extant examples range from the simpler square box-like cottages to quite complex medium-sized houses; and the same is true of Surrey and Kent. All the examples cited here are of the time of Johnson; for where regulations did not forbid it, the timber tradition was still a living thing and the carpenters showed a pretty adaptability in their more ambitious efforts, though the Essex cottage box is dreary enough. Perhaps the most marked difference between London then and now would be the greater proportion of red brick in the buildings extant in Johnson's time. In the late seventeenth century and in Queen Anne's reign red brick had been the favourite material, but after 1720 grey and yellow stocks begin to become popular, and by the middle of the century they were in possession of the field. Isaac Ware, whose *Complete Body of Architecture* of 1756 is a mine of information on all matters of building practice of his time, writes on this point:

We see many very beautiful pieces of workmanship in red brick; and to name one, the front of the green-house in Kensington-Gardens will be sure to attract every eye that has the least curiosity: but this should not tempt the judicious architect to admit them in the front walls of the building.

In the first place, the colour is itself fiery and disagreeable to the eye; it is troublesome to look upon it; and, in summer, it has an appearance of heat that is very disagreeable: for this reason it is most improper in the country, though the oftenest used there, from the difficulty of getting grey.

But a farther consideration is, that in the fronts of most buildings of any expence there is more or less stonework: now... there is something harsh in the transition from the red brick to stone, and it seems altogether unnatural; in the other, the grey stocks come so near the colour of stone that the change is less violent, and they sort better together.

For this reason also the grey stocks are to be judged best coloured when they have least of the yellow cast; for the nearer they come to the colour of stone, when they are to be used together with it, always the better.

Where there is no stone work there generally is wood, and this being painted white, as is commonly the practice, has a yet worse effect with red brick than the stone work; the transition is more sudden in this than the other: but, on the other hand, in the mixture of grey bricks and white paint, the colour of the brick being soft, there is no violent change.[1]

The one point in which Ware shows himself out of touch with the tendency of his time in this passage is where he decries bricks of 'the yellow cast', for as the eighteenth century went on these yellow Malms as they were called became increasingly popular. Mr. Lloyd has suggested[2] that this replacement of red bricks by grey and yellow coloured ones is perhaps due to the exploitation of the Kentish brick-fields at this time. Nowadays, when London buildings of the eighteenth century have been reduced to a common drab by the action of time and soot, it is hard to appreciate this change in the aspect of London at its original value.

The type of London town house of the mid-eighteenth century dates back, in plan at any rate, to the Restoration.

[1] Ware, *Complete Body of Architecture* (1756), p. 61.
[2] N. Lloyd, *History of English Brickwork*, p. 58.

THE BANK OF ENGLAND
The main building by George Sampson, with wings added by Sir Robert Taylor
From the painting by T. H. Shephard

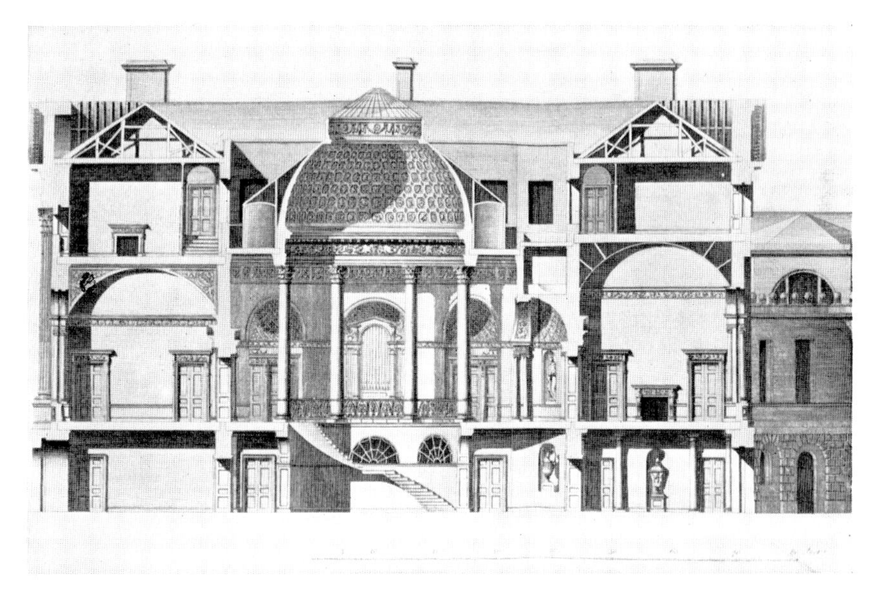

SECTION, FROM SOUTH TO NORTH, THROUGH THE CENTRE OF WARDOUR HOUSE
From Plans, Elevations, and Sections of Noblemen's Houses, *by James Paine, 1783*

The limitations of the long, narrow, street-fronted sites very early compelled the builders to an almost standard solution of their problem; and though in the 1750's and 1760's the influence of the more varied and ambitious planning that derived from a study of Roman architecture brought about some changes in the direction of curved forms (as bow-windows, apses to dining-rooms, &c.) in place of the monotonously rectangular room shapes of the earlier period, these are mainly found in the more ambitious houses by well-known architects. Dr. Heberden's house in Pall Mall, built by Paine in 1750, a house surely well known to Dr. Johnson, shows these tendencies in its elliptical staircase hall; but Robert Adam and his followers are, of course, the great exponents of this kind of planning. For more modest houses we must turn again to Isaac Ware, who has a long section on town houses, so valuable and informative that quotation in full needs no apology. Ware writes as follows:

The common houses in London are all built in one way, and that so familiar that it will need little instruction, nor deserve much illustration. The general custom is to make two rooms and a light closet on a floor, and if there be any little opening behind, to pave it.

Some attempt to make flower-gardens of these little spots, but this is very idle; plants require a purer air than animals, and however we breathe in London, they cannot live where there is so much smoak and confinement; nor will even gravel continue clean many days from the turning.

In this respect therefore, instead of borders under the walls, the best method is to lay the whole with a good sound stone pavement, and at the farther part to build the needful edifice, that cannot in London be removed farther off; and something of similar shape and little service opposite to it. An alcove with a seat is a common contrivance in the space between, but it is a strange place to sit in for pleasure: all this therefore is better omitted; and the young architect is to have a general caution on this head, that will serve him on many more, which is, that when there cannot be any proper ornament, nothing is so becoming as perfect plainness.

The lower story in these common houses in London is sunk entirely under ground, for which reason it is damp, unwholesome, and uncomfortable; but the excuse has weight: ground-rent is so dear in London that every method is to be used to make the most of the ground plan; but even in the most ordinary houses in the country, where some of the offices may be made without doors, it will always be best, instead of these totally under-ground floors, to have a basement story. . . .

In common houses the fore-parlour is the best room upon the ground-floor: the passage cuts off a good deal from this, and from the back parlour; this usually running straight into the opening, or garden as it is called, behind; but it is a much better practice to make the back parlour the better room. This may be done as we have proposed by making the fore room a hall or retaining it in form of a parlour; the passage into the garden may be from below, and consequently the breadth of the passage there taken in, which gives the back parlour a greater extent, and another window.

The first floor in these common houses consists of the dining-room, over the hall or parlour; a bed-chamber over the back parlour, and a closet over its closet.

This closet is usually a corner added to the building, and continued to the second story, not to the garrets.

In houses something better than the common kind, the back room upon the first floor should be a drawing-room, or dressing-room, for the lady; for it is better not to have any bed on this floor.

The two rooms on the second floor are for bed-rooms, and the closets being carried up thus far, there may be a third bed there.

Over these are the garrets, which may be divided into a larger number than the floors below, for the reception of beds for servants.

With all the care that can be taken in this article, often the number of servants cannot be lodged there; and in this case a bed for one man or two maid-servants is contrived to let down in the kitchen. But in this case the necessary care of those people's healths requires it should be boarded. . . .

Such a house as we have been here speaking of is to be built for six or seven hundred pounds, or it will cost upwards, according to a little more extent of ground, and a little more than usual ornament. The common builders of them work jointly, one doing his share of business in the other's house, according to their several subordinate professions; so that it is not easy for them to say what they cost, but they are generally ready to sell them for fourteen years' purchase, exclusive of ground-rent.[1]

Not the least interesting part of all this is the glimpse we get of the speculative builder's methods in the last paragraph. For the importance of their activities can hardly be exaggerated at a time when not only were new estates being developed but continual improvements were being made in the existing parts of the town, as the rebuilding of Westminster Bridge by Labelye from 1737 to 1747, which led to the lay-out of new streets and much new building about its approaches. The 'Weekly Summary' columns in such a newspaper as the

[1] I. Ware, op. cit., pp. 345–7.

London Chronicle (1757 seq.) are full of news of London improvements, such as street widening and the setting out of new squares. On one occasion in that paper there is an impassioned complaint against the City authorities for continuing to offer out-of-date buildings on repairing leases instead of insisting on rebuilding. The writer compares them unfavourably with private landowners in this respect. One of the qualities we most admire in eighteenth-century architecture is the orderly decency and neighbourliness of its street façades; this was promoted by public bodies, as an order of the Common Council of the City shows as early as the Restoration period (1667). 'That the surveyors take special care that the breast-summers of all houses do range of an equal height house to house. . . .' The same spirit appears in detail in the conditions of building leases and we hear for example in the *London Chronicle* of 1761 how a building contractor has been given a building lease of land 'on which to build a uniform row of houses'. It was the monotony of these 'uniform rows' when they were produced by the thousand under the stimulus of the industrial revolution that drew down much of the wrath of the early nineteenth-century romantic critics; and even as early as Ware there is a mild note of protest in his 'It is certain there is a sameness in modern buildings which takes off a great deal from their merit'. This, no doubt, is an anticipation of that movement towards greater restraint in detail and more enterprise in the general lines of composition, which becomes so marked among the architects of the generation after Ware, many of whom also took up land on speculation, the brothers Adam's Adelphi, and Leverton's houses in Bedford Square being only the most celebrated examples.

The changes which came over the external appearance of town houses in the eighteenth century were of course largely the result of the influence of such men as these, but one other factor should be mentioned, the London Building Acts. Of these the two most important are the Act of 1707 which forbade the wooden eaves-cornice and caused its gradual replacement by a brick parapet, and the ordinance of 1708 whereby 'no Door, Frame, or Window-frame of Wood, to be fixed on any house in London or Westminster and their Liberties shall be set nearer to the Outside Face of the Wall than 4 inches; nor shall any Brick work bear or be placed upon Timber . . . on Pain of three months' imprisonment, without bail or Mainprize.' In spite of these severe penalties it would seem that the ordinance did not command general obedience till some twenty years later. The implications of these two regulations are, first, the vogue of the parapeted front which conceals the roof; in many cases a parapet was added to houses that originally had overhanging cornices and often the brickwork of the two periods of building are indistinguishable; and, secondly, the disappearance of the broad white painted margin of the sash-framed window in favour of the set-back window, which in some cases was stuccoed and painted in the reveal to compensate for the lost margin. A further result in this case of the clause about brickwork bearing on timber was the tendency towards segmental tops to the window openings; for these, by reason of their arch-form, comply with the regulation and distribute the down thrust of the brickwork on either side of the window.

These London Building Acts have an importance far beyond that implied in their statutory limitation to London and Westminster; for apart from the influence of the houses built in compliance with them as being London work and therefore the fashionable example to provincial country builders, there is evidence that building clients adopted the provisions of the London Acts as a standard of workmanship in dealing with local contractors. And so we find houses with parapeted fronts, set-back sash-frames, and segmental-topped window openings appearing in country districts contemporaneously with older-fashioned work. In most parts of the country, red brick persisted long after the change to greys and yellows was well established in London. Further, brick became the fashion and is found almost everywhere (except in the Cotswolds), even in stone building countries and in the most surprising variety of local colourings—for example, the rich purple of east Dorset, the mixture of plain and grey vitrified bricks of Buckingham, and the brilliant reds of the Staffordshire-Shropshire borders, which Johnson must have known well. This preference for brick must have been due to fashion, almost certainly the example of London, for the evidence of William Halfpenny's *Useful Architecture in Twenty one new designs for country parsonages, Farm houses and Inns* (1752) goes to show that a house costing £208 in stone would work out nearly £50 dearer in brick. Halfpenny, however, gives no information as to how these figures were obtained and obviously there must have been wide differences from district to district.

The country builder was an enthusiastic patron of such books such as Halfpenny's, to judge by the number that were issued and the editions they went through. They supplied him with abundance of information as to the five orders, difficult bits of joinery, such as staircases, and, in addition, ready-made plans and elevations, which he could adapt to his purposes, just as the lower type of trade journal does to-day, only with rather more sense of responsibility. As an illustration of the range of such works one may cite William Salmon's *Palladio Londinensis* (1755) which in addition to more purely architectural information gives short cuts to mathematics; this is the heading of one section: 'To find the superficial content of a Cylinder. Note: that a Cylinder is a solid body such as is used in gardens for rolling the walks'. These *Builder's Pocket Treasures* (1763) and *Practical Builders' and Workmen's Assistants* (1774) and so forth are the real force behind eighteenth-century country building, rather than that mysterious phenomenon, the 'Wren Tradition', which if it had any real existence obtained only in the Cotswolds from which so many of Wren's masons were recruited. The authors of these books were most often tradesmen and describe themselves as architect and carpenter, though both Lightoller and Morris, who collaborated with Halfpenny on occasion, have left buildings as evidence of their quality in the former capacity.

A large part of Ware's book, from which we have already quoted so freely, and which is a much more authoritative work than the general run, deals with country building. Ware's scheme for a country parsonage is again worth quoting as an example of standard housing requirements in the middle of the century:

A house where nothing of this (i.e. farm buildings) is required, and which is for the reception of a small family, may be built without any under-ground work at all. Upon the level of the ground, if it be dry wholesome soil, may be an entrance from the principal door; and on each side of it a parlour. In front may be the stair-case; and over these lodging-rooms. Behind may be placed a kitchen and wash-house, which need be no more than sheds well covered; and, as most who devote themselves to a country life take the amusements of reading and of riding, beyond the right hand parlour may be a study, covered as the kitchen, and beyond the left a stable. The passage into the study being from the parlour, and the opening into the stable by a door outwards.[1]

The bedroom accommodation seems limited even for a small family and one is reminded of old Lady Townshend's comment, when she was shown over Horace Walpole's beloved Strawberry Hill: 'Lord God! Jesus! What a house! It is just such a house as a parson's, where the children lie at the foot of the bed.' These two quotations taken together help one to understand why so many country parsonages were rebuilt in the nineteenth century.

The country gentleman's house is perhaps the most typical of all rural buildings of the mid-eighteenth century. The classification is a wide one, for it varies from 'the most absolute necessaries of life without which a Gentleman of the smallest fortune thinks he makes no figure in the County', namely, 'one large room, a Serpentine river and a wood',[2] to something only a little less ambitious than the great monuments erected by the leaders of the architectural profession for eminent political peers. Of the larger kind that splendid establishment which was to crown with happiness the career of the heroine of *Grandison* may stand as an example.[3]

The situation is delightful. The house is very spacious. It is built in the form of an H; both fronts pretty much alike. The hall, the dining-parlour, two drawing-rooms, one adjoining to the study, the other to the dining-parlour, (which with the study, mentioned already, and other rooms, that I shall leave to Lucy to describe, make the ground-floor) are handsome, and furnished in an elegant, but not sumptuous taste; the hangings of some of them beautiful paper only. There is adjoining to the study, a room called The Music-parlour, so called in Sir Thomas's time, and furnished with several fine musical instruments. . . . The dining room is noble and well proportioned: it goes over the hall and dining-parlour. It is hung with crimson-damask, adorned with valuable pictures. . . . The best bed-chamber adjoining, is hung with fine tapestry. The bed is of crimson velvet, lined with white silk; chairs and curtains of the same. . . . The suite of rooms on the first floor which we just stept into, are each denominated from the colour of the hangings, which are generally of damask. Mrs. Curzon tells us, that, on occasion, they make fifteen beds, within the house,

[1] Ware, op. cit., p. 348.
[2] *Gent. Mag.*, 1739.
[3] Letter No. 5 (vol. vii, 1754, p. 21).

in which the best Lord of the land need not disdain to repose. . . . The offices are said to be exceedingly convenient.

Such places as this would be the work, if not of a London eminence, at least of some well-known provincial architect, such men as Carr of York, or one of the Bastards of Blandford, or the Hiorn family of Warwick. In Bath in Dr. Johnson's time at least four other architects beside the celebrated Wood are known, and considerable works recorded. One of them, Thomas Warr Attwood, is described as architect and plumber, but the Guildhall and the Old Prison there are evidences that his pretension to the grander title was not an empty one. Bath, of course, is an exceptional town, but a generally high standard of country town architecture is a characteristic of the age and seems to have been rather taken for granted. Johnson's own usual term of commendation for a country town is 'neat'. Towards the end of Johnson's life, and increasingly in the period immediately following, architects of reputation began to concern themselves with the design of the smaller types of gentlemen's house and the planning of these begins to improve very rapidly. Before 1780, however, this tendency is hardly noticeable, except perhaps in such places as Richmond or on the estates of great noblemen, where London architects would undertake such work, as Robert Mylne did for the New River Company's property. Otherwise the small to medium sized houses were left to the local builders, and the planning is the least admirable quality about them. Not that they are inconvenient so much as uninspired. To quote the inevitable Ware: 'It is true that the present general form of houses is alike: and it is also true that although this be a very commodious one, it is not the only shape that can be so; convenience in a house is not limited to the figure of a long square'.

The fifteen years from 1738, when Johnson first came to London, to 1753, the date of Lord Burlington's death, are not the period of the great patron's most important personal activity, which belongs rather to the preceding twenty years, the time of the buildings that bear his name as designer, the time of his own Chiswick Villa and the inception of Kent's great scheme for his friend, Coke, at Holkham, the time also of the fine series of publications that he organized and financed. The question of Lord Burlington's real claims to the authorship of his buildings is much disputed; we are fortunate in being exempt from such problems here. Our concern is with the school of architects to which he gave his name and with the influence he wielded, either directly through his followers or indirectly through their books and their example, on the whole architecture of the middle years of the century. By 1738, the year he was rebuffed in the matter of the Mansion House, the design being given to Dance in preference to Kent, family troubles and in some degree financial difficulties were curbing his own activities; but it is from this time on that we can really appreciate the thoroughness and wide scope of the change he had brought about in English architecture. The Mansion House itself with its 'Egyptian' hall and other Palladian features bears witness that, even where his advice was rejected, it was impossible to escape from his all-pervading influence. To quote Pope's well-known lines:

> Yet shall, my Lord, your just, your noble rules
> Fill half the land with Imitating Fools;
> Who random drawings from your sheets shall take,
> And of one beauty many blunders make; . . .
> Shall call the winds thro' long arcades to roar,
> Proud to catch cold at a Venetian door.

This is, of course, rather severe and cannot be applied to the eminent gentlemen whose works we are about to discuss. Of these are first the immediate entourage of Burlington—Kent, his life-long friend and collaborator who died in 1748, then Flitcroft and more obscure figures such as Morris and Daniel Garret, and, most important of all for us, Isaac Ware, from whose book we have already quoted. Ware began his career as a draughtsman to Burlington and his earliest published works are an edition of Palladio (1738), which Burlington himself revised and corrected, and *Designs of Inigo Jones and Others* (1743). Ware's most celebrated architectural work is Chesterfield House (1748); but there are other London houses as No. 5 Bloomsbury Square and No. 71 South Audley Street which show his powers equally well. His most important country house was Wrotham Park (1754), a design with a great pillared portico approached by curved flights of steps, and octagonal angle towers crowned with lead domes. In these buildings we can see in what the Burlingtonian contribution consists. The insistence on Palladio as the source of all, or almost all, worthy precedents for exterior features

BLACKFRIARS BRIDGE IN JULY 1766
From the engraving by E. Rooker

BLOOMSBURY SQUARE
From the engraving by R. Pollard and F. Jukes, 1787, after the drawing by E. Dayes

is combined with an admiration for Inigo Jones and a recourse to his example for plaster ceiling and chimney piece designs. But this is not all. Burlington and Kent had made free use of *motifs* derived direct from Classic Roman archaeology, and by their practice as well as by their publication of Palladio's plans of Roman Thermae had started their followers on the line of development in interior planning, which we have already touched on in reference to Dr. Heberden's town house. The importance of this can hardly be exaggerated; it is a turning-point in architectural history, second only in importance to the original introduction of Renaissance principles of design in the seventeenth century; for it meant the opening up of the possibilities of space composition in domestic architecture, hitherto almost confined to church building.

In one respect Ware is the last of the Burlingtonians of the pure blood, in the picturesque variety, that is, of his exterior compositions with their effectively grouped masses. Here he is the true follower of Kent, the author of Holkham and the Horse Guards; the Kent, of whom it is too often forgotten that he was originally a painter and besides being an architect was a pioneer in picturesque landscape gardening. Ware's successors, James Paine and Sir Robert Taylor, who, according to the well-known passage in Gwilt's *Life of Sir William Chambers*, 'before Mr. Robert Adam entered the lists . . . nearly divided the practice of the profession between them', had little of this enterprise in their exterior compositions. Paine at Wardour and Thorndon, and Taylor at Gorhambury produced just those square, well-proportioned, Palladian-dressed boxes, against which Robert Adam and his followers reacted with their striving after movement and variety of composition in mass. It is designs such as these which have brought on the Burlingtonian school the accusation of pedantic stodginess, though, as we have seen, against the work of the true Burlingtonians of the inner circle the charge will not hold. But if Paine and Taylor did not carry on the best traditions of their masters in exterior design, in the new developments within the house they worthily developed hints of Burlington and Kent. Paine's plans of Wardour and Worksop, and his first design for Kedleston (afterwards modified by Adam), and to a less degree Taylor's plan of Heveningham show a great advance in this respect.

Paine's great suites of square entrance, circular domed anteroom and Egyptian hall at Worksop, or pillared hall, elliptical staircase hall and circular drawing-room in the Kedleston plan, are in their scale and ambition something entirely new in English architecture. Both Paine and Taylor, who continued in practice till the 1780's, were considerably affected by Robert Adam's influence in their later works. Brocket Hall, which Paine seems to have begun about 1761, and which contains a typical Paine staircase feature (comparable with, but not as splendid as, that of Wardour), shows this very clearly in the rooms that were left to be finished last, after 1768 that is. The same influence of Adam can be traced in the town house erected by Taylor in Dover Street towards the end of his life. Another architect who shows a similar progress from a Burlingtonianism like that of Paine to a style largely influenced by Robert Adam, is Carr of York. At Tabley House, Cheshire, his style is very close to that of Ware, but after his work at Harewood, where he came into direct contact with Adam, the influence of the latter is very marked. In the works of other provincial architects, the Woods of Bath, we also see the influence of the Burlingtonian interior planning; but it would seem that in this case it hardly needed an outside influence to set either Wood on the way to ambitious and varied planning, for this seems with them a personal characteristic, whether expressed in the lay-out of streets and squares, or the planning of individual buildings.

The strength of the Burlingtonian school was largely founded on the support that it derived from the Italianate education of the upper classes. In the early part of the century the division between the architects and patrons who had been to Italy, and the upholders of the native baroque school, of which Hawksmoor and Vanbrugh are the great names, is very clearly marked and Lord Burlington as the leader of the Grand Tourists was a most important factor in the suppression of baroque in England after a short life of scarcely more than one generation. The facilities for foreign travel that came with the long peace of Walpole's administration, and the increasing wealth of the country bringing such opportunities for enjoyment and education within reach of an ever-widening public were all forces helping on the habit. One great objective of the Grand Tour was always Venice, where there were, in addition to gambling facilities and

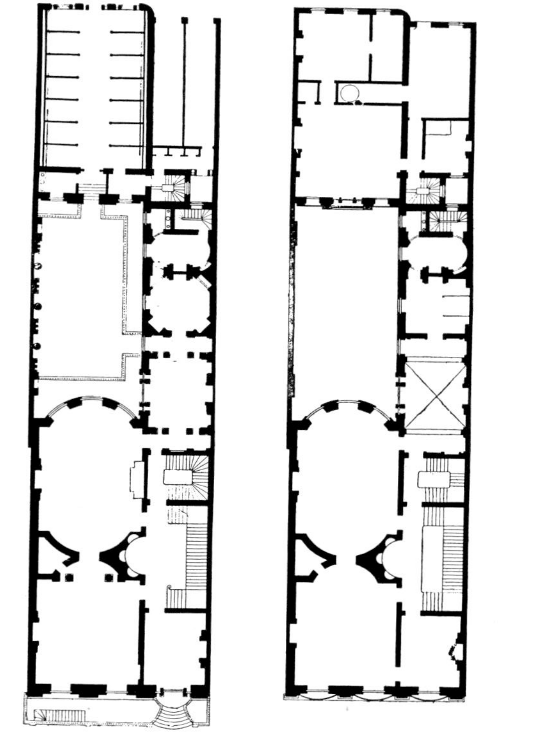

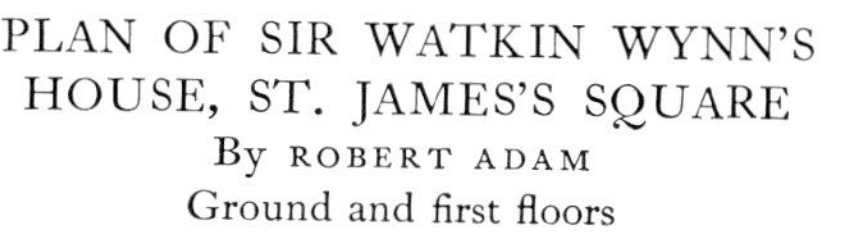

PLAN OF SIR WATKIN WYNN'S HOUSE, ST. JAMES'S SQUARE

By ROBERT ADAM

Ground and first floors

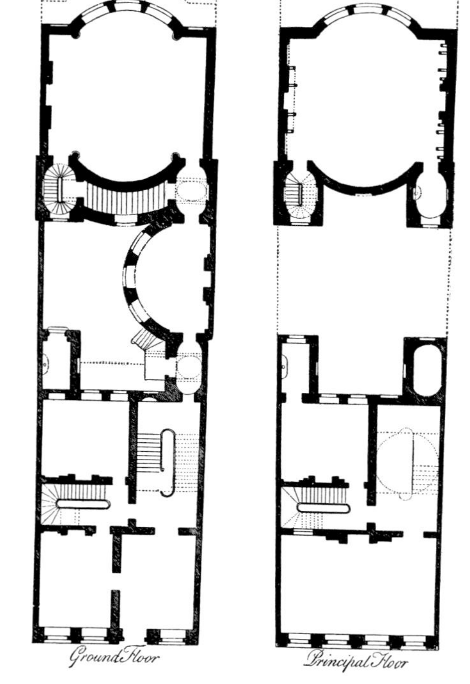

PLAN OF THE HON. THOMAS FITZ-MAURICE'S HOUSE, PALL MALL

By JAMES PAINE

Ground and first floors

pleasure parties, the most celebrated private collections of works of art and the remains of the last of the important schools of Italian painting. Moreover, within easy reach were Vicenza and Palladio's most celebrated villas, holy places to the architecturally-minded of that time. Even at a later date when Rome, the centre of the antiquarian and aesthetic ferment we associate with the name of Winckelmann, and Naples, which to social amenities could add the archaeological attractions of Pozzuoli, Herculaneum, Pompeii and even Paestum, were become the places of pilgrimage to all serious students of the arts, Venice remained the centre where men did their business with the antique dealers and engravers and draughtsmen that they employed to record the objects of their admiration, as we buy photographs.

This archaeological taste, which we have already noticed in the work of Kent and the inner Burlingtonian circle, was the fashion destined to supplant Palladianism in the years that followed Lord Burlington's death. Its source is to be found in the Rome of the 1740's and 1750's. There had always been an archaeological tradition in Rome, which descended through Pirro Ligorio and Palladio himself to the students of the French academy of the end of the seventeenth century whose greatest monument is the work of Desgodetz. But by the middle of the eighteenth century the tradition had been greatly reinforced. Herculaneum was discovered in 1719 and Pompeii in 1748 and in addition to these the Near East began to be opened up to investigators; Palmyra, Athens, Ionia, Paestum, Sicily were all visited by French or English enthusiasts during the middle years of the century. The significance of all this was that the charmed circle of the Renaissance masters as the sole interpreters of antiquity was broken. Henceforward the authority of the antique spoke with many voices, its prestige remained but its message was dubious. Moreover, at the same time there appeared other and stranger tendencies in the arts. The provinces of decoration, gardening, and the minor arts, which had formerly followed at a distance the lead of the great practitioners of the major forms of architecture, began to show a vitality of their own. The first considerations for these lesser branches of architectural design in the eighteenth century were novelty, variety, and the power to amuse—in a word 'chic'—and so we get that strange medley of fashions, rococo, the Chinese taste, and the Gothic. One may quote the words of an American designer's advertisement of 1759,[1] 'All sorts of Rooms after the manner of the Arabian, Chinese, Persian, Gothic, Muscovite, Palladian, Vitruvian and Egyptian', as an illustration. Of these the Gothic is generally treated as the most important, but this is in the light of future events and in Sir William Chambers's works at Kew the Gothic temple was only one, with the Pagoda and the Alhambra, among a great variety of exotic delights. Two considerable buildings, Kent's villa for Pelham at Esher and Strawberry Hill, are the only considerable Gothic designs of this period, with the exception of Robert Adam's Culzean in Scotland, and both of them partake of the nature of garden buildings. Their importance in relation to their own times has often been exaggerated.

For our purposes the whole of this ferment of ideas, archaeological and exotic, and its practical outcome, may be summed up in the careers of Robert and James Adam. Robert Adam's continental tour, 1753–8, brought him into contact with many of the leaders of the new movements abroad. Of these the most important was Piranesi, the engraver, and after him Clérisseau, the French architect and draughtsman, who accompanied him on his excursion into field archaeology, the expedition to survey Diocletian's Palace at Spalato in Dalmatia. Clérisseau in later years published a survey of the monuments of Nîmes, and it is probably due to him that Adam visited that city in 1754. For the younger brother, James Adam, whose tour began in 1760, we have much more information, thanks to the preservation of his diary of his travels. He was accompanied by Clérisseau throughout his tour. One or two points stand out in this document and deserve special mention. The first is his open-minded interest in medieval buildings, as the Duomo at Florence and Santa Maria della Spina at Pisa, but more illuminating than this is the long passage giving his impressions of Vicenza.

Walked out to see the different buildings of Palladio with which this city abounds, and of which I am no admirer. His private houses are ill adjusted both in their plans and elevations, as is also the Theatre Olympic, which is looked upon here as a *capo d'opera*. The seats are not convenient for the spectators: the order of them is pitiful. In the angles of the circular part the spectators cannot see the

[1] Francis Lenygon, *English Furniture* (1927), p. 37.

performers, and the seats begin much too high above the stage. The scena is the most crowded and ill adjusted thing I ever saw; and the alleys in perspective are perfectly childish. The Hotel de Ville is abominably *maigre* in every respect. What pleased me most of all Palladio's works, was his Villa Capra or Rotunda: it is about a mile from town, and is agreeably situated on a pleasant coline. The plan is pretty; but the fronts, the round room within, and indeed all the particular parts of it, are but very poorly adjusted. However, there is something to make a good thing of, which is more than can be said for most of Palladio's buildings. Near to this, on a neighbouring coline, is the Villa Valmarana, which is painted in fresco by Tiepolo, with a good deal of spirit and whim.[1]

To an English (if not to a Scottish) architect of a few years before such expressions as these would have been inconceivable blasphemy.

The Adam brothers' great period of success was the 'sixties. Mersham-le-Hatch, Syon, Osterley, Kedleston, Lansdowne House, Luton Hoo, Harewood, Kenwood, and Saltram were all undertaken during this decade, though in some cases the work lasted on well beyond it. In the earliest works the 'filagree' style of decoration in low relief plaster, based on the drawings of sixteenth-century arabesque decoration such as that of the Villa Madama, was not yet fully developed, but the complete Adam style matured very quickly and soon had an amazing vogue. These arabesques which are to be found before this time in the work of Kent, were of course an archaeological *motif* and had been introduced as such by the High Renaissance Italian masters. In James Adam's diary we find continual reference to them both in the revived forms of the sixteenth century and the original antique examples which he calls 'grotesques' after the 'grottoes', or partially excavated Roman buildings, in which they were found. All this has more to do with decoration than architecture, but the Adams and their followers were almost as much concerned with the one as the other. As regards the internal planning of their buildings they continued and refined upon the varied suites and geometrical forms of the late Burlingtonians; the plan of No. 20 St. James's Square (1772) and of Lord Bute's house, Luton Hoo, are veritable *tours de force* in this kind. Circular, elliptical, and apsed forms are all used freely and great play is made with screens of columns.

[1] Vide *Library of Fine Arts* (vol. iv, no. 9, Oct. 1831; vol. iv, no. 10, Nov. 1831).

Luton Hoo is one of the two works of Adam noticed by Dr. Johnson, whom Boswell records as having said, 'This is one of the places I do not regret having come to see. It is a very stately place, indeed; in the house magnificence is not sacrificed to convenience, nor convenience to magnificence. The library is very splendid; the dignity of the rooms is very great; and the quantity of pictures is beyond expectation, beyond hope.'

This exploitation of what we now call space composition, which moved even Johnson to admiration, and of which Luton Hoo is the most ambitious example in domestic architecture, has its counterpart externally in Adam's theory of movement. This is expounded in a well-known passage in the *Works* (1778).

> Movement is meant to express, the rise and fall, the advance and recess, with other diversity of form, in the different parts of a building, so as to add greatly to the picturesque of the composition. For the rising and falling, advancing and receding, with the convexity and concavity, and other forms of the great parts, have the same effect in architecture, that hill and dale, fore-ground and distance, swelling and sinking have in landscape: That is, they serve to produce an agreeable and diversified contour, that groups and contrasts like a picture, and creates a variety of light and shade, which gives great spirit, beauty and effect to the composition.[1]

All this is followed by an analysis of well-known examples as de Vau's Institut de France and Bernini's colonnades before St. Peter's, and concludes with a panegyric of Vanbrugh, a curious example of a back-to-baroque movement. But the most significant part of this quotation is its argument by analogy with painting. The discussion of the picturesque aesthetic belongs naturally to the section of this chapter on Gardening, but with the brothers Adam it had already affected architecture. Indeed, it may be maintained that it had already done so in the work of Kent at Holkham and elsewhere. Kent was an early exponent of the theory in gardening and himself a painter by early training. The real onset of the picturesque on architecture did not make itself felt till the end of the century and Reynolds's important 13th Discourse with its advocacy of 'variety and intricacy' in architecture was not promulgated until 1785. Adam's own most whole-heartedly picturesque composition was Culzean

[1] Adam, op. cit., p. 35.

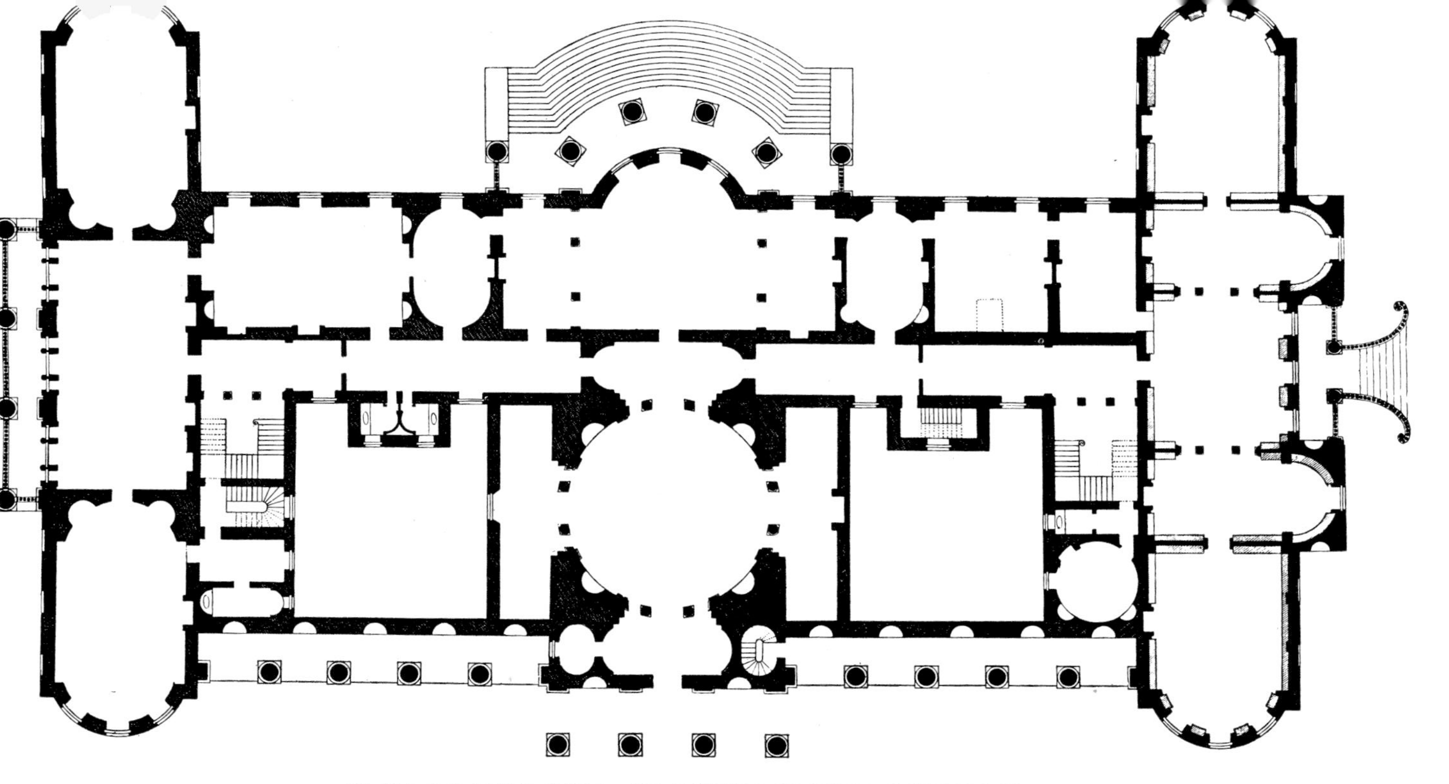

PLAN OF THE EARL OF BUTE'S HOUSE, LUTON HOO

By ROBERT ADAM

Ground floor

Castle (1787), a curious building classical in detail, medieval in grouping, after the manner of Vanbrugh's 'Gothic' designs, to which it would appear to owe a considerable debt, though perhaps Piranesi had a nearer and more direct influence on his friend. For the most part the picturesque in Adam is merely reflected in a rather more enterprising grouping of his masses than was usual with his contemporaries.

Of these contemporaries the most outstanding are Sir William Chambers and James Wyatt. Chambers returned from his Continental tour in 1755; while abroad he had also made the acquaintance of Clérisseau and had been considerably influenced by French work, especially that of the younger Gabriel. On his return he was employed to lay out Kew Gardens for the Dowager Princess of Wales, an appointment that was joined with that of drawing-master to her son, the future George III. This Court favour once attained was continued and proved the mainstay of Chambers's career, and in due course he became Controller of Works, in which capacity he was architect to the rebuilding of Somerset House. Unlike Adam or Wyatt he never attained great popular success or a large private practice and remained to the end of his life rather an official architect. With Sir Joshua Reynolds he was one of the founders of the Royal Academy. Consistent with all this is the conscious conservatism of his manner, a quality to be found in all aspects of his architecture. His planning, for example, is skilful, but shows a preference for rectangular forms and his exteriors have more in common with the Palladianists than the new fashions, though he is more eclectic and draws from larger sources of precedent than his immediate predecessors; and there is a liveliness and variety in his compositions that contrast with the severity sometimes amounting to dreariness of men like Paine. In his interior designs, again, though he uses low relief arabesques on occasion, his treatment is in general fuller and bolder than the fashionable 'filigrane toywork', to quote his own words of Robert Adam. Apart from Somerset House, and now that Carrington House, Pall Mall, has been destroyed, his best-known building must be the original block and forecourt of the Albany (1767), but country houses by him are extant and in Dublin he left distinguished works. He may be said to have founded a school there. Two books of Chambers deserve a special mention, his *Treatise On the Decorative*

Part of Civil Architecture (1759) and his book on *Chinese Gardening*. The influence of the first of these is acknowledged to have been immense and was an offset to the fashionable trivialities of his better-known rivals. The book on gardening has also its importance, but belongs naturally to the second section of the chapter. Chambers's activities in garden design are the exception to that conservatism we have chosen as his outstanding characteristic as an architect.

James Wyatt stands at the opposite pole to Chambers with his decorous conservative official style; he outbid Adam himself in the market for fashionable elegancies. His success, which was phenomenal, dates from the opening of the Pantheon in Oxford Street in 1772, six years after his return from study in Italy. This building, of which Johnson and Boswell expressed a temperate commendation—they preferred the Rotunda at Ranelagh—roused the enthusiasm of Horace Walpole, who was only too ready to snatch up any stick to beat the Adam brothers; and indeed it seems probable that Wyatt owed a considerable debt to the desire of the fashionable world to find an offset to those too successful architects, who were, moreover, Scotch and the protégés of Lord Bute. His style is closely related to theirs, though whether it was consciously adopted from them or derived from similar continental sources would be difficult to determine. The Adams themselves had no doubts; and, according to Horace Walpole, Robert Adam taxed 'Wyatt with stealing from him. But', he adds, 'Wyatt has employed the antique with more judgement and the Pantheon is still the most beautiful edifice in England.' It would seem that the exclusive claims to originality made in their *Works* (1778), which so affronted Sir William Chambers, were more probably directed chiefly against Wyatt. Whatever the rights and wrongs of this dispute, Wyatt was certainly a very gifted architect and well deserved to improve the position his first success had made for him. Whether by the persuasion of Horace Walpole or on his own motion, about the end of Johnson's life Wyatt began to turn his attention to the Gothic. His greatest achievement in this manner, Fonthill Abbey for the young William Beckford, lies outside the limits of our period; but already in 1782 he had been called in at Salisbury and begun there the works, which, together with those at Durham, were to earn for him the execration of nineteenth-century medievalists, and even before this, in 1780, he had been doing Gothic work at Lee in Kent upon the introduction of Horace Walpole. It should be added that in spite of these medieval excursions Wyatt continued to design admirably in the classic manner to the end of his career.

Besides these outstanding personalities of the architectural world there were a number of lesser but still well-known men, who seem to have followed the Adam brothers, at any rate as regards interior treatment. It was, indeed, the obvious road to success. Of these Thomas Leverton is best known for his houses in Bedford Square, in the planning of some of which he shows that he could learn more important things from the Adams than a mere fashion for low relief plaster work. 'Athenian' Stuart, who by his book on the *Antiquities of Athens* (1762) had so much influence on the taste of the second half of the century, took as much from Adam in the few buildings he actually architected, as he gave to him through the designs in his books. This is especially noticeable in the planning of No. 15 St. James's Square (1766) and the decoration of Mrs. Montagu's house (1781). One of the most successful of Adam's imitators was Henry Holland, an architect whose mature work belongs to the period after Johnson's death. Of his early buildings, such as Claremont, the exteriors have a rather stodgy Burlingtonian character and this applies almost equally to Broadlands, Hants (1783), where, however, he has attempted something like the fashionable Adam elegance; the same is true of some of the interiors of Brooks Club (1777). George Dance, the younger, is an architect whose name cannot be omitted from any such enumeration as this by reason of one building, Newgate Prison (1770–8). This extraordinarily able work with its dramatic composition and deliberate exploitation of all the associations of a prison stands alone in eighteenth-century architecture. In his smaller domestic buildings where Dance adopts some of the fashionable Adams' mannerisms, he gives no indications of any such remarkable gifts.

It is fitting at the last to mention two architects with whom Johnson himself had to do. John Gwynn we have met as his friend of the journey to Oxford and it was on his behalf that Johnson made his only excursion into architectural controversy. Gwynn's reputation, apart from a book on the town planning of London, rests on his ability as a designer of bridges. Magdalen Bridge, Oxford, is the best known, but he also built others at Shrewsbury, his native town, at Worcester, and at Henley. The occasion of the controversy was the competition design of 1759 for Blackfriars Bridge by Robert Mylne, a young Scotchman of twenty-five just back from Italy, where he had been at the same time as Robert Adam. The real points at issue were the rival merits of elliptical or semicircular arches and the seemliness of a cast-iron rail (Mylne's design had elliptical arches); but in the course of it Johnson snubs the young man, in his friend's interest, 'Let it not be presumed, that a prize granted at Rome, implies an irresistible degree of skill. The competition is only between boys, and the prize given to excite laudable industry, not to reward consummate excellence.' Johnson was heavy metal to bring against a young man of twenty-five and it is satisfactory to know that Mylne did erect the bridge and lived to become an architect of considerable distinction. The incident seems to have rankled with Gwynn, however, for in his book published seven years later we find this comment on foreign-trained architects, which after so much discussion of their antecedents and influence may well serve to conclude this account. 'Mr. Trowel is just arrived from Rome! You see everything is perfectly Italian, his drawings, his air, his cloaths, his servants, all Italian—Bravissimo! he must undoubtedly be a great genius, Mr. Trowel's name is up, and he may go to bed when he pleases.'

Gardens

In the time of Johnson gardening occupied a position in the world of ideas that we of to-day can scarcely understand, for all that our enthusiasm for gardening as a form of outdoor recreation has grown beyond anything imagined in the eighteenth century. Gardening was then the vehicle for a whole body of feeling that could find little or no outlet in the major arts of architecture and painting, confined as these were by the limitations of tradition and the Italianate taste of the time. Architecture was becoming more and more an expert's business and painting always had been so, for the day of the amateur sketcher was not yet; but every gentleman could 'improve' his garden and indulge in that pastime

SUPPER ROOM AT THE OAKS

Erected by ROBERT ADAM for the Fête Champêtre given by the Earl of Derby, 9th June, 1774

his individual taste, with a freedom impossible elsewhere. Moreover, eighteenth-century landscape gardening was no mere matter of feminine fripperies, whether medieval knots or modern rock gardens, but a serious activity, related on the one hand to the manly pursuits of planting and estate management and on the other to an appreciation of such masters of Italian landscape painting as Claude, Salvator Rosa, and Gaspar Poussin. In the first of these affinities landscape gardening shows itself very clearly as the art of a landowning class living on its estates—a point of importance, for it helps to explain its widespread popularity and amazing development in England, while on the Continent it always remained an exotic—*Le Jardin Anglo-Chinois*.

The popularity of landscape gardening and all that it implies only became apparent during Johnson's active life. In the early 1730's it was still mainly a hobby of the Burlingtonian aristocrats, but by 1738 Johnson himself could write

> There mightst thou find some elegant retreat,
> Some hireling senator's deserted seat:
> And stretch thy prospects o'er the smiling land,
> Then prune thy walks, support thy dropping flowers,
> Direct thy rivulets, and twine thy bowers.

The 'one large room, a serpentine river and a wood' as the minimum requirements of a gentleman dates from the following year, and about the same time a writer is 'always grieved to see the venerable Paternal Castle of a Gentleman of ancient family dwindle down into an imperfect imitation of an Italian villa, and the good old profitable Orchard laid out into a waste of green, bounded by fruitless trees'.[1] These of course were modest 'improvements'. The technique of landscape gardening was first developed at the great seats such as Holkham and Stowe and the Duke of Newcastle's Claremont. Stowe and Claremont had both originally been laid out by Vanbrugh and were later improved first by Kent and then by Capability Brown; but there is evidence that Vanbrugh himself was tending in the direction of the romantic and 'picturesque' garden, though of course his designs are in the main still of the French type; that is, immense semi-architectural settings for magnificent outdoor entertainments. Perhaps the earliest and most remarkable anticipation of the later taste in gardening is to be found in a letter

[1] *Gentleman's Magazine*, 1730.

of Vanbrugh's dated 1707 in which he pleads with the Duchess of Marlborough (unavailingly) for the retention of the ruins of old Woodstock Manor as an object of interest in the park of the new Blenheim '—were the inclosure fill'd with trees (principally Fine Yews and Hollies) Promiscuously set to grow up in a wild Thicket so that all the Building left (which is only the Habitable part and the Chapel) might Appear in two Risings amongst 'em, it wou'd make one of the most Agreable Objects that the best of landskip Painters can invent'.[1] The significance of this passage lies in the appeal to landscape-painting, for it is in the importation into gardening of ideas derived from landscape-painting that the eighteenth-century revolution consisted. Bridgeman (Vanbrugh's collaborator in his later years) is credited by Horace Walpole with the invention of the Ha-ha, or sunk fence, whereby the turf of the lawn could be separated from the cropped grass of the park by an invisible barrier which kept the cattle at bay without apparently confining the eye.

At that moment [says Walpole in his Essay on Modern Gardening] appeared Kent, painter enough to taste the charms of landscape, bold and opinionative enough to dare and to dictate, and born with a genius to strike out a great system from the twilight of imperfect essays. He leaped the fence, and saw that all nature was a garden. He felt the delicious contrast of hill and valley changing imperceptibly into each other, tasted the beauty of the gentle swell, or concave scoop, and remarked how loose groves crowned an easy eminence with happy ornament, and while they called in the distant view between their graceful stems, removed and extended the perspective by delusive comparison. . . . The great principles on which he worked were perspective, and light and shade. Groups of trees broke too uniform or too extensive a lawn; evergreens and woods were opposed to the glare of the champain, and where the view was less fortunate, or so much exposed as to be beheld at once, he blotted out some parts by thick shades, to divide it into variety, or to make the richest scene more enchanting by reserving it to a farther advance of the spectator's step. Thus selecting favourite objects, and veiling deformities by screens of plantation; sometimes allowing the rudest waste to add its foil to the richest theatre, he realized the compositions of the greatest masters in painting.[2]

It is possible that Walpole is attributing to Kent a developed landscape theory to which he hardly attained, for

[1] Vanbrugh, *Letters* (ed. Geoffrey Webb, 1928), p. 30.
[2] Walpole, *Anecdotes of Painting*, 2nd ed., 1782, vol. iv, pp. 289–90.

nearly all the important aspects of landscape gardening in its later phases are implied in this description. Moreover, it was written many years after Kent's time. But it is certain that the close connexion between garden lay-out and painting was emphasized by Kent and his friends, as the well-known story of the dead tree that he planted in Kensington Gardens bears witness. A dead tree is an obvious Salvator Rosa property, and we know that Kent himself possessed at least one picture by him; there is also the evidence of the few engravings after landscape designs by Kent, for example the decorations for Thomson's *Seasons*. It is typical of this first phase of the movement, when it was still in the hands of a small aristocratic Italian-educated clique, that gardening should be designed to remind clients of the pictures of the masters they so much admired. Stourhead, in Wiltshire, still exists as an almost perfect example of the 'Claude' garden (Walpole praises it for its perfectly managed grotto): every view is so arranged that the temples and garden buildings compose with the wooded hills and the valley dammed up into a series of lakes so as to make a series of Claudes to the visitor as he walks round the prescribed route. The importance of the prescribed route is amusingly illustrated by Johnson's story of the Lytteltons and their visitors to Shenstone at the Leasowes. 'They took care to defeat the curiosity which they could not suppress, by conducting their visitants perversely to inconvenient points of view, and introducing them at the wrong end of a walk to detect a deception; injuries of which Shenstone would heavily complain.'[1] This charge against the Lytteltons has been refuted. That the earlier idea of a garden as a setting for outdoor entertainments was not altogether lost sight of by these first landscape enthusiasts of the Kent school is shown in Walpole's description of Miss Pelham's fête at Esher, generally considered Kent's garden masterpiece:

The day was delightful, the scene transporting, the trees, lawns, concaves, all in the perfection in which the ghost of Kent would joy to see them. At twelve we made the tour of the farm in eight chaises and calashes, horsemen and footmen, setting out like a picture of Wouverman. My lot fell in the lap of Mrs. Anne Pitt, which I could have excused, as she was not at all in the style of the day, romantic, but political.... We walked to the belvedere on the summit

[1] *Lives of the Poets*: *Shenstone.*

of the hill, where a threatened storm only served to heighten the beauty of the landscape, a rainbow on a dark cloud falling precisely behind the tower of a neighbouring church, between another tower and the building at Claremont. . . . From thence we passed into the wood, and the ladies formed a circle on chairs before the mouth of the cave, which was overhung to a vast height with woodbines, lilacs, and laburnums, and dignified by those tall shapely cypresses. On the descent of the hill were placed the French horns; the abigails, servants, and neighbours wandering below by the river—in short, it was Parnassus, as Watteau would have painted it.[1]

Here is the English rococo with all the decorative gaiety we associate with that word, and here in Walpole's description in terms of painting—Wouvermann and Watteau—is the picturesque point of view; and, though Walpole as a connoisseur and almost a professional 'Kunstförscher' is too exaggerated an example to be typical of his age, he is symptomatic. There are other points, too—the threatened storm, the 'rainbow on a dark cloud falling precisely behind the tower of a neighbouring church and the building at Claremont', both of them Gothic buildings (for we may safely assume that Vanbrugh's medievalizing garden castle, the most prominent feature of the then Claremont, is the building referred to). Furthermore the villa itself, from which the party set out, was in the Gothic taste, as far as we know, the earliest complete house to be erected in that style in the eighteenth century, antedating Strawberry Hill by several years.

In 1750 Walpole, who had hardly begun Gothicizing his own villa, writes to Horace Mann, 'I am sure that whenever you come to England you will be pleased with the liberty of taste into which we are struck and of which you can have no idea—Grecian for public buildings, Gothic or Chinese for minor works and gardens'. Here is the Gothic revival put into its proper place and by its first great exponent; Esher and Strawberry Hill were Gothic because they were villas, minor works, whose function was to be amusing and to fit in easily with a picturesque and romantic lay-out. It is to a small place in the account of gardening, as an aid to picturesque effects that is, or to a more direct literary self-dramatization on the part of the spectator, that we must assign the Gothic taste in the time of Johnson. It played a

[1] *Letters*, May 19, 1763.

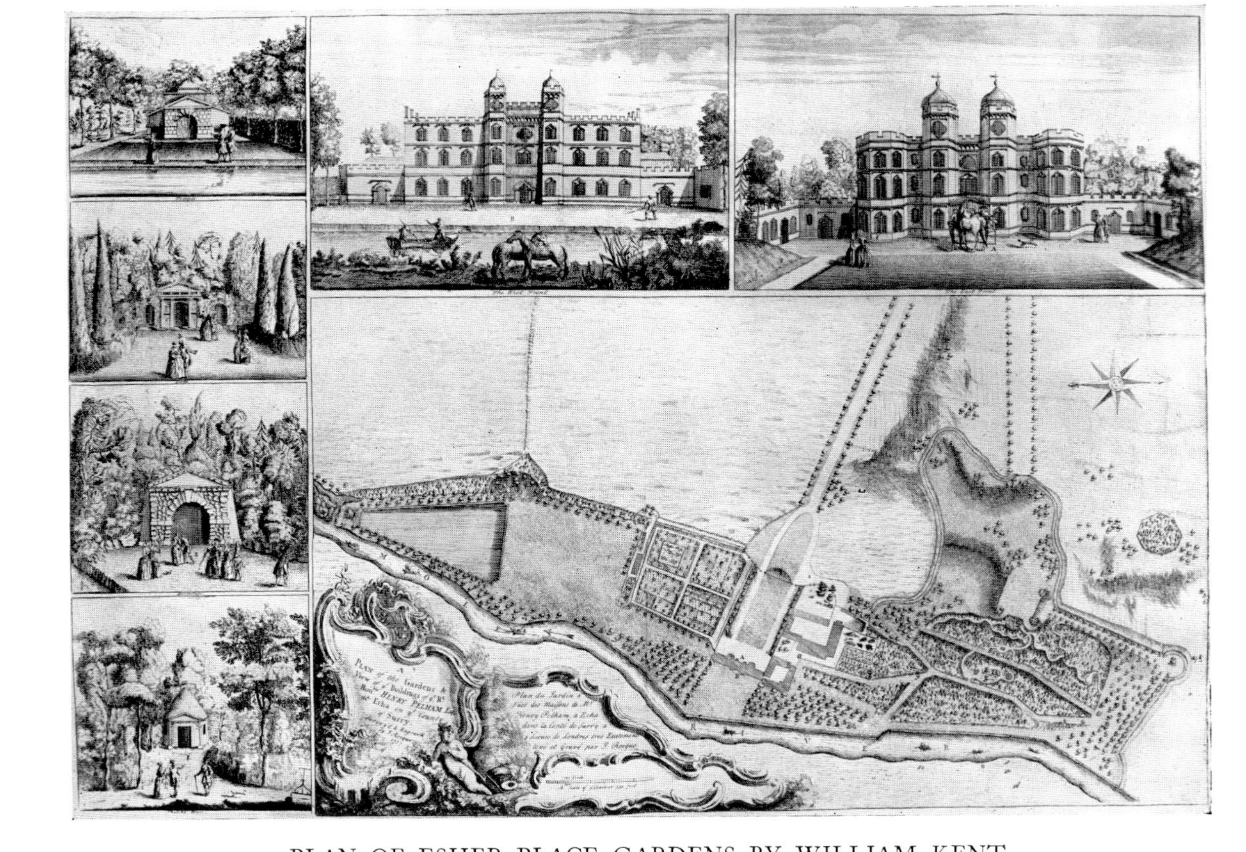

PLAN OF ESHER PLACE GARDENS BY WILLIAM KENT

From the engraving by J. Rocque

similar and equally minor part in the interior decoration and furniture designs of such masters as Chippendale. The distinction between picturesque effect and romantic self-dramatization is a convenient one, but many effects were intended to combine both appeals, and this the Gothic ruin could do most efficiently. The Classic temple is definitely architectural, its forms are clearly enunciated; but Gothic has a real tendency to dissolve its forms by multiplication and intricacy, and a Gothic building, when ruinated, or clothed with an overgrowth of ivy, has just that quality of 'form in dissolution' that the designers of picturesque landscape required. With their eyes fixed on the works of painters, whose preoccupation with the total visual effect led them to regard buildings as no more important individually than rocks or trees, the designers of the late eighteenth century required of their garden buildings, however important, that they should fit into the general 'over all' effect of the landscape rather than be self-sufficing works of architectural art. The full effect of this tendency on architecture proper was not apparent till the end of the century, and therefore falls outside the period of which we speak, but it has more than an antiquarian interest for us as the origin of those critical concepts of suitability to the site, 'seeming part of the landscape', 'local materials', &c., which persist to this day.

The other aim of eighteenth-century gardening, that of romantic self-dramatization, was equally well served by the Gothic, whether the mood to be induced was the melancholy romantic or the terrific. And there were other devices for attaining these effects beside Gothic ruins, as witness the following description:

We saw Hawkestone, the seat of Sir Rowland Hill, and were conducted by Miss Hill over a large tract of rocks and woods; a region abounding with striking scenes and terrific grandeur. We were always on the brink of a precipice, or at the foot of a lofty rock . . . the place is without any dampness, and would afford an habitation not uncomfortable. There were from space to space seats cut out in the rocks. Though it wants water, it excels Dovedale by the extent of its prospects, the awfulness of its shades, the horrors of its precipices, the verdure of its hollows, and the loftiness of its rocks: the ideas which it forces upon the mind are, the sublime, the dreadful, and the vast. Above is inaccessible altitude, below is horrible profundity. But it excels the garden of Ilam only in extent. . . . Hawkestone should be described by Milton, and Ilam by Parnell.[1]

These are Johnson's own words in 1774, and we see how profoundly even he, a man not especially interested in the visual arts, was affected by the current taste. The people who wanted this kind of pleasure from gardens were naturally dissatisfied and bored with the effects of the pure landscapists, and in 1772 an attack was launched upon the latter by Sir William Chambers in his *Dissertation on Oriental Gardening*.

At his first entrance, the stranger is treated with the sight of a large green field, scattered over with a few straggling trees, and verged with a confused border of little shrubs and flowers; upon farther inspection, he finds a little serpentine path, twining in regular esses amongst the shrubs of the border, upon which he is to go round, to look on one side at what he has already seen, the large green field; and on the other side at the boundary, which is never more than a few yards from him, and always obtruding upon his sight: from time to time he perceives a little seat or temple stuck up against the wall; he rejoices at the discovery, sits down, rests his wearied limbs, and then reels on again, cursing the line of beauty, till spent with fatigue, half roasted by the sun, for there is never any shade, and tired for want of entertainment, he resolves to see no more: vain resolution! there is but one path; he must either drag on to the end, or return back by the tedious way he came.

Such is the favourite plan of all our smaller gardens: and our larger works are only a repetition of the small ones; more green fields, more shrubberies, more serpentine walks, and more seats; like the honest batchelor's feast, which consisted of nothing but a multiplication of his own dinner; three legs of mutton and turneps, three roasted geese, and three buttered apple-pies.[2]

Chambers's remedy for all this tedium was more variety of garden buildings, each calculated to induce a different mood, as in his work at Kew, where in addition to the classic temples and the rococo Chinoiserie Pagoda (originally embellished from top to bottom with gilded dragons) there were Gothic and Moorish temples beside. He also advocated a greater exploitation of the element of surprise. It was in some sense a reversion to the old idea of a garden as a place of conceits and entertaining trifles. If, as Chambers suggests, the landscape garden could in bad hands degenerate into dreariness, his own recipe was far from being fool-proof, and

[1] *Diary of a Journey into North Wales* (1816), pp. 38–43.
[2] Chambers, *Dissertation on Oriental Gardening*, 1772, pp. v–vi.

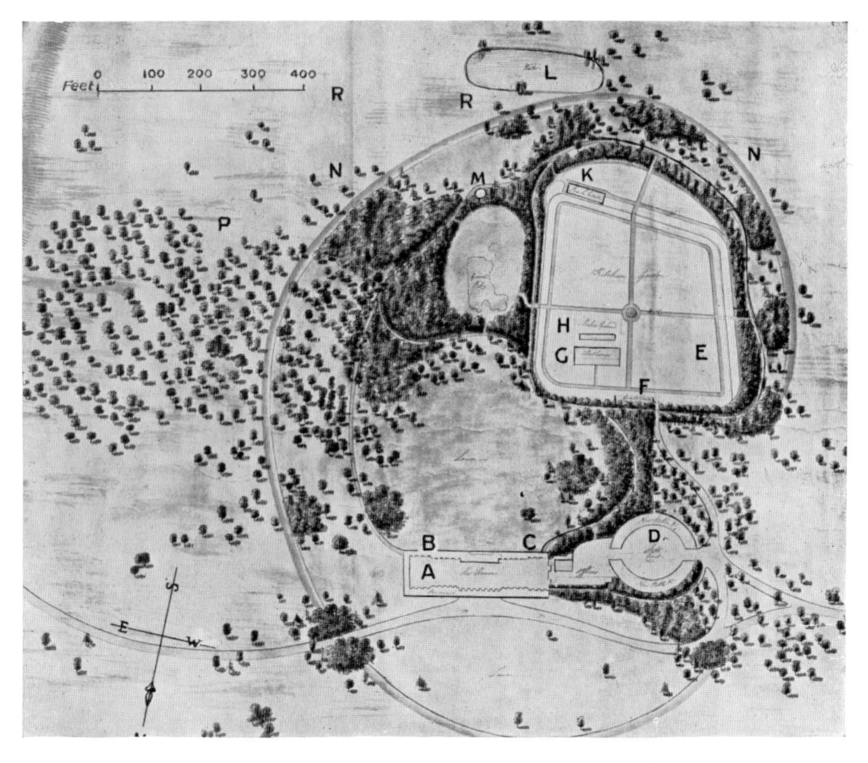

PART OF A DESIGN BY LANCELOT BROWN, 1781

From A Plan of Part of Heveningham, the Seat of Sir Gerard William Vanneck, Bart., with the intended alterations by L. B. 1781. *From* Country Life

we hear of more than one garden like that of Mrs. Thrale's neighbour, Mr. T., 'the clergyman who was a character I [Fanny Burney] could not but be diverted with, for he had so furious and so absurd a rage for building, that in his garden he had as many temples, and summer-houses, and statues as in the gardens of Stow, though he had so little room for them that they all seemed tumbling one upon another'.[1] Chambers's attack was supposed at the time to be levelled against Lancelot Brown (1715–83), the great Capability, on whose behalf there soon appeared the *Heroical Epistle to Sir William Chambers Knt.* (1773), certainly by William Mason, though Walpole was thought to have had a hand in it. This had an immense success, running to fourteen editions in four years and the victory may be said to have lain with the landscapists. In spite of all this Chambers's theories were not without their ultimate effect both in England and, perhaps even more, abroad; and if few gardens were actually planned to 'agitate the mind by a variety of opposing passions', at least by such extravagant means as he had suggested, yet there is an increased liveliness in the garden design of the end of the century which indicates that his complaint was felt to be justified and the ruin, the grotto, and the temple lived on and survive to this day in their degenerate descendant, the rustic summer-house.

In all these mid-eighteenth-century garden schemes and theories flowers are hardly ever mentioned. The whole idea of the landscape garden, whether you sided with Chambers or with Brown, was inimical to flowers, and it is very difficult to obtain any information as to the purely horticultural side of gardening in the time of Johnson. In the early part of the century when elaborate parterres were still in fashion, we find such books as Bradley's *New Improvements of Planting and Gardening*, which gives information as to the suitability of the plants for different parts of the garden as well as advice as to planting and propagating and an occasional picture of the garden practice of the time, such as this: 'Earwigs may be destroyed by hanging hogs-hoofs, the bowls of tobacco pipes or lobster's claws on the tops of the sticks which support the flowers, and killing the vermin which will lodge in them every morning'. But after the middle of the century gardening literature is concerned with much loftier themes

[1] Fanny Burney. Diary under date 1778.

than these. Bradley is considerably before Johnson's time, but the very neglect of flowers produced by the landscape enthusiasm makes it probable that methods did not change much. Of course, horticulture in the sense of the specialized cultivation of flowers continued quietly to make progress throughout the century, but then it is related rather to scientific botany than to gardening,[1] and we must go for information upon it to what are among the most charming of eighteenth-century books, the fine illustrated works on botany with coloured plates. It was studies such as these that made possible the reintroduction of flowers into the gardens of the nineteenth century and in a greater variety and splendour than Bradley could have dreamed of. Bradley, who was a Fellow of the Royal Society and tends rather to be encyclopaedic than brief, enumerates only thirty kinds of perennials, ten kinds of bulbs, and thirty annuals, these last including runner beans, which were grown for their decorative value in his day. These figures do not include all the varieties of each flower, but even counting them all the number of annuals would only rise to thirty-nine. By the end of the century the variety was immensely increased, and, what is more important, flowers were beginning to play a larger part in garden design, and with the nineteenth century came, in Mr. Hussey's words,[2] 'the introduction of hundreds of new plants for the display of which the bedding out system came into vogue'. Flowers were of course not completely excluded even by the most purist of landscape gardeners. The walled garden was always considered a suitable place, and some flowers were privileged to grow in plain view as Chambers's words 'verged with a confused border of little shrubs and flowers' suggest. These would be what Bradley describes as 'Wilderness', as opposed to 'Parterre', flowers, and would include daffodils, primroses, violets, perennial sunflowers and hollyhocks. To these must be added the flowering trees and shrubs of which Bradley gives eleven kinds, including the roses of which he notes, 'That curious and incomparable Patroness of Botany, the late Duchess of Beaufort, has told me of 16 different sorts.'

Timber trees were in a special sense the raw material of

[1] But Lord Bute, a great botanist, had a flower-garden at his country house near Kew, and Lady Mary Coke speaks of the multitude of exotic plants at Luton Hoo.

[2] Christopher Hussey, *The Picturesque* (1927), p. 184.

A VIEW OF ESHER PLACE, SURREY

From the engraving by L. Sullivan, 1759

the landscape gardener, for it was very largely on the variety of their foliage and that of the evergreens that he relied for his effects. In the later phases of the picturesque movement which fall outside the limits of this book, this aspect of gardening technique was immensely developed and the authorities of that time derided the work of Brown for the monotony and poverty of what we may call his palette. As compared with the amazing richness of their own effects the reproach was no doubt justified; yet, from our present-day standpoint, we do not feel the same sense of contrast as between our own immense resources and the poverty of the eighteenth century that must have struck every reader in respect of flowers. Indeed it would seem that there was very nearly as great a variety of trees in current use among the gardeners of Dr. Johnson's time as in our own. It is significant, too, that the only occasion on which Horace Walpole in his Essay on Modern Gardening descends to details of actual plants is in respect of trees.

> The introduction of foreign trees and plants, which we owe principally to Archibald duke of Argyle, contributed essentially to the richness of colouring so peculiar to our modern landscape. The mixture of various greens, the contrast of forms between our forest-trees and the northern and West-Indian firs and pines, are improvements more recent than Kent, or but little known to him. The weeping-willow and every florid shrub, each tree of delicate or bold leaf, are new tints in the composition of our gardens. The last century was certainly acquainted with many of those rare plants we now admire. The Weymouth pine has long been naturalized here; the patriarch plant still exists at Longleat. The light and graceful acacia was known as early; witness those ancient stems in the court of Bedford-house in Bloomsbury-square; and in the bishop of London's garden at Fulham are many exotics of very ancient date. I doubt therefore whether the difficulty of preserving them in a clime so foreign to their nature did not convince our ancestors of their inutility in general; unless the shapeliness of the lime and horse-chesnut, which accorded so well with established regularity, and which thence and from their novelty grew in fashion, did not occasion the neglect of the more curious plants.[1]

The last suggestion is almost certainly the right one. The earlier garden designers wanted evenness of colour in their trees for avenues and formal plantations, and it is another symptom of the painter's 'eye' that requires the dissolution

[1] Walpole, *Anecdotes of Painting*, 2nd ed., 1782, vol. iv, pp. 293–4.

of strict architectonic form into a general atmospheric effect, that the landscape gardeners should exploit the variety of foliage that exotics could give them, and thus bring into current use trees that before their time had been regarded merely as curious botanical specimens.

BIBLIOGRAPHY.—*Architecture.* ROBERT and JAMES ADAM, *Works in Architecture* (3 vols., 1778–1822). SIR R. BLOMFIELD, *History of Renaissance Architecture in England* (2 vols., 1897). A. T. BOLTON, *The Brothers Adam* (1922). BURLINGTON MAGAZINE MONOGRAPHS, *Georgian Art* (1929). SIR W. CHAMBERS, *A Treatise on the Decorative Part of Civil Architecture* (ed. Gwilt, 1825). JOHN GWYNN, *London and Westminster Improved* (1766). WILLIAM HALFPENNY, *Practical Architecture . . . representing the Five Orders with their several Doors and Windows* (1736); *Useful Architecture in Twenty-one New Designs for erecting Parsonages, Farm Houses and Inns* (1752). MISS M. JOURDAIN, *English Decoration and Furniture, 1760–1820* (1922). WILLIAM KENT, *Designs of Inigo Jones, &c.* (1727). FRANCIS LENYGON, *English Decoration and Furniture, 1660–1760* (1927). NATHANIEL LLOYD, *History of English Brickwork* (1925); *The English House* (1931). LONDON COUNTY COUNCIL, *Survey of London* (1926 et seq.). JAMES PAINE, *Plans and Elevations of the Mansion House, Doncaster* (1751); *Works* (1783). A. E. RICHARDSON, *Monumental Architecture* (1914); *The Smaller House of the English Renaissance* (1925). A. E. RICHARDSON and C. L. GILL, *London Houses from 1660 to 1820* (1911). H. A. TIPPING, *English Homes, Period VI, Vol. I* (1926). HORACE WALPOLE, *Letters* (ed. Toynbee, 19 vols., 1903–25). ISAAC WARE, *Complete Body of Architecture* (1756). J. WOLFE and W. GANDON, *Vitruvius Britannicus, Vols. IV and V* (1767, 1771).

Gardening. RICHARD BRADLEY, *New Improvements of Planting and Gardening* (1724). SIR W. CHAMBERS, *Dissertation on Oriental Gardening* (1772). KENNETH CLARK, *The Gothic Revival* (1928). CHRISTOPHER HUSSEY, *The Picturesque* (1927). SAMUEL JOHNSON, *Diary of a Journey into North Wales* (1816). BATTY LANGLEY, *New Principles of Gardening* (1728). LE ROUGE, *Les Jardins Anglo-Chinois* (1776). MANWARING, *Italian Landscape in Eighteenth-Century England* (1925). GEORGE MASON, *Essay on Design in Gardening* (1768). WILLIAM MASON, *The English Garden* (1772); *Heroic Epistle to Sir William Chambers* (1774). WILLIAM SHENSTONE, *Unconnected Thoughts on Gardening* (1764). HORACE WALPOLE, *Essay on Modern Gardening* (ed. Dallaway, 1826); *Letters* (ed. Toynbee, 19 vols., 1903–25).

XIX

THE INTERIOR OF THE HOUSE

By OLIVER BRACKETT

The regular progress of cultivated life is from Necessaries to Accommodations, from Accommodations to Ornaments. By your illustrious Predecessors were established Marts for Manufactures, and Colleges for Science; but for the Arts of Elegance, those Arts by which Manufactures are embellished, and Science is refined, to found an Academy was reserved for your Majesty.—*Dedication to* REYNOLDS'S *Seven Discourses* (1778).

ENGLAND is more fortunate than most nations of Europe in possessing numbers of houses of the eighteenth century which have been preserved, almost unspoilt, with their contemporary fittings and furniture. In almost every part of England can be found country houses, great and small, built and furnished in the mid-eighteenth century and still retaining their original appearance and character, except that conditions of modern life have introduced changes in such matters as drainage, baths, heating, and lighting, while time has sometimes destroyed such perishable things as curtains and ornaments. The architects, builders, decorators, and cabinet-makers of the day, steeped though they were in formula and classical tradition, were nevertheless essentially practical; and it is a tribute to their thoroughness and sound workmanship that these houses in spite of changes of fashion and habits have continued to serve their purpose as homes in which families can live from generation to generation. Had it not been so, neither the houses nor their contents would in most cases have been preserved. Thus we have a living record of the interior of the house of the period, a record which not only presents us with the facts, but enables us to catch something of that more elusive quality, the spirit of the time.

It is naturally in the country rather than in London that completely furnished houses can still be found. In London the case is different. Neither the few remaining great mansions built on the Palladian plan, nor the town houses of wealthy families erected in the streets of Mayfair, nor the many small houses of the middle classes in various districts, have been able to withstand the ruthless hand of progress. And although it is still possible to follow the planning and to some extent the decoration of London houses of the mid-eighteenth century from actual examples, it is necessary to rely on other sources of information to form a complete picture of the furnished home of the Londoner at the time of Johnson.

The published books by architects, builders, decorators, and furniture designers, Isaac Ware, James Gibbs, Matthew Brettingham, James Paine, Batty Langley, Robert Adam, Thomas Chippendale and many others assist in supplying information which is now sometimes lacking. Not only do they explain the arrangement of the house both in town and country and the original purpose of the rooms, but they discuss the causes of its decoration and illustrate the varied types of furniture which were fashionable at the time. Moreover, they unconsciously throw a light on the mentality of the men for whom the houses were built and the policy of the men who built them. Some of the writers of memoirs, again, can often give illuminating or vivid impressions of their social visits, though allowance must be made for the fact that they sometimes wrote from memory and with imperfect technical knowledge. In a similar spirit the painters of domestic scenes have a contribution to make to the history of the subject. More reliable, though less picturesque, are the inventories of the period, in which all the contents of the house from the garret to the kitchen are faithfully recorded, not only the paintings, furniture, and hangings, but the plate, china, glass, and ornaments, in short all the varied equipment of a typical house of the day.

It would not be possible to describe in general terms the interior of the house at the time of Johnson's working life, because a change took place in the national style during this period. Briefly this was the succession of the Palladian by the Adam School. It is true that this development was partly a question of evolution and that the Adam style by 1784 had made but little impression on the homes of the people. But the change is one that cannot be ignored. In order, therefore, within a limited compass, to obtain a grasp of the interior of the house of the period, it would cover the ground effectively to consider first the character of a typical house of the earlier style and to describe afterwards a London house of somewhat later date. It has already been pointed out that a house built in a London street had particular characteristics caused by its situation.

The typical house of the Palladian School of about the middle of the century was built on a rectangular plan with living-rooms on the ground floor leading one from another round a central hall; the upper floor was devoted to bedrooms and dressing-rooms, and on each side was a branching wing, one for stables and the other for the steward, house-keeper, and 'the lesser and inferior appendages'[1] as Brettingham described the servants. Next the hall was the dining-room communicating with a small drawing-room, and behind the hall a large drawing-room or saloon and a library, as well as a powdering closet or rooms for other purposes according to the standard of living of the owners. Isaac Ware in 1756 made a full description of such a house in the form of advice to a young architect, explaining both the arrangement and decoration in great detail:

> The decoration of the inside of rooms may be reduced to three kinds; first those in which the wall itself is properly finished with elegance; that is where the materials of its last covering are of the finest kind, and it is wrought into ornaments plain or uncovered; secondly where the walls are covered with wainscot; and thirdly where they are hung; this last article comprehending paper, silk, tapestry and every other decoration of this kind. For a noble hall nothing is so well as stucco; for a parlour wainscot seems properest; and for the apartment of a lady, hangings.[2]

These schemes of decoration, by stucco or panelled rooms or walls hung with silk and paper, were general both in town and country, until the Adam influence banished panelling from the larger houses. Ware made a great point of the fact that the whole scheme of arrangement was based on the most rigid system of calculation. The spacing of the apartments on the plan, the comparative height and length of rooms, the exact position of chimney-piece, doors, and windows were all arranged according to a definite scheme of proportion. If the hall was of stucco it would have a stone staircase with a flight of stairs on each side and a central balustrade. But frequently halls were panelled and had staircases of mahogany or painted pine or oak, with heavy column-shaped balusters and carved stair-ends. Behind the hall was invariably found a plain back staircase for the use of servants.

[1] Matthew Brettingham, *The plans, elevations, and sections of Holkham in Norfolk* (1773).

[2] Isaac Ware, *A complete Body of Architecture* (1756), pp. 469, 470.

The walls of the dining-room would be wainscoted in pinewood with long panels and a dado rail, all the surface painted white, blue, green, or brown, with carvings and mouldings gilded. In the middle of the long wall facing the windows was placed the chimney-piece. This was the central motive and the most decorative feature of the room. It was in two parts divided by a shelf, the overmantel having a carved pediment and frame inclosing a square opening for a painting—a portrait, landscape, or group of still life. Within the fire-place would be found a steel grate, with tongs, poker, shovel, and bellows. Commonly the dining-room had four doors with carved framework, one on each side of the chimney-piece and one in each of the short walls near the windows. The latter in height stretched from the cornice to the dado, and were closed by heavy sashes with small rectangular panes. In front of the windows hung curtains often of red or green damask looped up at the cornice into two festoons with tassels. The furniture of the dining-room was simple. One or more mahogany tables, a set of mahogany chairs with leather or hair-cloth seats fixed with brass nails, two mahogany sideboards with marble tops, a wine-cooler, a dumb-waiter, and a folding leather screen, were the main items which would be looked for.

The most important and ceremonial room in the house was the drawing-room which was both furnished and decorated in more lavish style. This was the room where the family entertained or spent their hours of leisure. It was therefore usually placed with a southern aspect to face the sun, and so arranged that the spectator could enjoy the beauty of the scenery from the windows. The best efforts of the carver and plasterer were lavished on the chimney-piece, door frames, and ceiling, and the richest materials in damask or satin would form the hangings or coverings of the furniture. Much of the furniture was gilded. Between the windows were placed tall mirrors richly carved and gilt with console tables below. Settees, arm-chairs, and stools of mahogany or white wood gilded were upholstered with damask or needlework. Tables were scattered about the room, the tripod table, the china table, and the card table to serve their various purposes. Commodes were among the richest and most decorative ornaments in the saloon. The most valued pictures hung on the walls. Glass chandeliers

PANELLED ROOM

from a house in Painswick, Gloucestershire, about 1755

suspended from the ceiling, wall sconces, and standing candle-stands contributed to the brilliance of the scene.

Mrs. Lybbe Powys, describing Eastbury in Worcestershire in 1760, gives the impression left on a careful observer by a house of this period newly furnished and decorated:

The building, as you see, thro' a fine lawn, may be styl'd an elegant fabrick; 'tis of stone, extending in length 570 feet, of which the main body of the house takes up only 144; the rest is arcades and offices. Having ascended a grand flight of steps, you come under a Doric portico, whose pediment extends 62 feet, with pillars 46 feet high; from thence you enter a noble hall, adorn'd by statues and busts, the saloon painted olive, the ornaments, as the cornice, etc. rich gilt; the sofas in this apartment are very fine tapestry. On one side the saloon is the common dining and drawing room, on the other the best drawing room, hung with and furnished with cut velvet; the state bed-chamber, hung with crimson velvet furniture; the same, the bed with gold, and lin'd with a painted India satin; the dressing room hung with green satin.

The *Managareth* or Chinese bedroom and dressing room in the attic storey, is excessively droll and pretty, furnish'd exactly as in China, the bed of an uncommon size, seven feet wide by six long.[1]

In London a few of the larger mansions were erected on the Palladian plan, but the bulk of the houses were built in streets or squares under different conditions. The value of land was high, so that in the planning of houses it was not expedient to place most of the living-rooms on the ground floor leading one from another round a central hall. The hall lost its importance, the drawing-room was placed on the first floor with bedrooms above and kitchens in the basement. James Paine, in 1783, published plans and elevations of several London houses of this type with explanatory notes. Numbers of such houses have been preserved and are familiar types at the present day, but Paine's descriptions help to explain the disposition and the original purpose of the rooms. Such is his description of the interior of Lord Petre's house in Park Lane:[2]

You enter from the street by three steps into a lobby or porter's hall from which you ascend three steps more and land in the best staircase. Upon the right you enter an anti-chamber, and from thence the dining room; behind the anti-chamber is a library (serving

[1] *Passages from the Diary of Mrs. Lybbe Powys, 1756–1808* (1899), pp. 62, 63.

[2] James Paine, *Plans, elevations, and sections of Gentlemen's Houses* (1783), pp. 24, 25.

also for his Lordship's dressing room) within which is a light closet, or powdering room. On the right hand side of the dressing room, through the back staircase is a room which serves for the clerk of the kitchen to change the courses from the table. . . . You are commodiously landed on the chamber floor by the circular staircase and enter a waiting room; from thence a dressing room, a drawing room, and . . . the principal bed chamber, within which is a light closet serving as a powdering room.

The second and attic floors contained bedrooms and a nursery, while the arrangement of the basement or office story was explained with much detail:

You enter the office story (which is partly under ground) from an area descending from the street 10 steps, and having two distinct entrances: the one into a common lobby for chairmen and visitors' servants to wait in; the other in the centre of the house, which is the general entrance; this communicates on the left hand with the servants' hall; and on the right hand with the Steward's parlour. Advancing farther, on the left hand of this passage is the housekeeper's room; and within this room is a china room; upon the right hand, beyond the Steward's parlour, is a store-room, . . . from whence proceeding to the end of the passage first mentioned, on the right hand leads through a larder to the kitchen; opposite the kitchen chimney is a passage at the end whereof is a good scullery and bakehouse, and larders.

It will be noticed that there was no bathroom in the house that James Paine described. The bathroom, in fact, was not placed in English houses of this date except in unusual cases. Holkham in Norfolk was an exception, for in this house bathrooms were found in 1773 as well as a system for supplying hot water by engines in the cellars.[1] But on the whole there is a curious reticence on this subject in the domestic history of England in the eighteenth century. The writers of the time, whether through modesty or lack of interest, have no comments to make either on the subject of washing or the bathroom. Inventories which chronicle the most trivial utensils found in the kitchen, fail to recognize or describe the common bath. In this respect there is a great difference between England and France at this date. French inventories frequently include the bath, sometimes plain and sometimes ornamented, in the list of household goods

[1] Matthew Brettingham, *The plans, elevations, and sections of Holkham in Norfolk* (1773).

belonging to some person of distinction.[1] So important was the bath that highly decorative examples are recorded as in the case of a famous design for a 'Baignoire en sofa' by De La Fosse which rivalled the most ornate specimens of furniture in its luxurious design. Moreover it was common enough for French artists to choose the bathroom as a background in depicting intimate scenes of domestic life.

At the time when Paine described Lord Petre's house in Park Lane discussed above, the influence of the Adam School was affecting both interior decoration and furniture. Robert Adam himself some ten years earlier had claimed an almost total change in the ornamentation of apartments,[2] the abandonment of the heavy tabernacle frame and compartment ceilings, in favour of elegant arabesques in stucco and painted medallions on pale grounds of white, green, or pink. But although these revolutionary schemes of decoration were almost universally adopted in important houses, they were but slightly reflected in the houses of the middle classes. The new influence in the ordinary house showed itself in more delicate mouldings, in chimney-pieces without overmantels, and in walls covered with textile materials and paper in place of carving and panelling. There was at this time a considerable variety in the fabrics used for wall-hangings, curtains, and coverings for furniture. The figured velvets of an earlier period as well as tapestries were out of fashion, and silk damask in crimson, blue, green, or purple was the most favoured material for covering of walls, usually finished with a gilt border below the cornice. Similar silks as well as satins were used for curtains strengthened with linings and ornamented with fringes. In Lord Hardwicke's house, No. 18 New Cavendish Street, 'very large white satin window curtains with pink satin ribbon binding, and pink silk broad fringes with white buttons' were supplied in 1784 by the firm of Gillow.[3] Cheaper and more homely stuffs, lutestring, moreen, tammy, cotton, and linen, were found in less ambitious circumstances.

Covering walls with paper was a common method of treatment at this date, but owing to the perishable nature of the material comparatively few rooms decorated in this

[1] Henry Havard, *Dictionnaire d'ameublement* (1887–90), vol. i, p. 233.
[2] Robert and James Adam, *Works in Architecture* (1778).
[3] MSS. in Soane Museum.

manner have survived the vicissitudes of time.[1] The flock wallpapers of the earlier period were intended to imitate in design, colour, and texture the figured velvets and silks which were then fashionable for wall-hangings and coverings of furniture. Commonly they had bold conventional patterns of diapers and floral designs in which the pomegranate was a familiar feature, and they were executed in a variety of rich colours, a deep red, blue, green, or yellow on a lighter ground.

After the middle of the century ordinary wall-papers became lighter both in design and colour, while the development of printing, in place of the earlier stencilling or hand colouring, put the industry on a different footing. Much has been made of the influence of J. B. Jackson of Battersea who advertised the process of printing from wood blocks in oil colour. In 1754 Jackson published a book which was intended to explain his policy, *An Essay on the Invention of Engraving and Printing in Chiaro Oscuro . . . and the Application of it to the making of Paper Hangings of Taste, Duration and Elegance.* In his ponderous introduction Jackson explained how the work of famous sculptors of antiquity could be represented by impressions from wood blocks on the walls of English houses for the benefit of those unable to afford the statues themselves. 'The Apollo of the Belvedere Palace, the Medicean Venus, the dying Mermillo, the fighting Gladiator, or the famous Group of the Laocoon, may be disposed of in so many Panels, and all the other Parts of the Paper correspond to this original Intent.' He further adapted his process to the reproduction of landscapes and views of cities. 'Or if Landscapes are more agreeable, for variety sake Prints done in this manner, taken from the Works of Salvator Rosa, Claude Lorrain, Gaspar Poussin, Burgher, Waverman, or any other great Master in the Way of Painting, may be introduced into Panels of the Paper, and show the Taste of the Owner.' This fashion of pasting prints on a wall had a certain vogue at this date. Horace Walpole showed some favour to this novelty, though with reservations, and the strange mixture of wall-papers which he chose for Strawberry Hill included an example of Jackson's experiment. In a letter to Sir Horace Mann in 1753 he wrote: 'Now you shall walk into the house. The bow

[1] C. C. Oman, *Catalogue of Wall-papers*, Victoria and Albert Museum (1929), p. 21.

window leads into a little parlour with a stone-colour Gothic paper and Jackson's Venetian prints, which I could never endure while they pretended, infamous as they are, to be after Titian, &c., but when I gave them the air of barbarous bas-reliefs, they succeeded to a miracle.'

The Chinese wall-papers found in England at this date, sometimes gifts from ambassadors and merchants, were painted by hand in brilliant colours. The representation of flowering trees and birds found in these papers were executed often with masterly skill. They appear to have been regarded by their English owners mainly as interesting and amusing curiosities, for they were commonly used to cover the walls of bedrooms, forming a background, as at Badminton and Nostell Priory, for lacquered furniture in the Anglo-Chinese style. A tribute to the remarkable skill shown by the Chinese artists in their delineation of natural forms is paid by Sir Joseph Banks in his Journal of 1770. 'A man need go no further to study the Chinese than the China paper, the better sorts of which represent their persons and such of their costumes, dresses etc as I have seen, most strikingly like, though a little in the caricatura style. Indeed, some of the plants which are common to China and Java, as bamboo, are better figured there than in the best botanical authors that I have seen.'[1] After the middle of the century scenes of native life, the cultivation of tea and the pleasures of the Chinese, were depicted on these papers.

The houses of the middle classes built in London streets, though simpler and less ambitious, were similar both in arrangement and decoration. With a dining-room and parlour on the ground floor, a drawing-room and bedrooms above and kitchen in the basement, they were based on a common plan which became traditional. Many of these rows of houses were the work of builders rather than of architects, and their panelling and staircases followed stock patterns, ornamental or plain, according to the means of the householder. Unless the interior of houses of this type had some eccentric feature like a Chinese or Gothic room they were too unimportant to interest the authors or journalists of the day. An observant Frenchman, however, M. Grosley, who lived in London after the middle of the eighteenth century, has recorded his impressions of the

[1] Francis Lenygon, *Decoration in England* (1914), p. 228.

habits and houses of the people. Things that to a contemporary Englishman would have been too obvious to notice attracted the attention of a Frenchman who was studying national character and comparing the English and the French. He commented on the smoky atmosphere of London due partly to excessive use of sea-coal fires in kitchens and factories, and the effect which it had on the interior of the house:

> The humid and dark air which enwraps London, requires the greatest cleanliness imaginable; and in this respect, the inhabitants of that city seem to vie with the Hollanders. The plate, hearth-stones, moveables, apartments, doors, stairs, the very street-doors, their locks and the large brass knockers, are every day washed, scowered, or rubbed. Even in lodging-houses, the middle of the stairs is often covered with carpeting, to prevent them from being soiled. All the apartments in the house have mats or carpets; and the use of them has been adopted some years since by the French.
>
> But what is an article of necessity in England, is mere extravagance in France. The houses in London are all wainscoted with deal; the stairs and the floors are composed of the same materials, and cannot bear the continual rubbing of feet without being cracked and worn. This renders carpets or coverings necessary. . . . The furniture of houses generally speaking consists of large chairs, the seats of which are in part stuffed up very full and covered with Morocco leather, and partly of mahogany tables. With regard to the walls, they are hung with cloth or printed paper by those who are not satisfied with plain wainscot; as for the beds, they are made of stuffs more solid than brilliant, and which require to be frequently renewed, if people prefer shew to solidity.[1]

M. Grosley also remarked on the insanitary drainage of the houses and the inadequate supply of water. Water was pumped from the Thames into underground pipes and thence distributed to the householder three times a week and kept in lead cisterns.

The house in Gough Square, off Fleet Street, where Dr. Johnson lived between 1749 and 1759, apart from its historical associations, illustrates the character of a small London house of the period with great completeness. The house is of symmetrical plan with a front door in the centre, approached by a short flight of steps with iron railings on

[1] M. Grosley, *A Tour to London; or new Observations on England* (translated) (1772), vol. i, pp. 46, 72, 73.

SCREEN, WITH NEEDLEWORK PANEL (PETIT POINT)
IN CARVED AND GILT FRAME
1755–60
Victoria and Albert Museum

each side. Surrounding the door is a carved doorway of about the date 1740. The interior of the house belongs for the most part to the first half of the eighteenth century, though there are signs that it was built on the site of an older building. The heavy front door leads into a small panelled hall. As a precaution against robbery or other dangers the door has two strong bolts on the inside and is fitted with a heavy chain which can be fixed at one end into a twisted hook; further protection from intrusion is offered by an iron bar with spikes placed across the fanlight above the door. A door on the right of the hall leads into the parlour, a small room covered with plain pine panelling, for there is no decoration throughout the house. Each of the two windows in the parlour is recessed and has a window seat, the sides of the recess holding the shutters which can be closed and barred. There is a solid iron grate within the opening of the chimney-piece. A door in the panelling between the chimney-piece and one of the windows connects with a small powdering closet with walls of white plaster and a niche on one side where the wig stand would be placed.

Opposite the parlour on the other side of the hall is the dining-room. This room is panelled in precisely the same manner as the parlour and has no distinguishing features, except that on one side of the chimney-piece there is a cupboard the back of which is entirely occupied, like a cabinet, with small compartments closed by hinged doors and intended evidently for the disposal of silver and glass and other articles of value used at the table. The staircase has balusters of column form and is built round a well in the centre. In ascending the staircase, a few steps from the bottom, a cupboard from which candles were taken at bedtime is found in the wall. The first floor is occupied by two rooms used as drawing-rooms or for similar social purposes but, like the rooms below, without ornament. The inner wall of each is in the form of a partition with two doors, and a peculiarity of the arrangement lies in the fact that the partitions can be swung round, making the rooms into one large salon, on occasions when space was required for the entertainment of numbers of guests. On the second floor are bedrooms, and ascending farther, the staircase ends in the spacious garret where the Doctor retired for the composition of his Dictionary. There is a description by James Northcote of an occasion in 1754 when Sir Joshua Reynolds took Roubiliac, the sculptor, to call on Johnson, in Gough Square:

> Johnson received him with much civility, and took them up into a garret, which he considered as his library; where, besides his books all covered with dust, there was an old crazy deal table, and a still worse and older elbow chair, having only three legs. In this chair Johnson seated himself, after having, with considerable dexterity and evident practice, first drawn it up against the wall, which served to support it on that side on which the leg was deficient.[1]

At the back of the hall is a door from which a short and plain staircase descends direct to a large and barren kitchen with walls of whitened plaster. On the ceiling are heavy oak beams which suggest that the kitchen may originally have belonged to an older house which was demolished and rebuilt at the beginning of the eighteenth century. Two open fire-places are found in the kitchen, used in one case for cooking joints from a jack and in the other for boiling kettles and other purposes. There is also an old stone sink, but the cistern, the pump, and the other furniture of the kitchen has not been preserved.

It has already been pointed out that the house of the average Londoner was only affected to a limited extent by the Adam School of decoration. It must also be borne in mind that both panelled rooms and furniture not infrequently had long lives, so that it would often happen that people of moderate means were living in houses which contained a mixture of the old and the new. Such was the case in a house in Lincoln's Inn Fields into which in January, 1774, Lloyd Kenyon (afterwards first Baron Kenyon) moved at the time of his marriage to his cousin Mary Kenyon.[2] Lloyd Kenyon, the famous lawyer, had known poverty but was making a good income at the date of his marriage. The house was evidently furnished practically but not extravagantly, for Kenyon was notorious for the economy of his habits. It is related that in the vacation he had been in the habit of dining with two friends, Dunning and Tooke, at a small eating-house near Chancery Lane for the sum of sevenpence-halfpenny.[3] 'As to Dunning and myself,' wrote Tooke, 'we were generous for we gave the girl who waited

[1] James Northcote, *Life of Sir Joshua Reynolds* (1818), vol. i, p. 75.
[2] L.C.C., *Survey of London*, vol. iii, 'St. Giles's-in-the-Fields' (1912).
[3] A. Stephens, *Memoirs of John Horne Tooke* (1813), p. 33.

on us a penny a piece; but Kenyon, who always knew the value of money, sometimes rewarded her with a halfpenny and sometimes with a promise.' The house which Kenyon rented at his marriage, No. 18 Lincoln's Inn Fields, has now been demolished. When the work of furnishing was almost completed Mrs. Kenyon wrote a long letter to her mother describing the interior of the house with much detail:[1]

The entrance is a broad lobby well lighted by a window over the door, and a staircase window. It is wainscot, painted white as far as the arch turned at the bottom of the staircase. On the left hand is a sweet pretty parlour, stuccoed and painted white—marble chimney-piece and hearth; two windows, and, at the lower end of the room, two pillars, on which stands a mahogany sideboard. On one side stands a *garde du vin*, on the other side a chair, which I think must be displaced and a small table set there. On the side, where the door opens, which is a long way from the window, stands our dining table, with one chair on one side, near the pillar. Between the windows is a very pretty round glass, ornamented with gilt paper-mache, in great taste, two chairs on each side the fire, a handsome cistern of mahogany, with brass hoops etc, under the sideboard, and a Turkey carpet. The back room has only one window, which looks into a little flagged court, twelve of my steps long and six steps broad, but quite entire and not overlooked by any window but our own, a marble chimney piece and hearth, a stove grate, the same to the other parlour; [it] is wainscot, painted white, has a larger dining table for great days, a wardrobe from Chambers for Mr. Kenyon's clothes, a wash-hand stand, a little closet, dark, but shelved very conveniently, and four chairs, the same as the dining parlour. The room behind that is white wainscot, has two windows, is as large as the little drawing-room, but has nothing at all in yet. There is a fire-place with a marble chimney-piece; but that and all the back-rooms are common fire-places. Behind that is the back staircase, and beyond that a butler's pantry with a dresser that has two drawers and a cupboard under it, shelves over it for glasses etc. a lead cistern and pipe with water.

So much for that floor. The front staircase is a very good one, with a neat mahogany rail to the top of the house. I must tell you, before I proceed further, there is a very handsome glass lamp in the passage, another upon the landing, and a third by the dining room door. The dining room is 21 feet and a half long, and 17 feet wide, has [a] marble chimney piece and hearth, a handsome steel grate, etc; it is to be new papered, this week, and have the furniture all in order; it is quite ready when the paper is put up. The paper is to be a blue

[1] *The Manuscripts of Lord Kenyon* (Historical MSS. Comm. 14th Report, App. IX, Part IV, 1894), p. 505.

small patterned flock; I will send you a bit of it. The back room has, at present, a bed in it, which is to be removed on Wednesday morning, and that room is to have the old blue flock paper we found in it, blue moreen curtains, chairs, a toilet, and a book-case—will not that be a nice breakfast room? In the little room behind that, which is wainscoted and painted white, is a blue moreen bed, a little chest of dressing drawers, and two chairs; then comes my little store room, which is about as large as half the little drawing-room, has two rows of shelves, a table across the end with drawers and cupbords under. In this place I keep china, glasses, and all my stock of groceries; the plate chest is to be kept there too, when it arrives. Through this closet is the water-closet, very convenient and sweet; it is over the stable.

Up the next story is our lodging room, over the dining room. It is hung with a green flock paper, has green moreen bed and window curtains, a large chest upon chest (so high, that I must have a step-ladder to look into the five top drawers) a dressing table and glass in one pier, a small chest of dressing drawers in the other pier, a night table, a wash-hand stand, and eight chairs. The back room is wainscoted and is to have the bed from Chambers in. A maid's room behind that and, over my own store room, another pretty closet with a linnen press, and a light large cupbord or small closet through it. The two back garrets have servants' beds in. The front is a landing. All the garrets have flat roofs, and are in every respect as good rooms as those below.

The house had evidently been built some twenty or thirty years before the Kenyons moved in, for it possessed decorative details of an earlier period. Mahogany staircases were familiar features in some of the houses in Lincoln's Inn Fields built about the middle of the century. The panelled rooms painted white were probably not new, but of the rooms on the first floor one was intended to have a new flock paper with the small type of pattern which was becoming fashionable, while in the other room on this floor the older flock wall-paper was retained. The furniture was evidently useful rather than remarkable, and it is interesting to note that Mrs. Kenyon experienced a difficulty in reaching the top drawers of a double chest-of-drawers without a step-ladder, a point which seems to have been overlooked by the designers of these popular but unpractical pieces of furniture.

Mrs. Kenyon seems to have been impressed by the glass lamps in the passage and landing, suggesting that this was a novel form of illumination. The usual method of lighting

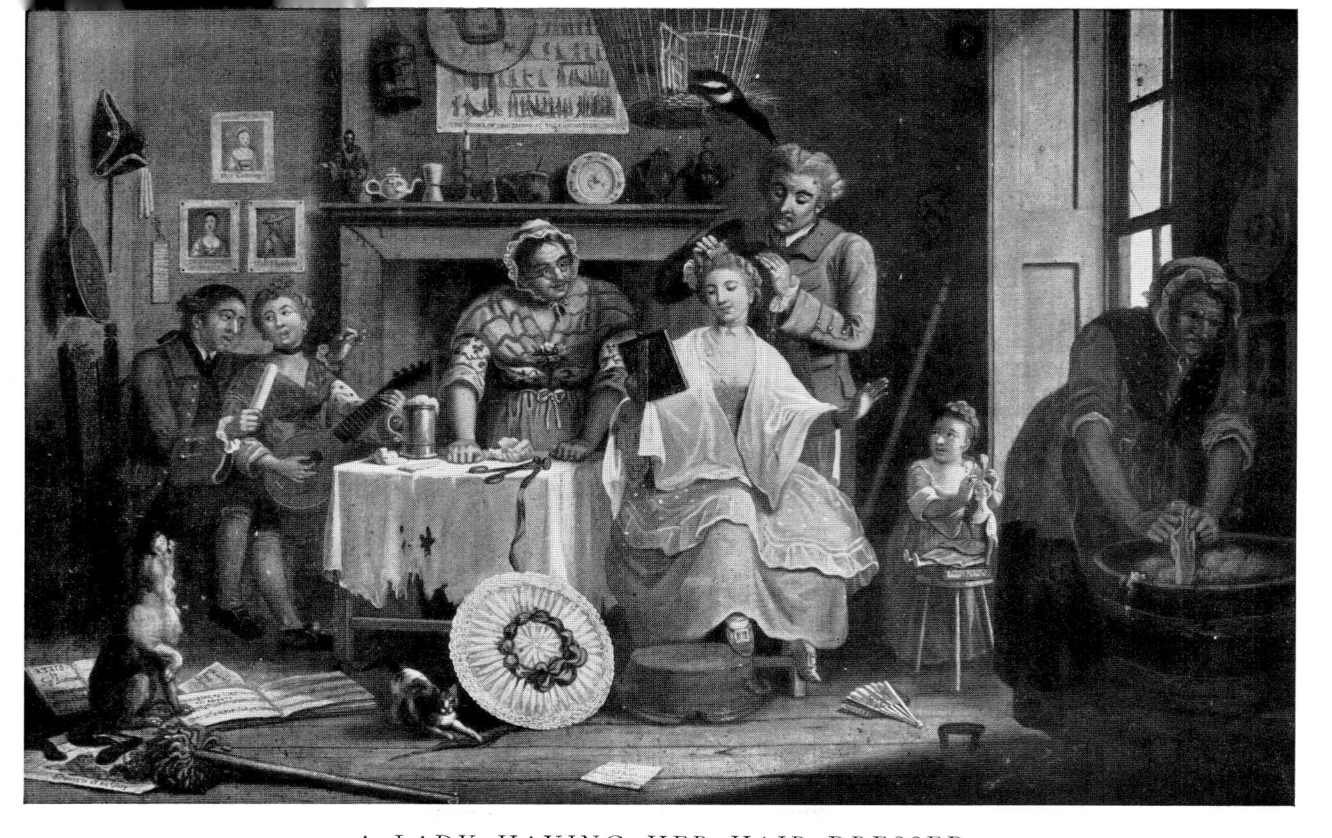

A LADY HAVING HER HAIR DRESSED

From the painting by J. Collett, 1763

halls and staircases at the middle of the eighteenth century was by glazed hanging lanterns with brass frames which were often chased. On the whole the lighting of houses must have been dim, depending for the most part on candles. But when drawing-rooms were lighted up for ceremony a flashing illumination could be obtained by glass chandeliers hanging from the ceiling and sconces on the walls, the brilliance of effect intensified by reflections in many gilded mirrors. Equally indifferent was the heating of houses, and the general use of open fires for this purpose is commented on by writers of the day. Mrs. Lybbe Powys on a visit to Old Buckingham House in March 1767 remarked: 'It being at that time the coldest weather possible, we were amazed to find so large a house so warm, but fires, it seems are kept the whole day, even in closets.'[1] Portable stoves were sometimes used as well as braziers; a large brazier in the centre of the Pavilion at Ranelagh Gardens was much commented on. Occasionally experiments were made in more scientific methods of heating. At Holkham in Norfolk, according to Brettingham's description in 1773, there was 'a Furnace beneath the Floor of the Hall, for the convenience of warming it; which it does by means of Brick Flues, that have their Funnels for the conveyance of Smoke carried up in the lateral Walls'.[2] This house, however, seems to have been almost before its time in its ambitious schemes for comfort in internal arrangements.

In remote country districts the furniture and decoration of farm-houses and the like were unaffected by changes of style or vicissitudes of fashion. Such was the case with the house of Dr. Daniel Dove in the Yorkshire countryside, described by Southey in the early part of the nineteenth century, but representing a traditional type of English country home found throughout the eighteenth century and earlier:[3]

The house consisted of seven rooms, the dairy and cellar included, which were both upon the ground floor. As you entered the kitchen there was on the right one of those open chimneys which afford more comfort in a winter's evening than the finest register stove; in front of the chimney stood a wooden bee-hive chair, and on each side was a long oak seat with a back to it, the seats serving as chests in which the oaten bread was kept. They were of the darkest brown and well

[1] *Passages from the Diary of Mrs. Lybbe Powys, 1756–1808*, p. 116.

[2] Matthew Brettingham, *The Plans, elevations, and sections of Holkham in Norfolk*, p. 1.

[3] Robert Southey, *The Doctor* (1834–7).

polished by constant use. On the back of each were the same initials as those over the door, with the date 1610. The great oak Table, and the chest in the best kitchen which held the house linen, bore the same date. The chimney was well hung with bacon, the rack which covered half the ceiling bore equal marks of plenty; mutton hams were suspended from other parts of the ceiling; and there was an odour of cheese from the adjoining dairy, which the turf fire, though perpetual as that of the Magi, or of the Vestal Virgins, did not overpower. A few pewter dishes were ranged above the trenches, opposite the door, on a conspicuous shelf. The other treasures of the family were in an open triangular cupboard, fixed in one of the corners of the best kitchen, half-way from the floor, and touching the ceiling. They consisted of a silver saucepan, a silver goblet and four apostle spoons. Here also King Charles's Golden Rules were pasted against the wall, and a large print of Daniel in the Lion's Den. . . . Six black chairs were arranged against the wall, where they were seldom disturbed from their array. They had been purchased by Daniel the grandfather, upon his marriage, and were the most costly purchase that had ever been made in the family; for the goblet was a legacy. Over the chimney-piece were two Peacocks feathers, some of the dry silky pods of the honesty flower, and one of those large 'sinuous shells' so finely described by Landor.

In his simple narrative Southey described also the garden, and the whole scene recalls one of those unchanging sides of English country life which even industrial revolutions cannot wipe away. It is interesting to note that according to Southey, tea was almost unknown in the country districts of Yorkshire at this time. The traditional form of life went on indefinitely. Families lived, as in the case of Dr. Dove, for century after century in the same house. Most of their furniture, the great oak tables, the settles with high backs, and the chests, served their purpose equally well two or three hundred years after they were made. Now and again, at the time of a wedding perhaps, some new piece of furniture of modern form was introduced, no doubt amid great excitement. The ornaments were treasured things of sentimental interest.

It would be outside the scope of a study of the interior of the English house at the time of Johnson to discuss the lives of the craftsmen and furniture-designers who contributed to its decoration. Some reference, however, must be made to Thomas Chippendale, not on account of the popularity of his reputation, but because his publication, *The*

Gentleman and Cabinet-maker's Director, explains the character of English furniture of the mid-eighteenth century more clearly and more graphically than any other source of information. Critics have been busy of late in disputing Chippendale's claim to be regarded either as the creator of a style or as a craftsman of superior distinction to many of his lesser-known contemporaries. First, it has been convincingly demonstrated that the larger proportion of the engraved plates in the *Director* bearing the author's signature were actually the inventions of other designers, in particular of Lock and Copeland.[1] This opinion receives support from the fact that the title-page of the *Director* omits to record that the designs were 'improved by the politest and most able artists', as was stated in an advertisement of the book inserted in the *Whitehall Evening Post* for June 9, 1753, the year before its publication.[2] It is further claimed that there were other cabinet-makers who were probably as well known as Chippendale in their own day but whose names are almost unknown to posterity because they did not publish books of designs. Some of the work of Benjamin Goodison and the firm of Vile and Cobb, for instance, has recently been identified from records and is distinguished for the fine quality of its workmanship.[3] Comparisons of artistic merit or skilful craftmanship are difficult in this case, because most of the authenticated furniture of Chippendale's firm belongs to a later phase of his career when he was associated with Robert Adam.

That Chippendale was a driving force and a great advertiser will hardly be disputed. Many of his contemporaries published books of designs, but none of them covered the whole field of the furnishing of the house with such thoroughness, nor illustrated such a variety of types. The *Director* was professedly intended to appeal to 'Persons in all Degrees of life', and its object was to present to the public the widest possible selection of models, both plain and decorated, although the latter predominated. Many of the models were drawn out to scale so that the trade might find it worth while

[1] Fiske Kimball and Edna Donnell, *The Creators of the Chippendale style* (Metropolitan Museum of New York) (1929).

[2] Oliver Brackett, 'Georgian Art', *Burlington Magazine* [Monograph III] (1929), p. 51.

[3] H. Clifford Smith, *Buckingham Palace: its Furniture, Decoration, and History* (1931).

to buy the book. In the third and fullest edition (1762) the great variety of chairs illustrated embrace the familiar types with a suggestion of French influence and the rarer Gothic and Chinese experiments, as well as small hall-chairs of solid mahogany which were beginning to come into fashion; for the drawing-room were large upholstered arm-chairs and sofas with carved frames, usually gilt. Many varieties of tables were shown. These included side-tables with marble tops, fragile china-tables with fret rims, small tables with hinged flaps (described as 'breakfast tables' but more commonly known as 'pembroke tables'), gilt console tables with mirrors, library tables and writing tables of varying forms. But a conspicuous omission of Chippendale's was the small tripod table with circular top. This was one of the most popular tables of the time and was used for various purposes in the daily routine of domestic life. The family groups shown in the paintings of Hogarth, Devis, Hayman, Zoffany, and others are usually seated at tables of this type taking tea or engaged in conversation. Nor were card-tables illustrated in the *Director*, in spite of the fact that the card-table was an essential element in the furnishing of an English house of any importance. Memoirs of the period make much comment on the excessive gambling which was common among people of wealth and fashion. Mrs. Lybbe Powys has left a graphic description of an important evening party which took place at Eastbury in 1777:

> They danc'd in the Saloon. No minuets that night; would have been difficult without a master of the ceremonies among so many people of rank. Two card-rooms, the drawing-room and eating-room. The latter looked so elegant lighted up; two tables at loo, one quinze, one vingt-une, many whist. At one of the former large sums pass'd and re-pass'd. I saw one (nameless here) lady of quality borrow ten pieces of Tessier within half an hour after she set down to vingt-une, and a countess at loo who ow'd to every soul round the table before half the night was over. They wanted Powys and I to play at 'low loo' as they term'd it, but we rather chose to keep our features less agitated than those we saw around us.[1]

The card-table with hinged flap and green baize top with places for counters and candles was a traditional form inherited from the time of Queen Anne, but at the middle of

[1] *Passages from the Diary of Mrs. Lybbe Powys, 1756–1808*, p. 186.

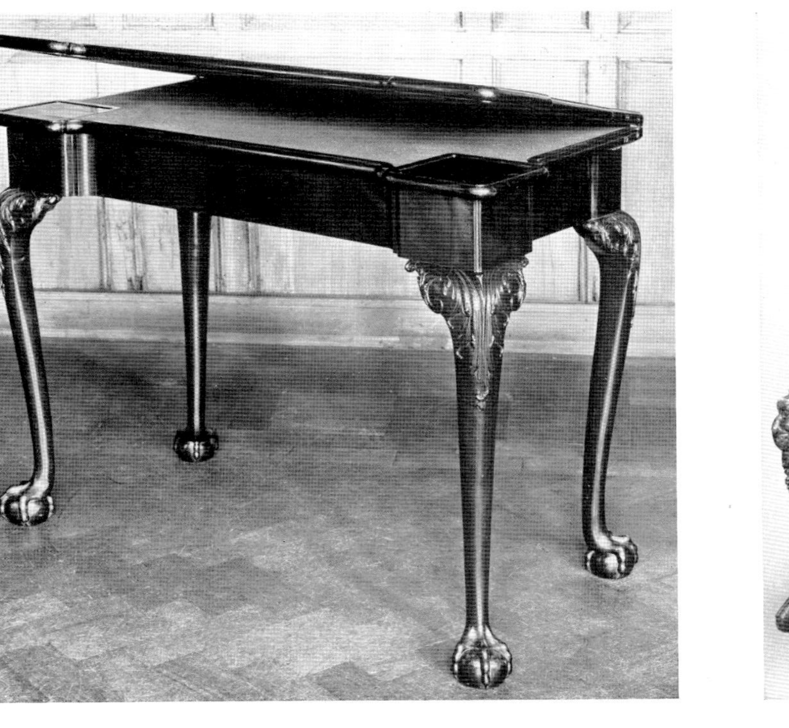

MAHOGANY CARD TABLE

1750–1760

Victoria and Albert Museum

MAHOGANY CHAIR

About 1740

At Nostell Priory, Yorkshire

the century it was made of mahogany and had straight legs in place of the claw-and-ball of an earlier date.

It was no doubt part of Chippendale's policy to ignore a few obvious types of furniture which had been in use for many years, and to concentrate on original designs which might attract the public by their novelty. He claimed that his ambition was 'to improve and refine the present Taste', though this was probably not much more than an effective stunt by his publicity department. Nevertheless the new types of furniture made for English homes at this date were considerable. The commode, for instance, became the most important and decorative feature of the drawing-room and was based on a French model which the English cabinet-makers had probably borrowed from the published designs of Meissonier, Pineau, and others. It was adapted by Chippendale and his contemporaries to satisfy the conditions of the English house, and was made at first of solid mahogany without the marble tops and ormolu mounts of the French model. Many varieties of gilt furniture, console tables with mirrors, fire-screens containing tapestry, girandoles, and candelabra, were directly inspired by French influence. New kinds of furniture, on the other hand, were made at this period not under foreign inspiration, but owing to social habits or fashionable pursuits of the day. The practice of collecting china was very general, so that hanging shelves and cabinets were required for the display of curiosities in porcelain, as well as carved and gilt stands to support large china vases. The spread of literature and the fashion for collecting books created a demand for book-cases, and as most houses of importance were built to include a library, glass cases of architectural design were needed for the walls.

In designing new types of furniture the cabinet-makers of the day were further assisted by the fact that some signs of a refinement in the habits of daily life were visible at this date. The period was a strange mixture of luxury and dirt. Although, as we have noticed, the absence of the bathroom was conspicuous in English houses there was evidence of some improvement in the fitting up of the bedroom. The four-post bedstead was a traditional form adapted to the style of the mid-eighteenth century. The posts were of mahogany, usually carved, while hangings were in velvet, damask, or other material, often with rich gold fringes.

David Garrick's bedstead in the Victoria and Albert Museum, of about the date 1775, has Indian cotton hangings printed in colours with the 'Tree of Life'. Dome bedsteads and Field bedsteads were new variations found after the middle of the century. Ladies' dressing-tables received much attention from Chippendale, although there was nothing very novel in their design, beyond a tendency to the elaboration of fittings, which increased as the century advanced. One of Chippendale's most distinguished designs for a dressing-table had a central mirror between two upright cabinets and was described as follows:

> A Design of a Dressing-Table for a Lady; the Drawer above the Recess hath all Conveniences for Dressing, and the Top of it is a Dressing-Glass, which comes forward with folding Hinges. On each Side is a Cupboard with Glass Doors, which may be either transparent or silvered; and in the Inside, Drawers, or Pigeon Holes. Two Dressing-Tables have been made of Rose-wood, from this Design, which gave an entire Satisfaction: All the Ornaments were gilt.

Both the finished examples referred to have been identified and are well known; one which belonged to Lady Arniston was sold at Christie's Sale Rooms on July 6, 1916, the other being in the possession of the Duke of Manchester at Kimbolton Castle.

The washstand was a new type of furniture and evidently began to come into use shortly after the middle of the century. Chippendale gives several designs for 'bason stands' as well as models which though described as 'shaving-tables' are actually washstands with mirrors attached. These designs are dated 1761 and are illustrated in the third edition of the *Director* (1762) but not in the first edition (1754), so that it may be assumed that the washstand as a definite piece of furniture, as far as England is concerned, was invented about this date. One model in the *Director* described as a 'shaving-table' is a cabinet on legs containing drawers and a cupboard, and fitted with basin, racks for razors, and compartments for soap balls; the mirror rises with a spring-catch and is worked by 'a scheme to bring the Glass forward, when a Gentleman is shaving'. This type of washstand was afterwards elaborated and became fashionable towards the end of the century. A contemporary description of such a washstand is given in the accounts rendered in 1784 by John Russell and Benjamin Parran for

MAHOGANY SIDE-TABLE WITH MARBLE TOP
About 1750
Worshipful Company of Coopers

SIDE-TABLE OF WOOD, GILT AND SILVERED
About 1775
Style of Robert Adam
At Harewood House, Yorkshire

the furnishing of the King's house at Newmarket.[1] 'A wainscote Bason stand with a Dressing glass to slide up and down in a frame with racks and a spring fastening, a white stone Bason, 2 Glasses for Soap and a Drawer in front with a brass pendant ring, a bottom shelf cut out with a turned ring for a bottle.'

The other type of basin-stand consisted of a wooden ring to hold the basin resting on a tripod stand, in the base of which was a circular depression for the bottle; in the middle was often a cone-shaped box containing a glass cup to hold the soap ball. A common opinion that these stands were powdering-stands cannot be supported. Both types of these washstands were of small proportion, measuring on the average not more than 2 ft. 9 in. in height. The basins, which were plain or decorated, were not more than about 9 in. in diameter, and the bottles, also, were of proportionate size. In the Blue Bedchamber at Strawberry Hill, Horace Walpole possessed on a lacquered cabinet 'an ewer and bason of blue and white Seve china; under it a blue and gold china bottle', and in the Red Bedchamber 'an ewer and bason of Chantilli porcelain'.[2] These miniature washing-stands, though picturesque, were curiously inefficient from the practical point of view, but no doubt their small proportions were due to the general inadequacy of the water-supply.

The cabinet-makers of the day found further opportunities for exercising their talents in originality by their experiments in the Chinese and Gothic styles. Chippendale published a number of designs for a variety of types of furniture in both these tastes, but many of them were fantastic compositions which were never carried out in the solid. Some of his contemporaries went further and specialized in either the Chinese or Gothic style or mixed them together. Edwards and Darly in 1754 published a comprehensive work entitled: *A new book of Chinese designs calculated to improve the present Taste, consisting of Figures, Buildings and Furniture, Landskips, Birds, Beasts, Flow^rs and Ornaments*, but most of the designs were borrowed from books of travel and were quite remote from their intended purpose. Neither of these styles in fact seems to have achieved the success that was

[1] P. Macquoid and R. Edwards, *Dictionary of English Furniture* [Washstand] (1924–7).

[2] Horace Walpole, *Description of the Villa at Strawberry Hill* (1784), pp. 28, 29.

anticipated. A certain number of enthusiastic or eccentric amateurs gave them their blessing, but the bulk of the public were not much inclined to be bitten, at all events as far as their own homes were concerned. Witty journalists found the Chinese and Gothic tastes an effective field for ridicule in the daily press. The two fashions were commonly classified together and were associated further with the rococo style, though human imagination could hardly conceive a more utterly incongruous trio. The Chinese style, on the whole, appealed to the public rather more than the Gothic. Bedrooms with lacquered furniture against a Chinese wall-paper made a consistent composition which was not discordant with an English house, and by the brilliance of its colouring formed an effective relief to the severity of the native style. But the Chinese taste flourished less in the home than in the Chinese pavilions and temples for which there was some vogue at this date, or the public places frequented by the people for entertainment. Carlisle House in Soho Square, where Teresa Cornelis, the notorious Venetian adventuress, entertained the fashionable side of society with masquerades, was furnished in the Chinese style, probably by Chippendale who was engaged in 1773 in a lawsuit with the proprietress in the Court of Bankruptcy.[1]

For furniture in the Gothic taste there was some demand in the Gothic houses built by Sanderson Miller and others at this date. Horace Walpole is commonly regarded as a pioneer in this movement, but he appears to have had conflicting scruples in the matter. On August 22, 1761, ten years after operations had started in his own Gothic villa, he wrote:

> Went again to Mr. Charles Hamilton's at Payne's Hill near Cobham to see the Gothic building and the Roman ruin. The former is taken from Batty Langley's book (which does not contain a single design of true or good Gothic) and is made worse by pendent ornaments in the arches, and by being closed on two sides at bottom, with cheeks that have no relation to Gothic. The whole is an unmeaning edifice. In all Gothic designs, they should be made to imitate something that was of that time, a part of a church, a castle, a convent, or a mansion. The Goths never built summer houses and temples in a garden.[2]

[1] Oliver Brackett, *Thomas Chippendale* (Appendix) (1924).

[2] Horace Walpole, *Journals of Visits to Country Seats* (1928), p 36.

And when in 1774 he came to explain his own Gothic house at Strawberry Hill, he was candid enough to confess: 'I do not mean to defend by argument a small capricious house. It was built to please my own taste, and in some degree to realize my own visions.'[1] This modest ambition was not shared by the builders and cabinet-makers of the day, who aspired to 'improve' the Gothic style 'in many grand designs'.[2] But neither the Chinese nor Gothic fashions survived the change in taste which coincided with the Adam influence in interior decoration after about 1770.

Robert Adam in 1773 summed up the change which he himself traced in interior decoration:

A remarkable improvement in the form, convenience, and relief of apartments; a greater movement and variety in the outside composition: and in the decoration of the inside, an almost total change.

The massive entablature, the ponderous compartment ceiling, the tabernacle frame, almost the only species of ornament formerly known in this country, are now universally exploded, and in their place, we have adopted a beautiful variety of light mouldings, gracefully formed, delicately enriched and arranged with propriety and skill. We have introduced a great diversity of ceilings, friezes and decorated pilasters, and have added grace and beauty to the whole by a mixture of grotesque stucco and painted ornaments together with the painted rainceau with its fanciful figures.[3]

This statement shows the general trend of Robert Adam's policy. It meant the abandonment of the Orders as a basis of architectural composition in favour of different schemes of decoration due to the study of other models. During the years when Robert Adam travelled on the Continent (between 1754 and 1758) he preferred to make drawings of the Baths and Palaces of Rome, Venice, and other cities, rather than the Greek and Roman Temples for which his predecessors professed a blind admiration. He was also much influenced by the ruined palace of the Emperor Diocletian at Spalato in Dalmatia of which, amid considerable difficulties, he made drawings in the company of Clérisseau, a French architect. He also found inspiration in the domestic buildings of the Italian Renaissance, in particular for the arabesque designs which were distinctive features in his schemes of

[1] Horace Walpole, *Description of the Villa at Strawberry Hill.*

[2] Batty Langley, *Gothic Architecture improved . . . in many grand designs* (1742).

[3] R. and J. Adam, *Works in Architecture* (1773), vol. i, p. 3.

decoration. Apart from the selected models which he himself chose for study, he lived at a time when new movements were changing public taste throughout Europe. Such an event as the discovery of Pompeii, for instance, could not fail to influence a mind as eager for new suggestions in decoration as that of this Scottish-born architect.

In the typical house of the fully-developed Adam style (after about the date 1770) are found large spaces of blank wall relieved by panels filled with fine arabesques, or medallions containing groups of classical figures, in plaster or painting. A feature of the style was the semi-circular alcove at one end of a room, and niches at intervals in the wall were characteristic. Ceilings were commonly divided into compartments containing pateras and rosettes[1]—flippantly described as 'chese cakes and raspberry tarts' by a contemporary critic—amid delicate festoons and scrolls. Chimney-pieces were of the 'simple' type, usually of marble and carved with extreme refinement. Among the designers of this school, the Italian Pergolesi had a great reputation, while Cipriani, Zucchi, and Angelica Kauffman achieved fame for their painted decoration on walls and ceilings.

Where Robert Adam's imagination showed itself was in his conception of the interior of the house as a consistent unity, in which the fittings and ornaments were part of one uniform composition. William Kent some thirty years earlier had, in his more limited way, worked on similar lines, but in a general sense the architects of the time planned and decorated their apartments without reference to the furniture, which was the affair of the cabinet-maker. It was Adam's ambition, on the other hand, not only to make the furniture part of the composition of the room, consistent with the decoration of walls and ceiling, but to include carpets and curtains in the general scheme. With the assistance, therefore, of his expert designers, he made a vast number of designs suitable for the houses which he built, designs for commodes, tables, couches, chairs, girandoles, and frames, as well as curtains and carpets, and such minor items as candlesticks and plate for the table. The bulk of these designs are preserved in the Soane Museum.

In order to be in unison with its backgrounds, it was necessary for this furniture to be lighter both in form and

[1] A. T. Bolton, *The Architecture of Robert and James Adam* (1922).

ornament than the heavy mahogany types which had been fashionable a few years earlier. Carving, therefore, tended to give way to inlay and painting. Favourite motives of decoration were medallions containing groups of figures, delicate festoons and scrolls, rams' heads, and borders of honeysuckle. For such medallions the talent of Wedgwood was sometimes made use of, and for ormolu mounts, Matthew Boulton, the famous metalworker, was much employed. There is little doubt in our opinion that in some of his designs Adam was influenced by the bronze furniture of Pompeii. In spite of the affinity of some of his furniture with the French School of Louis XVI, it is doubtful if Adam owed anything to this source. It has been suggested, on the other hand, with reason, that the typical Adam chair with oval back and straight legs was first evolved by him and afterwards adopted by the cabinet-makers of Paris.[1]

In houses built by Adam and intended for 'the parade, the convenience, and social pleasures of life' the types of furniture required were but few in number though highly ornamental in character. These fastidious models, however, were utterly remote from the habits and the desires of the bulk of the people. There is no doubt that the Adam tradition slowly and to a limited extent affected the furnishing of the homes of the middle classes. But the wants of their daily life demanded not even echoes of the magnificent commodes and candlestands of the new palaces, but simple and useful furniture for the house refined and improved under modern conditions.

In the furnishing of the house of the period were included a vast number of miscellaneous articles often of a purely utilitarian character. Many of these things, such as the utensils used in the kitchen, belonged essentially to the time or were relics of an earlier age, but have passed out of use with the advance of modern civilization. On April 19, 1777, a sale took place at the house of Sir Thomas Robinson, adjoining Ranelagh Gardens in Chelsea, and in the catalogue of the sale the contents of all the rooms were recorded in the most minute detail. Sir Thomas Robinson, of Rokeby, was a well-known figure in the social life of the day. Possessed of great wealth he travelled on the Continent, making a study of the fine arts, and subsequently had some claim to be

[1] H. A. Tipping, Robert Adam (in *Dictionary of English Furniture*).

considered as an amateur architect, although his achievements in this direction were not remarkable. Following the fashion of wealthy Englishmen of the day he aspired to be a patron of artists. It was Sir Thomas Robinson who proposed Chippendale for the Society of Arts, and there are good reasons for assuming that the famous cabinet-maker was employed on the furnishing and decoration of Rokeby in Yorkshire and Prospect House in Chelsea, although no documentary proof has up to the present been discovered. Sir Thomas was also celebrated for the extravagance of his entertainments.[1] The memoirs and letters of Horace Walpole, Lady Harvey, Lady Mary Coke, and others have frequent references to the balls, breakfasts, and masquerades which took place at his house in Chelsea, though often accompanied with a strain of ridicule, for Robinson, on account of his pompous and tedious manners, was a favourite target for the witty shafts of his more frivolous contemporaries. His tactlessness was proverbial. On one occasion, acting as a mediator for Lord Chesterfield, he roused the wrath of Dr. Johnson, by remarking that had circumstances permitted, he would have settled £500 a year on him.

Shortly after Sir Thomas Robinson's death, his house in Chelsea and all its contents were sold by auction. The value of the Sale Catalogue lies in the fact that it records in great detail the whole equipment of the house, from the garret to the kitchen, the furniture, plate, pewter, china, pictures, curtains, and carpets. The number of rooms in the house was considerable. There was a Front Hall, a State Room, an Assembly Room, a Ball Room, a Front Parlour, a Back Parlour, a Principal Dining Parlour, a Library, numerous bedrooms and dressing closets, a Housekeeper's Room, a Kitchen, a Knife Office, a Washhouse, and a Dairy. The furnishing of the various rooms brings back the manners and customs of the period with some realism. In the hall was found a mahogany claw table, a mahogany wig-stand, and five hall chairs, as well as an 'excellent porter's chair covered and lined with Spanish leather, and mahogany apparatus'—a type of furniture very characteristic of a period when the porter was obliged to sit for many hours in a cold and draughty passage. Other items in the hall which recall the life of the time were a brass frame hall lantern with shade

[1] *Dictionary of National Biography*, Sir Thomas Robinson.

LACQUERED COMMODE WITH ORMOLU MOUNTS
About 1770
Victoria and Albert Museum

DRESSING TABLE, WITH INLAY OF SATINWOOD, HAREWOOD AND OTHER WOODS
About 1775
Victoria and Albert Museum

and burner, twenty-four leather fire buckets, a blunderbuss, two pairs of pistols, a fowling-piece, two swords, a bayonet, and a dinner bell.

The State Room, evidently an imposing apartment used for entertainments and receptions, possessed an unusual feature in the form of 'a magnificent pavillion or canopy of Genoa crimson silk damask richly fring'd, tastefully decorated, with carv'd and burnish'd gold embellishments, also a large squab, two cushions and two bolsters', evidently a divan of somewhat oriental luxury, belonging to a type illustrated among the more extravagant designs of Chippendale and his contemporaries but not often chosen by the Englishmen of the day as a suitable or necessary part of the fitting of the house. The rest of the furnishing of the State Room was in keeping with this magnificent centre-piece. All the room was crimson and gold. The windows had crimson silk damask curtains festooned and lined, and the same material covered the sofas and chairs. Typical examples of the most expensive types of furniture of the period were found, such as a 'superb Commode' with ormolu mounts and top of Egyptian marble. The floor was completely covered with a large Scotch carpet. The brilliance of the scene was completed by valuable paintings hanging on the walls, among which were included pictures by Raphael, Vandyck, Watteau, Sir Peter Lely, and Rubens, as well as portraits of famous personalities.

The furnishing of the Principal Dining Parlour had the practical and utilitarian character which would be expected. The windows were hung with festooned curtains of crimson damask and the floor covered with a Wilton carpet. Within the fire-place—as was the case with most of the rooms—was a steel compass fender engraved and ornamented, with shovel, tongs, and poker. There were two mahogany dining-tables which could be joined together in the event of large dinner parties. The chairs were of mahogany covered with horse-hair fixed with brass nails. Against the walls were two side-tables with marble tops and painted frames, and a mahogany wine-cooler (described as a wine-cooper). The room was well lighted with a pair of glass chandeliers, and four metal branches for eight lights on the walls. The furniture of the typical dining-room seldom varied from this arrangement, though by this date, urns supported by pedestals sometimes flanked the principal sideboard, and dumb-waiters were in fashion. Tall screens of six or eight leaves were common, sometimes of leather painted with pastoral scenes in the French style, or of incised Chinese lacquer. It is to be regretted that the painters of domestic scenes did not on occasion depict their family groups at dinner. By such means all the equipment of the dining-table, the china and silver services, the knives, forks, and spoons, the silver salt-cellars, the glasses of varying form, the candlesticks and ornaments, would have been displayed in proper relation to one another, instead of as isolated portions of collections as they are mainly known to-day.

The walls of the Library in Sir Thomas Robinson's house were covered by seven mahogany bookcases of different sizes, with sliding shelves, glazed doors, and drawers underneath. Bookcases of this type were fixtures and formed a complete architectural composition, as opposed to the movable bookcase which was not necessarily designed for any defined position. Often these bookcases relied for their decorative effect on graceful mouldings, the proportions of which were calculated according to definite rules, and to brass drop-handles and escutcheons, richly chased. The Library at Chelsea had curtains of green damask, thus differing in colour from the curtains in the other rooms in the house. This was the room used for reading, writing, and smoking—a jar of herb tobacco was mentioned. The furniture consisted of a writing-desk with inkstand, a mahogany reading-desk on a claw to raise occasionally, a mahogany nest-of-drawers or receptacle for papers, an easy chair covered with leather, and a pair of library steps. On the floor was a circular Wilton carpet with fringe, and light was obtained from a pair of glass chandeliers, two pairs of metal branches for four lights and sockets on the walls, and a pair of carved mahogany candlestands. There was also an organ in this room, and another in the Saloon. Sir Thomas Robinson seems to have had a taste for chamber organs, and it may have been his influence that caused Chippendale to make so many designs for this type of musical instrument, for but few of them seem to have survived in private houses. After about 1770, on the other hand, small portable chamber organs were in common use.

The furniture of the bedrooms varied in importance.

BOOKCASE, CARVED, PAINTED AND GILT
Style of William Kent. About 1735
Victoria and Albert Museum

Sir Thomas's bedchamber was naturally the most imposing. The central feature consisted of 'a handsome bed of red copper plate cotion furniture lin'd thro' compleat, the bedstead with settee head and mahogany foot posts', with a white and a check mattress, three blankets, a bolster, and three pillows, as well as 'a very fine real Marseiles quilt'. Printed cotton curtains in festoons hung at the windows. The room contained a variety of chairs and a 'Péché mortel'[1] or couch, a chest of drawers, a screen, two dressing-glasses, and a set of 'India' dressing-boxes. No dressing-table, washstand, or wardrobe is mentioned. The floor was covered with floor-cloth and had small Wilton carpets or mats. Sir Thomas evidently kept canaries in his bedroom, for 'two fine canary birds with gilt wire cages and ornaments' were included in the sale.

The other rooms in the house were furnished in keeping with their purpose or importance. The kitchen contained a great number of utensils of a miscellaneous character. For purposes of cooking were found a jack, with line, pullies and iron weight, a pair of large spit racks, two spits, two gridirons, and a beef fork. In addition to the open fire-places there were tin Dutch ovens for cooking. Numbers of vessels used for preparing food and cooking are enumerated. Among them are mentioned stewing pans and dishes, saucepans, kettles, apple roasters, brass skimmers, lark spits, skewers, steelyards, and pewter plates and dishes. The wooden furniture consisted mainly of deal tables and plate racks, and a Dutch clock. In many kitchens of the period, a dresser with rows of pewter plates on shelves was a distinctive feature.

The lavish form of entertainment followed at Sir Thomas Robinson's house required that the china and plate should equal the furniture and decoration in fastidiousness and extravagance. At this date people of fashion who had travelled abroad and prided themselves on the distinction of their manner of living, sometimes affected the taste of collecting and using Oriental and Continental china, in preference to the home-made wares of Chelsea, Worcester, or Rockingham. Sir Thomas's habits seem to have lain in this direction. He had no less than three Oriental blue-and-

[1] 'Two Designs of Couches, or what the French call *Péché mortel.*' Chippendale's *Director* (3rd ed., 1762), Pl. xxxii.

white table services. One consisted of eight oblong dishes, three dozen plates, fifteen soups, a terrine, a cover and dish, two boats, and two salts. He also had a tea service of Dresden china which included a teapot and stand, a sugar dish and cover, a basin, a cream ewer, with coffee cups and tea-cups and saucers. There was further a white embossed tea and coffee equipage of Dresden porcelain. Throughout the house were large Oriental bowls and vases, sometimes placed on carved and gilded stands such as became fashionable after the middle of the century.

To the knowledge of the interior of the house of the period, the pictures of domestic scenes by painters of the day make an invaluable contribution. The human element, which in other records can only be vaguely felt, is here the predominating interest, and the furnished room takes its proper place as the background against which the scenes of daily life were acted. It is to be regretted, however, that in England there is not much variety in this source of information. The so-called 'Conversation Pieces' of Hogarth, Devis, Hayman, Pugh, Zoffany, and others are always attractive from the point of view of sentiment and usually skilful in technical achievement. Within their limitations they have bequeathed to posterity a truthful and picturesque aspect of the home of the wealthy and leisured Englishman of the time. But their purpose was to represent family groups posed in conventional attitudes, seated almost invariably in the drawing-room, engaged in taking tea or polite conversation. Only one room, therefore, is depicted, and in its representation by different artists a marked similarity is found. An atmosphere of intense refinement is always successfully suggested. It will be noticed that, in all cases, the rooms were sparsely furnished, containing no furniture which could be regarded as superfluous. This was the characteristic of a period which possessed a definite style in furnishing, and forms a marked contrast to the overcrowded rooms of the Victorian age, when the collecting of furniture of all periods and nationalities was becoming fashionable. The central feature of the room, round which the figures grouped themselves, was commonly a small circular table with tripod stand, a type which could be adapted to almost any purpose. If tea was served, the table was covered with a white linen table-cloth. The taking of tea was simple in its arrangement, for only

THE THOMLINSON FAMILY
showing a furnished interior of the period
From the painting by Arthur Devis, 1745

a tray with silver teapot, urn and cream jug, with small porcelain cups (without handles) and saucers would be found, while food was seldom served. At other times the lady of the house is shown engaged in embroidery with a work-basket on the table. The card-table which belonged essentially to the drawing-room, was often introduced. Sometimes a spinet or small piano was shown. The men and women, whose portraits were depicted, would be seated on chairs or a sofa upholstered usually with red, green, or yellow damask, walls being covered with similar material. The latter were hung with a few pictures, a mirror, or a pair of sconces, while a rich Turkey carpet on the floor would usually complete the composition.

Among subject pictures of the period, however, there is one series, Hogarth's 'Marriage à la Mode', which stands out by reason of the variety of scenes depicted. These satirical representations of 'Modern Occurrences in high life' depict, not groups of figures posed in conventional attitudes, but different aspects of contemporary manners, expounded with vigorous, if theatrical, handling. The backgrounds to the six scenes in which is unfolded the threadbare and somewhat trivial story of the impoverished peer who married his son to a rich alderman's daughter with subsequent disasters, are full of interest in a study of the interior of the house of the time. The pictures were painted in 1745 and thus belong to the earlier part of Johnson's period.

In the first scene, 'The Marriage Contract', the room contains a dark green domed canopy with pelmets. The gouty peer, one of whose feet is swathed in bandages, is seated on a heavy couch with gilt framework, pointing with one hand to his family tree painted on a scroll. The rich alderman studies the marriage contract at a circular table, on which is a heap of gold and notes as well as a silver tray with inkstand, glass, sealing-wax, and candlestick with lighted candle. Seated on a couch the future bride and bridegroom turn their backs to one another, the former conversing with Councillor Silvertongue, who plays an important part in the subsequent drama. The walls are covered with green material suggesting a marbled paper and are hung with pictures of a religious character.

The second episode, 'Shortly after Marriage', shows the famous apartment which is supposed to have been copied from the drawing-room of No. 5 Arlington Street. This is a spacious room divided into two parts by an arch supported on columns painted in imitation of dark green marble with gilt capitals. The front room has a stone chimney-piece of the 'continued' type, with a panel in the overmantel painted with Cupid blowing bagpipes amid ruins. On the mantelshelf are crowded a variety of oriental porcelain ornaments and figures, with a bust in the middle. The walls are panelled and painted dark green, while on one side hangs a large fantastic sconce with branching lights, ornamented with Chinese figures, foliage, and fishes, and fitted with a clock which shows the time of day to be twenty minutes past twelve. There is a fire burning in the hearth within a basket grate. The young peer and his yawning wife lounge on heavy cabriole chairs upholstered with red brocade, to the disgust of a steward who unsuccessfully attempts to draw attention to a bundle of bills; a small dog sniffs at a woman's cap protruding from the earl's pocket. By the lady's side stands a heavy tripod table with porcelain teapot and sugar basin on a tray. Near the fire-place is a screen with needle-work panel, and on the floor a Turkey carpet. The walls of the farther room are covered with a grey figured wall-paper or damask. From the ceiling a silver chandelier is suspended by a red cord with tassels. A sleepy man-servant is arranging card-tables after a night of gambling.

The story passes from this luxurious apartment to the disreputable abode of a quack doctor. The room has a Venetian window. A large cupboard with glazed doors, of the type commonly used for bookcases at the time, contains a skeleton and other anatomical material. The earl is accompanied by a young woman and with a sarcastic smile holds out a box of pills to an abortionist, a woman of vast proportions who with a look of hatred in her face touches the point of a surgical knife in her hands. The quack stands by her side, with a leering expression. Behind is a table covered with a cloth and against the wall a cabinet with drug pots on shelves.

The next episode, 'The Countess's Dressing Room', illustrates the practice among ladies of fashion of the time for entertaining visitors in their bedrooms. A concert, in fact, is taking place on this occasion. Within a round-arched alcove is shown a bed with canopy and curtains of red material. The countess, whose hair is being dressed by a valet, is seated beside a dressing-table, on which is a draped silver mirror, a pincushion, and other articles of the toilet. She is oblivious to the concert and is receiving a ticket for the 'Turk's Head Bagnio' from Silvertongue, who lounges on a sofa covered with figured red damask. Behind them is a tall screen painted with figure compositions. In the centre a coloured man-servant offers chocolate to a lady who leans forward engrossed in the singing of an Italian tenor accompanied on the flute by a German musician; near by sit three men, a variety of social caricatures, one with hair in curl-papers, another with a fan attached to his wrist, the third asleep. In one corner a heap of curiosities in a basket have been brought in from a sale. The tastes of the countess are shown by the pictures on the walls which include Susannah and the Elders, Ganymede, and Correggio's 'Jupiter and Io'.

The dramatic outcome of the visit by the countess and Silvertongue to the 'Turk's Head Bagnio' is unfolded in the fifth picture. The wall facing the spectator in this room is hung with tapestry, partly covered by two pictures. In one corner a bed is shown in shadow. The room is in confusion, tables thrust aside, a chair overturned, and on the floor a woman's mask, hoop, corset, and shoes. The young earl has discovered his wife and her lover together and has himself been killed as the result of a duel which followed. As he falls the countess kneels before him while Silvertongue in night-shirt escapes through the open window. The watch enters at the door holding up a lantern.

The background to the final scene, 'The Death of the Countess', seems never to have been clearly explained. Mr. Austin Dobson,[1] who summed up the conclusions of previous writers and authorities, assumed that after the catastrophe in the 'Turk's Head Bagnio' the countess went back to the house of her father, the rich City merchant. But the room depicted seems evidently to belong to an inn or third-rate hotel in the City. The row of hat-pegs, the corner-cupboard containing long clay pipes, the board hung with bells, all support this suggestion. It was an old room, moreover, with plain panelling and a bow window with small panes of glass with the Arms of the City of London inset.

[1] Austin Dobson, *William Hogarth* (1907).

From the window is seen a view of Old London Bridge. On the walls hang a brass clock, a few cheap prints, and an Almanack. The countess, having heard that Silvertongue has been hanged, takes poison. As she dies, a nurse holds up her child, evidently a weakling with legs in irons. Her father extracts rings from her right hand. Near by an apothecary is questioning a youth. On a circular table covered with a soiled table-cloth an unfinished meal is shown, with a handsome silver bowl, and pewter plates and dishes from one of which a starving dog is seizing a pig's head by the ear. There is no carpet on the floor of this bare and ill-furnished room, while the overturned chair belongs to a type which was made a century earlier than Hogarth's time.

MARRIAGE À LA MODE. PLATE IV. THE COUNTESS AT HER TOILET

From the painting by W. Hogarth

BIBLIOGRAPHY.—ROBERT and JAMES ADAM, *Works in Architecture* (1778–1822). A. T. BOLTON, *The Architecture of Robert and James Adam* (1922). OLIVER BRACKETT, *Thomas Chippendale: a study of his life, work, and influence* (1924); *Burlington Magazine* [Monograph III], 'Georgian Art' (1929). MATTHEW BRETTINGHAM, *The plans, elevations, and sections of Holkham in Norfolk* (1773). SIR WILLIAM CHAMBERS, *Treatise on Civil Architecture* (1768). THOMAS CHIPPENDALE, *The Gentleman and Cabinet-maker's Director*, 1st ed. (1754), 2nd ed. (1755), 3rd ed. (1762); Conversation Pieces, *Catalogue of Exhibition of English Conversation-Pieces, at 25 Park Lane, London* (1930). W. P. COURTNEY, Sir Thomas Robinson (in *Dictionary of National Biography*). SAMUEL CURWEN, *Journal and Letters* (late 18th cent.) (1824). MRS. M. C. DELANY, *Autobiography and Correspondence (1718–88)* (1861). P. H. DESTAILLEUR, *Recueil d'Estampes relatives à l'ornementation des appartements*, Paris (1863). LILIAN DICKENS and MARY STANTON, *An Eighteenth-Century Correspondence* (Sanderson Miller's correspondence, 1738–79) (1910). AUSTIN DOBSON, *William Hogarth* (1907). J. B. DU HALDE, *Description . . . de l'Empire de la Chine 1735* (English translation) (1741); *Dictionary of National Biography*, see Courtney, W. P. EDWARD and DARLEY, *A new Book of Chinese Designs, calculated to improve the present taste* (1754). J. A. GOTCH, *The Growth of the English House* (1909); *The English Home from Charles I to George IV* (1918); M. GROSLEY, *A Tour to London; or new Observations on England* (translated by Thomas Nugent) (1772). HENRY HAVARD, *Dictionnaire d'ameublement*, Paris (1887–90). Historical Manuscripts Commission, *The Manuscripts of Lord Kenyon*, 14th Report, Appendix IX, Part IV (1894). INCE and MAYHEW, *The Universal System of Household Furniture* (1762?). T. JOHNSON, *150 New Designs* (1758). M. JOURDAIN, *English Decoration and Furniture of the later 18th century* (1922). FISKE KIMBALL and EDNA DONNELL, *The Creators of the Chippendale style* (Metropolitan Museum of New York, 1929). FRANCIS LENYGON, *Decoration in England* (1914). LONDON COUNTY COUNCIL, *Survey of London*, vol. iii, 'St. Giles's-in-the-Fields' (Part I), 'Lincoln's Inn Fields' (1912). P. MACQUOID, *A History of English Furniture* (1905–8). P. MACQUOID and R. EDWARDS, *The Dictionary of English Furniture* (3 vols., 1924–7). R. MANWARING, *The Cabinet and Chair-maker's Real Friend and Companion* (1765). National Gallery (Millbank), *Catalogue of the British School* (1920). JAMES NORTHCOTE, *Life of Sir Joshua Reynolds* (2 vols., 1818). C. C. OMAN, *Catalogue of Wall-papers*, Victoria and Albert Museum (1929). JAMES PAINE, *Plans, elevations, and sections of Gentlemen's Houses* (1783). *Passages from the Diary of Mrs. Lybbe Powys (1756–1808)*, edited by E. J. Clemenson (1899). SIR THOMAS ROBINSON, *Catalogue of Sale* (1777). H. CLIFFORD SMITH, *Buckingham Palace: its Furniture, Decoration, and History* (1931). ROBERT SOUTHEY, *The Doctor* (1834–7). ABRAHAM SWAN, *The British Architect; or the Builder's Treasury of Staircases* (1758). H. A. TIPPING, *English Homes* (1920). HORACE WALPOLE, *Description of the Villa at Strawberry Hill* (1784); *Journals of Visits to Country Seats* (Walpole Society) (1928); *Letters (1736–85)* (19 vols., ed. Toynbee, 1903–25). ISAAC WARE, *A complete Body of Architecture* (1756). H. B. WHEATLEY, *Old and New London* (1891). G. C. WILLIAMSON, *English Conversation Pictures* (1931).

XX

THE DRAMA AND THE THEATRE

By W. J. LAWRENCE

The Drama's Laws the Drama's Patrons give,
For we that live to please, must please to live.
Prologue spoken at the Opening of the Theatre in Drury-lane, 1747.

That stroke of death (Garrick's), which has eclipsed the gaiety of nations, and impoverished the publick stock of harmless pleasure.—*Life of Edmund Smith* (1781).

In and about the mid-eighteenth century, the English theatre was the battle-ground of conflicting ideals. Relics of the old intellectual callousness and irresponsible individualism were at war with a steadily increasing social consciousness, to which impetus had been given by patriotic fervour. The struggle was between the cultivated idler, who to some extent was tradition-ridden and insisted upon the game being played strictly according to the rules, and the open-minded citizen with an ordered method of life and a simple desire for wholesome amusement. No longer was the theatre, as in Restoration days, the exclusive rendezvous of the aristocracy; exclusiveness of the old order was now only to be obtained at the Italian Opera House in the Haymarket, where an exotic entertainment lacking in popular appeal was kept alive by the subscriptions of the dilettanti. After a long abstinence, the middle classes had returned once more in full force to the play, and the influence of their unsophisticated tastes proved a vital factor in the shaping and colouring of contemporary drama. With their advent a cleansing, though somewhat enervating, breeze of puritanism began to flow steadily through the theatre. More desirous that their emotions should be played upon than that their intellects should be exercised, the middle classes gave their support to the new sentimental comedy whose main characteristics had been formulated by Colley Cibber and established by Steele, now growing generally popular because its pathetic tone appealed to the incipient humanitarianism of the hour, but especially to the liking of the *bourgeoisie* owing to its moralizations.

Best known when it was a living force and a source of controversy as 'Genteel' or 'High' comedy, the comedy of sentiment was not so much an extension of Thalia's old domains as virgin soil. In reality, it was the genesis of modern domestic drama. Had it been recognized for what it was, a new genre, and not, as was mistakenly thought, the highest form of pure comedy, much idle controversy would have been checked and encouragement could have been freely given to the writing of true comedy, whether the comedy of manners or of intrigue. Not that writing of the sort failed to persist, despite all opposition, but, the old aims being deflected by new concepts, it was mostly of a spineless order. Whatever the reason—possibly it was the aftermath of Collier's fulminations against the rank indecency of Restoration drama—the dramatic age was marked by a squeamishness hitherto uncharacteristic of the British people. The new sentimental drama was known indifferently as Genteel or High Comedy for the reason that it dealt with lords and ladies and eschewed low humour. Such was the horror professed by the coffee-house quidnuncs for all that was vulgar that the dramatist, fearing lest he should overstep the line, kept his vivacity so well within bounds that he ended by avoiding all humour whatsoever. Comedy had grown, like Niobe, all tears. The climax came with the production at Drury Lane in 1762 of Whitehead's *The School for Lovers*, a play in which the characters were all remarkable for elegance of sentiment, purity of expression, and propriety of manners, but in which there was not the slightest scintillation of wit or leaven of humour. To dramatist and manager alike, this cant phrase 'low' was a perpetual bugbear; but to those who took their courage in both hands and braved its terrors there occasionally came reward. When Garrick brought out a revised version of Jonson's *Every Man in his Humour* in 1749, he had his doubts about its suitability to the times and begged the audience

> With no false niceness this performance view,
> Nor damn for low whate'er is just and true.

But the old play had no storm to weather, and found at once safe anchorage.

This squeamishness very properly extended to matters of indecency, though, if hypocrisy is the homage that vice pays to virtue, one may doubt with Sheridan whether it was not in large measure hypocritical. When Dangle in *The Critic* remarked that even Congreve and Vanbrugh had to be bowdlerized to avoid outraging susceptibilities, Sneer replied, 'Yes; and our prudery in this respect is just on a par with the artificial bashfulness of a courtesan, who increases the blush upon her cheek in an exact proportion to the diminution of her modesty'. The secret, perhaps, is revealed by William Cooke in some reflections upon sentimental comedy made in his essay on *The Elements of Dramatic Criticism* in 1775. Cooke admitted that the age was free from great and leading vices, but characterized it as peculiarly marked by 'a slavish effeminacy of manners and universality of indolent dissipation'. In his view, people of fashion were averse from seeing themselves depicted in a true light, assumed a virtue they did not possess, and lauded abstract morality in inverse ratio to their observance of it. The masses took their cue from their betters, and fell into the same pose, 'so that between the two parties nature began to be called vulgar and everything partaking of the low, humorous, or vicious (principal ingredients in comedy)' grew to be despised, because the quality had an interest in decrying them, and the masses permitted themselves to be duped by the artifice.

Unhappily this spirit of deodorization led to the marring of many a masterpiece. It is a pity that the sound advice given by Arthur Murphy in 1776 had not been laid down as an edict by some person in authority (say, the Lord Chamberlain, then the final arbiter in affairs theatrical) some quarter of a century or so earlier. 'If new plays cannot be had,' wrote Murphy, 'let them revive the old, but be sparing of alterations. They may lop excrescences and remove indecency; but the form in which the fathers of the drama left their work shows their own frame of thought, and ought to be respected.' There was in this a lash that righteously fell across Garrick's shoulders. During his long term of control at Drury Lane, Roscius had been guilty of serious sophistication of many of the classic pieces he revived. Not content with purging an admired old play of offence, he frequently sought to bring its obsolete technique up to date, never hesitating in such cases to insert new scenes of his own. Nothing, indeed, could be more reprehensible than his ruthless treatment of Shakespeare. It would be a poor excuse to say that in this respect he had excellent precedent for his course, that he only did what Davenant and Dryden and

DAVID GARRICK

From the painting by T. Gainsborough

Tate had done before him. The times were different. Shakespeare the poet had won something beyond mere theatrical repute; scholarship had put its impress upon him; restoration of the decayed great Gothic edifice in which his thoughts and memory were enshrined had begun. To continue the maltreatment of his text on the boards was to underrate the intelligence of the age. Only a year or two before Garrick's emergence, Fielding's *Medley* had aptly summed up the situation in saying, 'For, as Shakespeare is already good enough for people of taste, he must be altered to the palates of those who have none'.[1] That was exactly what Johnson meant when he told Boswell that for him to praise Garrick for his Shakespearian revivals 'would be to lampoon the age'. He in nowise forestalled Lamb's long-accepted, but none the less fallacious, thesis concerning the unactability of some of Shakespeare's greater works when he said that 'many of Shakespeare's plays are the worse for being acted: *Macbeth* for instance'. He was simply passing judgement on the ill stage methods of his times.

Garrick's attitude towards Shakespeare was as inconsistent as it was reprehensible. When, in 1756, he compressed *The Winter's Tale* into the limits of an afterpiece (styled *Florizel and Perdita*), he mendaciously avowed in his prologue:

> 'Tis my chief wish, my joy, my only plan,
> To lose no drop of that immortal man.

Yet the drops eventually lost from Shakespeare by his constant handling of the scalpel would have made a streamlet. And the worst of it was that, as in the case of Dryden, of Davenant and Tate, the evil he did lived after him. Not all his ill tasks were ill performed: so neat and skilful was his abbreviation of *The Taming of the Shrew* that it held the stage to the utter exclusion of the original for a century. Happily, his other maltreatments of the master had a much shorter life. But, execrable as was the taste shown in his operatic versions of *A Midsummer Night's Dream* and *The Tempest,* in neither instance was the offence quite so grave as that committed in 1772, when, dazzled by the false lights held out by Voltaire, he strove to make *Hamlet* conform to the rules. A clean sweep was made of Osric and the Grave-diggers; Laertes underwent a sea-change and exuded sentimentality from every pore; Gertrude, overwhelmed by her

[1] *The Historical Register for the Year 1736,* Act III, sc. i.

sense of criminality, went mad; and the duel between Hamlet and Laertes was followed by another between Hamlet and the King. A new dying speech provided for Laertes met with so much applause when delivered by Aickin that Garrick, who himself acted Hamlet, emulated the spirit of Bottom the Weaver, and took it from him and dovetailed it into his own part.

Yet, such was the homage then paid to Roscius that no voice was raised in rebuke. On the contrary, *The Macaroni Magazine* actually praised him for his throwing of the play on the Procrustean bed and shaping it in accord with prevailing French opinion. After sanctions of this order, it is not surprising that he lost sense of the fitness of things and was foolish enough to include several of his Shakespearian perversions in the collected edition of his works. Judgement, however, had grown topsy-turvy owing to a settled idea in theatrical and journalistic circles that the great dramatic poet was fair quarry for the adapter. What liberties were conceded may be grasped from the amazing suggestion made by Francis Gentleman in *The Dramatic Censor* in 1770: 'Every alterer of Shakespeare should remember there were no female performers in his days, and improve accordingly to the present time such parts as necessity, not want of genius or knowledge, made him abbreviate.'

With the sentimental drama in the saddle, true comedy sat uneasy on the pillion. It was not until the last quarter of the century that the lineal successors of Congreve and Farquhar emerged. With his abundant wit and humour and his gifts of characterization, Foote had the capacity to place himself among the elect, and his commanding position as controller of the Haymarket would have enabled him to do so, had he not yielded to the temptation to take the line of least resistance. Led astray by the hallowing of the fashionable mob over his powers of mimicry, he pandered to a malicious age by concentrating upon personal caricature and frittered away a rare genius upon mere topicalities. Nothing dates so soon or dies so speedily as work of this order.

Yet, even while her throne was vacant, Thalia had her sporadic successes. At Drury Lane in 1761, George Colman the elder's *The Jealous Wife*, a skilful comedy written in terms of Farquhar, which Johnson underrated as simply a well-acted theatre piece, met with the triumph it deserved.

Five years later, Colman, in association with Garrick, repeated his success with *The Clandestine Marriage.* There was nothing factitious about the good fortune of either piece, even in those days of perpetual playhouse intrigue, and both won for their authors posthumous fame. Goldsmith, however, was the first dramatist of the century to question the validity of the coffee-house fiat which condemned humour as low and forbade its exemplification in the theatre. It was at Covent Garden in 1768 that he blew his trumpet-blast of defiance in the scene of the bailiffs in *The Good-Natur'd Man* (a comedy spoken of by Johnson, with the malice of a friend, as the best that had appeared since *The Provoked Husband*); and, though he had been compelled by the clamours of the sentimentalists to withdraw the scene, the challenge had served its purpose, and was reinforced by the restoration of the scene on publication of the play and by a preface in which the author expressed his fears that over-refinement would banish humour and character from the English stage, as it had banished them from the French. Had the fates only been propitious, that was a contingency his own genius was best calculated to avert. But it was not until 1773 that the first serious check was given to the steady encroachments of 'the mawkish drab of spurious breed' by the production of *She Stoops to Conquer.* Great moral courage was associated with that event, for Goldsmith and Colman,[1] the Covent Garden manager, both knew that they were rowing against the stream and were liable to be swamped. But full-blooded humour of a good old English quality carried the day. It was a triumph over many difficulties, for never since Shakespeare's day had an improbable story been made half so plausible.

Irishmen both, there were few points of contact between Goldsmith and Sheridan, but they were at one in their dislike of sentimentality. Much less firm in principle, Sheridan began by holding the candle to the devil. But he committed the grave mistake at the outset of halting between two opinions, and it is not unlikely that the temporary set-back he experienced on the first production of *The Rivals* was in part due to that cause. A play that combined a spice of

[1] Note the anecdote of Colman and Goldsmith on the first night of the play, related by Cooke and cited by Henry Saxe Wyndham, *The Annals of Covent Garden Theatre* (2 vols., 1906), vol. i, p. 193.

Congreve with a spice of Shadwell and coquetted with sentimentality was difficult to place. Circumstances alter cases. Where Gay had succeeded in *The Beggar's Opera*, Sheridan, because of the difference of genres, had failed. Polly Peachum is, as Mr. F. W. Bateson has pointed out, 'equally a real character of sentiment and a caricature of sentimentalism'.[1] Sheridan's Faulkland is a composite of much the same type, but the burlesque of lackadaisical introspectiveness is weakened by the juxtaposition of a time-serving sentimentality towards the end of the play. Sheridan was to achieve his purpose in *The School for Scandal* in a subtler and much more artistic way. After Foote's ineffectual bludgeoning of the sentimentalists in *Piety in Pattens*, he saw that nothing could get home save the deadliest of rapier play. His Joseph Surface is the irrefutable arraignment of the hollow insincerities of the sentimental school.

There was no weakening in the popularity of tragedy in our period, but its quality was visibly diminishing. This was apparent to all who had discerning eyes, because a standard of comparison was constantly afforded by the preservation on the acting list of the best work of Dryden, Otway, Lee, and Southerne. But, so potent and various were the forces operating against the creative spirit that the critics were powerless to stop the rot. Rousseau once said in effect that tragedy was a sadistic enjoyment, since its prime appeal lay in enabling us to see others suffer without suffering ourselves. But the time had now arrived when the sterner muse had lost the monopoly of that appeal. Sentimental comedy was poaching upon her preserves. It had the more telling pathos. The difference was between the woes of people in whom the spectator could take an interest and the woes of legendary characters whose ups and downs caused little stirring of the blood. There had been strange forewarning of this at the dawn of the century in the prologue to *The Fair Penitent*:

> Long has the fate of kings and empires been
> The common business of the tragic scene,
> As if misfortune made the throne her seat,
> And none could be unhappy, but the great.

Aware of the gulf that yawned, Lillo avoided it by re-creating the domestic tragedy of middle-class life, but,

[1] *English Comic Drama 1700–1750* (1929), p. 102.

despite the success of *George Barnwell,* his influence upon writers of tragedy in our period was surprisingly meagre. When *The Gamester* of Edward Moore was produced at Drury Lane in 1753, the critics, little recking that its vigorous prose would hold the stage for generations, complained of its low style and shocking catastrophe. Rather than emulate sound native examples, the age went a-whoring after strange gods. Pseudo-classical theory predominated; Voltaire's influence grew apace; poetical rhapsody was contemptuously ousted by intellectual precision. Great indeed must have been the acting that could give the semblance of life to the resulting frigidities. But it must at least be accounted unto Johnson for righteousness that, although he hearkened to French precepts in writing *Irene,* his was the subsequent pronouncement which gave its quietus to the Unity of Place.

Yet why, even in the circumstances, should pedestrianism have held undisputed sway? What evil star checked the emergence of the English Racine? These questions demand an answer. The canker lay in the rank dilettantism of the age. Deep down were the roots of that spirit, and custom had endowed it with privilege. Of all tories your old playhouse tory was the most uncompromising. In Caroline days, play-writing came to be looked upon by courtiers and university men as a gentlemanly pastime, but it was considered unbecoming and derogatory to take money from the players for the use of a play. Somehow, the fad of an hour developed into a convention and was instrumental in altering the whole trend of English dramaturgy. But for its persistence we should have had no Etherege, no Wycherley, and no Congreve. Yet, even in Restoration days, it was far from an unmixed blessing: a file of Ned Howards also marched. In Johnson's day, when mediocrity abounded, it was to prove a curse. Every gentleman with a smattering of taste and every scholar desired to figure as the author of at least one tragedy. Reynolds's Vapid echoed their sentiments: they believed that it was better to have even a damned play to one's credit than no play at all. Though divinity as a science is ill-calculated to shape the ends of the secular drama, divines were especially bitten by the mania. Home, Mason, Young, Hoadly, Brown, Townley, Delap, Bate Dudley, Francis, Francklin: all figure in the dramatic annals of the time.

The prime misfortune was that theatrical conditions in the Garrick era loaded the dice in favour of the aspiring amateur. The professional dramatist had no surety of foothold. His risks were great, and the possible rewards, particularly if much time had been expended over the work, seldom commensurate. Payment was purely by results, and, in those days of malice, intrigue, and caprice, the results were always problematical. The maximum reward that the dramatist could receive was the proceeds of three benefits, the third, sixth, and ninth nights of the run of his play, after the daily charges of the house had been deducted. At Drury Lane in 1757, the expenses were £90, but authors of new plays were charged no more on their benefit nights than 60 guineas. (Adaptors of old pieces had, however, to pay 80 guineas.) The managers demanded a guarantee against loss on the author's first benefit night, and those who were unable to make a deposit—the vast majority of writers by profession—were driven to the humiliating expedient of hawking about benefit tickets as soon as, and sometimes before, the play was produced. So common was the practice that benefit tickets came to be looked upon as an even greater nuisance than book subscriptions. Of the rebuffs received by the abased playwright, a graphic picture has been drawn by Fielding in *The Adventures of Joseph Andrews*, Bk. III, chap. iii. After all the labour of composition, the worry of attending rehearsals, the hawking of tickets, and the anxieties of the first night, the average professional dramatist was lucky if he made, say, £148 out of his play, precisely the sum gained by Aaron Hill from his three benefits when *Merope* was staged in 1749. The irony of the situation was that the well-to-do amateur was not only immune from the initial humiliations experienced by the professional, but, more often than not, received the greater recompense. While Johnson for his *Irene* got, in all (including the £100 paid for the copyright by Dodsley), but some £295 odd, Young, for his tragedy of *The Brothers* in 1752, received from his benefits alone £400, and magnanimously gave the sum (and more) to the Society for the Propagation of the Gospel.[1] Yet the merits of the two plays were about on a par.

There was good precedent for this ostentatious denial of the labourer's hire—not to speak of much earlier instances,

[1] Arthur Murphy, *Life of David Garrick* (1801), chap. xx.

Vanbrugh and Addison had done it—but practices of the sort suggested an invidious distinction which the author striving to live by his pen naturally resented. When the wealthy amateur responsible for the tragedy of *Zobeide* produced at Drury Lane in 1771 handed over his profits to Mrs. Yates the actress, Kenrick was moved to interject a bitter aside into a scurrilous satire on Garrick:

> Tho' modest Craddock scorns to sell his play,
> But gives the good-for-nothing thing away.[1]

In yielding to the pressure from high quarters on behalf of some importunate amateur or other, Garrick, as actor-manager of the leading theatre, laid up for himself a store of trouble. Few of the dilettanti had any sense of the theatre, and most of them who turned their attention to tragedy wrote academic exercises rather than plays. Often, it was a labour of Hercules to lick the amorphous mass into shape; and Garrick was the unacknowledged (and frequently resented) collaborator in half a hundred pieces. Use became with him so much a second nature that he could not find it in his heart to leave a classic untampered with, and, in the revision of new plays, an extraordinary metamorphosis now and again took place. When, in 1774, Burgoyne wrote *The Maid of the Oaks*, to exploit an unrevealed facet of Mrs. Abington's genius, it took the form of a pleasant little after-piece in two acts. But, by dint of padding it with extraneous entertainment, Garrick spun it out into five, thus evolving a new type of topical musical comedy whose spectacular features caused it to be acted twenty-five times. In nothing was the influence of the middle-class playgoer better shown than in theatre-pieces of this order. The characteristics of a play of that type were lambently set forth once by the Leviathan, when speaking of *High Life Below Stairs*. 'Here', he said, 'is a farce which is really very diverting, when you see it acted; and yet one may read it, and not know that one has been reading anything at all.'

But where the faults were in both warp and woof, not even the keen intelligence of a Garrick could transform a bad play into a good one. In tragedy, the fundamental weakness of our whole period was pithily characterized in 1752 by

[1] 'Love in the Suds; a town Eclogue, being the lament of Roscius for his Nyky' (1772).

Bonnell Thornton, when he complained of the French-cold correctness of our writers, with whom 'the tinsel pomp of declamation takes the place of passion and nature'. Six years later, a Drury Lane prologue (nothing less!) embroidered upon that stricture with:

> Modern tragedy, by rule exact,
> Spins out a thin-wrought fable, act by act.
> Prim and trim, and delicate and chaste,
> A hash from Greece and France, came modern taste.
> Cold are her sons, and so afraid of dealing
> In rant and fustian, they ne'er rise to feeling.

French influence proved most baneful in the predilection shown for long declamatory speeches in season and out. Apart from the resulting tedium, this often led to many absurdities. Fine poet as he undoubtedly was, Thomson had no sense of stage effect. In his *Tancred and Sigismunda*, the ill-fated heroine had to deliver four long speeches after she had received her death-wound. Mrs. Cibber greatly shone in this character, but the wonder is, with the many obstacles thrown in their way, that the players were able to carry the tragedy into safe harbourage. The essence of good acting is good listening, a difficult art when speeches run to excessive length. Thomson's lovers exchanged confidences alternately in speeches running to thirty or forty lines, imposing on each other, as Murphy pointed out, 'the task of listening in a mute attitude, much longer than consists with the ardour of a mutual passion'.[1] One result was, in such situations, that the player was apt to drop his role on becoming silent, and to gaze anywhere save at the speaker. What should have been a representation became a reading.

Apart from the influence brought to bear upon him, the secret of Garrick's fostering of the incompetent is revealed by Mason in his memoirs. We are told that Roscius, when at the height of his powers as actor-manager, refused to entertain any tragedy which did not enable him to display 'the expression of strong but sudden effects of passion; for, conscious of his peculiar strength, he was rather pleased to elevate, by his own theatrical powers, feeble diction and sentiment, than to express that in which the poet might be naturally supposed to have a share in the applause'.

In his *Case of Authors by Profession or Trade* written in

[1] *Life of David Garrick*, chap. ix.

1758, Ralph very properly complained that no other writer was hedged in by so many difficulties as the dramatist. So capricious and tyrannical were the managers of the two winter theatres that Goldsmith was driven to moot an impracticable project of a third house solely for the production of new plays. Worst of all, the best of authors had no surety of any return whatsoever for his work. Prejudice might be entertained against him on a side issue. Few new plays were judged solely on their merits. At Drury Lane in 1770, Kelly's capable comedy, *A Word to the Wise,* was damned after a sustained battle royal lasting over two nights by a cabal headed by Wilkes, purely for the reason that he had supported the Government with his pen.[1] Not that there was always as much as the shadow of a reason for the bludgeoning of a play. Bands of author-baiters existed, and the unhappy playwright who was powerless to raise a formidable party of playgoers in his support was wholly at their mercy. All the malcontents had to do, after unnerving the players by adroitly administered disapproval, was to prevent the announcement from the stage of the repetition of the play. Even if this were done on the second night, the destruction was complete: the author received no benefit. Not a penny accrued to him: the copyright of a damned play was valueless.

All sorts and conditions of people participated in these playhouse struggles. In 1758, Johnson repaired to Covent Garden on the first night of *Cleone* to lend a helping hand to Dodsley, but found, to his agreeable surprise, that the excellent acting of the company had quickly hypnotized the audience and nipped all opposition in the bud. Usually, however, the hunters were not to be baulked of their quarry, not even through any respect of persons. Not even the presence of the King and several members of the royal family prevented them from (as it happened, righteously) slaughtering Franklin's comedy, *The Contract,* when produced at the Haymarket in 1776. Now and again, there were extraordinary slips between the cup and the lip. In 1773, when Kenrick's *The Duellist* was brought out at Covent Garden, there was a very full first night's muster, but the author's friends, having borne out his cause to a successful issue and heard the play given out for a second time, were foolish enough to leave the house before the curtain rose

[1] Joseph Knight, *David Garrick* (1894), p. 254.

on the afterpiece. The consequence was that a faction in the gallery took advantage of their departure to insist upon the revocation of the announcement and the giving out of another play before they would allow the afterpiece to proceed.

There is prime significance in the fact that the afterpiece, as a convention, dated only from the second decade of the eighteenth century. Its establishment and development formed the main outcome of the happy return of the middle classes to the theatre. A second price at the close of the third act of the play had been regularly taken from post-Restoration days, and, while inclination counted for much, it was this practice that proved the deciding factor in inducing the masses to come back to their old love. For some years before, and during the Garrick period, it was customary for the doors to open at five and the curtain to rise at six: a long wait to those who went early to obtain good seats, though the tedium was to some extent dissipated by the three selections played at intervals by the orchestra, otherwise known as First, Second, and Third Music. Early resort of this order was seldom convenient for the middle classes, and it became obvious that if the solid support of the masses was to be maintained, something more substantial than the fag-end of a tragedy followed by a trivial farce must be proffered. This led to a remarkable development of the afterpiece. The second price public was regaled with a constant variety of entertainment, from petit comedy to ballad opera and pantomime. While the classes were giving their support to the rules, the masses were helping to break them down. Serious inroads began to be made for the first time on the Horatian five-act form. As afterpieces, delightful little comedies in two acts, such as Murphy's *Three Weeks after Marriage* and Macklin's *Love à la Mode*, won much popularity; but, because of their form, the critics excluded them from the category of comedy and insisted on their being called farces.

Throughout our period, the public at large evinced no great liking for unmixed music drama. Recitative, save in mock opera, it could not abide. Apart from the *cognoscenti*, taste extended no farther than to musical comedy. Arne's *Artaxerxes*, produced at Covent Garden in 1762, was the only 'grand' or serious opera to meet with full acceptance and

The Last Time of the Company's performing this Season.

At the Theatre Royal in Drury-Lane,

This present MONDAY, June 10, 1776,

The WONDER.

Don Felix by Mr. GARRICK,
Col. Briton by Mr. SMITH,
Don Lopez by Mr BADDELEY,
Don Pedro by Mr. PARSONS,
Lissardo by Mr. KING,
Frederick by Mr. PACKER,
Gibby by Mr. MOODY,
Isabella by Miss HOPKINS,
Flora by Mrs. WRIGHTEN,
Inis by Mrs. BRADSHAW,
Violante by Mrs. YATES.

End of Act I. The Grand GARLAND DANCE,
By Signor GIORGI, Mrs. SUTTON,
And Mr. SLINGSBY.

To which will be added a Musical Entertainment, call'd

The WATERMAN.

The PRINCIPAL CHARACTERS by
Mr. BANNISTER,
Mr. DAVIES,
And Mr. DODD.
Mrs. WRIGHTEN,
And Mrs. JEWELL.

To conclude with the Grand Scene of The REGATTA.

Ladies are desired to send their Servants a little after 5 to keep Places, to prevent Confusion.

The Doors will be opened at HALF after FIVE o'Clock.

To begin at HALF after SIX o'Clock. Vivant Rex & Regina.

The Profits of this Night being appropriated to the Benefit of The Theatrical Fund, the Usual Address upon that Occasion Will be spoken by Mr. GARRICK, before the Play.

gain lasting vogue. In the lesser realms, however, there was remarkable progress. By the end of our period, simple ballad opera had insensibly developed into full-blown comic opera. The distinction between the two was that whereas ballad opera was designed for the normal, musically-uneducated player with a passable singing voice, comic opera demanded the specially trained singer with some slight histrionic capabilities. In keeping with the English spirit of compromise, the transition from ballad opera, with its homely, sporadic airs and lack of musical structure, to comic opera, with its partial adoption of Italian form, was nicely graduated. This was due to the fact that, marked as was the tendency to ape or borrow Italian melody, the ballad opera system of adapting old English tunes, side by side with new compositions of the same type, persisted.

In 1761, a great impetus was given to musical progress by the accession to power at Covent Garden of Beard, the tenor singer, Rich's son-in-law. In the following year came the first comic opera, Bickerstaffe's *Love in a Village*, which, although nothing better from either a dramatic or a musical standpoint than a neat pastiche, won abiding popularity. Though the impress of Arne predominated, eighteen of the airs being his, all sorts of composers fell into the drag-net, from Handel, Galuppi, and Geminiani to Boyce, Howard, and Weldon. Bickerstaffe's aim is indicated in his dedication in his claim 'that the music is more pleasing than has hitherto appeared in compositions of this kind; and the words better adapted, considering the nature of the airs, which are not common ballads, than could be expected, supposing any degree of poetry to be preserved in the versification'. Progress in the achievement of greater uniformity was soon made, yet not without subsequent retrogression. For Bickerstaffe's *The Padlock* in 1768, Dibdin supplied an original score, which, though duly appreciated, was evidently considered a work of supererogation. In 1775, *The Duenna* of Sheridan could win an unprecedented success despite the fact that some of its music was stale. That England had now become a highly moral nation (while at the play) is shown by the fact that when *The Beggar's Opera* was revived at Covent Garden in 1777, retribution came at last to Captain Macheath, and, to the satisfaction of all, he was sent for three years to the hulks.

Little by little, the boundaries of the musical drama were extended. With the production at Covent Garden in 1764 (following its success in Dublin) of Kane O'Hara's *Midas*, there swam into play-lovers' ken a new genre, nothing less than an indigenous type of *burletta*, not so much reminiscent of its exotic prototype as of ballad opera. This was mythological operatic burlesque, and, as such, wholly sung. The airs were set to old ballad music, and the recitative on which they were strung was written in rhymed couplets. Later examples of this highly amusing genre were *The Golden Pippin* and *Tom Thumb*.

Still more composite and vastly more popular with all grades of playgoers was the pantomime. As established by the eccentric John Rich, himself the finest Harlequin of his century, this seductive entertainment was an extraordinary amalgam of disparates. Grand opera, mythological masque, elaborate mechanical spectacle, all had a place in its make-up, but the basic and most attractive element was the comic dumb show sustained by a narrow selection of *commedia dell'arte* types, in which Harlequin's magic bat figured at critical junctures as the modern equivalent of the god from the car. Always seasonable, though never of any particular season, as now, entertainments of this order were revived again and again, like any popular play. Apart from their operatic preludes, they were strictly things of dumb show during the first half-century of their course and justified the name by which they were called. It was not until almost a score of years after Rich's death that the anomaly of a speaking pantomime was known. The first of the kind, Dibdin's *The Touchstone, or Harlequin Traveller*, produced at Covent Garden in 1779, exploited a fantastic idea afterwards developed with advantage by Gilbert in *The Palace of Truth*. But the most brilliant of early 'dialogue pantomimes', as they were called, was Colman's *The Genius of Nonsense*, brought out at the Haymarket in 1780, and neatly characterized by the town as 'the nonsense of genius'. In it was clever incidental satire of Dr. Graham's *Temple of Health and Celestial Bed*, with Bannister as the counterfeit presentment of the king of quacks.[1] But the speaking pantomime had not come to stay. After 1786, there was a reversion to type.

[1] See *The Reminiscences of Henry Angelo* (1830), pp. 127–8.

The ever-increasing prominence of the musical play led in time to a salutary change in the methods of remunerating the author. This was due to the fact that composers were averse to payment by results and demanded hard cash. As recompense for his *burletta, Poor Vulcan,* Dibdin was given, in 1778, a single benefit at Covent Garden, which brought him about £95; but, afterwards, when he provided both the book and music of a new afterpiece, a less hazardous system of remuneration was adopted. For his two one-act pieces, *Rose and Colin* and *The Wives Revenged,* both produced on the one night, he was paid £140. But for a time managers halted between two opinions, and it was a matter of personal bargaining. Thus, for his highly successful satirical play, *The Mirror, or Harlequin Every-where,* of which again he was both author and composer, Dibdin, in 1779, was given a sixth part of the first six nights' receipts, amounting to no more than £130. But, henceforward, dramatists by profession who associated themselves with the fortunes of any particular house were generally paid by lump sum. In his dealings with John O'Keeffe, Harris, the astute manager of Covent Garden, bought not only the acting rights of the play (slender and unsatisfactory as they then were) but, to prevent publication, the copyright.

Prologues and epilogues were still maintaining their old popularity. The former were mostly *à propos des bottes,* and so little apposite that any prologue would have done for any play. According to Fielding, there were but three topics, abuse of the town, condemnation of all contemporary authors, and the extraordinarily high merits of the play about to be represented. But there was sound appreciation for good work, as is shown by the fact that Johnson's memorable prologue for the opening of Drury Lane under Lacy and Garrick's management in 1747 was often called for during the season. Garrick himself was an excellent prologue-writer, and some of his addresses evoked a similar compliment. As to the epilogue, ever since Physibulus in *The Spectator* had complained of 'the unnatural tack of the Comick Tail to the Tragick Head', repeated objection had been made to the conventional derision of the moral and pathos of tragedy. Many others made a stand. In 1753, Glover, in the epilogue to his *Boadicea,* refused to mitigate the severities, and rebuked the taste which demanded the effacing by 'Fancy's wanton hand' of compassion's tribute to the maze of sorrow. Similar protests were made in the epilogues to Home's *Douglas* in 1757 and Murphy's *Alzuma* in 1773. But the convention still persisted, and in its worst form. Nothing, surely, could have been more disillusioning than for an actress, who as the ill-fated heroine had committed suicide or been killed in the last act, to come on again at the finish and deliver an address jeering at the emotions she had striven so hard to evoke. A stale old device this, going back to the days of Nell Gwyn; yet we find it being resorted to in the epilogue to Dodsley's *Cleone* in 1758, and, exactly twenty years later, in the epilogue to Cumberland's *The Battle of Hastings*. Not all old conventions were quite so obstinate. At the beginning of the century all plays, even those in prose, had rhymed tags at the end of scenes and acts. The object of this artificial expedient was to enable the concluding speaker to make a neat exit. Progress towards naturalism, however, had so far advanced in our period, despite manifold drawbacks, that by 1770 all the tags had disappeared save the one at the end, generally addressed to the audience.

By the Licensing Act of 1737, theatrical regulation had been placed under Crown control, with the Lord Chamberlain as dictator. Playhouses were then strictly limited in number, and could be established only under royal letters patent. Apart from the King's Theatre in the Haymarket, otherwise the Italian Opera, there were, in our period, but two winter theatres of moderate size, Drury Lane and Covent Garden, and a smaller one in the Haymarket. But, if the Crown had its measure of control, so too the people had theirs: apparently it was the more potent of the two. At a trial following upon a riot in the Haymarket in 1738 over a visit from some French players, it was laid down magisterially 'that the public had a legal right to manifest their dislike to any play or actor; and that the judicature of the pit had been acquiesced in, time immemorial'.[1] That pronouncement became the playgoer's Magna Carta. He grew extremely sensitive concerning his rights, so much so, that any infringement of them was apt to arouse his latent but illimitable capacity for riot. Symbolic of its turbulent era was the row of iron

[1] Benjamin Victor, *History of the Theatres of London and Dublin* (1761), vol. i, pp. 55–6.

spikes which ran along the front of the stage of Drury Lane and Covent Garden in the mid-eighteenth century. It was needed. There were riots at Drury Lane in 1744 over Fleetwood's capricious advance of prices, and again both there and in Covent Garden in 1763, because an attempt had been made to abolish the custom of second price after the third act. Possibly, the most serious disturbance of all occurred at Drury Lane in 1755 on the sixth night of prolonged rioting over the appearance of a few French dancers in Noverre's ballet, *The Chinese Festival*, at a time when England was drifting into a war with France. On this occasion, the people of rank and fashion in the boxes supported Garrick, much to the incensement of pit and gallery. A free fight ensued. Gallants jumped down from the boxes into the pit, swords were drawn amid the screams of women, and blood was shed. Oddly enough, while Garrick was hesitating about his course, the Montagues and Capulets of the arena suddenly united forces, and proceeded to tear up the benches and demolish the scenery. To repair the damage cost £4,000.

In order that grievances might have expression and that excesses might be avoided, a spokesman for the public was appointed in or about 1744, and regularly attended the pit on all important occasions. He was known as 'Mr. Town', and the office was held for long by a Mr. Chitty. In 1753, when *Gil Blas* was produced at Drury Lane, the play was badly cast and indifferently acted, with the result that there were many sounds of disapproval on the second night. For a time it looked as if Edward Moore, the author, would be denied his benefit and so receive no recompense, but 'Mr. Town' very considerately begged the audience to allow the play to be given out for the next night, thus preventing disaster.

Playhouse accommodation was primitive. All the seats were backless benches and none were bookable. (One could secure a whole box in advance, but not a particular seat in that box.) Ladies had to send their footmen betimes to the theatre to take bodily possession of desirable seats and occupy them until they arrived. Queues being as yet undreamed of, crowds of a serious magnitude were to be seen struggling round the doors on important occasions at an early hour, much to the ruffling of the well-dressed. When Foote's *Piety in Pattens* was produced at the Haymarket in

THE PIT ENTRANCE, 1784

1773, enough people assembled in front of the house considerably before the opening hour to fill the little theatre three times over. Such was the pressure that women fainted, hats, swords, and cloaks were lost, and one girl had her arm broken. Finally, the doors were burst in, and many gained free ingress. Then, after all, the play greatly disappointed expectations, and the infuriated audience, by way of gaining compensation for the discomforts it had experienced, tore down the panels of the orchestra well and destroyed many of the pit benches.

Newspaper puffery of every possible kind was advanced to a fine art long before organized dramatic criticism secured a foothold. In its eagerness for revenue, the daily press allowed its privileges to be abused. It is significant that the Covent Garden account books, now in the British Museum, record a payment of six shillings on November 8, 1766, for a puff preliminary of the coming revival of the famous old pantomime of *Doctor Faustus*. Throughout our period, the theatrical press agent was a much more potent personage than the regular dramatic critic. That his office was well established by 1764 we have proof of in Puff's abuse of Dactyl in Foote's *The Patron*. Horace Walpole discounted newspaper praise of Garrick on the score that most of it came from his own pen. An anonymous pamphlet addressed to Roscius in 1772 accuses him of controlling the policy, by purchase, of half a dozen papers, practically all of any consequence. Not content with that, he sought to gain support for new productions by sending puffers to the various coffee-houses and court end of the town. Rational dramatic criticism first began in the monthly magazines at the beginning of the latter half of the century, and, though in a few years the daily press fell in line, it was in the magazines that the soundest judgement continued to find expression. Regular notices of new productions and important revivals, with keen appreciations of the acting, appeared in *The Universal Museum* in 1762. Especially remarkable is the excellence of the reviewing in *The London Magazine*. Only to-day, when the events of that time assume their proper perspective and can be viewed dispassionately, is it possible to savour the acumen and honest good sense with which, in January 1768 and May 1777, the merits of *The Good-Natur'd Man* and *The School for Scandal* were discussed in its pages.

It is more than passing strange that criticism of this high and helpful order should have been resented in professional circles. Colman, in the preface to *Polly Honeycomb*, poured contempt on the magazine reviewers, styling them 'the self-impanelled jury of the English court of criticism'. Newspaper criticism, when it came—and it was in pretty full force by 1768, when *The Public Advertiser* was looked upon as the theatrical gazette of the time—met with similar objurgation. Little short of amazing is the tone of Cumberland's rejoinder in 1775, when, replying to the accusations of plagiarism from Shadwell in his comedy, *The Choleric Man*, he moaned out in the preface to his play:

> When any play, like this now submitted to the public, meets with a favourable reception on its first appearance—the very next morning by break of day out comes your manifesto; unravels the whole plot and contrivance of the drama, dissects the characters, detects the plagiarisms, and kindly tells the town what it is to expect; and all this is the dark operation of one midnight hour; while the poor romantic author lies wrapt perhaps in golden dreams of happiness and success.

The mills of the gods grind slowly, but criticism was avenged for all time by the masterly portrait of Sir Fretful Plagiary.

It is customary to speak of our period as, pre-eminently, the era of great acting, but no historian who seeks to arrive at an individual opinion strictly on the evidence can accept that verdict without some qualification. Otherwise, a wholly erroneous idea is conveyed. It is true that no other half-century in the annals of the English stage presents such a constellation of histrionic genius. What names in any period of like duration can be compared with those of Garrick, Quin, Spranger Barry, Mossop, Woodward, Henderson, King, Kemble, Mrs. Cibber, Mrs. Pritchard, Kitty Clive, Peg Woffington, Mrs. Barry, Mrs. Abington, and Miss Farren? But simply to enumerate the famous—weighty as is the list—is to convey a false impression. The era was largely one of the soloist and duettist. Within living memory, star-acting has shown that while crowds may be drawn to see one or two characters in a classic brilliantly acted, the play itself has been rudely marred by the incompetence of the rank and file. Though not precisely a common experience, more to be observed earlier than later and oftener in tragedy than comedy, that was the weakness of eighteenth-century acting: a palpable lack of team work. The general defects of the time are best to be seen in the curious praise given to some of the great players. Murphy characterizes Mrs. Pritchard's acting as Mrs. Beverley in *The Gamester* as 'a specimen of the most natural acting that had ever been seen —she did not appear to be conscious of an audience before her—she seemed to be walking about in her own parlour in the deepest distress and overwhelmed with misery'. To-day that simple virtue is the A, B, C of the player's art and passes unobserved, but Mrs. Siddons, at a later period, was lauded for possessing it.

The truth is that, although Congreve, so far back as 1696, had formulated the law of the invisible fourth wall, that law had received no recognition, was to receive none until Leigh Hunt reinforced it. Acting was as much a thing of rhetoric as of representation. Many of the players were in the habit of dropping their characters when they ceased speaking, looking idly about the house, and only coming again into the picture on hearing their cues. The common practice in soliloquizing was for the actor to approach the pit and make the house a confidant of his thoughts. Henderson, first of metaphysical tragedians, was remarkable for his avoidance of this fault. Even Kitty Clive, fine comedian as she was, was not immune from vicious habits. Davies tells us that

> Mr. Garrick complained that she disconcerted him by not looking at him in the time of action, and neglected to watch the motion of his eye; a practice he was sure to observe in others. I am afraid this accusation was partly true, for Mrs. Clive would suffer her eyes sometimes to wander from the stage into the boxes in search of her great acquaintance, and now and then give them a comedy nod or curtsy.

If we are to believe Aaron Hill, most actresses of the time shirked all outward manifestation of deep sorrow lest they should distort their pretty features, and none would disfigure their features with make-up when the exigencies demanded it. To the latter charge, Peg Woffington alone was to prove the exception. What astonishes most of all is to find that even Garrick was not without his Achilles' heel. Davies points out that, after his prolonged tour abroad ending in 1765, Roscius had so far gained by his observation of Continental stage methods 'that he did not now appear so solicitous for applause as to disturb his own feelings and lessen the pleasure of his audience; that he entirely dropt that anxious exertion at the close of a speech, both in look and behaviour, which is called by the comedians a clap-trap. That there was certainly an alteration as well as an improvement in his style of acting, was noticed by the spectators in general'.

Though Garrick founded no school, his influence was none the less beneficial. If he had not Barry's gift of exquisite pathos, his acting was not marred by that excessive sensibility which was the only defect of Barry's quality. He was always as much master of himself as of his audience. Lacking powers of declamation, his excellence lay in his command of the entire gamut of the passions, in his unexampled range of characterization, and, above all, in his attainment of the art which conceals art. In his naturalness of style, he gave the players a salutary object lesson of which the more discerning were not slow to avail themselves. Less artificiality meant less playing for one's own hand and better team work. No plays had ever finer all-round acting than *The Clandestine Marriage, The School for Scandal,* and *The Belle's Stratagem* when first presented. The misfortune was that much of Garrick's good work was undone by the reactionary principles of his successors. Under his rule, the old monotony in tragic representation had been dissipated by variation of pace, with accelerated delivery in moments of passion; but, with the coming of Kemble and Mrs. Siddons, there was such a slowing down that the old performers who happened to be associated with them were so far deceived by their over-deliberate delivery and long pauses as to imagine they had forgotten their parts, and went the length of prompting them.

Johnson, who was typical of his time in having a profound contempt for players in the mass, admitted that Garrick had advanced the dignity of his art, and left the stage more respected than he found it. Perhaps in this he was simply drawing an inference from the fact that his old friend, being 'the first man in the world for sprightly conversation', had been received with open arms by Society rather than asserting a general amelioration, but, whatever the circumstances, the actual advance, judging by the light of after-history, was trifling. Genius apart, the player had a long row to hoe before he gained social enfranchisement. The

PEG WOFFINGTON

From the painting by J. G. Eccardt

attitude towards his class assumed by the mid-eighteenth-century audience was unworthy of so polite an age. Often, an actor who had given some offence was compelled to go down on his knees and crave pardon before a full house ere he could be allowed to resume his vocation. Even Garrick on occasion was scurvily treated. There was no consideration for the female sex: audiences thought nothing of receiving an actress of Peg Woffington's prominence with a shower of orange peel, if they conceived she had been in any way neglectful of her duty to the public.

One reason why few players could then call their souls their own was that all save the most illustrious were dependent on the bounty of the public for a portion of their livelihood. The principle of the annual benefit, which had sprung into being at the beginning of the century with the aim of eking out meagre stipends, brought with it many degradations, not the least of which was the keeping of the minor players in hopeless serfdom. Concerning the prevailing economic system, William Cooke, writing in 1775 in *The Elements of Dramatic Criticism,* complained that it compelled the rank and file to pay more attention to the making of good benefits than to the study of their art. Intimacy with a wide circle of playgoers became indispensable, and the consequent dissipation and expense opened the door to many bad habits. Success depended more on being a *bon vivant* than on sound and conscientious acting.

The age was ripe for scenic reform, calling for it, but nothing material could be effected so long as the stage was burdened with its Old Man of the Sea. Symptomatic of that calling and indicative of that incubus was a reflection indulged in by the anonymous author of *The Actor* in 1755:

> One thing more there is that hurts the truth of the representation more than all, the suffering a part of the audience to be behind the scenes. The keeping up of the illusion of carrying on an appearance of reality is the great merit of theatrical representation, but that is impossible under this disadvantage. Let the decorations of the house, the dress and deportment and recitation of the players be ever so proper, this destroys all. The head of some cropped beau among a set of full-bottomed conspirators destroys all the look of reality.

Here is censured a baneful custom in vogue since post-Restoration days, a custom which, because of the disturbances it gave rise to, had necessitated the constant placing of an armed guard on either side of the proscenium. Convinced of its noxiousness, Garrick, at the beginning of his co-management of Drury Lane in 1747, had decided to abolish it, and had advertised in his bills that admission behind the scenes would be no longer permitted. Characteristically enough, he failed to grasp his nettle. Opposition, strange to say, came from within as well as from without. The players persisted in their old practice of building up amphitheatres on the stage on benefit nights for the accommodation of their better-class patrons, and it was not until about 1764 that complete reform in this respect was effected.

Then began an era of richer scenic illusion. Progress, however, came in but slow increments, since only half-measures could be taken. The conventional arrangement of the stage with its solid proscenium doors, its curtained balconies and projecting apron—obstructive heritages from the Restoration theatre—perpetually called a halt to the reformer. In one respect, it had a utility that for long precluded any possibility of a drastic change. Without its proscenium balconies, it would have been impossible to stage the many engaging balcony and window scenes occurring in the old comedy of intrigue, save by resorting to built-up backgrounds of so cumbrous an order that they would have seriously delayed the progress of the play. On the other hand, it was found that the prevailing scenic system of simple flats and wings, so grateful because of its expeditiousness, was wofully inadequate to give the illusion of domestic interiors. Furniture could give little aid because it had to be reduced to a minimum: the most luxurious apartment seldom had more than a table and a couple of chairs. This was due to the fact that all changes had to be made in full sight of the audience. The old practice had been to keep the curtain up from the beginning to the end, and there was no possibility of an improvement until 1750 or thereabouts, when the system of dropping the curtain between the acts first began. To vary the monotony of the unillusive rows of wings, set-pieces were occasionally placed at the sides representing the fronts of houses (as in *All in the Wrong* at Drury Lane in 1761) or the walls of interiors. Then doors came to be provided in the back scenes, and entrances and exits ceased to be wholly made through the permanent proscenium doors, though these still continued to be employed. In

SCENE FROM 'THE DUENNA', 1775, showing the PROSCENIUM DOOR AND STAGE BOX

DESIGN FOR THE AUDITORIUM OF DRURY LANE, 1775

By ROBERT ADAM

Bickerstaffe's comic opera, *Love in the City*, at Covent Garden in 1767, there was an interior scene in which steps led up to a folding glass door opening on a back parlour. Greater attention was now being paid to accessories. At Drury Lane in 1760, in *The Way to Keep Him*, the scene of the Widow Bellmour's apartment in the third act was provided with a toilette table, a bookcase, a harpsichord, and several chairs.

One important alteration, due to Garrick's tour of the foreign theatres and made shortly after his return in 1765, revolutionized the whole scheme of stage lighting. He removed the half-dozen view-obstructing chandeliers which had long hung in front of the stage, substituting for them a number of unseen wing-lights. The very perceptible footlights were allowed to remain. One result was that the scenery, hitherto a dim and distant background, grew to be an environment of the action. Another was that some slight graduation in lighting could at last be effected during the traffic of the scene. Not much, of course, seeing that with candles and oil-lamps as the only media, unified control was impossible. Yet, despite the serious drawbacks, the latter end of our period witnessed the genesis of atmospheric effect. Of the progress made by 1782, we have an indication in a stage direction on Mrs. Brooke's Covent Garden operetta, *Rosina*:

> In the first act, the sky clears by degrees, the morning vapour disperses, the sun rises, and at the end of the act is above the horizon: at the beginning of the second he is past the height, and declines till the end of the day. This progressive motion should be made imperceptibly, but its effect should be visible through the two acts.

Much of the improvement in atmospheric effect was due to the innovating genius of Phillippe Jacques de Loutherbourg, the noted German battle painter. Loutherbourg came to England, in 1771, as Garrick's scene designer and scenic director, and very quickly made his influence felt. Spectacle reared its head, but was kept strictly in its place. Tragedy and comedy were for the most part soberly mounted, little but stock scenery being provided for either, but at Christmas and Easter, special theatre pieces were brought out with profuse and overshadowing embellishment. In Garrick's *The Christmas Tale*, in 1773, Loutherbourg astonished the town by suddenly transforming a summer landscape into an autumn one, a piece of hocus-pocus brought about by filtering light through movable silk screens of various colours. But his lasting influence on English stage mounting was in giving greater variety and a new picturesqueness to the plantation of the scene by the use of ground rows and raking pieces: devices which served the grateful purpose of giving a moderate-sized stage much greater apparent depth. One of his best arrangements of this order was seen at Drury Lane in 1777 in the opening scene of Dibdin's comic opera, *The Quaker*, where Lubin appeared at the back of an irregular hill and slowly advanced to the front, sometimes perceptible and sometimes concealed by the shrubbery.

Throughout the greater part of our period the dressing of plays was a haphazard business. It is much to be doubted indeed if, in matters of appropriateness of attire, any particular advance had been made on the methods which obtained in the Elizabethan age. Even when any glimmering of a rule is to be perceived, the rule does not appear to have had any rational basis. Thus, while certain characters in Shakespeare's historical plays, such as Falstaff, Richard III, and Henry VIII, were always given their correct attire by convention, all their associates appeared in mid-eighteenth-century dress. Judging by the evidence afforded by the quaint illustrations in Rowe's *Shakespeare*, there is good reason to believe that, these exceptions apart, the principle of playing Elizabethan drama in the dress of the hour in which it was being represented had been followed from Burbage's day to Henderson's. In this respect, Macklin was the first to make serious innovation. When, in the ripeness of his years, he appeared as Macbeth at Covent Garden in October 1773, he dressed the character in Scots habit, and all the supporting players were garbed in similar attire. As acted by Garrick and Barry, the Thane of Cawdor had all the trappings of an Hanoverian officer. When Garrick captured the town as King Lear in 1761, it was as a beardless monarch he was shown, with a white wig, a short robe of velvet trimmed with ermine, white silk hose, lace ruffles, high-heeled shoes and diamond buckles. His Romeo and his Benedick might have stepped on the stage straight from Ranelagh. Quin and Barry had played Othello in military uniform, but Garrick was sensible enough to follow Foote's example in dressing the character in Moorish attire. Such,

SPRANGER BARRY AND MISS NOSSITER IN THE BALCONY SCENE OF *ROMEO AND JULIET*

From an engraving in the J. R. Bath collection

however, was the habituation of the town to conventional absurdities that he received nothing but ridicule for his pains. There was no standard of judgement. His arraying of Hotspur in a laced frock and a Ramillies wig was carped at by the critics, not because of the inappropriateness of the costume, but on the score that it was 'too insignificant for the character'. Possibly, these experiences were at the back of his mind when, in response to Benjamin West's urgings for a wholesale reform in matters of dressing, he replied that if he attempted it he would be assailed by a shower of missiles from the gallery. But the real secret of his *non possumus* attitude, considerable as had been his ponderings over the question, was that he had arrived at the conclusion that the public was well satisfied with things as they were, and that he dreaded fostering a taste that might prove in the end to be both exacting and expensive.

In these old days, when players sought more for showiness of attire than propriety—when Cato and Caesar were adorned with fine flowing full-bottomed wigs and the maid was dressed as sumptuously as the mistress—the curse of the theatre was its stock wardrobe, wherein all might rummage. Yet, as long as the repertory system ruled, the stock wardrobe remained inevitable. New plays might bring new dresses, but new dresses became old stock, to be indiscriminately used. There was lavishness enough, if there had only been a prevailing sense of fitness. In a pamphlet addressed to Garrick in 1747 it is complained that

> there was a time when the best Actors contented themselves with a new suit at each new Play, and then too thought they were very fine in Tinsel Lace and Spangles; but some of our present heroes must not only have a new habit for every new part, but several habits for the same part, if the play continues to be acted for any number of nights: I have taken Notice of one in particular, who is rarely seen twice in one Garb.

Players have always been more prone to follow the line of least resistance than any other class of purposeful people. It was largely due to the temptations of the stock wardrobe that period dressing of revivals became an impossibility. Even as late as 1767, it was not unusual to see the various members of the same family arrayed in the attire of half a dozen different countries. The women were as indifferent about the proprieties as the men. Whatever the role, give the tragedy queen a heavily-embroidered robe, a coiffure of lace and feathers, and a page to dangle after her carrying her court train, and she was happy. It is true that Miss Bellamy, when she first gave life to Dodsley's *Cleone* in 1758, had the courage to discard the hooped petticoat, but no one followed her example. The heroines of ancient Greece had to await the second advent of Mrs. Siddons before they received their proper garb.

Reform in costuming was perpetually being mooted, but there was a diversity of opinion as to what should be done. A critic, writing in 1759, pleaded for some degree of accuracy in historical plays, but he was not so particular about the treatment of old comedy. He thought that a Restoration comedy should not have Restoration dressing, that the characters should be garbed in the fashion of the hour of its revival. The curious thing was that no one until near the close of our period saw that the dimly recognized claims of appropriate costuming involved also the wholly unrecognized claims of appropriate scenery. The first to perceive that scenic architecture and period costuming were interdependent was George Steevens, the Shakespearian scholar. Writing anonymously in 1782, as one of the contributors to the *Biographia Dramatica*,[1] Steevens, in the account given of Home's tragedy, *The Fatal Discovery*, a Drury Lane production of 1769, begins by exercising his powers of sarcasm on the acting of its athletic young hero by the gouty Barry and on the inappropriateness of its scenery and costume. He then goes on to say: 'These circumstances sufficiently prove that a manager ought to be conversant with the customs, habits, arms, and architecture, peculiar to various countries, that, when he supplies theatrical decorations, he may avoid anachronisms and absurdities.'

From this pronouncement the modern theatre may be said to date. The relics of medievalism which had hitherto subsisted debar us from placing its genesis any earlier. A decade after our period ended, Kemble and Capon pioneered the way for the stage archaeologist and the later nineteenth century placed him on the throne. All the qualities of Steevens's ideal manager were possessed to the full by Charles Kean and Sir Henry Irving.

[1] Malone's annotated copy of this edition, now in the Bodleian, reveals the authorship. See *The Review of English Studies* for July 1929, p. 288.

BIBLIOGRAPHY.—For the drama and histrionics of the period, see ALLARDYCE NICOLL'S *XVIII Century Drama, 1750–1800*; ERNEST BERNBAUM, *The Drama of Sensibility* (1915); J. W. KRUTCH, *Comedy and Conscience after the Restoration* (1924); the various Lives of David Garrick by (1) THOMAS DAVIES, 1780, (2) ARTHUR MURPHY, 1801, and (3) JOSEPH KNIGHT, 1894; *An Apology for the Life of George Anne Bellamy*, 1784 (which, although abounding in inaccuracies, gives a valuable picture of the times); *The Memoirs of Tate Wilkinson* (1790); the History of the English Stage compiled by R. J. SMITH (15 vols.) (British Museum Library, press mark, '11826 r'); PERCY FITZGERALD'S *The Life of Mrs. Catherine Clive* (1888); EDWARD ABBOTT PARRY'S *Charles Macklin* (1891).

No exhaustive investigation of the theatrical architecture or the staging and costuming and general theatrical conditions of the period has been made, but some incidental treatment of these subjects will be found in ALLARDYCE NICOLL'S *The Development of the Theatre* (1927); and, in respect to Shakespearian mounting, reference should also be made to GEORGE C. D. ODELL'S *Shakespeare from Betterton to Irving*. For details of the progress of stage lighting, see *The Stage Year Book* for 1927, W. J. LAWRENCE'S article on 'Early English Stage and Theatre-Lighting (1580–1800)'. Among magazine articles dealing with the eighteenth-century stage, particular attention is demanded by WALTER H. GODFREY'S study of 'The Apron Stage' in *The Architectural Review*, vol. xxxvii, pp. 31–5. Others likely to prove serviceable are W. J. LAWRENCE'S 'A Century of Scene Painting' in *The Gentleman's Magazine* for March 1888, and his 'Stage Scenery in the Eighteenth Century' in *The Magazine of Art* for August 1895.

XXI

MUSIC

By SIR HENRY HADOW

The delight which Music affords seems to be one of the first attainments of rational nature; wherever there is humanity, there is modulated sound. The mind set free from the resistless tyranny of painful want, employs its first leisure upon some savage melody. Thus in those lands of unprovided wretchedness, which Your Majesty's encouragement of naval investigation has brought lately to the knowledge of the polished world, though all things else were wanted, every nation had its Music; an art of which the rudiments accompany the commencements, and the refinements adorn the completion of civility, in which the inhabitants of the earth seek their first refuge from evil, and, perhaps, may find at last the most elegant of their pleasures.—*From Johnson's dedication—perhaps his last published work—to Burney's Account of the Commemoration of Handel* (1785).

'SIR,' said Johnson, 'I might as well have played on the violoncello as another; but I should have done nothing else.' It is a pleasing picture which is here evoked: Johnson taking the bass in a sonata with Giardini and Barthélémon; but it remains a dream unfulfilled; indeed the same conversation (April 7, 1778) recalls the failure of his only musical experiment. 'I once bought me a flagelet,' he says, 'but I never made out a tune.' On the other hand, he took a sincere if puzzled interest in the gift which he did not share.

There is nothing, I think, [he said to Goldsmith] in which the power of art is shown so much as in playing on the fiddle. In all other things we can do something at first. Any man will forge a bar of iron if you give him a hammer; not so well as a smith, but tolerably. A man will saw a piece of wood, and make a box, though a clumsy one; but give him a fiddle and a fiddle-stick and he can do nothing. (April 15, 1773).

And again in 1775:

After having talked slightingly of musick, he was observed to listen very attentively while Miss Thrale played on the harpsichord, and with eagerness he called to her, 'Why don't you dash away like Burney?' Dr. Burney upon this said to him, 'I believe, Sir, we shall make a musician of you at last.' Johnson with candid complacency replied, 'Sir, I shall be glad to have a new sense given to me.'

This may serve as a pendant to his reception of Boswell's exaggerated raptures (Sept. 23, 1777):

In the evening our gentleman-farmer, and two others, entertained themselves and the company with a great number of tunes on the fiddle. Johnson desired to have 'Let ambition fire thy mind', played over again, and appeared to give a patient attention to it; though he owned to me that he was very insensible to the power of musick. I told him that it affected me to such a degree, as often to agitate my nerves painfully, producing in my mind alternate sensations of pathetick dejection, so that I was ready to shed tears; and of daring resolution, so that I was inclined to rush into the thickest part of the battle. 'Sir, [said he] I should never hear it, if it made me feel such a fool.'

His most intimate circle included two men who were not only musicians but the most eminent musical historians of their time. With Dr. Charles Burney, organist of Chelsea Hospital, he was for many years on terms of close friendship: Sir John Hawkins, a distinguished amateur, acted as his executor, and, to Boswell's great indignation, wrote his biography. We have vivid descriptions of both; Burney in Madame d'Arblay's *Diary*, Hawkins in a letter of Horace Walpole. We can see Burney, amiable and absent-minded, coming much elated to his audience with George III, forgetting every word of his carefully prepared speech, wholly oblivious of the Queen's presence, discoursing 'eagerly and warmly' upon his travels, pulling out two dirty books from his pocket, and expatiating on their merit and rarity. 'I would not take fifty pounds for that,' he said, as if he had meant—but he had no such meaning—'Don't hope for it to your own collection.'[1] Hawkins was of a more saturnine cast, 'full of minute facts that delight antiquaries', 'so exceedingly religious and grave as to abhor mirth, except it is printed in the old black letter', thinking nothing sublime but an anthem, and Handel's choruses, 'heaven upon earth'. 'However,' concludes Walpole, 'he writes with great moderation, temper, and good sense, and the book is a very valuable one.'[2] It is significant that England should offer these rivals an equal welcome, and that they should comprise between them almost the whole range of our eighteenth-century music.[3]

There is a notable passage in Burney's *History* [vol. iv,

[1] Madame d'Arblay's *Diary* (ed. Barrett, 1905), vol. iii, p. 159.

[2] Walpole, letter to the Countess of Ossory, Dec. 3, 1776.

[3] Hawkins's five volumes were published together in 1776: Burney's four, at irregular intervals, from 1776 to 1789. Johnson wrote the 'Dedication to the Queen' of Burney's *History*.

p. 532], which clearly indicates the general condition of our public taste as set forth by its ablest exponent.

> As the OPERA [he says] includes every species of Music, vocal and instrumental, its annals, if faithfully and amply recorded, seem nearly to comprise the whole history of the art: for here we have the most varied and impassioned composition, the most refined singing, the completest orchestra, with the occasional use of every species of solo-instrument; and though the general style of opera Music is necessarily dramatic, yet that of the Church or chamber is not precluded. Choruses and solemn scenes of splendid sacrifice or funereal sorrow, in the ecclesiastic style, as well as scenes of simplicity and social gaiety, are here frequently admitted with propriety. Indeed, the opera is not only the union of every excellence in the art of Music, but in every other art. . . .

We shall find later on the means of testing and interpreting this opinion; it is enough at present to note its prevalence. During the period with which we are dealing operatic music came first in popular regard; all other forms of the art were secondary and even ancillary to its purpose.

When Johnson came to London in 1737 opera was passing through one of its periodic crises. Many of the old controversies were over: Buononcini had left England in disgrace; the 'two fighting cats' Cuzzoni and Faustina had ceased from troubling; the Royal Academy of Music, irridescent with the colours of the South Sea bubble, had been shattered, partly by its own extravagance, partly by the impact of the *Beggar's Opera*; Farinelli had just retired to Spain, with a fortune accumulated, as he said, from 'England's Folly'. But sufficient causes of controversy remained, and were reinforced by a political quarrel which invaded from outside the doors of the playhouse. For many years the King and the Prince of Wales had been at daggers drawn. George II favoured Walpole, the Prince set up a party against him. George II was a devotee of Handel; the Prince organized at Lincoln's Inn Fields a rival opera with Pepusch as general director, and Porpora and Hasse as composers in ordinary. Handel in 1737 made one of his tactical blunders. He endeavoured to disarm opposition by writing an anthem for the Prince's marriage and found that he had bought reconciliation at too dear a rate. The King withdrew his patronage; Covent Garden closed its doors and went into bankruptcy. Handel with indomitable courage paid off his debts and re-

A CONCERT AT MONTAGU HOUSE, 1736

From a drawing by Marcellus Laroon in the British Museum

opened, but his public was irresponsive and a further blow was struck when in 1740 his enemy, the Earl of Middlesex, took over the direction of the theatre. From that time forward he wrote no more operas.

He was succeeded by Galuppi, an amiable and melodious Venetian, under whose easy régime opera passed into a further period of decadence. Handel could fill the absurd conventions with magnificent music and direct them with such unity of purpose as the conditions allowed: after him there was no one who could bend the bow of Odysseus, and the suitors who crowded to the attempt, often distinguished in their own fields, were hampered by their converging multitude. It augurs ill for the dramatic ideal that the new opera-house was opened with a Pasticcio—*Alessandro in Persia*—compiled by Galuppi, and composed by Leo, Hasse, Avena, Pescetti, Lampugnani, and Domenico Scarlatti; still worse, that this collaboration was accepted with great applause, and specially commended for its variety of style. Clearly opera had come to be accepted as a miscellaneous entertainment in which drama counted for nothing. Its subject was alien, its language unknown, its plot non-existent, its characterization restricted to a few broad types; and the whole cramped in a conventional scheme, from which the understanding was excluded, the whole attention being fixed on the splendour of pageantry and the prowess of an individual singer. In tragic opera there were three acts, each with a statutable number of lines, six characters arranged by custom into three pairs of lovers, five classified types of aria, presented in a settled order of sequence, a few perfunctory choruses at the fall of the curtain: nothing in the entire plan to stimulate intelligence or arouse expectation. Only in the lighter comedies and *intermezzi* was there any scope for human interest or freedom of movement, and these were usually held of so little account that they were often played between the acts of *opera seria* as intervals of welcome if incongruous relief. From Galuppi to Lampugnani, from Lampugnani to Paradies, from Paradies to Giardini and Bertoni, this preposterous system prevailed, and, though it was partly redeemed by the beauty of certain separate numbers, it was disastrous to any organic growth and progress.

Nor had England yet roused itself to the consciousness that

music had an intrinsic meaning apart from its appeal to the senses and the emotions. The subtleties of style and construction, through which the notes of a perfect melody form as vital an organism as the measures of a perfect verse, had no doubt been intuitively perceived by the great composers; they had not yet penetrated the ears of the listening public. On this point Burney is conclusive. He is maintaining [vol. iv, p. 226] that opera in an unknown language is not more irrational than a concert, and continues:

> Now it may be asked, what entertainment there is for the mind in a *concerto, sonata,* or *solo*? They are mere objects of gratification to the ear, in which, however, imagination may divert itself with the idea that a fine *adagio* is a tragical story; an *andante,* or *grazioso,* an elegant narrative of some tranquil event, and an *allegro* a tale of merriment.

To him the whole significance of music lies in an interpretation of the scene or emotion that it depicts: in other words he ignores the one aspect which to us gives it claim to a place among the arts—the absorption of the sensuous and emotional elements into the understanding spirit which is above them both.[1] It is worth noting that when these words appeared Haydn had been writing symphonies for over thirty years and Mozart for over twenty.

Our eighteenth-century Oratorio has a curious history. In 1720 Handel, then attached to the household of the Duke of Chandos, wrote for the private theatre a masque of six scenes entitled *Haman and Mordecai*. Twelve years later it was revived by Bernard Gates, organist of the Chapel Royal, presented to Handel as a birthday surprise, and so well received that it was offered for public performance at the Haymarket. It was prohibited by Dr. Gibson, Bishop of London: Handel remodelled it with additional words, renamed it *Esther*, and gave it under Royal patronage without scenery or action. The success was so great that he followed it up with two other examples—*Deborah* and *Athaliah*—and included all three in the programme of his triumphant visit

[1] Johnson, however, says in his Dedication to Burney's *History of Music* (1776):

'The science of musical sounds, though it may have been depreciated, as appealing only to the ear, and affording nothing more than a momentary and fugitive delight, may be with justice considered as the art that unites corporal and intellectual pleasure, by a species of enjoyment which gratifies sense, without weakening reason.'

to Oxford in 1733. Then the London audience wearied of its new toy. *Saul* in 1739 fell flat, notwithstanding the 'Envy' chorus, the Dead March, and the superb 'organ concerto' overture: *Israel* had to be mutilated to suit the popular taste, and even so did not hold the house. More notable still, *The Messiah*, successfully produced at Dublin in 1741, met, on its transference to England, a storm of disapprobation. The nobility censured it as dull, the clergy as irreligious; the general public thought nothing about the matter, but followed the line of least resistance.[1] The work was withdrawn after three performances; Walsh, the publisher, made for the score a derisive offer of £20, which Handel indignantly refused; not until its revival at the Foundling Hospital in 1749 did it begin to assume the position which, in this country, it has ever since maintained.

Handel had impaired the Royal favour by one political event; he regained it to the full by another. The defeat of the Jacobite Rebellion in 1745 gave opportunity for a great outburst of national rejoicing. For it Handel compiled the 'Occasional Oratorio' and wrote *Judas Maccabaeus*, the latter of which was by far the most immediately successful of all his works in this form. George II, who had already been partly conciliated by the Dettingen Te Deum, restored him to the full sunlight of his favour, and gave him *carte blanche* for the music of the next public display—the celebration of the Peace of Aix-la-Chapelle. Handel responded with a gigantic piece of pageantry—an open stage in the Green Park, a spectacle of unexampled magnificence, a blaze of fireworks and an orchestra of over a hundred performers, reinforced by musketry and cannon. We are told that at the rehearsal, in which the music alone was given, twelve thousand people paid for admission, and held up the traffic for three hours.

[1] It has sometimes been supposed that there is an allusion to *The Messiah* in Horace Walpole's letter to Sir Horace Mann, Feb. 24, 1743.

'Handel has set up an Oratorio against the operas, and succeeds. He has hired all the goddesses from farces and the singers of *Roast Beef* from between the acts at both theatres, with a man with one note in his voice and a girl without ever an one; and so they sing and make brave hallelujahs.'

This, however, is impossible, for *The Messiah* was not produced until March 23. Walpole's allusion is to the oratorio of *Samson*, which was successfully produced on Feb. 18 and had a run of eight nights.

Dr. Beattie tells us that at the first performance of *The Messiah* some of the audience were impressed, including the King, who rose to his feet at the Hallelujah Chorus. But they were few in number and were powerless to withstand the combined forces of bigotry and frivolity.

Nothing in the course of our eighteenth-century music is more significant than the fluctuation in its treatment of Handel. His earlier operas—*Rinaldo, Teseo, Radamisto*—were played to crowded houses; the later, not dissimilar in merit, were usually left to shiver under a *succés d'estime. Esther* and *Athaliah* were triumphant exponents of a new form; of his other oratorios—and he wrote twenty-four in all—only *Samson* and *Judas Maccabaeus* were successful at their first presentation. 'Where'er you walk' could not save *Semele,* nor the 'Golden Lyre' *Alexander Balus*; even at the height of his popularity, when the acclamation of the Firework Music had hardly died down, *Susanna* and *Solomon* attained but seven performances between them, and his favourite *Theodora* was so sparsely attended that, as he said, 'You could have danced there'. He was periodically pressed for money, he was three times bankrupt, he was the victim of persistent intrigue and opposition; yet we are told that he brought back four thousand pounds from his visit to Oxford, that he raised another thousand by a single benefit concert, and that he left a fortune of twenty thousand at his death. Lord Chesterfield once left the theatre, not because the music was over, but because he was 'unwilling to disturb the King at his privacies'. The centenary festival of 1784 filled Westminster Abbey for three days, and was attended by the most brilliant concourse of people that had ever assembled to honour a composer.[1]

Apart from the theatres, at which both opera and oratorio were presented, there were three chief places of musical resort: New Spring Gardens at Lambeth, which afterwards borrowed a name from the neighbouring estate of Vauxhall, Ranelagh adjoining the grounds of Chelsea Hospital, and Marylebone Gardens beside the Rose tavern in the High Street. Of these Ranelagh, the latest in date, was specially famous for masquerades [see Walpole, letter to Sir Horace Mann, May 3, 1749], but its musical reputation was sufficient to secure Burney as organist and to attract a flying visit from the young Mozart. Marylebone was celebrated for *burlettas* and comic operas—among others *La Serva Padrona,*

[1] An account of this, with a life of Handel, was written by Dr. Burney: *An Account of the Musical Performances in Westminster Abbey and the Pantheon . . . in Commemoration of Handel* (1785). The 'Dedication to the King' was written by Johnson.

adapted by the elder Storace from Pergolesi. The leader for many years was Defesch, who is immortalized in Hogarth's caricature of 'The Chorus', and who was succeeded in 1770 by Barthélémon. But the place had been of doubtful repute—Gay selects it as the haunt of Macheath and his marauding crew—and it never took the same rank as its two contemporaries. Greatest, both in achievement and in popularity, were the New Spring Gardens, which, since the middle of the seventeenth century, had been the favourite pleasure-ground of the London citizens. The proprietor at this time was Tom Tyers, the audacious jester who delighted Johnson by comparing him to a ghost ('Sir, you never speak until you are spoken to') and whose most notable *coup* was the rehearsal of Handel's 'Firework Music' before its production in the Green Park. The director of the orchestra was Arne, the one English composer of the eighteenth century who most nearly approached to genius. Mrs. Arne was engaged as principal singer; the band included some of the most celebrated virtuosi of the day; the programmes were light, varied, and entertaining; they were enhanced by every device of brilliant spectacle and material comfort; the usual price of admission was one shilling; and the gardens were open every evening during the summer months. Johnson, in company with Goldsmith, Boswell, and Mrs. Thrale, was an occasional attendant and, though we may conjecture that he was not much affected by the music, he seems to have enjoyed on the whole his experience of 'mingling with the pleasures of the people'.

These popular entertainments aided in two respects the cause of our native art. First, they brought into prominence the claims of English singers and English players. We have already mentioned Mrs. Arne; besides her there were Miss Faulkner, Miss Catley, and Miss Brent at Marylebone; at Ranelagh John Beard, the tenor, and Parry, the harp-player; at Vauxhall came after Mrs. Arne, Mrs. Weichsell, herself famous, and the mother of a more famous daughter, Mrs. Billington, and a succession of English artists whose names, recorded in Grove, run over the limits of the century. No doubt some of the impulse may have been given by partisan motives; Burney tells us that in 1745 there was a rebellion against the opera singers, 'who being foreigners were mostly Roman Catholic'; but at least the opportunities came and the country showed that it was abundantly able to profit by them. Secondly, the tide moved, largely through the influence of the Gardens, in the direction of simple and popular melody. *The Beggar's Opera* had owed its success partly to political satire; it set a brief fashion which produced nothing memorable and died about 1735. The second period of Italian domination was wearying even its devotees; public taste gradually turned from these 'intricacies of laborious song' and prepared to welcome an art of which both words and music were more readily intelligible. Hence came the vogue of Ballad Opera which was prevalent during the last half of the century and which was one of England's most distinctive contributions to the history of music. It started with Arne's *Love in a Village*, which was produced with unstinted applause in 1762 and followed by a line of succession from Shield and Dibdin to Stephen Storace and Michael Kelly. The revulsion may be illustrated by two significant comments. Madame d'Arblay, writing in 1783, tells us that Pacchiarotti, the last great male soprano, once occupied an entire concert in singing 'most deliciously' a number of little airs and ballets, including English and Scottish. Horace Walpole, when the Italian opera-house was burned in 1789, openly rejoiced and expressed a hope that it would never be rebuilt.

As the pleasure-gardens gave entertainment to the public at large, so did the Routs to a more exclusive and fashionable coterie. Among these the most famous was that organized by Madame Cornelys, at Carlisle House, Soho, which opened about 1761, reached its zenith some eight years afterwards, and about 1785 declined into the usual bankruptcy. It combined many sorts of appeal—dancing, card-playing, assembly—Madame Cornelys was specially noted for the excellence of her commissariat—but the chief interest for us is in the concerts. These were directed by J. C. Bach and Abel, son and pupil respectively of John Sebastian, and grew so powerful that in 1771 they could organize a party against the Haymarket. Carlisle House was indeed the resort of many celebrities. Angelo, the fencer, lived there; so did Bartolozzi the engraver; Bach and Abel lived next door; among the *habitués* were Garrick, Colman, Sheridan, Cipriani, Gainsborough, and Sir Joshua Reynolds; and though Johnson stood aloof and disdainfully asked, 'Pray, sir, who is

The Orcheſtra, Grand Walk, &c. — *in Marybone Gardens.*

London Printed for Robt. Sayer, at the Golden Buck in Fleet Street.

this Bach? Is he a piper?', there is reason to believe that the doctor's ignorance was rhetorically assumed. It was not, at any rate, shared by any other member of The Club.

Two musical societies of this period deserve a special mention. The Academy of Ancient Music was established at the Crown and Anchor in 1710, and for eighty-two years maintained a high standard both of selection and of performance. Its first patron was the Duke of Abercorn, its first director Dr. Pepusch, who left it the best part of his valuable library; Handel and Geminiani took frequent part in its concerts; and it marked the executive proficiency of the time by appointing an amateur, Henry Needler, as its first violin. The Noblemen's and Gentlemen's Catch Club was started in 1761 with a galaxy of patrons, and soon found its doors besieged by applicants. Among its earliest members were the Duke of Kingston, the Marquess of Lorne, Lord Bolingbroke, Lord Ashburnham, and Lord George Sutton; among the later were the Prince of Wales, the Duke of Clarence (afterwards William IV), and the Dukes of Cumberland, York, Cambridge, and Sussex. From 1763 to 1794 it offered annual prizes for Glees, Canons, and Catches, and so established on a firm foundation that school of glee writers who, more even than the composers of ballad opera, constitute England's distinctive national form. The prize winners included Arne, Stafford Smith, Webbe, Lord Mornington, Steevens, Callcott, and many others—a hive of sweets over which the words 'in tenui labor at tenuis non gloria' might be placed as an inscription.

A word should be here added on the technique of musical performance. It is clear that there was a great improvement in vocalization, for Burney says that Farinelli's execution, 'which excited such astonishment in 1734, would be hardly thought sufficiently brilliant in 1788 for a third-rate singer at the opera' [*History*, vol. iv, p. 413]. In 1748 Geminiani revolutionized the art of violin playing, to such purpose that before the end of the century Paganini was covering three octaves on a single string and performing marvels of dexterity which would have been sheer impossibilities a generation before. Other instruments, too, had their special proficients: Parkes on the oboe, Snow on the trumpet; in 1740 a Dublin playbill announced the first appearance of the clarinet; in 1738 the band at Marylebone Gardens included 'two grand or double bassoons, the greatness of whose sound surpasses that of any other bass instrument whatsoever'.[1] Of more importance is an announcement from Covent Garden (May 16, 1767), that Miss Brickley is to sing a song from Arne's *Judith*, 'accompanied by Mr. Dibdin on a new instrument called a Piano Forte'. Next year J. C. Bach introduced it as a solo instrument to the London public; it gradually made its way into prominence, and in 1773 Clementi as composer and John Broadwood as maker established its superiority over the harpsichord.

These technical developments of violin and clavier had their effect in the domestic music of the period. Many of the principal musicians, English and foreign, were teachers and gained a part of their livelihood by giving instruction to the daughters of their patrons. The harpsichord stood in every house; even Squire Western provided one for the use of Sophia; and the pieces composed for it were commonly known by the significant name of 'lessons'. Handel in 1720 and 1733 wrote for the daughters of George I two volumes of pieces, the second of which includes the mythologically named 'Harmonious Blacksmith', and followed them at intervals with a succession of fugues and lyric numbers. Stanley, the blind organist of the Temple, published as his Opus I a set of six sonatas; Nares of the Chapel Royal is chiefly memorable for his harpsichord lessons, one of which, printed by Mr. Fuller Maitland,[2] is worthy of all the praise that has been bestowed upon it. The arrival of J. C. Bach in 1762 marks a turning-point. His first two opus numbers, 1763 and 1764, are definitely inscribed 'pour le Clavecin' (i.e. the harpsichord); in Opus V, 1768, he writes 'pour le Clavecin ou le Pianoforte', and thenceforward as in the Progressive Lessons, the latter instrument is always desig-

[1] Handel's typical orchestra consisted of twenty-five to thirty-five performers, balancing a chorus of the same number. The staple was made up of strings, largely reinforced by oboes and bassoons: the other instruments, e.g. flute and trumpet, were kept for special effect of drama and pageantry. Throughout Handel's career the balance remained almost unimpaired—at the Commemoration Festival of 1784 the numbers of the band were 250 as against a chorus of 275. He introduced horns into *Radamistro* (1720) and trombones into *Saul* (1738), both very sparingly. The general use of the clarinet did not come until after Handel's time. It must be remembered that he accompanied his oratorios on the organ, and that Mozart's 'additional accompaniments' to *The Messiah* were written for a hall in which no organ was provided.

[2] *Oxford History of Music* (2nd. ed., 1931), vol. iv, pp. 329–38.

nated. His father had disliked it, his elder brother had dismissed it as 'fit only for rondos'; it is to him that we owe the recognition of a medium which passed successively into the hands of Clementi, and through Clementi of Cramer and Mozart and Beethoven.[1]

Of concerted chamber music our earliest examples are again from Handel who, in the early part of the century, wrote trios for wind or stringed instruments with a bass, and five violin sonatas, two of which are of special value. Among contemporaries and successors are Geminiani and his pupil Dubourg, Michael Festing the Londoner, who directed the orchestra at Ranelagh, Giardini, a prolific composer of sonatas and concerti, Barthélémon, who divided his time between London and Paris, and Wilhelm Cramer, a poor composer but a superb virtuoso, who for five and twenty years directed the Opera and the King's band and who led the orchestra at the Handel Festival of 1784. The concerted chamber works were called 'Sonatas' and laid out on the plan, adopted by Purcell, of two violins and a bass. They were usually simple and artless, consisting sometimes of two, and sometimes of three movements apiece, their material not yet very clearly organized, except in fugues, dance numbers, and variations, and their chief interest concentrated on the violin technique, which grew in range and variety as the century proceeded. On a larger scale were the *concerti grossi*, in which the soloists—strings or organ or oboe—were reinforced by an acompaniment of ripieno strings. These, as with Corelli, were in four contrasted movements and in scheme and volume of sound formed a sort of transition between the chamber and the orchestra. Geminiani was a notable writer of concerti and led the way to the orchestral overtures of J. C. Bach.

No account of our domestic music would be complete without some record of the English song-writers. Of all musical forms lyric song has the most direct appeal, it drives straightest to the heart, it touches the sympathy and comprehension of the largest number. It has been said that in this respect the eighteenth century falls short of its predecessor, that it has nothing to rival Playford in one field

[1] The history of the piano-forte has recently been written by Miss R. E. M. Harding (*The Piano-Forte*, 1933). Its use in England is fully dealt with. It appears to have been well established in England by 1760.

and the Orpheus Britannicus in another. Even if this is true (and such comparisons are always tiresome and often inconclusive), it does not touch the fact that during this dark period we have a considerable store of native melody; the tapers in our home windows burn with a light which if slender is unquenchable. Many of these began on the operatic stage or in public entertainments; they soon made their way through collections and anthologies into the common property of the nation. Such were Arne's Shakesperian lyrics, 'Where the bee sucks' and 'Blow, blow thou winter wind'; such were Dibdin's 'Tom Bowling' and Davy's 'Bay of Biscay' and Hook's 'Lass of Richmond Hill', and the traditional melodies of 'Polly Oliver' and 'Admiral Benbow'. These and their like did more than anything else to sustain the love of music among the people at large. The pageantries of opera and oratorio were too remote and too costly; not one man in a thousand could afford to enjoy them: these knocked at every man's door and were admitted to every man's household.

Three patriotic songs attained in this period a special celebrity: Arne's 'Rule Britannia', Boyce's 'Hearts of Oak', and, most memorable of them all, the National Anthem. The authorship of this tune has been veiled in a long and obscure controversy; Carey's improbable claim is now wholly discredited, and there is no one else to whom it can be assigned with certainty. The most likely conjecture traces it to a seventeenth-century galliard of Dr. John Bull, which it closely resembles and the manuscript of which was in Dr. Pepusch's library; but there are other conjectures and we may well be contented to await further enlightenment. All we know is that the first public performance took place simultaneously at Covent Garden and Drury Lane on September 28, 1745, when news came of Sir John Cope's disaster at Prestonpans; that it was sung there and at the other theatres for several nights; that it was printed, words and music, in the *Gentleman's Magazine* next month; that it rapidly grew from popular to national favour; and that in 1790 it was adopted, with acknowledgements to its English origin, as the melody of 'Heil dir im Siegerkranz'. Since then it has passed into the national repertoires of nineteen or twenty countries besides our own.[1] It is noticeable that

[1] See Grove (3rd ed., 5 vols., 1927), s.v. 'God save the King', vol. ii, pp. 406–8.

A MUSIC PARTY ON THE THAMES AT FULHAM

GRANVILLE SHARP and MEMBERS of the SHARP FAMILY

From the painting by J. Zoffany in the possession of Miss Olive Lloyd-Baker

the anthem was not commissioned from Handel or from any other 'official' composer, and that it was not written to celebrate a victory, but was inspired by a defeat.

We have seen that in most of the larger fields of composition England was, during this period, content to take a secondary place. Our *opera seria* never rose above *Artaxerxes*;[1] our oratorios were pale reflections of the Handelian style; to the development of the great instrumental forms we contributed virtually nothing. In the liturgical music of the Church we struck a firmer note and maintained, for a time not unworthily, the tradition of Blow and Purcell.

The record gathers chiefly round the names of three men: Maurice Greene (1695–1755), William Boyce (1710–79), and Samuel Arnold (1740–1802). Greene was educated at the choir school of St. Paul's Cathedral, to the organistship of which he succeeded in 1718. During the early years of his tenure he was a close friend and follower of Handel, for whose organ-improvisations he used to blow the bellows: later he was swept into the dispute with Buononcini and unhappily took the wrong side. In 1727 he was appointed organist and composer to the Chapel Royal, and three years later Professor of Music at Cambridge, choosing for his exercise Pope's *Ode on St. Cecilia's Day*. The libretto was afterwards offered to Handel who, by now estranged, refused it on the ground that it had already been set by 'mein bellows-blower'. In 1735 he was made Master of the King's band, and in that capacity produced the usual tale of ceremonial odes and cantatas. Eight years later he published the volume of *Forty Select Anthems* on which his reputation as a composer principally rests and then, in full middle life, retired. He continued to perform his routine duties for a few more years; in 1750 he inherited an estate in Essex and devoted his leisure to a compilation of anthems and services which he left to his pupil Boyce for completion.

He was a man of undoubted gifts, but of indolent and unstable temper. His finest anthems, 'Lord, let me know

[1] Arne's opera, the book translated from Metastasio, was produced in 1762, as a direct challenge to the Italians. It was successful and held the stage intermittently until the first quarter of the nineteenth century. The part of Mandane, originally written for Miss Brent, was long accepted as a test-piece for soprano singers, and three of the songs—'The soldier tired of war's alarms', 'In infancy our hopes and fears', and 'Water parted from the sea'—remained famous after the rest of the work had disappeared.

mine end', for example, and 'Lord, how long wilt thou be angry?', are among the classics of their kind: the former was long adopted for the funeral ceremonies in St. Paul's, Westminster Abbey, and St. George's, Windsor, and might well be restored to its place. His verse-anthems are on the whole less successful; the lighter texture wears thin at times, and begins to show traces of conventional and perfunctory work. But in his treatment of full choral masses he is of the great school, expressive, dignified, austere, and imbued with the noblest spirit of the English service. Dr. Walker[1] sums up a most judicious account of his music by saying that our impression of him 'is that of a man who, somehow, neglected and more or less frittered away a very splendid talent; for natural genius his name certainly ranks among the foremost few in the list of English musicians of the last two centuries'.

He was succeeded, both at the Chapel Royal and in the mastership of the King's band, by his pupil William Boyce, who is at once his complement and his antithesis. Boyce had greater learning, greater industry, a sincerity beyond impeachment, and a wide command of resource, but his writing is never 'stung by the splendour of a sudden thought'; it is deliberate, persuasive, reasonable, the work of an orator rather than of a poet. He was a typical product of the mid-century: his sonatas, we are told, had a wider vogue in England than any since the days of Corelli, he was much in demand as a conductor, both of the three-choir festivals (Gloucester, Worcester, and Hereford) and at the festival of the Sons of the Clergy, his burly presence filled for nearly fifty years an honoured place in the history of the art. At his death forty-six of his anthems, with five services, were collected for publication, and we can still hear with pleasure such examples as 'By the waters of Babylon', 'If we believe', and the chorus, 'O praise our God, ye people', which he wrote for his exercise at Cambridge.

His chief monument is the Corpus of Cathedral Music which he took over from Greene, largely augmented, and published in three volumes from 1760 to 1778. There had been nothing like it since Barnard's *Select Church Music* of 1641, it remained for another century our golden treasury of liturgical music from Tallis and Byrd to Blow and Purcell and Croft. It was dedicated to George II, printed by sub-

[1] *History of Music in England* (2nd. ed., 1924), p. 220.

scription, and rapidly circulated not only through Cathedral and Collegiate churches but among the libraries of wealthy patrons. To it more than anything else we owe the maintenance of that standard which, even in its feeblest days, the music of the English Church has never entirely discarded.

Greene left special injunctions that no composition of his should be included: Boyce adopted the same self-denying ordinance. These omissions were partly supplied by the four additional volumes which appeared in 1790 under the editorship of Samuel Arnold. The harvest of Arnold is more jejune, and there are some tares mingled with the wheat, but it keeps in remembrance many works which are well worth recording and a few of conspicuous and distinguished merit. As a composer Arnold was ruined by his own versatility. He wrote lavishly in almost every known form, operas, oratorios, chamber music, anthems and services for the Chapel Royal, but he aimed at the popularity of the moment, and his name chiefly survives in his *Cathedral Music* and his historic edition of Handel.

An almost exact contemporary, Jonathan Battishill, deserves mention both for his genuine talent and for the tragedy which cut short its early promise. Born in 1738, he began his career as assistant to Boyce; then, after an interval at Covent Garden, where he collaborated with Arne in light opera, he was appointed to the organistship of a City church. He returned to the study of ecclesiastical music and produced his two masterpieces, 'Call to remembrance' and 'O Lord, look down from heaven', which in massiveness and austerity may rank with the best of Greene. In 1777 his life was shattered by a domestic sorrow, he withdrew into complete seclusion, and though he lived twenty-five years longer he wrote no more. It was a conspicuous piece of ill fortune that brought so promising a career to so tragic and premature a close. But for this the Church music of the century might have ended on a strain of nobility as high as that with which it began.[1]

[1] Another career, full of early promise, and cut short by a disastrous end, was that of Thomas Linley (1756–78), the contemporary and intimate friend of Mozart. He was the son of a meritorious composer under whom he made his début as violinist at the age of eight, studied chiefly at Florence, and on his return was appointed leader of the orchestra successively at Bath and at Covent Garden. He was attaining a considerable reputation both in opera and in sacred music when he was accidentally drowned at the age of 22. Two volumes of his collected works were posthumously published, but they have now passed out of account.

'When a man is tired of London he is tired of life,' said Johnson, 'for there is in London all that life can afford.' This does less than justice to other districts throughout the country, in many of which there were active centres of social life; and these, so far as they concern music, may well be included in our general survey. In Newcastle, for instance, Charles Avison, organist of St. Nicholas, headed a revolt against Handel and established a rival school which was 'of importance in its day'. Like his master Geminiani, he was a well-known writer of concertos, and the *Essay on Musical Expression* (1753), in which he expounds the principle of his school, was widely read and aroused a vivacious controversy. In East Anglia Burney was for nine years organist of King's Lynn; and after him the music of the entire region was dominated by Joseph Gibbs of Ipswich, whose reputation extended far beyond its bounds and whose violin sonatas are among the most remarkable of their time. Far more important and more enduring was the group which gathered round the three western cathedrals of Gloucester, Worcester, and Hereford. From the beginning of the century their choirs had been accustomed to meet annually for combined performance: in 1724 an official festival was inaugurated at Gloucester, and since then the rota has been continued unbroken up to the present day. At first the music was restricted to anthems and services: in 1737 Boyce was appointed conductor, and under his guidance the scheme was extended to include secular and instrumental compositions. A landmark was passed when in 1759 *The Messiah* was given in Hereford Cathedral. In 1743 it had been condemned as irreligious by the London clergy.

Wales came into the field with the blind harper, John Parry of Ruabon, notable not only as a virtuoso but as a collector of Cambrian folk-songs. His volume of *Ancient British Music* was published in 1742, became immediately popular, and was followed by several others. They did incalculable service in revealing and disseminating a number of first-rate tunes, the value of which is not impaired by the extravagant and uncritical belief expressed in their antiquity. The 'March of the Men of Harlech' for example, every bar of which bears the signature of the eighteenth century, was long and seriously attributed to the capture of Harlech Castle in the reign of Edward I. But they largely enriched our store of national melodies, and they received later a royal welcome when Haydn, who was interested in folk-songs, furnished many of them with accompaniments.

Johnson was debarred from music by two causes. One was the physical disability, which he has shared with many men of letters from Swift and Pope in his own time to Darwin and Tennyson in ours. The other was the emptiness and frivolity which marked the general taste in the London of his day. Music was declared to be an 'art of luxury'—a sort of audible confectionery which dispensed with the understanding. It was of no use to ask, 'Sonate, que veux-tu?' when its leading exponent had already asserted that it meant nothing. It says much for Johnson's integrity that he should have been willing to admit the possibility of 'a sixth sense', and of his tireless inquiry that he should have spent some time in the endeavour to ascertain its nature. If we sometimes think of him as rejecting the art with gruffness and impatience we may well recollect that the most tender of his poems is written to the memory of a musician:

> Phillips, whose touch harmonious could remove
> The pangs of guilty power or helpless love;
> Rest here! distressed by poverty no more,
> Here find the calm thou gav'st so oft before;
> Sleep, undisturbed, within this peaceful shrine,
> Till angels wake thee with a note like thine!

BIBLIOGRAPHY.—The chief authorities for this chapter, apart from Boswell, may conveniently be arranged under four heads.

1. *General histories of Music.*

Sir JOHN HAWKINS's *History of the science and practice of Music* (1776), vol. v, and BURNEY's *A General History of Music* (1776–89), vol. iv, are the main contemporary sources. BUSBY's *History of Music* (1819) is largely, though not entirely, a compilation from Burney and Hawkins. GEORGE HOGARTH's *Musical History* (1835) is a more original work and contains some valuable information on the status of English singers, the growth of music-publishing, and the progress of musical education in England. Among more recent books the most important are J. A. FULLER MAITLAND's volume on 'The Age of Bach and Handel' (*Oxford History of Music*, 2nd. ed., 1931, vol. iv); H. DAVEY's *History of English Music* (1895), a little extravagant in claim but full of information; and ERNEST WALKER's *History of Music in England* (1907, 2nd ed. 1924), to all of which this chapter is deeply indebted.

2. *Dictionaries.*

REES's *Encyclopaedia* (1819) is notable for the articles on music written by BURNEY: see especially that on Arne. F. J. FÉTIS' *Biographie Universelle des Musiciens* (1837–44) is rather scanty in its treatment of England, but contains many useful facts, and, in the first edition, an admirable introductory essay.

Two supplementary volumes were added by POUGIN in 1878. RIEMANN'S *Musik-Lexicon* (translated with additions by Shedlock) appeared in 1882 and has passed through many editions. The dictionary of *British Musical Biography* by BROWN and STRATTON (1897) is still, and is likely to remain, a standard work on the subject. GROVE'S *Dictionary of Music and Musicians* (3rd ed., 1927) is indispensable.

3. *Biographies.*

The first part of this period gathers round the career of Handel. Chief among his biographies is that of F. CHRYSANDER (1858–67), who was also the principal editor of the monumental *Handel-Gesellschaft* edition from its inception in 1856. Other volumes which may be specially commended are those of VICTOR SCHOELCHER (*Handel et son temps*, 1857), W. S. ROCKSTRO (1883), R. A. STREATFEILD (1909), ROMAIN ROLLAND (1910), and NEWMAN FLOWER, the last of which appeared in 1923, and sums up the results of previous research.

For the last half the central figure is J. C. BACH, whose life and times have been definitively portrayed in 1929 by C. SANDFORD TERRY. Reference should also be made to the short but appreciative chapter on JOHN CHRISTIAN in C. H. BITTER'S *Emanuel und Friedmann Bach und deren Brüder* (1867), though this has more to do with general criticism than with history.

4. *Brochures, Monographs, Miscellaneous works.*

ARBUTHNOT'S *Harmony in an Uproar* (1732) is an amusing satire on the quarrels at the Italian Opera in the time of Handel and Buononcini. CHARLES AVISON'S *Essay on Musical Expression* (1753) contained, in its first edition, a vigorous defence of Geminiani against Handel, which was answered by Dr. WILLIAM HAYES, the Professor of Music at Oxford, and modified in this, the second edition. HAWKINS in 1770 published a history of the Academy of Ancient Music, BURNEY in 1785 an account of the Handel commemoration at Westminster Abbey. Madame D'ARBLAY produced her *Memoir of Dr. Burney* in 1832: there are also many references to music in her *Diary* (1842–6), as there are in the *Letters of Horace Walpole* (see Mrs. Paget Toynbee's edition, 16 vols., 1903–5). Handel's visit to Dublin is commemorated in a short monograph by TOWNSEND (1857). C. F. POHL'S *Mozart in London* dates from 1867 (compare JAHN'S *Mozart*, English translation, vol. i, pp. 38 et seq.), together with his *Haydn in London*, which, besides a valuable bibliography, contains a chapter on the condition of English music at the time of Haydn's first visit. References to newspapers and periodicals (e.g. FAULKNER'S *Dublin Journal*, *The Public Advertizer*, *The Gentleman's Magazine*, *The Harmonicon*, *The Musical Quarterly*) are too many to be here enumerated, but commendation should be given to two articles on Arne (by F. G. EDWARDS), which appeared in the *Musical Times* for November and December 1901. Among special monographs, honourable mention should be given to J. S. BUMPUS'S *History of Cathedral Music* (2 vols., 1908) and to LYSONS' *Annals of the Three Choirs* (1864–95).

R. EITNER'S *Quellen-Lexikon* (1900 et seq.) should be consulted throughout.

XXII

EDUCATION, SCHOOLS AND UNIVERSITIES

By SIR CHARLES MALLET

At a great school there is all the splendour and illumination of many minds; the radiance of all is concentrated in each, or at least reflected upon each. But we must own that neither a dull boy, nor an idle boy, will do so well at a great school as at a private one.—*Tour to the Hebrides* (22 Aug. 1773).

Sir, while you are considering which of two things you should teach your child first, another boy has learnt them both.—*Life of Johnson* (28 July 1763).

THE teaching of Dr. Johnson's day had its roots far back in history. The classical revival and the educational changes which accompanied the Reformation had set on foot a vigorous advance. Great schemes for 'teaching everybody everything', girls as well as boys and poor as well as rich, appealed to the educational reformers of the seventeenth century. Comenius brought a schoolmaster's knowledge to bear on the new philosophy of Francis Bacon. Milton pleaded for a far more generous education than the Schools and Universities of his day could give. The Royal Society introduced the world to science. William Petty advocated utilitarian teaching. John Locke would have had education include not only virtue, wisdom, breeding, but manual training and almost all branches of human knowledge. Yet by the middle of the eighteenth century English education had advanced but little beyond the methods of the century before. With all the plans for improving and diffusing it, there was still little provision for instructing the mass of the people.

From medieval times indeed there had existed in England not only Grammar Schools in the full sense, but simple schools of an elementary type where children might be taught to read and write. Latin reading was commoner than writing. Cathedrals and Monasteries, Colleges and Collegiate churches, religious and industrial guilds, had often made provision for such teaching. Priests who served chantries had not infrequently found time to keep small schools. And probably some rudimentary private schools for boys and girls existed also. But all schools under ecclesiastical control suffered inevitably when the Reformation attacked ecclesiastical foundations. After that day, though a few elementary schools were founded by private persons, too little was done in the sixteenth and seventeenth centuries to replace what had been lost, and to establish any organized system of education for the poor. Yet the population grew, in the towns especially. The need of elementary teaching, in English, and in reading, writing and arithmetic, became more obvious than ever. The Nonconformists, inheriting democratic sympathies from the Puritans, and finding their educational ambitions often checked by the prejudice of Churchmen, took an active part in the endeavour to meet the need. Men of a liberal and philanthropic spirit would have gone far to make the State responsible for supplying primary education. But, in default of a lead from the State, voluntary effort had to do what it could. Little schools, humble little dames' schools especially, were maintained in many places. Johnson attended one at Lichfield. Shenstone, who went up to Pembroke College, Oxford soon after Johnson, thought that they existed everywhere. He depicted his old school-mistress, attired in an apron blue as a harebell and a cap whiter than driven snow, dwelling in a lowly cottage set round with garden flowers, teaching 'virtuous lore', hating the Pope, enforcing discipline, birching offenders, and rewarding the diligent with sugared cakes. Goldsmith, born a few years later, has as kindly a picture of a village schoolmaster, who could out-argue the parson with long and thundering words, and who was skilled to rule, and kindly if severe. Village schools of the same type figure also in Fielding's books. A Committee of the House of Commons estimated that 50,000 children still attended dames' schools in 1816.

But much more in the way of elementary education was required. In the last forty years of the seventeenth century, a period of substantial progress in education, attempts to meet the deficiency were made. Private benevolence set up a charity school for twenty boys in Lambeth. Dr. Busby paid for the instruction of poor children in Westminster. A Blue Coat School of fifty boys was founded also in Westminster. Colonel Colchester, one of the originators of the Society for Promoting Christian Knowledge, established an elementary school at Westbury-on-Severn for sixty-seven boys and girls. Edward Colston in Queen Anne's reign established two new schools for poor boys at Bristol and

A PARSON'S SCHOOL
about 1750

contributed handsomely to others. A remarkable movement, fostered in early days by Tillotson and Baxter, created a large number of new schools in Wales. Beyond that, Colonel Colchester was associated with Dr. Thomas Bray in the plans which the new Society adopted for establishing 'Catechetical Schools' in every parish in and round London. The early eighteenth century saw these Charity Schools already famous. There were fifty-four of them in London and Westminster, containing over 2,000 children, in 1704. In the last year of George I Charity Schools existed in every county in England: 22,000 boys and nearly 6,000 girls were among their pupils. To Addison in their beginnings they seemed to be 'the glory of the age'.

The teaching given in the Charity Schools was gratuitous. It was open to boys and girls alike. The age of the pupils was from seven to twelve. The chief object was religious, to teach the beliefs and the catechism of the Church of England. But to religious and moral instruction the three simple arts of reading, writing and arithmetic were added, and these necessities thus became the recognized elements of elementary education. It should be added, however, that arithmetic was often regarded as a superior accomplishment to which comparatively few pupils would attain, and for girls generally sewing took its place. The weakness of the Charity Schools seems to have lain in an excessive attention to pious formulas and in a want of intelligence on the part of the teachers. If they gained at first, they suffered afterwards, by their close connexion with the Church. Though Dissenters helped to establish them, their teaching sometimes tended to exclude Dissenters, and the whole system was presently overtaken by the apathy which the ecclesiastical politics of the eighteenth century produced.

The same desire, however, to promote the moral and religious instruction of poor people led, before the eighteenth century was over, to a general movement for founding Sunday Schools. In these schools, besides the elements of religion, a certain amount of reading, a little writing, and still less arithmetic was taught; and their organization, which may be dated from about 1780, came to be regarded as an important element, by some indeed as the only necessary element, in the education of the poor. Schools of Industry, which 'mixed labour with learning', followed; and the success attained by

Hannah More, with her sister's assistance, in establishing Sunday Schools and Schools of Industry in Somersetshire illustrated again the powers which won Dr. Johnson's esteem. Yet, as she wrote to William Wilberforce, the farmers told her that they did not want their ploughmen made wiser than themselves; and one farmer's wife, who could not read, added that the lower classes were fated to be ignorant and wicked, and that we 'could not alter what was *decreed*'. But Hannah More herself did not intend to make working people into scholars and philosophers. She taught the girls only such work as might fit them for servants. She did not encourage writing for the poor. Even to some educational reformers of Sir Robert Peel's day public education seemed to be a charity to be conceded by legislators of the upper classes for the benefit of those below.

Secondary education, as we now call it, was a different matter. In that field it cannot be said that the efforts of reformers had by the time of Dr. Johnson had much practical effect. The old Grammar Schools of England were established, many of them, long before the Reformation: the King's School at Canterbury has traced its beginnings back almost to Augustine. Elizabethan writers claimed that Grammar Schools with liberal endowments existed in most 'corporate towns', two or three hundred possibly before the days of Edward VI. In the sixteenth century some important new ones were founded; Merchant Taylors' in London, Holt, Oundle and Tonbridge, Rugby and Harrow are cases in point. The teaching of Latin was the basis of their system; and the tenacity with which they clung to the old classical tradition may have been one cause of their decline. As late as 1805 Lord Eldon ruled that modern languages and even mathematics could not legally be introduced into the curriculum of an endowed Grammar School. They suffered inevitably when private schools sprang up to teach modern subjects. Moreover, it is possible that Royalists long remembered that Hampden, Cromwell and Milton had all been educated at Grammar Schools. The standards and methods of some of the masters employed in them during the eighteenth century did not increase their reputation. Chief Justice Kenyon at the end of that century described them as 'empty walls without scholars', where everything except the receipt of salaries was neglected. In old days they had attracted the best-witted boys: in the eighteenth century, it has been said, they had to be content with the leavings.

The teaching probably had not altered substantially in 200 years. Booksellers could still sell fresh editions of the Latin Grammar which, in its earliest form, Lily had written with help from Erasmus for Colet's new school. The writings of seventeenth-century schoolmasters, like John Brinsley in the days of James I and Charles Hoole who made his reputation during the Civil War, show that efforts were not altogether wanting to lighten and widen the teaching given. Attempts were made to teach English, but they were only partially successful. Writing and arithmetic were not regarded as the school's concern. Hebrew crept in, under Puritan influence, to encourage the study of the Bible. Greek was of some importance; Greek grammar, Xenophon, Homer, Sophocles, Euripides, figure in Hoole's curriculum of Sixth Form teaching. But Latin is the paramount business: Latin grammar and translation, Aesop's Fables, Cicero's Letters, Caesar's Commentaries, Ovid, Livy, Virgil, Horace, Pliny, Juvenal, Plautus, are among the subjects taught. Hours were very long, from 6 to 11 and from 1 to 5.30 in Brinsley's scheme; and one of the characters in his dialogue regrets the two breaks of fifteen minutes allowed at 9 and 3. But between Brinsley's day and Hoole's the advance in method was very slight; the 'good old waie of teaching' still prevailed; and another half-century, though it may have seen some changes in hours and in school-books, probably left the old system in essentials little altered. Hartlib's attack on the methods of seventeenth-century Grammar Schools as 'clogged with much labour, wearinesse and difficulty' was not untrue of George II's day. His complaint that grammatical teaching was 'a stoppage and a let to studies', and a torturing of ingenuous minds, is in effect echoed a century later by Robert Lloyd, who acted for a time as usher at Westminster School;

> Still to be pinioned down to teach
> The syntax and the parts of speech,
> Or perhaps what is drudgery worse,
> The links and points and rules of verse.

It is supported by Joseph Priestley's statement that 'the severe and proper discipline of a grammar school' had become 'a common topic of ridicule' in the early days of George III.

The Grammar Schools fell into some disfavour. It is estimated that over 170 new ones were established between 1660 and 1730, but very few under George II. They still, however, existed in large numbers, and offered to a wide public at least the elements of a classical education. Some of them, of course, did much more. Several expanded into Public Schools. Others, though still ranking as Grammar Schools, grew rich: Christ's Hospital and Dulwich, Bedford and Birmingham are notable examples. Birmingham School was rebuilt in 1734 and rose to new importance in the years which followed. Christ's Hospital early in the nineteenth century was providing education for 1,000 boys and 65 girls. It had developed a mathematical side as early as 1673. Some of the Grammar Schools, the newer ones especially, enlarged their teaching, realizing that arithmetic and modern subjects were desired. English became the language for instruction. At St. Olave's School in London most of the boys gave up the classics. At Beverley and Rotherham the teaching of 'pettyes', simple things like writing and arithmetic, was recognized long before the eighteenth century began. Some famous classical schools like Banbury possibly owed their decline to their unwillingness to expand or modernize their teaching. The fortunes and endowments of the Grammar Schools varied greatly. Reading School, for instance, in the latter part of the eighteenth century was in great repute, while Abingdon and Newbury were seriously declining. Dorchester was reduced to ten boys, Buckingham to six, Buntingford to four. At Berkhampstead one Master took in a few boys while his assistant resided in another county. At Sevenoaks no free scholars could be found.

But others told a different story, and in the North especially there were many signs of growth. Good Masters often drew a good type of pupil. Sedbergh under able Masters numbered 122 boys in the days of George I: it had great fame and won many distinctions at Cambridge in the early years of George III, though there were fluctuations later. Bradford prospered under Benjamin Butler from 1728 to 1784, though the hours were long, from 7 a.m. to 5 p.m., and the teaching severely classical. Writing, arithmetic and modern subjects only came in there in 1784. Wakefield numbered 160 boys in 1717, and, helped by scholars from Trinity, Cambridge, became a famous school in Johnson's day. Manchester secured a great reputation. There were troubles to face in the first half of the eighteenth century. But William Purnell, a devoted Master, carried the School successfully through them. The numbers rose to 170 in the early years of George III. Between 1749 and 1784 Manchester sent to the English Universities 183 boys, of whom 153 had been boarders in the School, and of whom several won mathematical honours. Among these Grammar School pupils and Masters not a few distinguished names were found. Richard Bentley was educated at Wakefield and taught as a Master at Spalding. Samuel Johnson was a pupil, well if roughly taught, at Lichfield, served for a short and miserable time as an usher at Market Bosworth, and tried for one or two masterships elsewhere. Samuel Parr entered Harrow at the age of five and was afterwards a Master at Colchester and Norwich. Vicesimus Knox as Head-master of Tonbridge showed what a classical education could be made.

Public Schools, the greatest development of the Grammar School system in this country, were famous long before the days of Dr. Johnson, but were by no means universally popular with parents. Critics like Swift saw clearly enough the mischiefs which often accompanied education in rich homes, the inefficient tutors, the lack of discipline, the spoiling and coddling of boys 'taught from the nursery' that they were to inherit a great estate, the folly of supposing that accomplishments were all that a gentleman needed and that the study of Greek and Latin was a loss of time. Locke impressed the Whig gentry when he reminded them of the poor quality of some masters, of the 'mixed herd of unruly boys', of the 'tyranny' of Latin grammar, themes and verses, of the lax morals and the rowdy ways, in which, at a very early age, they were asked 'to hazard their sons' innocence and virtue'.

William of Wykeham's great foundation held the primacy in years if not in fashion, and Eton had been established on the Winchester model and started on its career by a Winchester man. Both were still governed by ancient, inelastic statutes, perhaps more inelastic at Winchester than anywhere else. Each had its Warden or Provost, its body of Fellows, its seventy Scholars on the foundation, its Commoners or Oppidans, and at Oxford or Cambridge another College in close connexion with the School. The Scholars in both cases had the minimum of supervision and comfort. In cold weather they probably suffered real hardship. Bullying and brutality were clearly not unknown. At Eton in 1766 the boys were 'supposed to breakfast' after 8, or on holidays after 9. Collegers dined at 12, supped generally at 6, and went to bed, or at any rate were locked up for the night, soon after 8. The Dames' boarding-houses possibly had some civilizing influence on other boys. At Winchester through most of the eighteenth century bread and beer were thought enough for breakfast: tea and coffee were not recognized till 1838. The food was often coarsely cooked. There was for long reluctance on the part of the Fellows to spare money enough for the comfort of 'the children'. But in 1712 the Fellows did, 'out of their tender Care', consent to increase the commons of Collegers by 2¾*d.* a week. And in 1776 they agreed to give them butter at breakfast and some 'garden stuff' with their meat. Till 1708 Collegers at Winchester had to make their beds and sweep out their chambers. The hour for morning chapel was 6 in the summer until the nineteenth century was far advanced. But at Eton and elsewhere hours were growing easier, and plenty of time was allowed for play.

Many of the boys were very young, though Scholars were rarely admitted under eight. The education, founded on Latin, was severely classical. The Eton Latin Grammar was an abbreviation of Lily's ancient book: the Westminster Grammar was to Sydney Smith 'a most atrocious monument of absurdity'. Mathematics and modern languages were no part of the school routine. Writing, English and other 'accomplishments' could be picked up in spare time. The staff and pay of masters was often insufficient, the level of teaching not invariably high. Numbers fluctuated. The Scholars often fell below 70. At Winchester in 1717 there were only 20 Commoners, with the Duke of Hamilton at their head. But under Dr. Burton their number rose rapidly and reached 123 in 1734. Then they declined as quickly. In the middle of the century Scholars and Commoners together numbered only 78, the lowest figure for 400 years. At Eton under Edward Barnard, Head-master from 1754 to 1765—a popular and able man whom Horace Walpole

ETON COLLEGE FROM THE PLAYING FIELDS

called 'the Pitt of schoolmasters'—the number of Oppidans rose largely. Numbers ran up to 500 and more. Men of fashion sent their sons there: in 1766 the Duke of Hamilton headed the Eton aristocrats. Pitt and Fox, Walpole and Wellesley became familiar names in Georgian days. At Winchester Joseph Warton, Head-master from 1766 to 1793, was a literary man of interest and distinction, who would occasionally stand up to Dr. Johnson. But he had no special qualifications for a Head-mastership, and his reign at Winchester was marked by three mutinies among the boys. It can hardly be said that either Winchester or Eton satisfied in those times any educational ideal.

Westminster claimed an even older origin, though Henry VIII and Elizabeth had founded it afresh. But the old buildings of the monks of St. Peter's long supplied a home for the Westminster Scholars. They numbered forty. Choristers enjoyed a preference. Pensioners were boarders. Oppidans, day-boys, came in from outside. At Christ Church, Oxford, and Trinity College, Cambridge, scholarships were reserved for Westminster. In the eighteenth century it rivalled Eton: in the last year of George I it numbered 434 boys. Dr. Busby had greatly increased its reputation, and in the Georgian era William Cowper, Warren Hastings, Gibbon and Bentham were added to its roll. Dr. Nicoll, Head-master from 1733 to 1753, maintained the School's reputation, and the imposing Dr. Markham, who succeeded him, won high ecclesiastical honours. Westminster was famous for its Greek. It was hardly less famous for its neglect of modern subjects, its hard discipline, its fagging. Latin was still the Scholars' official language. English, arithmetic and writing were outside the regular curriculum. Cowper had an inborn taste for literature, and Westminster, at any rate, permitted him to read. But in his *Tirocinium* he deplored the pedantic training, the noise and vice and lying, the wild excursions and quarrels of the boys—Westminster and Eton, Winchester and Harrow would sometimes break into open rebellion—the loss of home life and affections at a very early age. Supervision was very lax. Games were little organized. Football was played, but was not yet popular: a great Head-master at Shrewsbury thought it fit only for butchers' boys. Cricket was beginning: the first Public School cricket match was played, between Eton and Westminster, in 1796. Cowper played both cricket and football, but his memory lingered upon simpler games. Gray remembered hoops at Eton; and marbles, hop-scotch and puss-in-the-corner speak of Public Schoolboys who were very young. Gibbon, happily quartered in his aunt's boarding-house, was less critical of Westminster than Cowper. He thought Public Schools 'adapted to the genius and constitution' of our race.

The Free Grammar Schools of Shrewsbury, Rugby and Harrow date from the same era, but Shrewsbury originated under Edward VI. Rugby and Harrow were endowed later by private persons, Rugby by a merchant who happily owned a few acres close to London, Harrow by a substantial yeoman who loved the hill on which Charles II told his courtiers to look for the Visible Church. Rugby and Harrow in the eighteenth century were making way. But Shrewsbury, after a great start with Philip Sidney for a pupil, had since the Civil War fallen upon evil days. Its Puritan Head-master had been imprisoned after the Restoration. A scholar like George Jeffreys had done nothing to restore its fame. Inadequate Head-masters let the School decline. In the eighteenth century numbers fell more than once to very low figures. It was not till 1798 that a thorough reorganization saved it, and under Dr. Samuel Butler its best days began. Rugby emerged from obscurity under a Head-master, Henry Holyoake, who had shared the persecution of the Magdalen Dons by James II. He made the School respected in the county before he died in 1731. But some twenty years later, when it acquired its new School House, its income was only £116, and there were well under 100 boys there in 1778. Then Dr. James's vigorous administration brought the numbers up to two or three hundred, and raised its reputation to the highest point as yet attained. Harrow also won prosperity under Thomas Brian, who gathered 140 boys there by 1721. And after some vicissitudes Dr. Thackeray and Dr. Sumner, with their Etonian traditions, raised the School again. When Dr. Heath in 1785 gave place to Dr. Drury, there were not far short of 200 boys. Rodney was there before he went to sea in 1732. Wellesley was removed after a riot in 1771, and took his fame and his brother's to Eton. Scholars like Samuel Parr and William Jones were there in 1753. But the best days of Harrow, Rugby, Shrewsbury were still to come. The classics ruled in all alike. At

Harrow arithmetic and writing were taken for granted, religious instruction was almost entirely neglected, and the French master, we are told, 'lived the life of a dog'.

Of the Public Schools in the City of London St. Paul's had the earliest celebrity. Its foundationers were more than twice as numerous as Winchester's or Eton's. Colet's 153 boys still, in the eighteenth century, lived on the same cramped and noisy site, followed the same customs, and learned the same Latin Grammar. Milton and Marlborough, Pepys and Halley had added to their fame. But the Mercers' Company were indifferent Governors. When they fell into financial troubles they borrowed the funds of the School, and their patronage threatened to convert it into 'a mere charitable foundation'. The foundationers had fallen to fifty or less when George Thicknesse was appointed High Master in 1748. Thicknesse restored the numbers and the reputation of the School. But a new site and new methods were needed to do full justice to a great bequest. Merchant Taylors' School, founded in 1561, suffered from some of the same difficulties. Rebuilt after the Fire of London, it still had no more than a small paved court for the boys to play in, which Clive's adventurous spirit must have found inadequate in 1737. The connexion with St. John's College at Oxford gave the School some Scholars of distinction. But under a Jacobite Master numbers fell severely. Then in 1760 James Townley set to work to restore the ground lost, and to bring up the numbers to the proper figure of 250 boys. He tried in vain to modernize the curriculum. But, a friend of Garrick, he was more successful in encouraging dramatic performances in the School. Charterhouse School, which had started work in 1614, was younger, but was more fortunate in the space at its disposal. John Wesley used to run thrice round the green in the morning. In later days he wondered why all the squares and buildings looked so small. The younger boys in Wesley's day were often, it seems, robbed of their rations. William Blackstone may have fared better: he was head of the School in 1738. The Jenkinsons were Charterhouse boys and Georgian statesmen, and other pupils of distinction were not wanting in these London Schools. But in all alike the want of proper supervision and of organized games led to abuses. Charterhouse in George III's day held its own better than some of its contemporaries, but tales of neglect and bullying, of drinking and misconduct, cannot be altogether set aside.

The best summary of the education given, even in Public Schools where some demand for modern subjects might have been expected, is probably that drawn up by Thomas James, an Etonian of 1766, who became Head-master of Rugby later. The hours of work were not in his day excessive. At Eton Tuesday was usually a whole holiday, Thursday a half-holiday, and Saturday a 'Play-at-four'. On a full working day lessons generally lasted from 8 to 9, from 11 to 12, from 3 to 4, and from 5 to 6. Lower boys began work earlier, especially in summer. Eton perhaps had more holidays and festivals than some other Schools. The 'business' of the School included grammar, composition, the reading of Greek and Latin authors, and enough history and geography to understand what those authors wrote. The Head-master's Division read Homer, Lucian, Virgil, Horace, the *Scriptores Romani*, the *Poetae Graeci*, the *Epigrammatum Delectus*, and other books. Dictionaries and lexicons were in universal use. In their leisure hours these older boys were expected to read Cicero, Ovid, *Spectator*, Milton, Pope, Roman and Greek history, Potter's *Antiquities*, 'and all other books necessary towards making a compleat scholar'. Latin themes and Latin verses, Greek iambics, repetitions from Virgil, Horace, and the Greek Grammar, declamations and speeches and map-drawing were also among the studies of the upper school. But only the Sixth Form wrote iambics and were permitted to speak and to declaim. The Fourth Form read Ovid, Aesop, Caesar, Terence, a little Greek Testament, and some other books. They too indulged in repetitions and verses, to a greater extent perhaps than they desired.

The lower forms were less ambitious. Form I learned little but Latin Grammar, and learned it by heart. Form II added the Latin Testament, the Catechism and Phaedrus. Form III began Greek Grammar, and the next promotion was to Latin verse. Holidays and half-holidays were utilized for short lessons in subjects which the school routine neglected—writing and mathematics, a little algebra and Euclid, a little geography, drawing and French. For geography at Eton, Pomponius Mela was the favourite author. To these studies dancing and fencing might be added. At Eton in 1766 the famous family of Angelo already kept a fencing-school, and the interest of drawing was enchanced by learning it from a natural son of Peter the Great. James apparently introduced at Rugby and recommended to Shrewsbury a weekly English exercise and some study of spelling. But for private reading he seems to have preferred selections and abridgements to anything else. The presumption which ran through education was that Latin and Greek were the only subjects to which serious attention need be given. A few small preparatory schools were beginning to be established, to teach young children the elements necessary before they could enter on the classical training of the Public Schools.

The defects of the endowed schools gave great opportunities to private teachers, and it seems that private schools and academies may claim a good deal of the credit for the improvement in education which the eighteenth century shows. In this improvement the Nonconformists, harassed as they were under Charles II and Queen Anne by ecclesiastical prejudice and penal legislation, took a leading part. It was not, it is true, till 1779 that Dissenters secured a general permission to teach, and even then the permission did not apply to most endowed schools. But decisions in the Law Courts limited the Bishops' powers of interference, and many Georgian Bishops had no wish to enforce them. The Nonconformist academies were alive to the need of modernizing education. They appreciated the demand for commercial instruction, for arithmetic, geography, history and drawing. Daniel Defoe found in Charles Morton's academy at Newington good teaching in languages, mathematics, history and logic, and nothing regarded as 'dangerous to monarchical government' even in the days of Charles II. For his *Compleat English Gentleman* Defoe himself proposed an education which should dispense with Greek and Latin, but include natural and experimental philosophy, history, geography, mathematics, astronomy, and even navigation. Richard Frankland's academy at Rathmell was long recognized as an admirable recruiting-ground for Dissenting Ministers in the North of England. It developed into the Manchester Academy after his death in 1698.

In the eighteenth century Nonconformist academies flourished for a time at Whitehaven and Kendal. Dr. Ashworth made Daventry Academy an important centre, and the

July, 1777.

WARRINGTON ACADEMY.

THE TRUSTEES of this ACADEMY beg leave to recommend it to public notice, as affording peculiar advantages for the liberal and virtuous education of youth in general, whether intended for commercial life, or for any of the learned profeffions.

The terms, per feffion, are:

Commons, exclufive of breakfaft, 17 l. Rent of a feparate apartment in buildings erected for the ufe of the ftudents, 3 l. 3 s. A courfe of lectures, which is completed in five years, on theology, ethics, logic, &c. by the Rev. John Aikin, D. D. 3 l. 3 s. Claffics, Greek and Roman, by the fame, 3 l. 3 s. A courfe of lectures on the principal branches of mathematics, and on natural philofophy, theoretical and experimental, by the Rev. William Enfield, LL. D. 3 l. 3 s. A courfe (by the fame) on the following fubjects, Geography, hiftory, commerce, the theory of language, elocution, the principles and feveral fpecies of compofition, 3 l. 3 s. N. B The two preceding courfes are completed in three years each. Lectures on chemiftry, by Mr. Aikin, Surgeon, 2 l. 2 s. On anatomy, by the fame, 1 l. 1 s. N. B. Thefe lectures are read alternate years. French, by Mr. Hulme, 3 l. 3 s. Arithmetic, writing, drawing, by Mr. Bright, 1 l. 1 s. each. Book-keeping and furveying, by the fame, 2 l. 2 s. each. Each ftudent attends fuch lectures only as his friends appoint. Entrance 2 l. 2 s.

Mr. Aikin propofes to give to any gentlemen who are defigned for the medical profeffion, a courfe of private inftructions preparatory to the regular ftudy of phyfic.

The fees for tuition are paid at entrance; thofe for board and apartment at the middle and end of the feffion. The feffion commences on the 10th of September, and continues without interruption to the end of June.

No ftudent is admitted under 13 years of age.

Letters addreffed to the Rev. Dr. Enfield, Warrington, will be duly anfwered.

From the *London Chronicle*, 1777.

Warrington Academy established in 1757 attracted teachers like Joseph Priestley and William Enfield. Two great churchmen of the eighteenth century, Bishop Butler and Archbishop Secker, owed most of their education to Dissenting teachers. Secker has left an interesting account of his own education. He passed from a Free School at Chesterfield to a Nonconformist academy at Sheffield, where he lost most of the Greek and Latin which he had already learned. But after an interval of tutoring in London, largely in geometry and mathematics, philosophy and French, he recovered his classics in another Nonconformist academy at Gloucester, and added to them some Hebrew, Syriac, and Chaldee. With his master, Samuel Jones, he moved to Tewkesbury, where, however, the reputation of the school declined. After that he studied medicine in London, Paris and Leyden, and finally acquired an Oxford degree.

Most private schools reflected the feeling against a narrow classical education, and they were free to try experiments of their own. Boarding Schools for boys sprang up in many places. In the North of England, in Yorkshire in particular, a modern education in a boarding school could be obtained at a low price. Thomas Sheridan had a successful school in Dublin. A teacher of repute could generally, it seems, depend on finding pupils, though Priestley's attempt to establish a boarding school failed, and Johnson's can hardly be called successful. When Johnson started a school at Edial near Lichfield in 1736, to board young gentlemen and teach them the Latin and Greek languages, he hoped to instruct them 'in a method somewhat more rational than those commonly practised', and he set himself to ascertain the practice of Charterhouse and Westminster and other famous schools before drawing up his plan. The list of books which he recommended to a young friend included, for Greek, Cebes, Aelian, Lucian, Xenophon, Homer, Theocritus, Euripides, and, for Latin, Terence, Tully, Caesar, Sallust, Nepos, Velleius Paterculus, Virgil, Horace, Phaedrus. His scheme for the classes of a grammar school prescribed, when the formation of nouns and verbs had been 'perfectly mastered', Corderius by Mr. Clarke, and then Erasmus, with an English translation by the same author; for Class II, Eutropius and Cornelius Nepos or Justin, with the translation; and for Class III, Ovid's Metamorphoses in the morning, Caesar's Commentaries in the afternoon, practice in the Latin rules till the boys were perfect, and then in Mr. Leeds' Greek Grammar. Afterwards this Class should proceed to Virgil and Horace and the writing of themes and verses. A good deal of time was allotted to learning rules and being examined in them. It cannot be said that Johnson's plan showed any marked originality in education, and his boarding school did not attract the public or continue for very long. Though it included David Garrick, it seems never to have counted more than eight pupils. But, as the eighteenth century proceeded, the system of private schools made progress. Dr. Rose and Dr. Charles Burney shared in a successful school at Chiswick during Johnson's later days, and Dr. Burney established one of his own at Hammersmith in 1786. Early in the next century private schools existed in large numbers, and many people seem to have regarded them as free from the defects which still persisted in the Public Schools and Grammar Schools of the time.

Among girls of all classes education was still backward. Efforts indeed were made, mostly very modest efforts, to enable poor girls to share in the instruction provided for poor boys. Apart from the opportunities offered in village schools, girls were admitted to the Charity Schools up and down the country. Christ's Hospital had its contingent of girl pupils. The Grey Coat School at Westminster, the Yellow School at Cirencester, the Free School at Great Marlow, a seventeenth-century foundation, and Colonel Colchester's school at Westbury-on-Severn, included a certain number of girls. But their education was largely utilitarian. Handicrafts like sewing, knitting, spinning, lace-making were almost as important as reading and writing. Arithmetic and advanced studies of that nature working girls were not thought to require. Even the upper classes expected women's education to be confined to simple subjects. Some authorities thought the study of the English language specially well suited to the female mind. But Swift declared that not one young gentlewoman in a thousand was taught to read or spell, and that anything beyond books on devotion or domesticity was regarded as likely to turn a woman's brain. Governesses were generally inefficient, boarding schools sometimes not much better. Even Lady Mary Wortley Montagu, who could not think it 'criminal' to improve her reason, studied Latin surreptitiously, thought scholarship the business of professional men, and advised women to conceal their learning as they would conceal a physical defect. Rousseau's *Emile*, published in 1762, had a profound effect in many ways on French and English education. But Rousseau's prescription for a woman's education was to study what was useful and agreeable, not abstract subjects or the works of genius. Women must learn docility, to endure inconvenience and restraint. The ideal for a mother was to be 'a recluse in her home'. Madame de Genlis found that a taste for the sciences rendered women singular and sundered them from the simplicity of domestic life. Dr. Gregory's *Legacy to his Daughters* advised them in 1774 to be cautious in displaying their good sense.

If you happen to have any learning, keep it a profound secret, especially from the men, who generally look with a jealous and malignant eye on a woman of great parts and a cultivated understanding.

It would never do for women to be thought to 'assume a superiority' over the company they met.

Gradually, however, the demand for women's education increased. Even in Charles II's day Mrs. Bathsua Makin had been bold enough to advocate teaching girls arithmetic and science, and her schools at Putney and at Tottenham for young gentlewomen had inaugurated newer methods. Before the end of the seventeenth century there were prosperous girls' schools in Manchester and York, and in the eighteenth century many boarding schools for girls grew up. They varied, no doubt, widely in usefulness and value. Mrs. Whitney's Boarding School for Young Ladies at Buckingham may have been typical of the cheapest. It offered, about the year 1770, board, lodging, washing, reading, plain and fine needlework for 12 guineas a year. There was another guinea a year if tea and sugar were required. We hear of parlour boarders elsewhere at 25 guineas yearly. But there were better-class schools also and higher fees. Miss Pinkerton's academy is not wholly a caricature. Most girls of the upper classes were taught, either at home or at school, English, writing, arithmetic (for keeping household accounts), drawing, dancing, needlework and a little French. The writing and spelling were often indifferent. Some girls' schools made a point of teaching Italian. In 1777 one preceptress announced that dancing, French and Italian were essential for any female whose parents had the least pretensions to taste. In Johnson's age the teaching of girls as a whole was still among the poorer classes lamentably deficient and among the middle and upper classes largely superficial. For most young ladies a smattering of accomplishments rather than a thorough education was the end in view. But there was at least some desire to learn, which girls of intelligence might hope to satisfy, and which even the eccentricities of fashion or the inadequacy of teachers could not permanently repress.[1]

But if in the eighteenth century the schools of England had many elements of weakness, it cannot be said that the Universities made up for their defects. Alike at Oxford and at Cambridge routine and lethargy reigned. The old forms survived but the old life had gone out of them, and the stirrings of the new life were hardly yet beginning to show. Students disinclined for study found teachers often equally indifferent. Some hard workers of course there were, though many undergraduates went down without degrees. But zeal and enthusiasm were generally out of fashion. At Oxford the statutes of Archbishop Laud still governed the University. It was not till 1760 that the right to amend them was allowed. The Hebdomadal Board, the Vice-Chancellor, Proctors and Heads of Houses, had become all-powerful. The business of the old Congregation of Regent Masters was practically confined to dispensations and degrees. Convocation, with its reserve of non-resident voters, could generally be relied on to oppose innovations, and was always inclined to oppose the Hebdomadal Board. The new impulse given to science in the seventeenth century seemed to have received a check. Clerical traditions still dominated thought. Even in the nineteenth century Newman reminded his contemporaries that Scripture believed the earth to be stationary, and Keble maintained that when God made the stones He also made the fossils in them.

At Cambridge in the same way ancient statutes, dating from the days of Elizabeth, still held the field. Designed originally to repress 'the increasing audacity and excessive licence of men', they had in effect taken the government of the University out of the hands of the younger Regent Masters. An academic oligarchy, entitled the Caput,

[1] Johnson himself gave Latin lessons to Queeney Thrale and for a time to Fanny Burney. Mme D'Arblay's *Diary*, vol. i, pp. 243 and 427.

appointed by Heads of Colleges and Doctors, ruled. But Cambridge, as compared with Oxford, was less conservative and clerical in feeling, and both in education and in politics was readier to welcome new ideas. The influence of Newton was already proving irresistible. Newtonian mathematics were soon to be paramount in the Schools. By 1774 the champions of the classics were driven to take refuge in skits.

> See Euclid proudly spurns the Mantuan muse,
> While gentle Horace wipes Maclaurin's shoes.
> There Homer learns the theory of light,
> And tortured Ovid learns to sum and write.

Bentley, the prince of classical scholars, was ready to welcome the new studies. He defended religion by appealing to science. He built an observatory at Trinity for the first Plumian Professor of Astronomy. He fitted up a laboratory for the first Professor of Chemistry. He helped to found the first Professorship of Botany. And quarrel as he might continuously and scandalously with his Fellows at Trinity, abuse his position as he undoubtedly did, his zeal for education cannot be denied. Bentley's troubled reign at Trinity ended in 1742, and few other Cambridge Heads in the eighteenth century attained a like distinction. But John Covel of Christ's College, an octogenarian of George I's day, had a reputation for travel, languages and science. Thomas Sherlock, for a short time Master of St. Catharine's, developed into a great churchman. Daniel Waterland at Magdalene was not only a vigorous theologian, but a notable tutor and Master of his College. Edmund Law, Master of Peterhouse in 1756, won fame both as philosopher and as divine. William Powell, Master of St. John's in 1765, instituted College examinations, and greatly strengthened the position of his Society. Isaac Milner, towards the end of the century, upheld both education and evangelicalism at Queens'. These and others may be set against such academic figures of the eighteenth century as contributed little in intellect or breeding to the fame of the University they served.

At Oxford old loyalties were too persistent and polemics too engrossing to make a healthy atmosphere for education in early Georgian days. Cambridge of course had its Jacobites. In 1717 twenty-two Fellows of St. John's College were deprived for refusing the oaths to the Government. But Whig feeling generally prevailed. George II visited

Cambridge and gave £2,000 towards the completion of the Senate House. At Oxford there could be no visits from Hanoverian Sovereigns. The old capital of the Cavaliers still hankered after the divine right of Stuart Kings. With a Whiggish Constitution Club, considered 'insolent' in its adherence to the new dynasty, there were bound to be outbreaks of Jacobite feeling in 1715 and other unsettling years. Indeed there were said to be only three Colleges in Oxford where the Heads were not violent and disloyal Tories. Atterbury, who passed from Christ Church to a Bishopric in 1713, was closely associated with the Jacobite party. Dr. Shippen, Principal of Brasenose from 1710 to 1745, was the brother of the Jacobite leader in the House of Commons. In some respects a quarrelsome and untrustworthy ruler, he had at least one boon companion among contemporary Heads. Dr. King of St. Mary Hall persisted for years in advertising his Jacobite opinions, and found some undergraduates ready to echo them too noisily as late as 1748. But after George III's accession even Dr. King had to admit that the cause was dead. Other College Heads were less actively polemical. Dr. Leigh, appointed Master of Balliol by what some thought a scandalous job in 1726, was content to let his College decline into reaction and obscurity for fifty years. Dr. Charlett at University had friends and correspondents in every political party. Provost Lancaster of Queen's and his immediate successors were preoccupied in rebuilding their College. Dr. Gardiner made some struggle against abuses at All Souls. Dr. Newton at Hertford showed the zeal of a reformer. But types of academic energy were rare. Quarrels over College elections were only too common. Just before the end of the seventeenth century Humphrey Prideaux, asked to recommend a College for his nephew, had replied that most rulers of Colleges in Oxford were 'such as I could scarce committ a dog to their charge'. Half a century may have brought improvement, but it would have been hard to find among them any figures of outstanding dignity and power.

In October 1728 Samuel Johnson went up from Lichfield to Pembroke College, Oxford, a boy of nineteen, very conscious of his poverty, rather fierce and bitter in his independence; and there he learned to know his Homer, his Horace, his Euripides, dipped into metaphysics, read widely on all sorts of subjects, and dreamed ambitiously of travelling abroad. Six years later Thomas Gray went up from Eton to Cambridge. He became a Pensioner at Peterhouse, but it was in Pembroke that he ultimately found a home. Gray read classics, principally Statius and Propertius, wrote graceful Latin verses, learned Italian, steadily eschewed metaphysics and mathematics, and went down, like Johnson, without taking a degree. Johnson revisited Oxford a quarter of a century later and became a welcome guest in College Common Rooms till the end of his life. Gray was a Professor of History at Cambridge when he died. For both the education offered was little more than a continuance of the classics learned at school, with 'the rudiments', as Thomas Sheridan put it, 'of logick, natural philosophy, astronomy, metaphysics and the heathen morality' thrown in.

The old tests and exercises of medieval days remained. But most of them had lost their meaning. The old disputations were still the principal requirements for degrees. *Disputationes in Parviso* were disputations in grammar and logic, three days a week in full term, continued for several terms. *Answering under Bachelor* meant more disputations, in which a Bachelor acted as Moderator—questions in logic, grammar, rhetoric, politics or ethics, taken twice in the third or fourth year. And the public *Examination* meant *viva voce* questions in grammar, logic, ethics, Latin, Greek and other subjects, put to candidates by three Regent Masters nominated by the Senior Proctor. *Determination*, the ancient ceremony on Ash Wednesday, was followed by more disputations by Determiners during Lent. Candidates for the Master's degree had then to fulfil certain further requirements, in which disputations, at Oxford especially, played the largest part, and to take an oral examination similar to the Bachelor's, but embracing philosophy and history, astronomy and Hebrew in its scope. At both Universities there had long crept into these old ceremonies certain elements of farce. At Cambridge the Tripos had a curious history. The tripos-verses, Latin compositions bearing on questions propounded for disputation, had replaced the speech of the old Bachelor seated on a three-legged stool, who had formerly disputed with the questionists seeking a Bachelor's degree. About 1748 the Moderators, who supervised the disputations, began to print the lists of successful candidates on the back of the tripos-verses. The lists became known as the Tripos, and from them the name was transferred to the examination itself. Wrangler and Optime are in the same way terms derived from the old disputations. Both at Oxford and Cambridge the ancient practices led to licence. The gibes and innuendoes of the *Terrae Filius* became almost unendurable to College Heads whose proceedings were not above reproach. At Oxford the anniversary of the *Act* was frequently suppressed. At Cambridge in 1740, ten years after the new Senate House was opened, the authorities forbade the mocking of the disputants with unseemly jokes. But the disputations of the old Act[1] continued for long to be the chief test of academic distinction, and the growing predominance of mathematics at Cambridge tended to make the statutory exercises there less and less satisfactory as a test of genuine work.

Reforming spirits—and there were such even in eighteenth-century Colleges—were fully alive to the faults of the system. John Napleton, a vigorous tutor of Brasenose, freely denounced its 'lifeless unedifying formalities' in 1773, and going to the root of the matter demanded real examinations, to be held at fixed dates under proper conditions and followed by class-lists of successful students. Dr. Jebb of Peterhouse about the same time proposed, though vainly, to establish for all students at Cambridge an annual examination in a wide range of subjects, including classics, history, mathematics and philosophy, and Vicesimus Knox a little later published a slashing attack upon the Oxford ways. The greatest dunce, he declared, could get his *testimonium* signed 'with as much ease and credit as the finest genius'. The candidates had little books of stock questions, and the examiners knew just what to ask. Sometimes the questions were deliberately farcical. Sometimes the examiners were 'pot companions of the candidate'. The antiquated forms were 'contemptible minutiae'. The examination for the Master's degree at Oxford was no more serious than that for the Bachelor's. Knox begged the Prime Minister to call in Parliament to revise University Statutes, to get rid of useless forms and needless oaths, to insist on longer residence and better discipline, to put down undesirable privileges, to increase the pay of College tutors, to make the education offered more worthy of the name. At Cambridge other voices

[1] The elaborate ancient ritual of Inception to the Master's degree.

were already echoing these sentiments, and urging that the admission of Nonconformists to the Universities could no longer be reasonably denied.

The days of Dr. Johnson were not destined to see large reforms at Oxford. But the demand for better methods quietly gained ground. Men like John Eveleigh, elected Provost of Oriel in 1781, Cyril Jackson, appointed Dean of Christ Church in 1783, and John Parsons, who succeeded to the Mastership of Balliol later, gave the movement powerful support. In the year 1800 a new Examination Statute at last established a real examination and an Honours list. At Cambridge the University examinations became effective at an earlier date. The modern system really began when it was realized that the test of merit offered by the old exercises needed to be supplemented by examinations, and when examinations, at first oral but afterwards written ones, began to count for more than the disputations of the past. The Senate House Examination, when the Moderators took to summoning doubtful candidates, probably dates from the reign of George I; in the middle of the century its importance was admitted. In 1753 the division of candidates into Wranglers, Senior Optimes and Junior Optimes appeared. Ten years later the examination had become the recognized way of determining places, and the old exercises were regarded as a rough preliminary test. Another ten years saw the practice of dictating questions for written answers established. But for long the Mathematical Tripos was the only one: and it is surprising to find how often men brought up in classical schools won high places in it after a short training. Paley is alleged to have gained a Senior Wranglership on little more than twelve months' work. Even in Porson's University the Classical Tripos was not established till 1822.

The level of teaching in the eighteenth-century Universities was not generally very high. While at Cambridge mathematics overshadowed classics, at Oxford antiquarian and oriental studies won some prominence: Anglo-Saxon made progress: English literature, French and Italian, music and dancing, had votaries too. But in the first sixty years of the century several new Professorships were established—new Cambridge Chairs in chemistry, astronomy, experimental philosophy, anatomy, botany, Arabic, geology, geometry:

new Oxford Chairs in poetry, botany, Arabic, experimental philosophy, and Common Law. Among University prizes, which were more numerous at Cambridge than at Oxford, some encouragement of classics appeared. Chancellors at both Universities gave medals or prizes for them. The Cambridge Members gave prizes for Latin Prose. And in 1774 Sir William Browne's medals for Greek and Latin odes and epigrams indicated a certain change in classical taste. At Oxford scientific subjects struggled to assert themselves. Gregory and Keill, as Savilian Professors, did their best to maintain the stimulus which Wallis had given. Chemistry, anatomy and botany attracted students, but found it difficult to secure fair play. Joseph Bankes of Christ Church proposed in 1760 to import a botany lecturer from Cambridge. In 1724 the Crown endowed Professorships of History in both Universities, from whose modest emoluments teachers in modern languages had to be paid. But it was noticeable that comparatively few of the Professors lectured. Spence in the new History Chair at Oxford, had little inclination to do so. Gray, who held the same post at Cambridge, 'constantly intended to read lectures', but his intention was defeated by indifferent health. Sibthorpe, Sherardian Professor of Botany for thirty-six years, is reported to have lectured once. Blackstone, on the other hand, lectured finely at Oxford on the Common Law; and Richard Watson, elected Professor of Chemistry at Cambridge in 1764, though he 'had never read a syllable on the subject nor seen a single experiment', lectured with remarkable success. But when appointed Professor of Divinity later—a subject of which he knew as much 'as could reasonably be expected'—he plunged into ecclesiastical studies, and as Bishop in Llandaff and resident in Westmorland could not reasonably be expected to teach pupils in Cambridge. Even Thomas Warton, the most popular member of a well-known academic family, could find little time for lecturing, though he spent his life at Trinity, Oxford. Professor successively of Poetry and of History, Poet Laureate, and one of the representative literary figures of his day, Warton was at home in every Common Room. He loved his jokes, his ale and his tobacco, and the riverside watermen and his cronies in the taverns. And he loved literature and politics, Tory politics especially, with all his heart.

Lively critics did not hesitate to draw attention to the weaknesses of the educational system. Cowper, whose brother was a Cambridge undergraduate, wrote about 'ignorance in stilts'. Joseph Butler of Oriel found Oxford teaching in 1715 so frivolous that he thought of migrating to Cambridge. But even at Cambridge lectures could be 'odious beyond conception', to a man like Gilbert Wakefield sixty years later on. Amhurst, a bitter young Oxford satirist, talked of debauchees acting as Professors of Moral Philosophy, and of astronomy teachers who had never in their lives looked soberly upon the stars. Adam Smith, a lonely student at Balliol in 1745, declared that most Professors 'had given up altogether even the pretence of teaching'. Gibbon, a Gentleman Commoner of Magdalen in 1752, found the Oxford Professors 'secure in the enjoyment of a fixed stipend, without the necessity of labour or the apprehension of control'. It was not a complete answer to urge, as Dr. Parr urged forty or fifty years afterwards, that few Cambridge Professors were 'disgraced by notorious incapacity or criminal negligence', or to plead, as James Hurdis pleaded at Oxford, that nine of the twenty Professors there were then lecturing regularly, that five others might be for aught he knew, that three were lecturing once a term, that two others would do so if they had any audiences, and that one was shortly going to begin.

But if University teaching failed, there was more hope in the Colleges and in the tutorial system which was quietly growing up. The tutor's responsibility for discipline and conduct was increasingly recognized in the seventeenth century. He had often a twofold responsibility, to his College and to his pupil's parents. The system had its dangers. A bad tutor might become a toady. In Universities staffed by clerical celibates there were too many Fellows waiting for livings, too many tutors with an eye on ecclesiastical preferments which young men of rank or their relatives might be able to confer. Moreover, College teachers were sometimes inadequate. Bentham thought his a gloomy sort of Protestant monk. Johnson rudely said that his tutor's lecture on logic was not worth half the twopenny fine imposed for missing it. But in other tutors a different spirit prevailed. John Wesley, elected in 1726 to a Fellowship at Lincoln, proposed at once to be busy as long as he lived, and would have thought himself 'little better than a highwayman' if he had not lectured on every weekday in the week. Tutors of that stamp could even in the eighteenth century win response. Dr. Waterland's *Advice* to young students at Cambridge, republished at Oxford in 1755, showed, it is true, little freshness in the training recommended, and was contented with a range of classical studies little beyond the powers of a fourth- or fifth-form boy at school. But, nevertheless, Cambridge tutors like Waterland at Magdalene, Laughton at Clare, Law and Paley at Christ's College, Jebb at Peterhouse and Powell at St. John's, laboured hard to make teaching a reality. College examinations did a good deal to make up for the University's defects. And at Oxford a number of able tutors, including men like John Burton at Corpus, who struggled to introduce Locke's teaching, Francis Thompson at Queen's, who was said to understand Newton's *Principia* better than Newton himself, Conybeare at Exeter, and several others, kept teaching and scholarship alive, until Eveleigh and Jackson and Parsons and their contemporaries could carry through the University their educational reforms.

Sketches of the two Universities remain to us, drawn by observant foreigners in the eighteenth century. Von Uffenbach, a German traveller, visited first Cambridge and then Oxford in 1710. At Cambridge he wondered at the paucity of lectures, and at the Fellow-Commoners served by poorer men. He was specially interested in libraries. He had some good words for Wren's magnificent library at Trinity: the College hall he thought ugly and smoky and smelling of bread and meat. He admired also the fine Master's Lodge at Trinity, the new buildings of Clare and the organ in King's College Chapel. But he found Magdalene a very old and mean building, and the books in its library 'overgrown with mould'. The library at Caius' was in a 'miserable garret', little visited and thick with dust. The University library was kept in two mean rooms, one of them half empty; the librarian was absent, as, apparently, his custom was. And some other College libraries visited, those at Trinity Hall and Peterhouse, at Christ's and Pembroke and St. John's, yielded little but disappointment and dust. Von Uffenbach was equally critical at Oxford. Certain new buildings, the new Chapel at Trinity, the new College at Queen's, he approved.

Christ Church hall, he admitted, was 'exceedingly large and lofty'; but again the 'stench of bread and meat' in it, the dirty tablecloths, the wooden platters, made it a place in which no German gentleman could eat or live. All Souls was just planning its great library: Von Uffenbach was indignant that any one should have given £10,000 for 'a palace for these lazy *socios*'. At All Souls and elsewhere he found some unreadiness to show him what he wished to see. The Bodleian was intolerably noisy, and seemed to regard as its chief objects of interest two worm-eaten loaves from the siege of Oxford and one of Queen Elizabeth's shoes. The visitor evidently failed to discover the real treasures there. The Ashmolean Museum was equally disappointing. The Physic Garden showed the same traces of neglect. There were grounds, no doubt, for some of the criticisms passed. But a young Danish visitor of those days, Lewis Holberg, who stayed in Oxford longer and learned to know it much better than Von Uffenbach, has drawn a pleasanter picture of the society he found, of its talk, its hospitality, its love of humour, and of the kindness which it was ready to show to any foreigner adopted as a friend.

Von Uffenbach's disparaging criticism of Cambridge may be balanced by Bentley's characteristic boast that he had found Trinity brick and left it marble.

> The College chapel, from a decayed, antiquated model, made one of the noblest in England; the College hall from a dirty, sooty place, restored to its original beauty, and excelled by none in cleanliness and magnificence.

But the chief work done at Trinity in the eighteenth century consisted in repairs and improvements, in the beautifying of the Master's Lodge, the stuccoing of the Great Court, the reconstruction by James Essex, a remarkable architect, of Nevile's Court and the Combination Rooms. At Cambridge during that century no new Colleges were built. But Clare completed its beautiful buildings and designed a new Chapel. Peterhouse and St. Catharine's added new blocks. Magdalene established Pepys' library in its new home. King's College invited Hawksmoor and Wren to plan a great quadrangle, but finally entrusted the task to Gibbs. Several Colleges carried out important alterations, improved the Lodges—sometimes encroaching on the space required for students—introduced sash windows, panelled walls, handsome fire-places, and other signs of comfort, adorned their halls and chapels and gardens, rebuilt the bridges over the river, and cased their ancient courts in stone, imposing, after the fashion of the day, a full Italian dress on the old walls beneath. At Oxford there were larger architectural changes and threats of others larger still. The rebuilding of Queen's proceeded vigorously after 1704. Worcester College was founded in 1714, and in the ancient grounds of Gloucester Hall new buildings presently appeared. Hart Hall was converted into Hertford College about 1739 by the indefatigable Dr. Newton, a genuine eighteenth-century reformer. Christ Church, Oriel, University, Jesus, Pembroke and several other Colleges added notably to their buildings and quadrangles. A Music Room was opened in 1748. Bocardo[1] vanished in 1772. Old buildings were remodelled, old inclosures swept away, old gardens beautified afresh. Battlements replaced gables, fire-places the old braziers of the past. Hawksmoor built the Clarendon Building, Gibbs the Radcliffe Camera. And Hawksmoor, who was mainly responsible for the new College at Queen's and the new quadrangle at All Souls, also drew magnificent plans for rebuilding Brasenose, Magdalen and Christ Church. There was no limit to the grandiose ambitions of the advocates of the Palladian style.

One feature of University life in the eighteenth century no observer could overlook. It was the predominance of rich and idle undergraduates, called Gentleman-Commoners at Oxford and Fellow-Commoners at Cambridge, young men of rank and fortune, who lived a life of pleasure, not of work. The grant of special rights to privileged persons, a fault which our Public Schools had avoided, led to inevitable abuse. There were gradations among these privileged Commoners. But they all stood on a different footing from ordinary undergraduates, wore handsomer dresses, paid higher fees, spent two or three times as much money, had servants as well as servitors to wait on them, were admitted to the Fellows' table, the Fellows' Common Room, even the Fellows' cellar. They resided or not, read or not, as they pleased. At one Oxford College early in the century a

[1] The medieval prison over the Bocardo gate of the city in which in the past scholars of the University had expiated their offences. Cranmer spent part of the period of his imprisonment there.

notorious don drank with a young Duke, a boy of fifteen, till two in the morning. Another young Duke was given a Doctor's degree as a compliment, and Nell Gwyn's grandson received an M.A. at a special Convocation called for the purpose. At Cambridge, in days when the Colleges were poorly filled, Fellow-Commoners were more numerous than they had ever been before. Gray speaks of 'the Bucks' running mad, breaking into shops and setting women on their heads in the street. Two prominent members of the class were with him at Peterhouse, Lord Euston, afterwards the Duke of Grafton, and James Lowther, afterwards the first Earl of Lonsdale. Gray's old schoolfellow Horace Walpole was hardly less conspicuous at King's.

Most young men of fashion entered the Universities as Gentleman or Fellow-Commoners. William Pitt went up in that capacity to Trinity, Oxford, in 1727. Four Norths, with one future Prime Minister among them, forsaking the family tradition at Cambridge, joined the same Oxford College in the eighteenth century. Five future Prime Ministers may be counted among the Gentleman-Commoners of Oxford between 1730 and 1776. At Christ Church Gentleman-Commoners were specially plentiful. The House was at the height of its glory in Dean Jackson's day. Charles Fox was a Gentleman-Commoner at Hertford, fascinating every one, at the age of fifteen. But, unlike most students of that type, he read voraciously, 'as if his bread depended on a Fellowship', to the complete bewilderment of his tutor. At Cambridge the politicians were hardly less conspicuous, and they interfered more conspicuously in University affairs. Thomas Pelham Holles, afterwards Duke of Newcastle, was at Clare in 1709, and was Chancellor of the University for many years later, just as Lord North, another unfortunate Prime Minister, was for years Chancellor at Oxford. Newcastle had a genius for jobbery and intrigue. He intervened constantly in University and College politics, even in small matters like the election of a Craven Scholar. The younger Pitt, runs the entry at Pembroke, 'anno aetatis suae decimo quarto nondum completo admissus est ad Mensam Sociorum': he came up soon afterwards with a tutor and a nurse. William Wilberforce at St. John's was given to understand that assiduity in learning was not expected from young men of fortune. Even Wordsworth's companions at St. John's spent their time in 'invitations, suppers, wine and fruit'. There were of course serious and thoughtful boys among Gentleman-Commoners: Charles Fox and William Pitt are evidence of that. But Vicesimus Knox's charges of immorality, drunkenness, idleness, ignorance, cannot be lightly dismissed. Organized games were still at a discount, cricket and football hardly developed, systematic boating not yet begun. And boys with too much money and too little occupation found racing, gambling, cock-fights, prize-fights, bull-baitings and all kinds of frolics difficult to resist. It is significant that College Fellows too often encouraged ideas of licence. At Cambridge in the middle of the century dons were conspicuous in opposing the Chancellor's efforts at reform.

At the other end of the social scale were the Servitors or Sizars, eking out a scanty income by doing small menial services for the richer men. Oxford caricaturists drew descriptions of them, cleaning shoes and doing exercises for the more fortunate, calling them in the morning, carrying in their meals, inheriting perhaps their old clothes and books. A servitor might be very humbly born, he might lodge wretchedly and toil hard. He might hate, as Whitefield, Wesley's follower, did at Pembroke, to go round calling men on dark mornings, lest the Devil should be lurking at the top of the stair. But the services did not in most cases differ widely from the services rendered by school fags, and the odd shillings which they brought in made all the difference. At Cambridge one experienced critic recommended parents of limited means to send their sons to Trinity as sizars. They got better fed there than the commoners, from the rich leavings of the Fellows' table, and paid nothing for their food. Sizars at Cambridge were, it seems, rather better off on the whole than servitors at Oxford, though their status was practically the same. Both in the eighteenth century were numerous. At Jesus, Cambridge, Sterne's College and Coleridge's, the sizars about 1750 were almost two-thirds of the College. Dr. Caryl, Master in 1758, started as a sizar. So did Isaac Milner, President of Queen's in 1788, and many another eminent man. At Oxford Dr. Potter, Archbishop of Canterbury, Dr. Lancaster, Provost of Queen's, Dr. Royse, Provost of Oriel, and many students destined for academical distinction, were servitors in their early days. It was not so

THE INTERIOR OF THE RADCLIFFE LIBRARY

From The Oxford Almanack, *1751*

much the difference of work or dress or condition which made the position difficult. It was the poverty contrasted with the wealth around them which sometimes perhaps embittered servitors and sizars alike.

Oxford and Cambridge were still preserves of the Church. Theology was still in theory the chief of their studies. And religious questions played their part in the Universities of the eighteenth century. But the controversies of Cambridge theologians cannot be treated here. The liberal-minded philosophy which preferred common sense to zeal and latitude to dogma, and which is reflected in the writings of Edmund Law and William Paley, had an important influence with Cambridge divines. The freedom of thought and the inclination towards Unitarian beliefs, attributed to men like William Whiston, Samuel Clarke and Conyers Middleton, became towards the end of the century to some extent identified with advanced political opinions. But it did not prevent the growth of a strong and earnest Evangelical party, in which Charles Simeon, at King's College in 1779, became a leading figure. Oxford took its share, a subordinate share, in Deistic and speculative controversies. Dean Prideaux was alarmed by the Atheists, Deists, Socinians, Arians, and other Sectaries 'set, as in battle array against us'. In 1729 the Vice-Chancellor thought it necessary to issue a warning against the advocates of pretended human reason who attacked the Christian creed. The University also took a curious interest in the efforts of John Wesley and his followers to introduce some method of strict religious practice into undergraduate life. But the Oxford Movement of the early eighteenth century never made a wide academic appeal. Enthusiasm so peculiar was generally condemned. In 1768 a little group of Methodist students was expelled. Even Dr. Johnson, who respected Wesley personally, felt that in the University of Oxford such practices were out of place.

It was in 1754 that Johnson's later visits to Oxford began. They gave him a Master's degree, in which he delighted, and he found friends of all kinds there—College Heads like Dr. Adams of Pembroke, dons like Thomas Warton, who looked up points for him at the Bodleian, undergraduates, young men of fashion, who routed him out in the Temple at dawn. He had a special group of friends at University

College, where Dr. Wetherell made him welcome, and where Robert Chambers, a distinguished tutor and afterwards in India a distinguished judge, introduced him to the two young Scotts, who were soon to be the glory of the College. There in the Common Room Johnson held sway, and dons bowed willingly or unwillingly before him. The talk ranged far and wide. The Doctor would allow that discipline was needed; 'subordination is sadly broken down'. But he would not have the old order attacked. Religious tests must stand. 'Our Universities were founded to bring up members for the Church of England.' As for lectures, they were 'unnecessary now, when all can read'. There might be in Oxford some 'labefactation' of principle, but that was common enough elsewhere. They would talk about the Oxford Press and Shakespeare and Milton. They would talk too about their contemporaries, Charles Fox and Burke and Warren Hastings. Johnson became almost an Oxford institution as the years went on. In 1782 Hannah More met him at Jesus College, where his host, Dr. Edwards, had gathered a party of all that was 'most learned and famous in this University'. The old man showed her round his own old College. Two years later he was paying his last visit. And, as Johnson passed from the scene at Oxford, the University prepared itself for a new world and new ideas.

BIBLIOGRAPHY.—*On education generally*: Useful books illustrating the educational progress of the eighteenth century among all classes are J. W. ADAMSON'S *Pioneers of Modern Education, 1600–1700* (1905) and *Short History of Education* (1922); O. BROWNING'S *Introduction to History of Educational Theories* (1881); J. LOCKE'S *Conduct of the Understanding* (ed. T. Fowler, 1890) and *Some Thoughts concerning Education* (1693); J. E. G. DE MONTMORENCY'S *Progress of Education in England* (1904); J. PRIESTLEY'S *Essay on a course of Liberal Education* (1765); T. SHERIDAN'S *British Education* (1756); FOSTER WATSON'S *Beginnings of the teaching of modern subjects in England* (1909), and articles in the *Gentleman's Magazine* on 'The Education of the Early Nonconformists' (Sept. 1901), 'Unlicensed Nonconformist Schoolmasters', 1662 and onwards (Sept. 1902), and 'Schoolmaster Followers of Bacon and Comenius' (Nov. 1903); H. WOTTON'S *Essay on the Education of Children*, &c. (1753).

Among books dealing with upper class education, J. L. COSTEKER'S *Fine Gentleman* (1732), D. DEFOE'S *Compleat English Gentleman* (ed. Bülbring, 1890), Lady MARY WORTLEY MONTAGU'S *Letters and Works* (ed. Lord Wharncliffe and W. M. Thomas, 1887), and J. Swift's essays *On Modern Education* and *Of the Education of Ladies* (Works, ed. Scott, 1814) may be mentioned. Information as to humbler forms of education will be found in the *Account of the Charity Schools* (6th ed. 1707) and W. HENDLEY'S *Defence of the Charity Schools* (1725); in T. GARRARD'S *Edward Colston, the Philanthropist* (1852); in W. ROBERTS' *Memoirs of Hannah More* (3rd ed. 1835); in C. WASE'S *Considerations concerning Free Schools as settled in England* (1678); in T. WILSON'S *True Christian*

Method of Educating the Children both of the Rich and Poor (1729); and in poems like O. GOLDSMITH'S *Deserted Village* (1770) and W. SHENSTONE'S *Schoolmistress* (1742). E. H. W. MEYERSTEIN'S *Chatterton* (1930) contains an account of Colston's school with much original material.

On the Grammar Schools: A. F. LEACH'S volumes on *English Schools at the Reformation* (1896) and *Educational Charters and Documents* (1911) are of value for the early history. N. CARLISLE'S *Concise Description of the Endowed Grammar Schools in England and Wales* (1818) gives some account of schools existing at that time, and the *Report of the Schools Inquiry Commission* (1868) has useful facts. Books like J. BRINSLEY'S *Ludus Literarius* (1612), C. HOOLE'S *New Discovery of the old art of teaching schoole* (1660), and FOSTER WATSON'S *English Grammar Schools to 1660* (1908) explain methods of teaching which survived. F.B.'s (BROKESBY'S) *Of Education with respect to Grammar Schools and the Universities* (1701) and J. CLARKE'S *Essay upon the Education of Youth* (1720) illustrate some eighteenth-century views; and R. AINSWORTH'S *Thesaurus Linguae Latinae Compendiarius* (3rd ed. 1741), T. HAYNE'S *Grammatices Latinae Compendium* (1680), and J. WARD'S *Short Introduction of Grammar* (1752) illustrate the books in use. But fuller information on particular schools will be found in the histories of Bradford Grammar School by W. CLARIDGE (1882), of Christ's Hospital by E. H. PEARCE (1901), of The King's School, Canterbury (*Memorials*) by C. E. WOODRUFF and H. J. CAPE (1865), of Lichfield by P. LAITHWAITE (1925), of Manchester by A. A. MUMFORD (1919), of Sedbergh by H. L. CLARKE and W. N. WEECH (1925), of Wakefield by M. H. PEACOCK (1892), of Warwick by A. F. LEACH (1906), and others.

On the Public Schools: There are now books of value on the history of most leading schools: e.g. on *Charterhouse Old and New* by E. P. EARDLEY WILMOT and E. C. STREATFIELD (1895); on Eton, Sir H. C. MAXWELL LYTE'S *History* (1875); on Harrow, the *History* by P. M. THORNTON (1885) and *Harrow School*, ed. by E. W. HOWSON and G. T. WARNER (1898); on Merchant Taylors', the *History* by H. B. WILSON (1812); on Rugby, the volume by H. C. BRADBY (1900) and the *History* by N. H. NICHOLAS (1826); on St. Paul's, the *History* by M. F. J. MCDONNELL (1909); on Shrewsbury, the *Annals* by G. W. FISHER (1899); on Westminster, the *Annals* by J. SARGEAUNT (1898); on Winchester, the *Annals* by T. F. KIRBY (1892) and the *History* by A. F. LEACH (1899). W. COWPER'S *Tirocinium* (1784) gives a side-light on Westminster, and A. K. COOK writes pleasantly *About Winchester College* (1917).

On the two Universities: See the *Historical Registers* (1900 and 1910); the University Histories, *Cambridge*, by J. B. MULLINGER (1873, &c.) and *Oxford*, by C. E. MALLET (vol. iii, 1927); the *College Histories* published by F. E. Robinson & Co.; V. KNOX'S essays *On Some Parts of the Discipline in our English Universities* (1778) and *Liberal Education* (1781); H. PRIDEAUX'S 'Articles for the Reformation of the two Universities', printed in his *Life* (1748); J. E. SANDYS'S *History of Classical Scholarship* (1903–8); L. STEPHEN'S *History of English Thought in the Eighteenth Century* (1876); D. WATERLAND'S *Advice to a Young Student* (1730); CHRISTOPHER WORDSWORTH'S *Social Life at the English Universities in the Eighteenth Century* (1874) and *Scholae Academicae* (1877).

On Oxford: Interesting information will be found in N. A.'s (AMHURST'S) *Terrae Filius* (1726); J. AYLIFFE'S *Antient and Present State of the University* (1714); BOSWELL'S *Life of Johnson* (ed. G. B. Hill, 1887) and *Johnsonian Gleanings* by A. L. READE (1909, &c.); G. COX'S *Recollections* (1868); E. GIBBON'S *Memoirs* (ed. G. B. Hill, 1900); A. D. GODLEY'S *Oxford in the Eighteenth Century* (1908); J. R. GREEN'S *Studies in Oxford History* (1901); T. HEARNE'S *Collections* (11 vols., 1885 onwards), and other publications by the Oxford Historical Society, e.g. *Collectanea* (2nd Ser. 1890, and 3rd Ser. 1896), J. R. MAGRATH'S *Flemings in Oxford* (1904, &c.), and L. M. QUILLER-COUCH'S

Reminiscences of Oxford 1559–1850 (1892); J. NAPLETON'S *Considerations on the Public Exercises* (1773); R. NEWTON'S *University Education* (1726); D. MACLEANE, *A History of Pembroke College* (1897); SIR C. H. FIRTH, *Modern Languages in Oxford 1724–1929* (1929).

On Cambridge: See also T. BAKER'S *History* of St. John's College (ed. J. E. B. Mayor, 1869); C. H. COOPER'S *Annals* (1842–1908) and *Alma Mater* (1827); R. CUMBERLAND'S *Memoirs* (1806); E. W. GOSSE'S *Gray* (1882); A. GRAY'S *Cambridge University* (1926); J. GREEN'S *Academic or Disputation on the State of the University* (1750); H. GUNNING'S *Reminiscences* (1854); J. E. B. MAYOR'S *Cambridge under Queen Anne* (1911); G. PEACOCK'S *Observations on the Statutes* (1841); G. WAKEFIELD'S *Memoirs* (1792); WILLIS and CLARK'S *Architectural History* (1886); D. A. WINSTANLEY'S *University of Cambridge in the Eighteenth Century* (1922).

For foreigners' impressions of the Universities, see *Travels of Zacharias Conrad von Uffenbach* (ed. W. H. and W. J. C. Quarrell, 1928) and C. MORITZ, *Travels through various parts of England in 1782* (ed. P. E. Matheson, 1924).

XXIII

SCIENCE, MATHEMATICS, AND ASTRONOMY

By E. J. HOLMYARD

Never think, my Sweet, that you have arithmetick enough; when you have exhausted your master, buy books. Nothing amuses more harmlessly than computation, and nothing is oftener applicable to real business or speculative enquiries. A thousand stories which the ignorant tell, and believe, die away at once, when the computist takes them in his gripe.—*To Sophia Thrale* (24 July 1783).

You, Sir, whose curiosity is so extensive, will easily conceive with what pleasure a philosopher, furnished with wings, and hovering in the sky, would see the earth, and all it's inhabitants, rolling beneath him, and presenting to him successively, by it's diurnal motion, all the countries within the same parallel.—*A Dissertation on the Art of Flying*: *Rasselas* (1759).

'LET it be remembered,' wrote Joseph Priestley (1733–1804), 'that a taste for science, pleasing, and even honourable as it is, is not one of the highest passions of our nature, that the pleasures it furnishes are even but one degree, above those of sense, and therefore that temperance is requisite in all scientifical pursuits.' The learned Dr. David Hartley (1705–57) was even more severe. 'Nothing,' he says in his *Observations on Man*, 'can easily exceed the vain-glory, self-conceit, arrogance, emulation, and envy, that are found in the eminent professors of the sciences. . . . Temperance in these studies is, therefore, evidently required, both in order to check the rise of such ill passions, and to give room for the cultivation of other essential parts of our natures.'

These illuminating quotations throw into clear relief the two most prominent features of the state of science in the eighteenth century. On the one hand, there was an enthusiasm for scientific investigation, and on the other hand a growing uneasiness was felt lest the progress of science might lead to a neglect of the calls of piety, or, worse, to free thought, rationalism, and atheism. As long as the Church was able to find an ally in science—as she had done in the seventeenth century—protesting voices were few and feeble; but the expansion of scientific discovery in the succeeding century began to give new weapons to advanced thinkers, and science was quickly perceived to be the ultimate basis of the criticisms of dogma that were already producing a genuine anxiety in the minds of religious men. The antagonism grew as time went on, to reach a climax in the nineteenth century; but for most of the period with which we are concerned the thought that they were playing with a dangerous toy was insufficient to quench the ardour even of the many clergymen numbered among the host of amateur natural philosophers.

The cult of science was indeed widespread among the educated classes. When Boswell made his first entry into Johnson's library, he 'observed an apparatus for chymical experiments, of which Johnson was all his life very fond'. In this taste for recreative and unofficial science, as in so much else, Johnson was typical of his age, when chemistry, physics, biology, and similar studies were pursued with eager delight by the leisured dilettante and intelligent lover of the curious. Natural philosophy had become a fashionable hobby, and since the qualitative sciences had not yet assumed that complexity which they were later to develop, any educated man with dextrous fingers could acquire without difficulty a sufficient command of the subject to experience the thrill of standing at the threshold of the unknown. The work of the Hon. Robert Boyle (1627–91) in chemistry and of Sir Isaac Newton (1642–1727) in astronomy and physics had shown —much to the surprise of contemporaries—that there was infinitely more to discover in Nature than had been suspected by classical antiquity or taught by medieval scholasticism; while the new interest in philosophy aroused by the semi-scientific metaphysical speculations of Descartes (1596–1650) and Gassendi (1592–1655) had slowly succeeded in creating an intellectual atmosphere favourable to a juster appraisal of the worth of scientific knowledge. The happy upshot was that parson and prelate, lawyer and scholar, author and schoolmaster, burgess and aristocrat, found their fingers burn with the itch to experiment: to what end may be realized from the fact that, of the noteworthy advances in science made during the latter part of the eighteenth century, perhaps a half were due not to the professional man of science but to the ingenious and inquiring amateur.

Though the Royal Society then, as now, was the principal focus of scientific activity, there were also enthusiastic local associations and societies, where exchange of information and ideas between the members supplemented the diffusion of knowledge effected by the *Philosophical Transactions* and the few other learned journals. One of the most fruitful of these provincial clubs was the Lunar Society of Birmingham, founded by Matthew Boulton, Dr. Erasmus Darwin, Dr. William Small, and their friends, about 1766. The 'Lunatics', as they were irreverently called in the servants' hall, met for dinner every month on the Monday nearest to the full moon, 'in order to have the benefit of its light in returning home': hence the name of the society. After a convivial dinner at two o'clock, each member contributed the results of his own observations, reported news of recent discoveries, and joined in the discussion of literary and scientific topics until the meeting broke up at about 8 p.m. The moving spirit of the society was Erasmus Darwin, famed as physician, philosopher, and poet, and 'extremely speculative'. Though the demands of his practice at Lichfield frequently prevented him from attending the monthly dinners, his insatiable interest in science and his energetic personality combined to keep the Lunar Society in fervent life; and enforced absence would draw from him some such characteristic letter as the following:

Dear Boulton,

I am sorry the infernal divinities who visit mankind with diseases, and are therefore at perpetual war with doctors, should have prevented my seeing all your great men at Soho [Birmingham] to-day. Lord! what inventions, what wit, what rhetoric, metaphysical, mechanical, and pyrotechnical, will be on the wing, bandied like a shuttlecock from one to another of your troup of philosophers! while poor I, I by myself am I, imprison'd in a post-chaise, am joggl'd, and jostl'd, and bump'd, and bruised along the King's high-road to make war upon a stomach-ache or a fever.

Erasmus Darwin.

Among the members of the society were poets, authors, physicians, engineers, theologians, botanists, chemists, mathematicians, and at least one printer, namely John Baskerville, inventor of the admirable Baskerville type. In this catholicity of composition, where men of the most diverse callings found a common tie in their love of scientific investigation, the Lunar Society exemplifies the widespread character of eighteenth-century interest in natural phenomena.

How different from the preceding century, when Newton wrote that efforts to found a scientific society in Cambridge had failed, owing to the fact that no one there seemed to be willing to try experiments!

All branches of science benefited from the new orientation of talent, but as in the seventeenth century physics made the most spectacular leap forward, so in the eighteenth century chemistry held the centre of the stage. Electricity showed premonitory symptoms of future greatness, physiology, botany, and zoology were in steady growth, and the other sciences were by no means stationary; yet activity was most intense and growth most vital in the investigation of the problems of chemistry.

Until the days of Boyle, chemistry had been practised either as a supposed means of obtaining the philosopher's stone—that elixir which should turn the base metals into silver and gold—or as a branch of pharmacy, with the object of preparing drugs and remedies for use in medicine. Boyle, however, had successfully urged that, though alchemy might be possible and medicinal drugs were certainly useful, chemistry ought more rightly to be regarded as a distinct and noble branch of natural philosophy, with the advancement of knowledge as its principal aim. By his overthrow of the Aristotelian theory of the four elements—fire, air, water, and earth—as the common constituents of all substances, he did much to clear the way for the establishment of a reasonable chemistry; and by a fortunate coincidence the first grand chemical generalization was made almost simultaneously by the German physicians Johann Joachim Becher (1635–82) and Georg Ernst Stahl (1660–1734).

Stahl, elaborating a suggestion of Becher's, propounded the theory that all combustible bodies owed their inflammability to the presence in them of a quasi-material substance, which he called *phlogiston* or 'fire-stuff'. On combustion, he supposed, this substance was driven off into the air, only an earthy residue or ash being left. Easily inflammable substances he regarded as rich in phlogiston, while metals and similar bodies, that could be burned only with difficulty, were correspondingly deficient in phlogiston. The phlogiston theory, though from its inception it encountered certain difficulties, was so successful in bringing to a common denominator not merely the chief phenomena of combustion, but other, apparently unrelated, chemical facts, that it gained universal credence; it became, indeed, so thoroughly established as to command allegiance until the closing years of the eighteenth century.

Contemporaneous with the dissemination of Stahl's ideas upon combustion was the rapid development of a satisfactory technique for the study of gases. Though the celebrated iatrochemist, J. B. van Helmont (1577–1644), had been able to demonstrate the existence of at least two varieties of gas different from ordinary air, the difficulty of manipulating such tenuous matter had been so great as to prevent any close investigation of gaseous substances. It was consequently still believed by the majority of men of science that air was the gaseous element *par excellence*, and that the other effluvia they encountered in the course of their researches were nothing more than atmospheric air contaminated with various impurities. This conception, it is true, persisted almost to the year 1800, but the discovery of methods of collecting gases and of investigating their properties gradually led to the epoch-making events that revolutionized chemistry in the last three decades of the eighteenth century.

Prominent among the 'pneumatic chemists' were Stephen Hales (1677–1761)—an Anglican clergyman; Joseph Black (1728–99)—a professor of chemistry at Glasgow and Edinburgh; Henry Cavendish (1731–1810)—a scion of the Duke of Devonshire's family; and Joseph Priestley—a nonconformist minister: three amateurs to one professional. Hales was the perpetual curate of Teddington in Middlesex, the parish register of which he occasionally enlivened with such notes as the following:

> James Parsons who had oft eat a shoulder of Mutton and a peck of Hasty Pudding at a Time, which caused his Death, buried March 27, 1744. Aged 35. Stephen Hales. Minister.

A keen botanist, Hales in 1724 engaged upon a comprehensive study of the physiology of plants, and in 1727 embodied his results in a book entitled *Vegetable Staticks*. Believing that 'a considerable quantity of air is inspired by plants', he conducted a series of experiments upon the fermentation and distillation of vegetable substances, and, improving upon an earlier device of Boyle's, invented the first recognizable form of the now familiar 'pneumatic trough'. It would be hard to over-estimate the importance of this apparatus in the subsequent history of chemistry. Still further improved by Priestley, it led directly to the discovery of many new substances and, in due course, to the establishment of facts that rendered the phlogiston theory untenable and a complete reorganization of chemistry inevitable.

By means of his ingenious apparatus, Hales was able to collect several different gases, but he did little to study their individual properties. The first important step in this direction was made by Joseph Black, the son of a Scottish wine-merchant residing at Bordeaux. As an undergraduate at the University of Glasgow in 1746, Black was fortunate enough to begin the study of chemistry under the capable instruction of Dr. William Cullen, one of the best known physicians of the century. When Cullen was appointed professor of chemistry at Edinburgh in 1756, Black succeeded to his chair at Glasgow, and ten years later again followed him at Edinburgh. In his chemical research, Black made a valuable innovation by adopting quantitative methods in his fundamental experiments. Previous chemists had usually contented themselves with purely qualitative results, and if changes in weight were incidentally noticed, they were regarded as unimportant or, at most, merely curious. By the careful use of the balance, Black succeeded in elucidating the composition of chalk, the relationship between quicklime and the mild alkalis (e.g. washing-soda), and the reason for the milky appearance assumed by lime-water on exposure to the atmosphere. He proved that, when strongly heated, chalk gave off a peculiar gas (which he called 'fixed air' and we now call carbon dioxide), and that small quantities of this gas were present in the air. He showed also that 'fixed air' was liberated from chalk by the action of a dilute acid, and that a given weight of chalk yielded the same weight of fixed air when treated in this way as when strongly heated. The investigation as a whole was a model of logical thought, exact and careful manipulation, and unprejudiced interpretation of experimental results. To claim it as the earliest example of chemical research carried out upon modern principles of scientific method would scarcely be an exaggeration; for Black's tacit admission that fact rather than

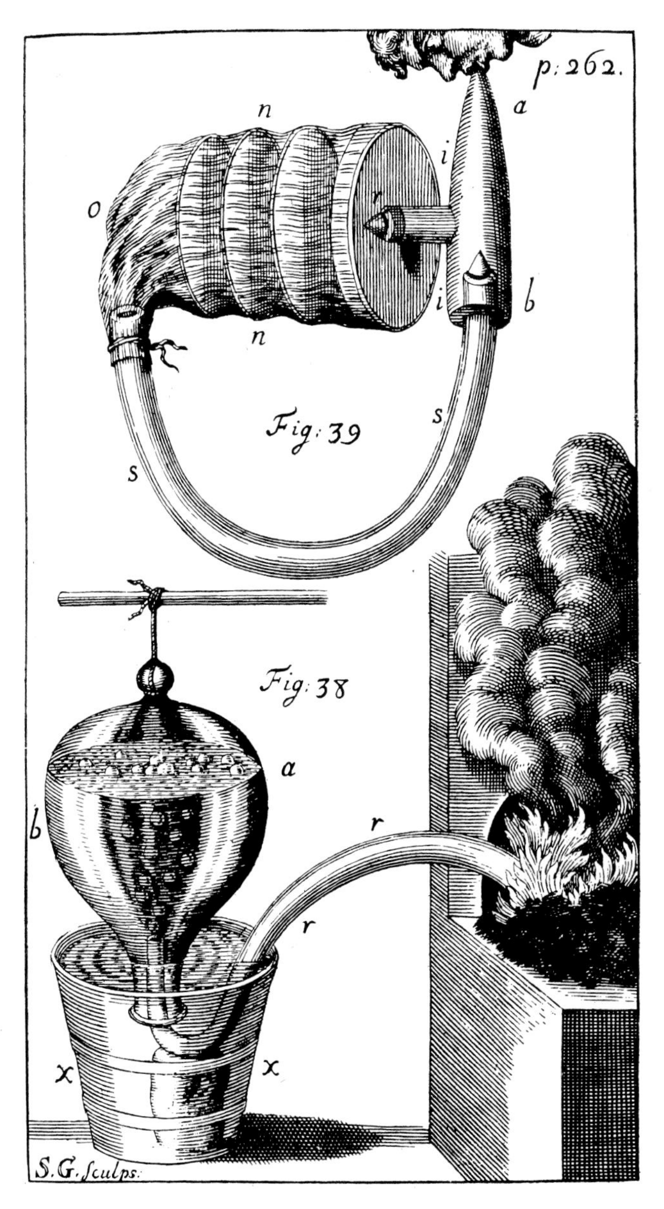

STEPHEN HALE'S APPARATUS FOR COLLECTING GASES

From Vegetable Staticks, *1727*

theory must be the final criterion of truth marks an epoch in the history of chemistry.

When it became generally recognized that Black's 'fixed air' was a distinct chemical individual, the path lay open to a more accurate conception of the nature of gaseous substances, and—though the term 'air' was not completely replaced by 'gas' until many years later—atmospheric air was dethroned from its unique position. Very soon, indeed, we begin to hear of inquiries into the composition of the atmosphere: a question that would have appeared meaningless in earlier times. To the triumphant solution of this great problem, the crowning achievement of eighteenth-century science, we shall return shortly. Meanwhile, we must follow the fortunes of the phlogiston theory of combustion, since the vicissitudes it suffered are intimately connected with the work that was being carried out upon gases.

According to the disciples of Stahl, metals were to be regarded as binary compounds of phlogiston with a metallic earth or calx. Upon combustion of a metal, the phlogiston was driven off and absorbed by the surrounding air, while the calx or ash was left. This explanation accounted very well for the facts that metals cannot be burned in a vacuum (since there would be no air to take up the phlogiston), or indefinitely in a limited volume of air (since after a time the air would become saturated with phlogiston), and that metallic calces may be reconverted into metals by heating them with charcoal (since charcoal was supposed to be rich in phlogiston, some of which it yielded to the calx). There was, however, a difficulty, the seriousness of which became fully apparent when quantitative methods were at length duly appreciated. This difficulty was the indisputable fact that, upon combustion of a metal, the calx invariably weighed more than the original metal: a phenomenon the exact opposite of that which would have been expected if the metal indeed lost a constituent, as the phlogistians affirmed. Various hypotheses were advanced to explain this awkward behaviour (it was even suggested that phlogiston had *negative* weight), but all were unsatisfactory. The successes of the phlogiston theory had nevertheless been so striking that no one appears to have had any suspicion of its broad truth.

It was the Rev. Dr. Joseph Priestley who made the discovery

that, in other hands, was to prove the key to the whole situation—rendering the phlogiston theory obsolete and at the same time revealing the true nature of the atmosphere. Born about six miles from Leeds, in 1733, Priestley packed so much intellectual activity into his seventy-one years that he has nearly as much claim as Johnson himself to be chosen as the epitome of his age. In political and philosophical opinions, the two men were completely antipathetic: Johnson the staunch Tory and steadfast upholder of the Established Church; Priestley the Radical, open sympathizer with revolutionary thought in France, and author of theological doctrines that Boswell was by no means alone in denouncing as pernicious. As a nonconformist minister, as a theologian, as a philosopher—the three capacities in which he might be described as a professional—Priestley has to-day little fame. His immortality rests solely upon the scientific experiments that formed his chief recreation, and that furnished him with pleasures 'but one degree, above those of sense'. So difficult is it for a man to judge the ultimate value of his own work.

In spite of his abhorrence of Priestley's theological and political tenets, Johnson was generous enough to give him honour for his discoveries in chemistry.

Chymistry was always an interesting pursuit with Dr. Johnson. Whilst he was in Wiltshire, he attended some experiments that were made by a physician at Salisbury, on the new kinds of air. In the course of the experiments frequent mention being made of Dr. Priestley, Dr. Johnson knit his brows, and in a stern manner enquired, 'Why do we hear so much of Dr. Priestley?' He was very properly answered, 'Sir, because we are indebted to him for these important discoveries.' On this Dr. Johnson appeared well content; and replied, 'Well, well, I believe we are; and let every man have the honour he has merited.'

The honour that Priestley merited was considerably greater than Johnson could have imagined. On August 1, 1774, he had concentrated the sun's rays upon red calx of mercury, and very much to his amazement had obtained metallic mercury and a gas endowed with the most extraordinary properties. Priestley was one of the most faithful adherents of phlogiston, and was completely at a loss to account for the extremely unexpected results of his random experiment. The problem as he saw it was this: calx of mercury is mercury *minus* phlogiston. How comes it, then, that upon heating this unpromising substance without admixture, metallic mercury is regenerated? Whence came the necessary phlogiston? And—a still greater puzzle—whence came the gas? Brilliant as an experimentalist, Priestley was not a fertile thinker, and he never succeeded in evolving satisfactory replies to his own questions. The gas he isolated upon this fateful occasion supported life and combustion very much better than ordinary air, but the only conclusion he was able to draw was that, by some means or other, he had managed to obtain a specimen of atmospheric air from which the phlogiston normally existing in it (as a result of the combustion of coal, wood, &c.) had been removed. He argued that, as a completely dry sponge would absorb more water than the same sponge when already damp, so air from which phlogiston was completely absent would support combustion better than air already partly saturated with it. Consequently he named his new gas 'dephlogisticated air'.

In October 1774 he accompanied Lord Shelburne—to whom for a time he acted as literary companion—upon a visit to Paris. There he dined with the celebrated young French chemist, Antoine Laurent Lavoisier (1743–94), and casually mentioned his discovery of dephlogisticated air. Lavoisier had himself conducted experiments upon the calcination of metals and upon the composition of the atmosphere, and had tentatively concluded that, far from yielding anything to the air, a metal when burned absorbed something from the air. He knew further that only a part of the air was thus concerned in combustion, and drew the legitimate deduction that the atmosphere was composed of at least two different gases. When he heard of Priestley's dephlogisticated air, his scientific genius perceived with a flash of inspiration that 'the ponderous old nonconformist' had accidentally prepared a pure specimen of the active constituent of the air. At the time, he made only conventional remarks of interest, but during the winter of 1774–5 he shut himself up in his laboratory at the Arsenal and feverishly repeated and extended Priestley's experiments. By the following Easter he was able to show that the phlogistians had been entirely mistaken in their scintillating theory. Combustion, in the light of his experimental results, could be satisfactorily explained only upon the hypothesis that when a substance burned, it combined with a certain gas in the atmosphere. This gas formed about one-fifth of the whole, the remaining four-fifths being composed of a second gas which would support neither combustion nor life, and for which he therefore proposed the name *azote*. The active gas was identical with 'dephlogisticated air,' but since Lavoisier's investigations proved phlogiston to be a myth, Priestley's term was clearly obsolete, and a new name had to be invented. Having discovered that 'active air' was a constituent of most acids, Lavoisier felt that the designation *principe oxygine* or 'acidifying principle' was eminently suitable for it, and so the gas received its present name, oxygen.

Lavoisier's work marks the effective birth of modern chemistry, and, from the point of view of science, is probably the most significant individual episode in the eighteenth century. The metamorphosis it effected extended far beyond the bounds of chemistry itself, and profoundly influenced the development of physiology, botany, zoology, physics, astronomy, and indeed all other branches of science. Indirectly, it played a great part in the Industrial Revolution, while the flourishing chemical industries of the nineteenth and twentieth centuries ultimately owe their existence to that historic dinner in Paris in the autumn of 1774. Lavoisier himself fell a victim to the guillotine during the Terror; but he had lived long enough to see his views accepted by the whole of the scientific world—except Priestley, who remained obdurately faithful to phlogiston until his death, in Pennsylvania, in 1804.

Further important work upon the chemical nature of gases was carried out by that eccentric personality Henry Cavendish, of whom it is related that he invariably dined upon leg of mutton and spoke fewer words than a Trappist monk. Wealthy, but leading a life of almost unbroken seclusion, Cavendish was perhaps the most capable English scientist of the eighteenth century. His discoveries were as numerous as important, but, caring nothing for personal aggrandizement, he frequently failed to publish them, so that their full extent became known only when his private papers were edited by Clerk Maxwell in 1879 and, more completely, by Sir J. Larmor and Sir Edward Thorpe in

1921. His principal discovery was that water, instead of being an element as had been universally believed up to that time, was a compound of Priestley's dephlogisticated air with a second gas, 'inflammable air', i.e. in modern terms, of oxygen and hydrogen. He also showed that the air contains a third constituent, besides oxygen and azote [nitrogen], occupying rather less than one-hundredth of the whole. This apparently unimportant substance attracted no further attention at the time, and was not rediscovered until a century later, when it received the name argon.

Although progress was most rapid in chemistry, the lifetime of Johnson witnessed remarkable developments in several other departments of science. To a contemporary, one of the most fascinating subjects must have been the startling experiments made in quick succession upon the peculiar properties of electrified bodies. It had been known since ancient times that amber, when rubbed, has the power of attracting light objects, such as feathers and bits of straw, but until the eighteenth century this strange phenomenon received little close investigation. Queen Elizabeth's physician-in-ordinary, William Gilbert, had discovered that many other substances possessed the same property as amber, but his interests lay mainly in magnetism, on which he wrote the first great scientific treatise. Boyle, in the company of 'two beautiful ladies' who wore false hair, had made the acute observation that the ornamental locks were easily electrified. One of the ladies gave him leave to satisfy himself more fully. 'Desiring her to hold her warm hand at a convenient distance from one of those locks taken off and placed in the free air, as soon as she did this, the lower end of the lock, which was free, applied itself presently to her hand.' Newton and Otto von Guericke, the burgomaster of Magdeburg, had also noticed certain electrical phenomena, but it remained for Francis Hauksbee to make the first efficient electrical machine, which he described to the learned world in 1709. Hauksbee's machine consisted of a glass globe, so mounted on an axis with pulleys that it could be rotated very rapidly. Upon exhausting the globe with an air-pump, and electrifying it by holding his hand upon it as it was quickly whirled, he observed a strong light on the inside. Here was the germ of modern work upon the ultimate constitution of matter, though nearly two hundred years were to elapse before the real significance of this electrical light was perceived.

Hauksbee's machine was also capable of yielding electric sparks, yet notwithstanding these important and promising discoveries, a period of twenty barren years followed in which electrical experiments seem to have been entirely discontinued. In 1729, however, a pensioner at the Charterhouse, named Stephen Gray, showed that the attractive power of electrified objects could be transmitted to others by contact, and that a charge applied to a limited area of certain bodies (such as metals) was instantaneously transmitted to all other parts. Substances through which the attracting power freely passed were later called conductors, while those that exhibited the opposite property were known as insulators. Gray discovered that silk, hair, rosin, and glass were insulators, but that the human body was a conductor; and on April 8, 1730, he carried out his celebrated experiment of electrifying a boy by suspending him in a horizontal position on threads made of hair and bringing a charged object near his feet. It was then observed that the boy's head acquired the characteristic power of electrical attraction, and that this power could be conveyed along rods held in his hands.

Thrilled by accounts of Gray's experiments, the Frenchman du Fay enthusiastically plunged into electrical research. Having got himself suspended on silk lines, he observed that, as soon as he was electrified, the near approach of another person caused pricking shoots, crackling noises, and fiery sparks to issue from his body. Among the spectators of this mystery was the Abbé Nollet, another keen student of natural philosophy, who wrote that he would never forget the surprise which the first electrical spark ever drawn from the human body excited both in M. du Fay and in himself. Du Fay further discovered that 'there are two distinct kinds of electricity, very different from one another', which he called *vitreous* and *resinous*. Two bodies electrified with the same variety of electricity were found to repel one another, while if they were electrified with unlike varieties they attracted one another.

Meanwhile, great improvements were being made in the machines for producing electricity by friction, with the result that even more spectacular phenomena astonished a

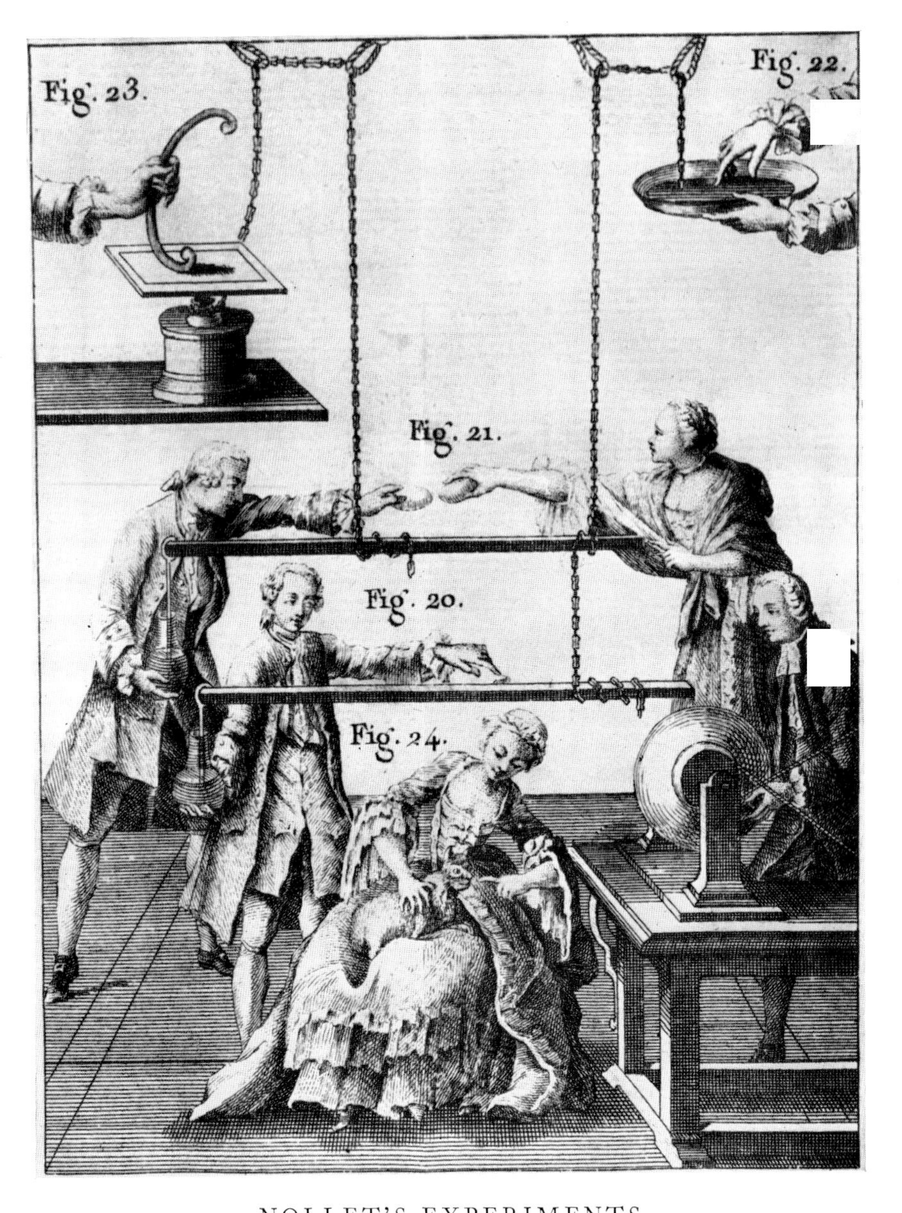

NOLLET'S EXPERIMENTS

From J. A. Nollet, Leçons de physique experimentale (1749–64)

public whose appetite for electrical wonders was by this time thoroughly whetted. In 1744 Dr. Ludolf of Berlin succeeded in inflaming ether by means of an electric spark, while Winckler, a professor of classics at Leipzig University, went one better by setting fire to brandy with a spark from his own finger. The commercial instinct was aroused, and by 1745 public exhibitions of electrical experiments were attracting crowds of eager sightseers. In the following year, a Dutch physicist named Pieter van Musschenbroek attempted to electrify water in a bottle, in his laboratory at Leyden. A friend, Cunaeus, assisted him by holding the bottle in his hand. When the water was imagined to be fully charged, Cunaeus proceeded with the other hand to disengage the wire connecting the bottle to the electrical machine. Much to his surprise and discomfiture, he received a violent electric shock in his arms and breast.

It is extremely curious [says Priestley in his excellent *History of Electricity*] to observe the descriptions which philosophers, who first felt the electrical shock, give of it; especially as we are sure we can give ourselves the same sensation, and thereby compare their descriptions with the reality. Terror and surprise certainly contributed not a little to the exaggerated accounts they gave of it; and, could we not have repeated the experiment, we should have formed a very different idea of it from what it really is, even when given in greater strength than those who first felt this electrical shock were able to give it.

Musschenbroek, who repeated the experiment that had so unexpectedly disturbed his visitor, felt himself struck in his arms, shoulders, and breast, lost his breath, and took two days to recover. He emphatically remarked that he would not take a second shock for the kingdom of France. Priestley, who always found it difficult to resist moralizing, reproves the cowardly professor. 'Far different from these were the sentiments of the magnanimous Mr. Boze, who with a truly philosophic heroism, worthy of the renowned Empedocles, said he wished he might die by the electric shock, that the account of his death might furnish an article for the memoirs of the French academy of sciences.'

It was quickly discovered that a jar coated inside and outside with tin foil was more efficient than a bottle filled with water, and such an apparatus was known as the Leyden Phial. The ingenuity of men in England, France, Germany, Holland, and even America was exercised in exploring the possibilities of the novel apparatus, and when Nollet constructed the first specimen in Paris, 'the report of it instantly spread through the court and the city, from whence all ranks of men crowded to see this new kind of thunder, and to experience the effect of it'. To satisfy the King's curiosity, the versatile Abbé administered the shock to one hundred and eighty of the Guards simultaneously; then, as a further improvement, he bethought himself of the community of Carthusian monks. History does not relate what persuasive arguments he employed, but one day the members of the Grand Convent found themselves arranged in a line a mile long, while the irrepressible Nollet dashed hither and thither to see that they were conscientiously holding the iron wires that connected each monk to his neighbour on either side. At length everything was prepared; the Leyden jars were charged, and Nollet made the necessary connexion. With ludicrous unanimity, the whole company gave a sudden spring into the air, and Parisians enjoyed one of those free entertainments so dear to their hearts.

From a study of the Leyden Phial, Bishop Watson of Llandaff arrived at the conclusion that all bodies contain electricity, and that in their normal or uncharged state the amount present is at an equilibrium level. The process of electrification he regarded as the removal of electricity from one body and its addition to another, so that the 'vitreous' and 'resinous' varieties might be nothing more than excess or deficiency of the normal amount of a single electricity. A similar theory was held by the celebrated American investigator, Benjamin Franklin (1706–90), who suggested that a vitreously electrified body contained an excess of the 'electric fluid' above its equilibrium amount, and that a resinously electrified body, on the contrary, had less than its normal share. The former was therefore described as 'positively' charged and the latter as 'negatively' charged, though Franklin himself admitted that it was impossible to be certain that this arbitrary nomenclature ought not, in reality, to be reversed.

Franklin's principal contribution to the science of electricity lay, however, not in his 'one fluid' theory, but in his proof of the identity of lightning and the electric spark. He was not the first to suggest this identity, but, noting that the two agree in their swift, crooked motion, in giving coloured light, in being conducted by metals, in firing inflammable substances, and in several other respects, he conceived the crucial experiment of attempting to draw electricity from thunderclouds. In 1752, placing himself under a shed to avoid the rain, he flew a kite during a thunderstorm, insulating the twine from his hand by holding it with a silk ribbon. Where the twine and silk joined, a key was attached. For some time he obtained no success; then, presenting his knuckle to the key, he drew from it a strong spark. Afterwards, he was able to charge Leyden jars from the key, and so had incontrovertibly demonstrated the identity of atmospheric electricity with that obtained from the frictional machine and in other laboratory ways. Franklin's dangerous experiment was repeated in other countries—with fatal results in at least one instance, the courageous Richmann being struck dead at St. Petersburg in 1753 by the shock from his kite-string.

The discovery that lightning was nothing more than a gigantic electric spark had immediate practical application in the construction of efficient lightning conductors. Knowing that electricity was conducted very readily by metals, and that the electric discharge passes most easily to or from points, Franklin erected pointed metallic rods upon houses and other buildings, burying the ends in the earth so that the lightning might be safely conducted to the ground and there harmlessly dissipated. Though the protection his rods afforded was not complete, their success was so marked that lightning conductors rapidly came into general use. King George III, after he had purchased Buckingham Palace from the Duke of Buckingham in 1761, gave instructions that lightning conductors were to be installed upon it, but hearing that certain English men of science recommended ball-ended rods instead of Franklin's pointed ones, he commanded that knobs should be placed upon them. This decision gave a welcome opportunity to a political wit of the time, who epigrammatically declaimed:

> While you, great George, for knowledge hunt,
> And sharp conductors change for blunt,
> The nation's out of joint.
> Franklin a wiser course pursues,
> And all your thunder useless views,
> By keeping to the point.

In 1766, one of the most fundamental laws of electricity was discovered by Priestley. Upon electrifying a hollow metallic sphere, he observed that there was no charge upon its inner surface, and that small, light objects inside it experienced no force, either of attraction or repulsion. Assuming, from experimental results already familiar, that the charge would be uniformly distributed over the surface of the sphere, and remembering that Newton had shown that no gravitational force existed within a uniform hollow sphere of matter, Priestley argued by analogy that electrical force must obey the same law as gravitational force. But the gravitational attraction between two bodies varies inversely as the square of the distance between them; hence, if the analogy is justified, the force of attraction or repulsion between two electric charges is also inversely proportional to the square of the distance between them.

Priestley's discovery of the Law of Inverse Squares, in its application to electric charges, was experimentally confirmed about ten years later by the French engineer Charles Augustin Coulomb, of whom it was said that the correctness of his mathematical investigations was equalled only by that of his moral character. Coulomb proved that the gravitational law was even more closely resembled by the electrostatic law than Priestley had realized; for just as the gravitational force between two bodies varies as the product of their masses, so the electric force between two charged bodies varies as the product of their charges. In the meantime Cavendish, in his customary silent fashion, had been attentively following the new discoveries in electricity, and supplementing them by brilliant original investigations of his own. Unfortunately he never bestirred himself to publish them; consequently the fact that he had arrived at conceptions of specific inductive capacity, potential, and other ideas of cardinal importance was not revealed until long after their independent rediscovery by such able physicists as Faraday in the nineteenth century.

Among the effects of electric charges, the physiological symptoms that followed administration of a shock continued to arouse the keenest interest. It is not surprising that John Wesley, for whom the art of medicine had a strong and perennial appeal, should have sought diligently to discover whether the electric shock had any curative power in

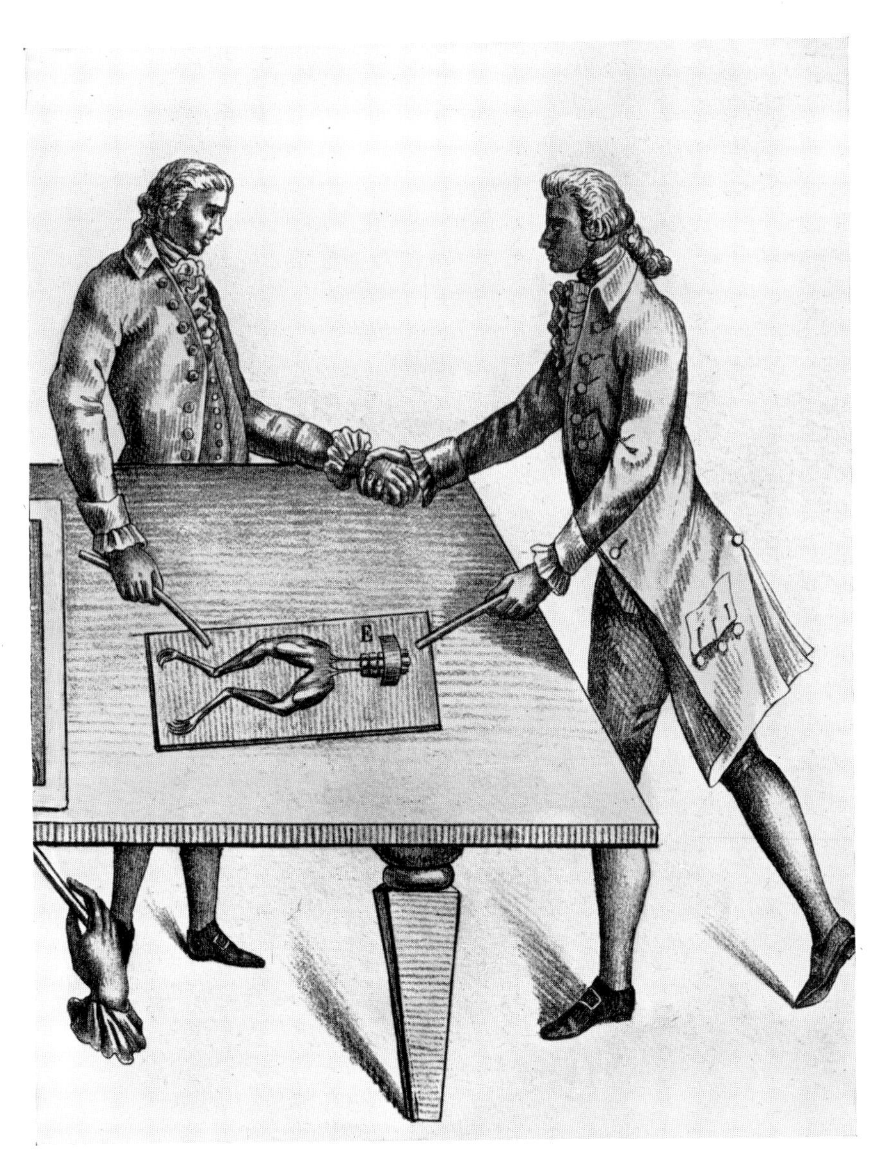

GALVANI'S EXPERIMENTS

From L. Galvani, Opere Edite ed Inedite, 1841

cases of disease. Perhaps, in the excitement of the pioneer, he was too optimistic about the results, but he maintained that he had scarcely ever known an instance in which shocks all over the body failed to cure a quotidian or tertian ague, and mentions cases of blindness, dropsy, palsy in the tongue, and deafness that had been cured or at least relieved by similar methods. For hysteria, he recommended that the patient should sit on a cake of rosin and submit to electrification for at least half an hour morning and evening; after which sparks should be taken from him and shocks of a suitable strength administered. We may well imagine that such heroic treatment 'has seldom failed of the desired effect'.

Four years before Johnson's death in 1784, animal electricity gave rise to another—and this time well authenticated—phenomenon of an astonishing character. Luigi Galvani, public lecturer on anatomy at Bologna, happened to be giving a lesson to a student on the anatomy of the frog. One of these animals, dead and skinned, lay stretched out upon the laboratory table, when by pure accident the student touched the main nerve of its hind leg with a steel scalpel. To his utter bewilderment the leg began to kick! Fortunately the days of witch-hunting were over, or Galvani would certainly have ended his life at the stake. As eager as his pupil to learn the cause of this curious occurrence, Galvani at length surmised it to be an electrical effect, as there had been an electrical machine upon the dissecting-table, and when this was removed the convulsions could no longer be induced. Subsequent experiments, in which he hung frogs' legs upon an iron trellis during a thunderstorm, proved that the surmise was correct; and a few years later his countryman Volta discovered that the electricity was produced by the saline liquid in the legs and the metals brought into contact with it. He was thus able to dispense with the frogs altogether, and generated the first continuous electric current by immersing two different metals (zinc and silver) in a solution of salt. This primitive electric battery formed the point of departure for all subsequent work upon current electricity; and with it we must leave physics in order to inquire into the progress made by the biological sciences during the century.

In 1732 a peculiar figure might have been seen traversing the desolate wastes of Lapland. His clothes consisted of a light coat of linsey-woolsey, leather breeches, a round wig, a green leather cap, and a pair of half-boots. He carried a small leather bag, containing one shirt, two pairs of false sleeves, two vests, an inkstand, a pen-case, a gauze gnat-cap, a comb, a fowling-piece and, most surprising of all, a microscope and telescope. It was the celebrated Swedish botanist Carl Linnaeus, whose services to botany were such that the principal botanical society of to-day is named after him. A keen collector, he roamed far and wide in search of specimens, and when he was appointed professor of natural history at Upsala he extended his field by inducing his students to undertake expeditions to distant regions. Linnaeus's greatest achievement was the establishment of a simple and useful system of classifying and identifying plants. Based merely upon the characteristics of the stamens and pistils of flowers, it was far from being a thoroughly scientific arrangement, and Linnaeus himself foresaw its supersession; but it rendered identification easy, and accompanied as it was by his division of plants into *genera* and *species*, it proved of incalculable assistance to his fellow botanists. It was Linnaeus, too, who secured the general adoption of the binomial system of nomenclature in biology, according to which every species of plant or animal is succinctly defined by two words—first the generic name and second the specific name. Thus *Ranunculus bulbosus* defines the bulbous species [of buttercup] belonging to the genus *Ranunculus*.

In France, Buffon, who succeeded du Fay in 1739 as director of the Jardin du Roi (now the Paris Zoo), occupied himself for half a century in writing a voluminous *Natural History* in forty-four quarto volumes.[1] In spite of its pompous style (which provoked Voltaire to say that the *Histoire Naturelle* was 'pas si naturelle'), Buffon's treatise diffused the taste for a sympathetic study of the animate world, and is further noteworthy as adumbrating the theory of organic evolution. No greater contrast could be found than that which exists between this popular and intelligible work and Goldsmith's *Animated Nature*, which justly caused Johnson to remark that if its author could tell a horse from a cow, that was the extent of his knowledge of zoology.

Yet biological studies were being successfully prosecuted

[1] 1749–1804. The last few volumes appeared posthumously.

in England. Gilbert White's *Natural History and Antiquities of Selborne* (1789) was a masterpiece of its kind, while the fruitful comparative method yielded valuable results in the hands of John Hunter (1728–93) and others. In the course of an active life, Hunter dissected over 500 different species of animals, as well as countless plants, and may be regarded as one of the principal founders of the science of comparative anatomy. It was, moreover, largely due to his influence and personal example that the establishment of natural history museums became general, his own collection—acquired by the Royal College of Surgeons in London in 1799—being a model of reasoned and systematic arrangement.

Of all the biological sciences, perhaps that which manifested most radical development in the eighteenth century was physiology. In particular, the work of Albrecht von Haller (1708–77), professor of anatomy, botany, and medicine in the University of Göttingen, marked 'the dividing line between modern physiology and all that went before it'. As far as our own country is concerned, the investigations of most moment were those carried out by Priestley upon respiration. He showed the close resemblance between respiration and combustion, and formed a very clear idea of the former process, except that, thinking as he did in terms of phlogiston, his conception was, so to speak, inverted. After Lavoisier's discovery of the real nature of combustion and of the composition of the air, Priestley's views had only to be re-translated in terms of the new theory to show how near he had come to the truth. It was, however, Lavoisier himself who proved that, during respiration, some of the inspired oxygen reacts with the blood to form carbon dioxide and water, and that this change is indeed the vital part of the process.

The broader outlook and more intensive study common to all the sciences we have hitherto considered was shared by astronomy. The achromatic telescope invented by John Dollond in 1758, and presented by him to the Royal Society, caused no little excitement in the scientific world. Similar instruments, together with enormous reflecting telescopes constructed by William Herschel (1738–1822), enabled far more numerous and far more accurate observations of the heavenly bodies to be made, and among the immediate results was the discovery of the planet Uranus. When he first observed this distant member of the solar system, Herschel must have felt recompensed for the laborious hours spent in polishing his concave mirrors—hours when he could not be brought to leave his work, but subsisted upon food placed in his mouth by his sister.

Though astronomical discoveries were frequent, the chief characteristic of eighteenth-century astronomy was the full and careful way in which the details implied by the Newtonian system were confirmed and its corollaries developed. This necessary completion of Newton's sublime achievement was rendered less difficult, not merely by the improved instruments now at the disposal of astronomers, but, more especially, by the great advances in mathematical procedure effected by the genius of Euler (1707–83), Lagrange (1736–1813), and Laplace (1749–1827). Euler, a native of Basle, wrote the first complete and accurate treatise on analytical calculus, improved the contemporary methods of algebra, trigonometry, and other branches of mathematics, and made important contributions to astronomy and physics. Though mathematicians commemorate him by the equations and algebraic expressions that bear his name, he is remembered by the layman for the solemn way in which he scored a joke at the expense of Diderot. Diderot, somewhat in disfavour with the Czarina on account of his irreligion, was informed while at St. Petersburg that Euler was in possession of an algebraical demonstration of the existence of God, and would like to give it him before all the Court. Diderot politely agreed, whereupon Euler, in a tone of perfect conviction, said gravely:

$$\text{Monsieur, } \frac{a+b^n}{n} = x, \text{ donc Dieu existe; répondez!}$$

Diderot was no mathematician and could not disguise his embarrassment; his request to return to France immediately was granted, to the accompaniment of peals of laughter on every hand.[1]

Lagrange, a true cosmopolitan and like most cosmopolitans a lover of Paris, was the most brilliant mathematician of his age. He invented the calculus of variations, vastly developed the subject of differential equations, and made

[1] It was, however, not Euler, but the waters of the Neva that caused Diderot's return. See M. Tourneaux, *Diderot et Catherine II* (1891), vol. ii, pp. 459 *et seq.*

JOSEPH PRIESTLEY'S LABORATORY

From Joseph Priestley, Experiments and Observations on Air, 1775

HENRY CAVENDISH

contributions of prime importance to mechanics, while his astronomical work included attacks upon the extremely difficult problem of calculating the gravitational effects that three bodies produce upon one another. Though he had a modest disposition, his fame could not be hidden, and in 1776 Frederick the Great invited him to become mathematical director of the Berlin Academy, so that 'the greatest King in Europe' might have 'the greatest mathematician in Europe' at his Court. In later life, Lagrange returned to France, where Napoleon conferred upon him the rank of count.

The work of Laplace, though much of it was carried out in the eighteenth century, mostly falls without the period that especially concerns us. Broadly speaking, it was a continuation and development of the Newtonian system; so that, although England could boast of no great mathematical geniuses in the century that followed Newton's death, she might at least point to the fact that the leading mathematicians of other countries had worked for a hundred years without exhausting the fabulously rich mine he had opened for them. Well might Dr. Johnson maintain the superiority of Newton over all foreign philosophers. If one figure more than another may be said to pervade the intellectual atmosphere of eighteenth-century science, that figure is Newton's, who, if he 'had flourished in ancient Greece, would have been worshipped as a Divinity'.

It is a deep step down from Newton to Priestley, yet if, after this brief sketch of the scientific work in Johnson's age, we ask ourselves who best typifies the English man of science of the time, our choice can fall on no other than the unassuming minister whose accidental discovery of oxygen changed the face of civilization. He spent arduous years in the selfless pursuit of knowledge, frankly admitted his own errors and faulty observations, and was ever willing to give others the full benefit of his knowledge. Robert Hall said of him, in words that are as graceful as true: 'His enlightened and active mind, his unwearied assiduity, the extent of his researches, the light he has poured into almost every department of science, will be the admiration of that period when the greater part of those who have praised and those who have blamed him will be alike forgotten.'

BIBLIOGRAPHY.—Many of the principal scientific articles of the century were published in the *Philosophical Transactions* of the Royal Society. Among other primary authorities, the following may be mentioned: S. HALES, *Vegetable Staticks* (1727); J. PRIESTLEY, *Observations on Different Kinds of Air* (1790); J. BLACK, *Experiments upon Magnesia Alba, Quicklime, and some other Alcaline Substances* (1756); A. L. LAVOISIER, *Traité de Chimie* (1789); J. PRIESTLEY, *History and Present State of Electricity* (1767); J. A. NOLLET, *Leçons de Physique Experimentale* (1749–64); B. FRANKLIN, *New Experiments and Observations on Electricity* (1750); L. GALVANI, *De viribus electricitatis in motu musculari commentarius cum Joannis Aldini dissertatione et notis* (Modena, 1792); C. LINNAEUS, *Systema Naturae* (tenth edition, 1758); G. WHITE, *Natural History and Antiquities of Selborne* (1789); G. L. L. BUFFON, *Histoire Naturelle* (1749–1804); J. HUNTER, *Works* (1835); A. von HALLER, *Anfangsgründe der Physiologie des Menschen* (1759); E. DARWIN, *Zoönomia* (1793); W. HERSCHEL's account of Uranus is to be found in the *Philosophical Transactions* (1782, &c.).

Some of the most useful secondary authorities are the following:

Chemistry: E. VON MEYER, *History of Chemistry* (1906); I. MASSON, *Three Centuries of Chemistry* (1925); H. C. BOLTON, *Correspondence of Priestley* (New York, 1892); ANNE HOLT, *Life of Joseph Priestley* (1931); J. A. COCHRANE, *Lavoisier* (1931); E. J. HOLMYARD, *Makers of Chemistry* (1931).

Physics: E. HOPPÉ, *Historie de la Physique* (Paris, 1928); F. CAJORI, *History of Physics* (New York, 1929); D. M. TURNER, *Makers of Science: Electricity and Magnetism* (1927).

Biology: C. SINGER, *Short History of Biology* (1931); E. NORDENSKIÖLD, *History of Biology* (1929); J. REYNOLDS GREEN, *History of Botany in the United Kingdom* (1914); HESKETH PEARSON, *Dr. Darwin* (1931); A. E. CLARK-KENNEDY, *Stephen Hales* (1929).

Astronomy: W. WHEWELL, *History of the Inductive Sciences* (1837); R. WOLF, *Geschichte der Astronomie* (1876); A. BERRY, *History of Astronomy* (1898); J. L. E. DREYER, *History of the Planetary Systems* (1906).

Mathematics: D. E. SMITH, *History of Mathematics* (Boston, U.S.A., 1923–5); F. CAJORI, *History of Mathematics* (New York, 1919); W. W. ROUSE BALL, *A Short Account of the History of Mathematics* (6th ed., 1915).

XXIV

MEDICINE

By SIR D'ARCY POWER

Whether what Temple says be true, that physicians have had more learning than the other faculties, I will not stay to enquire; but I believe every man has found in physicians great liberality and dignity of sentiment, very prompt effusion of benevolence, and willingness to exert a lucrative art where there is no hope of lucre.—*Life of Garth* (1781).

MEDICINE had not shaken itself free from the trammels of classical tradition when Johnson was born; when he died the old order had passed away completely, the work of William Harvey and Thomas Sydenham[1] had become the commonplace of physicians. The royal gift of healing was still practised in his childhood, and Dr. Johnson himself was touched for the King's Evil by Queen Anne upon the recommendation of Sir John Floyer, then a physician in Lichfield. He told Mrs. Piozzi long afterwards that he had a confused but solemn recollection of the Queen as a lady in diamonds and a large black hood. Learned physicians of the old school like John Arbuthnot (1667–1735) could hold their own in wit and repartee with Pope and Swift, Gay and Parnell. Radcliffe left a fortune to the University of Oxford;[2] Richard Mead, the Maecenas of his generation, made a princely collection of books and manuscripts, statues and coins. These men treated the disease and not the individual. Dr. Johnson said of Mead that 'he lived more in the broad sunshine of life than almost any man'; and he spoke of William Heberden the Elder (1710–1801) as 'ultimus Romanorum', the last of the learned physicians.

When Johnson died the plague was a thing of the past; small-pox had been mastered by Jenner, and better hygiene had lessened gaol-fever. The learned physician had given place to the clinical physician; men like Isaac Lettsom and the Pitcairnes, uncle and nephew, who treated the individual, had replaced those who, like Armstrong and Akenside, were

[1] Johnson wrote the Life of Sydenham prefixed to the translation of the latter's Latin works.

[2] The munificence of Dr. Radcliffe gave Oxford her Observatory, the Infirmary, opened in 1776, and the medical travelling Fellowships. His humanity was also shown by the bequest he made to St. Bartholomew's Hospital 'to improve the diets of the poor patients'.

more at home in literary circles than at the bedside. This change of type came chiefly from Holland and Germany; many of the younger physicians in the middle of the eighteenth century had been pupils of Herman Boerhaave (1668–1738) at Leyden, and of Albrecht von Haller (1708–77) at Göttingen. Both were great teachers and both had encyclopaedic knowledge. Both, too, added experimental physiology to their work at the bedside. Boerhaave, with a world-wide reputation, remained human and unspoilt to the end. He knew his pupils individually, and maintained a lively and inspiring correspondence with many of them. Haller was an expositor and a careful describer of facts. He caused his students to think for themselves; allotted to them subjects for theses; strove to make them avoid generalities and taught them to become exact in detail. Haller, perhaps, had the more intimate connexion with British physicians. He had visited England, and knew personally the leaders of science and medicine—Sir Hans Sloane, James Douglas, Cheselden, and Pringle. The teachers in the Edinburgh Medical School, which was beginning to come into prominence, were in many instances pupils of Boerhaave. Amongst these students was John Fothergill (1712–80), a Quaker, born in Wensleydale. He came to London without influence; made a very large practice; was a leader, and to a large extent a founder, of the School of practical physicians.

The progress in surgery and midwifery was as great as in medicine, but was even more rapid and revolutionary. Old beliefs were swept away, and methods were adopted which could not be improved upon until chemistry, physics, and optics enlarged their bounds. The rank and file of the medical profession had begun to feel early in the eighteenth century that they were insufficiently educated, and some, on their own initiative, sought to gain more knowledge by attending private classes and themselves paying the fees.

It had never been obligatory in England for a medical man to submit himself to examination before beginning to practise, unless he wished to enter the Navy or the Army, to live at Oxford or Cambridge, or in one of the towns like London, Newcastle, York, or Bristol, where a Barber's Guild or Company was in control. From 1540 until 1745 the licensing of those who intended to practise surgery in London or its immediate neighbourhood, that is to say within seven miles of the City, had been in the hands of the United Company of Barbers and Surgeons. The teaching provided by the United Company had been good and sufficient in its early days. The lecturers had been chosen from the best talent available, and were usually graduates from Oxford or Cambridge. The positions of lecturer and demonstrator were held to be honourable. They were well paid, were often the stepping-stone to success in practice, and were, therefore, much sought after.

The teaching became stereotyped in process of time, for it was wholly by lectures, and at the end of the seventeenth century it had fallen into disrepute. A feeling had also arisen that the practice of surgery should no longer be allied to the trade of a barber. Surgeons who had been taken prisoners by French and Spanish warships in 1744 complained that they were treated as privates and not as commissioned officers because their captors said that they were barbers. Little by little a succession of teachers of anatomy took upon themselves to infringe the monopoly of the United Company, and to give practical courses in anatomy and surgery where the student could see and handle things for himself instead of merely listening to a set discourse. George Rolfe gave such a course in 1701, and afterwards went to Cambridge as Professor of Anatomy. Dr. James Douglas was lecturing in 1706, and from this time onwards private teachers became so numerous that the United Company was obliged to take official notice of their existence. William Cheselden (1688–1752) was selected for the purpose, and a Minute appears in the records of the court of Assistants under the date March 25, 1714, that:

Our Master acquainting the Court that Mr. William Cheselden, a Member of the company did frequently procure the dead bodies of Malefactors from the place of execution and dissect the same at his own house, as well during the Company's Public Lecture as at other times, without the leave of the Governors and contrary to the Company's By-Laws in that behalf, By which means it becomes more difficult for the Beadles to bring away the Companies Bodies and likewise draws away the Members of this Company and others from the Public Dissections and lectures at the Hall. The said Mr. Cheselden was thereupon called in. But having submitted himself to the pleasure of the Court with a promise never to dissect at the same time as the Company had its lectures at the Hall nor without the leave of the Governors for the time being, the said Mr. Cheselden was excused for what had passed with a reproof for the same pronounced by the Master at the desire of the Court.

William Cheselden was at this time twenty-six years of age, was full of enthusiasm, and was already becoming prominent as an anatomist and a surgeon. It was for this reason probably that he was chosen for a public warning rather than another of the private teachers. He became a surgeon at St. Thomas's Hospital, and was the most expert operator of his generation. He was so dexterous and friendly that he was able to deprive an operation of some of its horrors. He often extracted a stone from the bladder in less than half a minute; and it is told of him that he once promised a child some sweetmeats if he would lie still while he cut him for the stone. The operation over, the child sat up and at once asked for the promised reward. He was, in addition to his skill as a surgeon, a wit, a patron of sport, and something of an architect, for it is said, though incorrectly, that he drew the plans for old Putney Bridge. Pope coupled his name with that of Dr. Mead in the *Imitations of Horace*, when he wrote:

> Late as it is I put myself to school,
> And feel some comfort not to be a fool;
> Weak though I am of limb and short of sight,
> Far from a lynx and not a giant quite,
> I'll do what Mead and Cheselden advise
> To help those limbs and to preserve those eyes.
> Not to go back is somewhat to advance,
> And men must walk at least before they dance.

It is clear, indeed, that Cheselden was also a man of humane feeling, for he says:

> If I have any reputation I have earned it dearly for none ever endured more anxiety before an operation, yet from the time I began to operate all uneasiness ceased and if I have had better success than some others I do not impute it to more knowledge but to the happiness of a mind that was never ruffled or disconcerted and a hand that never trembled during any operation.

The strain of an operation to an educated surgeon was always very great. John Abernethy, a generation later, rarely undertook a serious operation without vomiting. The ordeal was perhaps less severe for the patient. Operations were only undertaken as a last resource, when the patient had often suffered months or years of anguish. He was buoyed up with the hope of recovery or, at the worst, of relief from pain. It was not usual to drug him, but he was generally given a glass of brandy or other stimulant; neither was he bound, though the surgeon usually had three or four assistants in attendance for purposes of restraint. The tolerance of pain, too, was certainly greater when people lived more in the open air and were less introspective than nowadays. Several accounts exist in which the patient has described his feelings during an actual operation before anaesthetics were in use. They all agree that although the pain was great it was not insupportable. It caused sweating but not fainting; the operation was done quickly and the worst of the pain was soon over.

The new era in teaching began when the Company of Barber Surgeons was dissolved in 1745 and the Surgeons' Company was formed. The private classes continued to be held and were attended by increasing numbers of students. Samuel Sharp (1700–78), Cheselden's favourite pupil, carried on his class when the great surgeon became too busy in his profession to continue teaching. But all these classes were quickly eclipsed by the success of the Hunterian School.

In 1743 a young Scotsman named William Hunter (1718–83) visited the Anatomy schools in Paris, and on his return lodged with Tobias Smollett, the novelist, in Downing Street, Westminster. William Hunter advertised that on Monday, October 13, 1743, he would begin a course of anatomical lectures, to which 'would be added the operations of surgery, with the application of bandages'. The day is for ever memorable because it marks the beginning of scientific surgery in England. The great feature of the work was that Hunter made his pupils dissect a body with their own hands. They were thus enabled to verify the statements made by their teachers instead of looking at pictures or having the structures pointed out to them by a demonstrator as they were mentioned by the lecturer reading from a book. The results were satisfactory, and a story is told, but not on very good authority, that after the first lecture William Hunter proudly carried home 70 guineas under his cloak, telling a friend on the way that it was the largest sum he had ever possessed. Hunter helped the more needy of his pupils so liberally with these fees that he had no money left to advertise the third course of his lectures.

The success of William Hunter led him to call his youngest brother from Scotland. John Hunter (1728–93) answered the call, came to London, and converted surgery from a trade into a science. He endeavoured, with considerable success, to illustrate life in all its forms. Of the two brothers, William was the more widely gifted; John, the greater genius. The results of William Hunter's labours are preserved in the University of Glasgow, a magnificent collection of books, coins, manuscripts, and specimens illustrating the development of the embryo. John Hunter's work is represented by the Museum at the Royal College of Surgeons in London. It shows comparative anatomy in all its forms, comparative physiology, and much anthropology, for he collected his materials from many countries. The school which the brothers founded, known as the Hunterian or Windmill Street School, prospered exceedingly. William Hunter soon retired; but John Hunter gathered around him all the surgical and teaching talent of the day, and to his pupils and these colleagues he was affectionately known as the 'dear man'. Amongst the teachers was William Cumberland Cruikshank (1745–1800), one of the most brilliant of the younger men, a well-educated Scotsman, able to hold his own in literary and anatomical circles, and an excellent surgeon. He attended Dr. Johnson in 1783, when it was thought there might be need for an operation, and again during his fatal illness in 1784. Johnson loved him, described him as 'a sweet-blooded man', and recommended him unsuccessfully to Sir Joshua Reynolds as Professor of Anatomy at the Royal Academy in succession to Dr. William Hunter. He presented him with a set of the *Lives of the Poets,* and directed in his will that he should be allowed to choose a book from his library.

Medicine and surgery were so widely separated throughout the seventeenth century that the physician merely advised and attended when an operation had to be performed, but did not himself operate. The surgeons in England served an apprenticeship. The physician graduated at a university, and was usually a fellow of the Royal College of Physicians if he practised in London. Foreign degrees were accepted by the English Universities on an *ad eundem* basis, and it was the custom for the younger physicians to take the M.D. degree in Italy, Holland, France, Germany, or more rarely in Scotland, where the medical school was beginning to thrive under the influence of Monro, Cullen, and Pitcairne. The reading of a thesis in Latin was obligatory upon those who wished to obtain a degree in any university. The thesis was afterwards printed, and was supplemented in many cases by an oral examination. This examination was conducted by the assembled professors of the Medical Faculty. At the University of Leyden, and at the Royal College of Physicians in London, this examination lasted four or five hours, fruit and wine being provided. It was more perfunctory in the smaller universities, where it was preceded by a visit of the candidate to the examiners, a present—usually of gloves—and sometimes a dinner. In every university the oral examination was conducted in Latin, which placed native and foreign candidates upon an equality as regards language. There were several methods of escaping an examination at Oxford and Cambridge, where the medical degree could be obtained by favour—royal or otherwise. The degrees of foreign universities were accepted in England more freely than Scottish and Irish degrees.

A licence in surgery was sometimes granted at Oxford on proof that the applicant had treated a certain number of poor persons, but the surgeons in that city usually became 'privilegiati', like other tradesmen, on showing that they held a licence from a Barber-Surgeons' Company. This licence of the Barber-Surgeons' Company was granted after an oral examination in English and did not require a thesis. Smollett in *Roderick Random* gives a somewhat exaggerated account of the examination, but it must be remembered that he failed to pass for a Surgeon's Mate in 1740.

The apothecaries, that is to say the Freemen of the Society of Apothecaries in London, carried on much of the general practice amongst those who could afford to pay a fee. They were subordinate to the physicians, who exercised the right of visiting their shops once in every year and of casting into the street any drugs which fell below an arbitrary standard of excellence. For some years the physicians had tried to get a share of the lucrative practice of the apothecaries by establishing dispensaries or, as they would now be called, out-patient departments, where the poorer classes could be treated. Their efforts were resisted, and the wordy 'battle of the Dispensaries' ensued. The worst of the battle was over in Dr. Johnson's time, but as late as 1741 it was worth while for the publishers to issue a tenth edition of *The Dispensary*, a mock-heroic poem by Sir Samuel Garth, M.D. The apothecaries consolidated their position and continued to make a good living by selling medicines to their patients. It was not until 1811, as the result of a friendly lawsuit between John Fuller, apothecary to St. George's Hospital, and the executors of 'Old Q.', the fourth Duke of Queensberry, that they became lawfully entitled to charge for advice as an item separate from the medicines supplied. The situation was odd and complicated, though it only occurred in London and the larger towns. The custom was for the apothecary to see the patient and then go to the coffee-house, where he found the physician whom he was accustomed to consult. He described to him the symptoms and received 'a bill' or prescription, written in Latin, with directions as to what should be done for treatment. The apothecary went back to the patient when he had made up the medicine ordered and provided himself with the clysters, purges, and emetics which had been recommended. These he administered himself, but, if bleeding were required, the barber-surgeon was called in, and when cupping was necessary a 'cupper' was summoned. From first to last the physician never saw the patient except in very serious cases. His fee was one guinea a visit, or two-thirds of a guinea a mile if he had to make a journey. The distinction remained until the advent of motor-cars, for until then many of the older medical firms made a distinction in their ledgers between a 'visit' and 'iter', a journey.

Below the apothecary again came the unlicensed practitioners, who were not attached to any of the corporate bodies. They were usually humane men, who treated the poorest of the poor at their own homes in a spirit of philanthropy. Robert Levett, Dr. Johnson's friend, was a fair example of this class. Kind-hearted, and charitable, he had been a waiter in a Paris café, but had no professional knowledge except what he had learned from casual acquaintances.

It thus came about that there was a very clear differentiation in the medical profession during the whole of the eighteenth century. There was, first, the physician, cultured and educated in medicine, without any knowledge of surgery; then the surgeon, rougher and less cultured, but a master of the technical side of his profession. Both physician and surgeon were looked up to with respect by their patients and the public generally. The barber-surgeon was the surgeon holding no hospital appointment. He did much of the general practice in the town and shared it with the apothecary. He came from a lower class and was usually equal to all emergencies, though he fell back on the physician and the surgeon when he required more skilled advice. In the villages it was not necessary for the medical practitioner to have given any evidence of his professional education, but it was usual for him to have obtained a licence after serving an apprenticeship. Before the Scottish graduates began to invade England the doctor was generally spoken of as 'Mr.', 'surgeon', or 'the 'poticary'; later, when Scottish graduates became numerous, these simple titles were replaced by the term 'Dr.'

The state of midwifery in England may be estimated by the great excitement caused in 1726, when even the educated public discussed the burning question whether a poor woman, Mary Tofts by name, living at Godalming, was or was not delivered of rabbits, some alive and others dead. It was a clear case of gross imposture, but feeling ran so high that Caroline of Anspach, then Princess of Wales, ordered Sir Richard Manningham to inquire into the truth of the matter. Sir Richard was one of the chief teachers of midwifery in England, and has the credit of setting aside a few beds for lying-in women when the St. James's Parochial Infirmary was opened in 1739, a proceeding which marked a new era in the treatment of pregnant women.

Dr. William Smellie (1697–1763) came from Lanarkshire to London about 1740, and from that time onwards taught midwifery so admirably and so practically that it soon displaced the old haphazard methods of the midwives. He went to Paris and learnt from Grégoire how to teach by means of the 'phantom', making use of forceps in his demonstrations. He does not, however, stand alone in introducing the use of forceps. They had long been employed, with a certain amount of secrecy, by several generations of the Chamberlen family, and Dr. Burton vaunted the great superiority of his own pattern in 1751. It was this Dr. John Burton (1710–71) who is held up to ridicule by Sterne in *Tristram Shandy* as 'Dr. Slop'. He is there represented as an ill-tempered, ill-mannered and vulgar Papist. In reality he had been educated at St. John's College, Cambridge, had studied medicine at Leyden, and was an able scientific obstetrician, a prominent citizen of York, a founder of the York County Hospital, a highly distinguished antiquary, and the author of a standard work on Midwifery. In days when the man-midwife was looked down upon, Burton was known as a gentleman and a scholar. The forceps which he invented is still to be seen in the rooms of the York Medical Society. Smellie and Burton developed the practical side of midwifery. Dr. William Hunter, who soon abandoned the drudgery of teaching anatomy, took a wider view and was more concerned with the scientific aspects. He published a wonderful series of plates which showed for the first time the true anatomy of pregnancy.

Lying-in hospitals were quickly founded when midwifery began to attract the attention of such men as John Douglas, Smellie and William Hunter. In London the post of physician-accoucheur was created at the Middlesex Hospital, and was filled by Dr. William Hunter in 1748. The British Lying-In Hospital was opened in 1749; the City of London Lying-In Hospital in 1750; Queen Charlotte's in 1752; and the Royal Maternity Charity for delivering poor married women at their own habitations in 1757. The newly established county hospitals and infirmaries set apart special beds for maternity cases; but at Newcastle-upon-Tyne there was a maternity hospital as early as 1760, though it was many years before other provincial towns followed the example.

Irregular medical practice was rampant throughout the eighteenth century, and pure impudence carried many of its professors to success. Foremost amongst the quacks was the Chevalier John Taylor (1703–72), who called himself 'Opthalmiator Pontifical, Imperial and Royal, who treated Benedict XIV, Augustus III, Frederick V, King of Denmark and Norway, and Frederick Adolphus, King of Sweden.' He was a man of distinguished appearance who, with a firm hand and good instruments, operated with great dexterity. He had, too, the natural gift of speech, and knew several languages. But his knowledge of Latin was rudimentary. He once challenged Samuel Johnson to talk Latin with him. Johnson responded with a quotation from Horace which Taylor took to be 'something of his own composition'. 'He

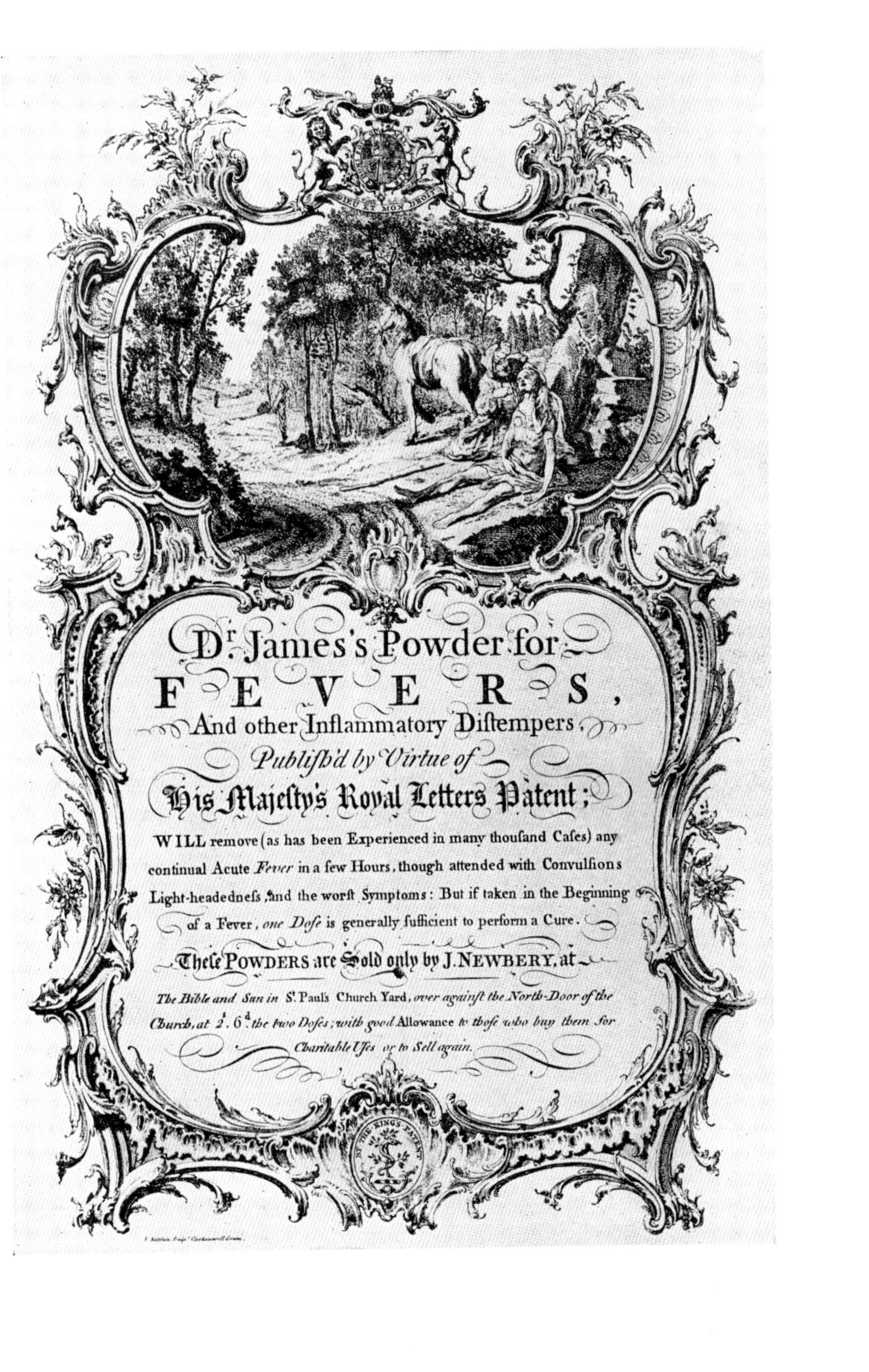
DIEU ET MON DROIT
Dr. James's Powder for
FEVERS,
And other Inflammatory Distempers,
Publish'd by Virtue of
His Majesty's Royal Letters Patent;
WILL remove (as has been Experienced in many thousand Cases) any continual Acute Fever in a few Hours, though attended with Convulsions Light-headedness, and the worst Symptoms: But if taken in the Beginning of a Fever, one Dose is generally sufficient to perform a Cure.
These POWDERS are Sold only by J. NEWBERY, at
The Bible and Sun in St. Paul's Church Yard, over against the North-Door of the Church, at 2s. 6d. the two Doses; with good Allowance to those who buy them for Charitable Uses or to Sell again.
BY THE KINGS PATENT

said a few words well enough', Johnson afterwards remarked when relating the story to Boswell. He gave it as his opinion that Taylor was 'the most ignorant man I ever knew, but sprightly: Ward the dullest.' Haller, on the other hand, when he made his funeral oration was in doubt whether to call him a quack or a genius. The son of the Chevalier succeeded his father, practised as an oculist, and is described

Doctor *FREDERICK*,
Lately come from *Germany*.

BEGS leave to acquaint the Publick, that he undertakes to Cure the Gout, and Rheumatiſm, without any return; being the firſt perſon that ever could Cure the Gout in *London*; Likewiſe, Cures the yellow Jaundice, Stitching in the Side. He likewiſe Cures any Body who is bit by a Mad Dog: Gentlemen and Ladies, I call myſelf Maſter; in a Word if you will make Trial where the Public may find great Benefit. No Cure no Pay.

Direct to me at Mr. *Compton's*, the *Crown* and *Featherſ*; in *Holbourn*, near *Red Lyon Street*, LONDON.

as 'an illiterate and cunning scoundrel without the redeeming qualities which made his parent amusing'.

Joshua or 'Spot' Ward, who was born in 1685 and died in 1761, is said to have begun life as a dry-salter in Thames Street, and was returned to Parliament as the member for Marlborough. He was unseated when examination showed that he had not received a single vote. He fled to St. Germain for political reasons and was pardoned by George II about 1733. He then began business as a quack doctor with an antimonial pill, a paste, and drops. The paste was afterwards adopted by the Faculty and appeared in the Pharmacopoeia as confection of black pepper. He also had a 'headache essence', which is still used, and is known as compound camphor liniment. He advertised that he 'performed many marvellous and sudden cures on persons pronounced incurable in several hospitals'. He fulfilled his promise by the simple device of hiring patients at half a crown a week and instructing them in the symptoms of the disease they were to simulate. A better class came in coaches and sat in his consulting room at five shillings a day, Ward paying the coach hire.

A new method of advertising was invented by Van Burtchell, who rose to notoriety from small beginnings as a quack doctor to a prominent position as a dentist. His wife died in 1775 and he caused her body to be embalmed by Cruikshank, probably at the suggestion of John Hunter. Van Burtchell then advertised that 'his dear departed' could be seen in his sitting room, where she was preserved in a glass case dressed in a fine gown of linen and lace, 'any day between 9 and 1 o'clock, Sundays excepted'. The exhibition continued until Van Burtchell married again, when the second wife banished the remains of the first to John Hunter's Museum. She can still be seen at the Royal College of Surgeons in a somewhat dilapidated state.

Robert James (1705–76) climbed into reputation by means of a secret remedy known as 'Dr. James's Fever Powder'. It consisted of antimony and phosphate of lime. It was a dangerous remedy on account of its depressant action, and was used extensively as a febrifuge when as yet 'fever' meant any condition in which the skin felt hot and the patient shivered. It was extolled by Horace Walpole and may have hastened the end of Oliver Goldsmith. It was sold by John Newbery, the bookseller in St. Paul's churchyard, at a cost of half a crown for four doses. Dr. James was educated at Lichfield and was an early friend of Dr. Johnson,[1] who wrote the dedication to Dr. Mead and a few articles in a large three-volume *Medicinal Dictionary, with a History of Drugs*, which Dr. James published in 1743–5.[2]

Women were as successful as men in irregular practice. Joanna Stevens, an ignorant and vulgar woman, induced Parliament to pay her £5,000 to disclose the secret of a remedy for the cure of stone. It consisted of a powder of calcined egg-shells and snails; a decoction of soap and swines' cresses; and pills of snails, alicant soap, and honey. Sir

[1] Johnson also 'helped' James in writing the *Proposals for printing a Medicinal Dictionary* (1741). One paragraph written by Johnson begins: 'Physic is an Art which every Man practises, in some degree, either upon himself or others.' Johnson numbered many doctors among his friends, and he was interested both in the physicians and in their physic. See, for example, J. D. Wright, *Some Unpublished Letters to and from Dr. Johnson* (Manchester: Bulletin of the Ryland's Library, vol. xvi, No. 1, January, 1932).

[2] There is an article on Dr. James's Powder by Professor Bruce Dickins in *Life and Letters*, vol. ii, no. 8, 1929. See also Charles Welsh, *A Bookseller of the Last Century* (1885), in which Newbery's autobiography is printed (pp. 118–59), and where there are references to Dr. James's Powder.

Robert Walpole took a course of this treatment, and it was calculated that he had consumed 180 pounds of soap and 1,200 gallons of lime water before he died.

Mrs. Mapp, known as 'crazy Sally', was equally successful in her time, but less fortunate. She herself was fat and ugly, but her sister is said to have been the original of Polly Peacham. Mrs. Mapp practised as a bone-setter at Epsom, and drove once or twice a week to the Grecian coffee-house in London in a four-horse chariot with outriders in gorgeous liveries. She appears in Hogarth's print, 'The Undertaker's Arms, or Consultation of Physicians', and is placed in the top row between Chevalier Taylor and Joshua Ward. She took to drink and died in poverty at Seven Dials. Percivall Pott, Surgeon to St. Bartholomew's Hospital, says of her:

> Even the absurdities and impracticability of her own promises and engagements were by no means equal to the expectations and credulity of those who ran after her, that is, of all ranks and degrees of people from the lowest labourer up to those of the most exalted rank and station, several of whom not only did not hesitate to believe implicitly the most extravagant assertions of this ignorant, illiberal, drunken female savage, but even solicited her company, or at least seemed to enjoy her society.

It is difficult to realize the deplorable condition in which the poorer inhabitants of the larger cities and towns lived during the eighteenth century. Rapid expansion was taking place in London and the buildings were erected in the form of narrow lanes, courts, and vents, without a plan and with the desire of crowding as many tenement houses as possible on any ground which happened to be vacant. These houses were let out to families who lived in single rooms and often carried on piece work requiring utensils and instruments which encroached upon the already insufficient floor space. The window tax of 1696 was made more stringent in 1746, and the numerous occupants of the cellars and attics lived for the most part in darkness, and foul air. Their very sky-lights were taxed, and ventilation was impossible. The water supply was drawn from surface wells, which were so infrequent that resort was usually made to the parish pump, and water carriers were employed in many parts of London. The common privy was placed over an open cesspool at the foot of the basement stairs; the cesspool was often damaged, leaking, and overfull, for there was no system of emptying it.

Overcrowding was normal, and two or three people usually occupied a single bed. Personal cleanliness was unknown. When it was urged against Kit Smart, the poet, that he was no lover of clean linen, Dr. Johnson confessed that he had no passion for it himself. Yet following Ovid's maxim, 'Video meliora proboque, deteriora sequor', he said on another occasion, laughingly, 'I have often thought that if I kept a seraglio, the ladies should wear linen gowns—or cotton; I mean stuffs made of vegetable substances. I would have no silk; you cannot tell when it is clean; it will be very nasty before it is perceived to be so. Linen detects its own dirtiness.'

The difficulties of being personally clean were very great. Sir John Floyer (1649–1734), a friend and adviser of Dr. Johnson, published *An Inquiry into the Right Use of the Hot, Cold, and Temperate Baths in England*, which ran through six editions between 1697 and 1722. It was intended to be exhaustive, but makes no mention of bathing for the sake of cleanliness.[1] A bath still exists at Hampton Court which was installed in the time of William and Mary, and it is possible that a few existed in some of the larger houses in England. At St. Bartholomew's Hospital in London a small swimming bath was provided when the south wing was built in 1736. At the Royal Infirmary in Edinburgh it was reported in 1778 that one cold bath and two hot baths had been placed in the west wing with their respective dressing rooms, and that in the east wing a bath had been provided for the patients of the house, so that it may be used occasionally as a cold or hot bath. The Report continued: 'Those in the West Wing are intended for people of the City; no patient in the Hospital having at any time admittance to them'. Professor Comrie, who draws attention to the Report, adds that these three baths seem to have been the only provision in the middle of the century by which the inhabitants of Edinburgh could carry out complete ablution otherwise than in a stream or in the sea. The College of Physicians at a slightly earlier date had established a cold bath in the

[1] When Wickins, a Lichfield draper, was with some pride showing Johnson his cold bath, the latter recommended him to 'let well alone, and be content', and added, 'I hate immersion'. It was said of the eleventh Duke of Norfolk, whose objection to clean linen was notorious, that he was never thoroughly washed except when he was so drunk that his servants were able to place him in the bath without his being sensible of it.

ET PLURIMA MORTIS IMAGO
The Company of Undertakers
Beareth Sable, an Urinal proper, between 12 Quack-Heads of the Second & 12 Cane Heads Or, Consul-
-tant. On a Chief Nebulæ, Ermine, One Compleat Doctor issuant, checkie sustaining in his
Right Hand a Baton of the Second. On his Dexter & sinister sides two Demi-Docters, issuant
of the second, & two Cane Heads issuant of the third; The first having One Eye conchant, to-
wards the Dexter Side of the Escocheon; the Second Faced per pale proper & Gules, Guardent. —
With this Motto —— Et Plurima Mortis Imago.

From the etching by W. Hogarth

garden of their Hall near the Cowgate; the Incorporation of Surgeons also instituted a bath about the same time.

The streets were as deplorable as the houses. They were ill paved, badly lighted, and usually had a central channel filled with garbage which was carried away by the rain in wet weather and was distributed as an evil smelling dust in the summer. It is not surprising, therefore, that drunkenness was a usual vice, starvation common, and epidemics frequent. But out of evil came good. The reign of George II marks the beginning of a care for public health in association with the names of Richard Mead (1673–1754), John Pringle (1707–82), James Lind (1716–94), and perhaps the Rev. Stephen Hales (1677–1761), who insisted on the value of ventilation and pure air. These glimmerings of the dawn of sanitary science appeared as early as 1720, when Dr. Richard Mead published *A Short Discourse concerning Pestilential Contagion and Methods to be used to prevent it*. He advocated the establishment of a central Council of Health, and the isolation of those sick of epidemic disease instead of shutting up the whole house, as was then the custom during outbreaks of the Plague. A generation later John Howard put hygienic precepts into practice in the village of Cardington, three miles from Bedford, and soon made it a model village, for he spared neither pains nor money. He began by building a number of neat cottages on his estate, annexing to each a little land for a garden and other conveniences. These cottages he peopled with the most industrious and sober tenants he could find, and he was careful to provide them with employment, to assist them in sickness and distress and to educate their children. He was also concerned to preserve their morals, and obliged them to attend regularly their several places of worship, to abstain from public houses, and to abandon such amusements as he thought pernicious. He secured compliance with his rules by making them tenants at will. How very far Howard was in advance of his time is shown by the notorious aftermath of the Session held at the Old Bailey in May 1750. The Court became infected by gaol-fever, 'killing Judges, Counsel, and others to the number of forty without making allowance for those of a lower rank whose death may not have been heard of'. Two years later, in 1752, Sir John Pringle published his book, *Observations on the Diseases of the Army*, the result of his observations during the Flanders campaign of 1742–3. The work was a classic and began hygienic reform, both in the British Army and amongst the civil population, by giving valuable hints as to the manner in which typhus and enteric might be avoided. Dr. James Lind, who was a physician at the Haslar Hospital, wrote in 1753 of the *Means of Preserving the Health of Seamen*. His declared object was to provide a plan of directions for 'preserving British seamen from such distempers as prove much more fateful to their corps than all the other calamities incident to them at sea. For', said he, 'the number of seamen in time of war who die by shipwreck, capture, famine, fire, or sword, are but inconsiderable in respect of such as are destroyed by the ship diseases and by the usual maladies of an intemperate climate.' The good work for the Navy thus begun by Lind was continued by Gilbert Blane (1749–1834), who published his book on *Observations on the Diseases of Seamen* in 1785, and obtained, amongst other things, free issues of soap and medicines to seamen. The name of Captain Cook must also be held in honour with that of Lind and Blane, in the history of naval hygiene. By a flash of genius—for it could be nothing else in a man who had been born in a labourer's cottage at Marton and had slept in an attic in Church Street, Whitby, when he was an apprentice—he solved the problem of keeping men healthy on a long sea voyage by insisting on cleanliness, and providing fruit and fresh water as often as they could be obtained.[1]

It is not surprising, considering the conditions under which the poor lived, that the eighteenth century had more than the usual share of epidemic disease. The plague had disappeared, but a heavy toll of human life in the poorer classes was taken by fever. London had almost reached its maximum of overcrowding and deaths were so numerous, especially amongst children, that it was said with some degree of truth there was no third generation of true Londoners. The population was only maintained by a constant flow of persons from the country districts. It is difficult to differentiate the fevers, for the same fever was called by different names. Post-mortem examinations were not usual and the patients were treated by the lowest class of medical men. No fee was obtainable, and the epidemics swept away the poorest whole-

[1] Cf. *supra*, vol. i, p. 118.

sale, while the sufferers were rarely, if ever, seen by a physician. The registration of deaths was incomplete, and there was no satisfactory certification of disease. Out of the welter of names come the terms continued fever, spotted fever, putrid fever, intermittent fever, and relapsing fever. Some of the epidemics were certainly enteric, but typhus was not distinguished from typhoid, nor was typhoid distinguished from relapsing fever and febricula. What we now know as typhoid was also called brain fever and low fever. The deplorable housing conditions in which the poor lived may possibly have caused some fevers which are now unknown, for they died out when better hygienic conditions prevailed.

It was quite different with small-pox. The disease had long been known as a definite infection, varying in its incidence and intensity. It was so especially a disease of children during the first half of the eighteenth century that about 1720 the Duchess of Argyll, writing congratulations to the Countess of Bute on the birth of a daughter, and on having already two fine boys in her family, adds, 'he that has had the small-pox is as good as two, so mortal as that distemper has been this year in town was never known.'

The exact incidence is unknown, but small-pox appears to have been a disease of the upper classes, while fever ravaged the poor. As is usual in small-pox, the several epidemics of the disease in the course of the eighteenth century varied greatly in virulence, and it is probable that during one of these outbreaks with a low mortality Bishop Berkeley's tar-water gained its reputation as a remedy.

In 1713, Dr. Emmanuel Timoni had drawn the attention of Dr. Woodward, then Gresham Professor of Medicine in London, to the value of inoculation as a preventive of small-pox. He stated that Circassians, Georgians, and other Asiatics had brought the practice to Constantinople, where it had been followed for forty years with the greatest advantage to many thousands. The method was noted, but little use was made of it until 1721, when Lady Mary Wortley Montagu induced King George II to order the inoculation of three men and three women, convicts lying in Newgate. The inoculations were performed by Dr. Maitland, a Scottish physician, who had been attached to the Embassy at Constantinople and had inoculated Lady Mary's elder boy in March 1717–18. Other experimental inoculations having been performed and all proving successful, the Princess of Wales caused Claudius Amyand, the sergeant surgeon, to inoculate two of her own children—the Princess Amelia, aged eleven, and the Princess Caroline, aged nine. It was considered for many years that inoculation required a long course of preparatory treatment. It was, therefore, only used by the wealthy, until gratuitous inoculations were introduced about 1746. The Middlesex County Hospital for Small-pox was founded in London in that year, and various hospitals for preparatory treatment were opened between 1750 and 1768. These hospitals were used chiefly by adults, for they did not receive children under seven years of age. Dr. Maty in 1767 called attention to the advantages of early inoculation, but it was not until 1775 that Dr. Lettsom seriously took up the practice of inoculating infants in London, and started a society for inoculation at the homes of the people. In 1779 he also opened a general inoculation dispensary for the benefit of the poor throughout London, Westminster, and Southwark without removing them from their own habitations. Local opposition prevented these institutions from being successful; but good work on similar lines was done in Newcastle-upon-Tyne, Chester, and Liverpool.

A great wave of philanthropy swept over England during the life of Dr. Johnson, and from it emerged the system of county hospitals. In London and Southwark the Royal Hospitals of St. Bartholomew and St. Thomas had been sufficient for the needs of the people, but more accommodation had to be provided as the population increased and the town grew. The Westminster Hospital was founded in 1720, Guy's in 1724, St. George's in 1733, the London in 1740, and the Middlesex in 1745. During the 125 years subsequent to 1700, no less than 154 hospitals and dispensaries were established in the British Isles, and of these seventy-four were opened in the provinces, beginning with Bristol in 1735. Others followed in rapid succession, built and equipped at the costs of merciful men and women who thus tried to alleviate the sickness and suffering by which they were surrounded. Some of these institutions were known as county hospitals; others were called infirmaries. They provided accommodation which was adequate according to the standard of the time, but the inmates were thought and spoken of as 'poor objects' of pity rather than as indi-

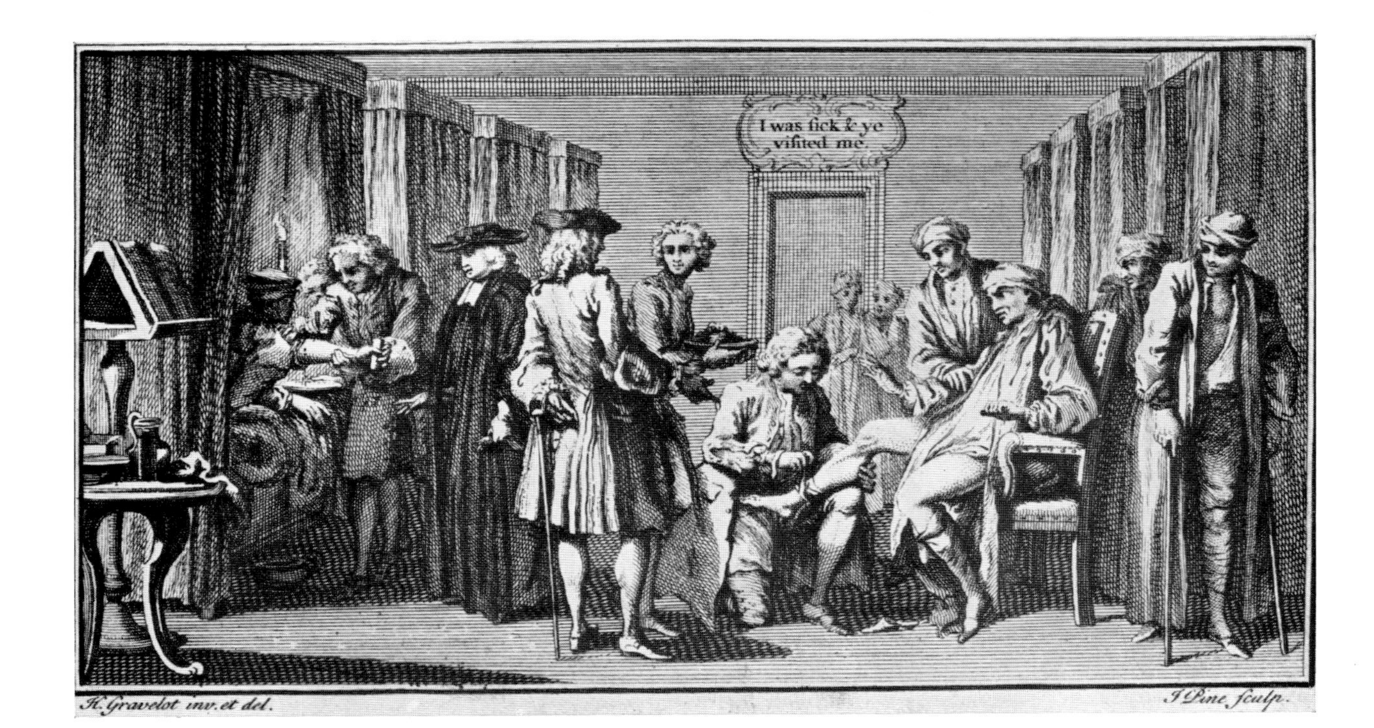
I was ſick & ye viſited me
H. Gravelot inv. et del.
J. Pine ſculp.

A HOSPITAL IN THE EIGHTEENTH CENTURY

From a print, after H. Gravelot, in the Library of the Royal College of Surgeons

vidual men and women. Patients were admitted suffering from every kind of disease—infectious and non-infectious alike—and, except for separation of the sexes, no attempt was made at segregation and classification.

All hospitals were free at first to any applicant who was

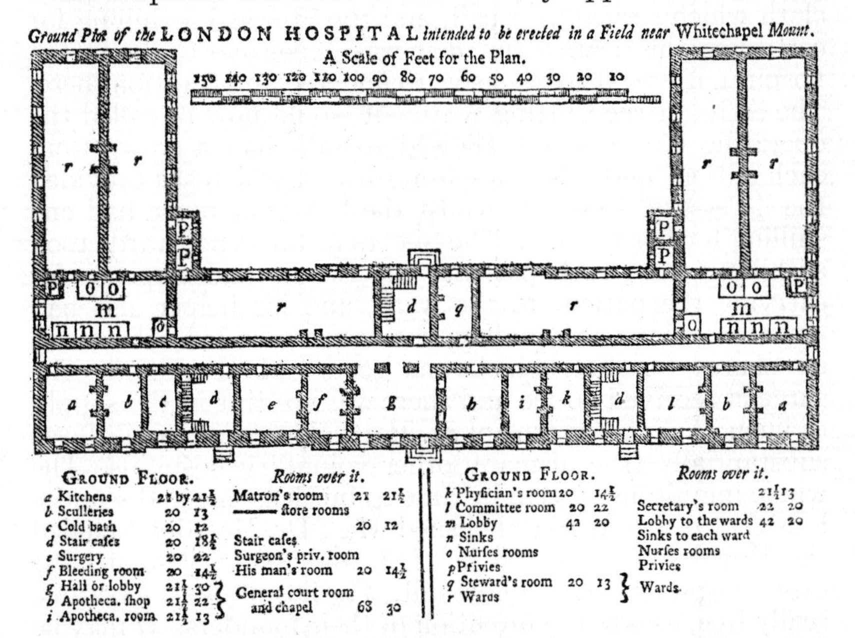

ill, provided that he had obtained a letter of recommendation from a Governor or subscriber, a matter of no great difficulty when towns were small and the inhabitants were personally known to each other. In process of time a vexatious system of red-tape and fees grew up which made it almost impossible for a really poor applicant to gain admission; and it is only recently that 'subscribers' letters' have been done away with. The system was most highly developed in the Royal Hospitals of St. Bartholomew and St. Thomas, which had existed for centuries. The procedure at St. Bartholomew's was highly complicated in the eighteenth century where documentary evidence exists to show the details. A patient had first to obtain a Governor's letter recommending him for admission. If he had no letter he had to deposit the sum of 19*s*. 6*d*. for burial fees, returnable, of course, were he fortunate enough to recover. If he died the Beadle received one shilling for giving notice of death to the friends; the porter demanded a shilling for the certificate to the parish where he was to be buried; the bearers of the corpse were paid two shillings for carrying the body to the hospital gate and 'no further'. A shilling was claimed by the Matron for the use of a black cloth which served as a pall, and the Steward a shilling for certifying the death. But if it was expensive to die in the hospital, it was also expensive to undergo an operation there. The Sister of the Cutting Ward—it would now be called the operating theatre—was allowed to take half a crown from each patient under her care in return for which she provided the necessary dressings, whilst the helper or nurse had one shilling for her trouble. The Sisters in the other wards took a shilling from each patient; the Beadle had sixpence for carrying the patient to the ward, and his helper also had sixpence. Here, fortunately, the expense ended; there was no charge for diet, which was good and abundant. The surgeon received no fee and there was no stint in the supply of linen. What was true of St. Bartholomew's Hospital was substantially true of many other voluntary hospitals. The whole iniquitous system became so burdensome and scandalous that it was at last abolished when Dr. Marsden founded the Royal Free Hospital in 1828, and for very shame the other hospitals had to follow suit. The hospitals then became really free, as was the intention of their founders. It may be said, however, of the voluntary hospitals, even when they were at their worst, that they provided comfortable beds, kept their patients clean, nursed them well, and treated them according to the best methods in vogue at the time.

Much undeserved censure has been cast upon the nursing in the voluntary hospitals. Contemporary evidence shows that in the larger and better managed hospitals it was good. The nurses in charge of the wards were drawn from the lower middle class; they lived in their wards, they scrubbed them clean, and made nursing a lifelong occupation. Dealing with an uneducated and outspoken class, they were themselves no doubt often heavy-handed and rough in speech. A searching inquiry was made into the conduct and duties of every person in the employ of St. Bartholomew's Hospital and in the report made to the Governors on July 16, 1747, it is said, 'There being no complaint made of any misbehaviour of the Sisters or Nurses of this Hospital, your Committee is of opinion that the Sisters and Nurses have done their duty.' Their enthusiasm sometimes carried them to considerable lengths for they once combined against the sheriff's officer, thrust him out of the hospital gates and rescued a patient whom he had seized. The Sisters were allowed to call in additional helpers in times of stress who were paid at the rate of a shilling a night. These occasional women were often careless and intemperate; it was from them that the regular nurses got a bad name which was wholly undeserved. The 'wicked and barbarous' parish nurses are in a different category from the hospital nurses; there can be no doubt of their enormities.

None of the good things found in the voluntary hospitals came in the way of the unfortunate persons afflicted with mental disease. Their treatment and their very features are preserved in the eighth scene of Hogarth's 'Rake's Progress'. They were chained, whipped, starved, and otherwise ill treated by the keepers, who were men of the lowest class. Any person on the payment of twopence was allowed to wander through the wards unattended, to tease the patients, stimulate their ravings, and make them a public exhibition. Dr. Johnson visited the Bethlehem Hospital (better known as Bedlam) on May 8, 1775, and his attention was arrested by a man who was beating his straw bed very furiously, supposing it to be William, Duke of Cumberland, whom he was punishing for his cruelties in Scotland in 1746.

Bethlehem was situated in Moorfields, just outside the City boundary. The scenes made by sightseers in the hospital became so objectionable that the Governors were obliged to take notice of them officially, and it was ordered in 1766 that 'the doors be kept locked on public holidays against all visitors'. This wholesome rule was not strictly enforced, and in 1770 it was further ordered 'that the admission of visitors be henceforth only by ticket and that accredited visitors be accompanied by an attendant'. Earlier attempts had been made to ameliorate the unhappy conditions of the patients; they were first spoken of as 'patients' in 1700, and 'curable' and 'incurable' wards were opened in 1725–34. Public opinion was stirring slowly in their favour, but it was not until 1750 that St. Luke's Hospital for Lunatics was established on Windmill Hill, nearly opposite Worship Street in London. Dr. Battie was appointed physician to the Hospital, and pupils were admitted to study the treatment of patients under his care, a privilege which had always been discouraged at Bethlehem Hospital. Incurable patients were admitted to St. Luke's Hospital on payment in 1754, and in 1782 a new hospital was built at the corner of Old Street and City Road, a low prison-like building which has only just been pulled down, but which at the time of its opening was far in advance of the amenities of Bedlam.

The death of Dr. Johnson, followed as it was nine years afterwards by that of John Hunter, marks no epoch in the history of English medicine. The work begun in their day went forward steadily. The teaching of the Hunterian school was imitated on a more comprehensive scale, and organized medical schools became attached to many of the larger hospitals in London and the provinces. Pressure from within and without made medicine a profession, with a regular course of study, tested by examination, and recognized by the State. Public health became a subject of great importance; the old epidemics disappeared, but were replaced by cholera as a warning that much still had to be done both for housing and for sanitation. Jenner, the pupil and friend of John Hunter, discovered the value of vaccination by following his master's advice, 'Don't think—try'.

BIBLIOGRAPHY.—WILLIAM MACMICHAEL, *The Gold Headed Cane* (1827). It has been reprinted several times, and contains an account of Radcliffe, Mead, Askew, Pitcairne, and Baillie. HESKETH PEARSON, *Dr. Darwin* (1930)—an account of Dr. Erasmus Darwin and his circle. STEPHEN D'IRSAY, *Albrecht von Haller. Eine Studie zur Geistesgeschichte der Aufklärung*, Arbeiten des Instituts für Geschichte der Medizin (Leipzig, 1930). HINGSTON FOX, *Dr. John Fothergill and his Friends* (1919). D'ARCY POWER, *The Craft of Surgery in England* (1886). SIDNEY YOUNG, *The Annals of the Barber Surgeons of London* (1890). GEORGE C. PEACHEY, *A Memoir of William and John Hunter* (Plymouth, 1924). JOHN GLAISTER, *Dr. William Smellie and his Contemporaries* (Glasgow, 1894). ALBAN DORAN, *Burton (Dr. Slop), his Forceps and his Foes* (Manchester, 1913). T. J. PETTIGREW, *The Medical Portrait Gallery* (no date). Vol. iii contains an account of W. C. Cruikshank. C. J. S. THOMPSON, *The Quacks of Old London* (1928). Capt. JAMES COOK, 'The Method taken for preserving the Health of the Crew H.M.S. The Resolution during her late Voyage round the World' (*Philosophical Transactions*, vol. lvi, 1776, Appendix, p. 39). Sir JOHN PRINGLE, *A Discourse on some late Improvements for preserving the Health of Marines delivered at the Anniversary Meeting of the Royal Society, November 30th, 1776*. (Reprinted by Dr. Andrew Kippis in *Six Discourses*, 1783.) JAMES LIND, *A Treatise on the Scurvy* (1752); *Essay on the means of preserving the Health of Seamen* (1757). SIR JOHN SIMON, *English Sanitary Institutions* (1890). The Rev. E. G. O'DONOGHUE, *The Story of Bethlehem from the Foundation in 1247* (1914). M. DOROTHY GEORGE, *London Life in the Eighteenth Century* (1925), chapters i and ii.

XXV

THE LAW AND THE LAWYERS

By SIR F. D. MACKINNON

Lawyers know life practically. A bookish man should always have lawyers to converse with. They have what he wants.—Boswell's *Life of Johnson*, vol. iii, p. 306.

SIR WILLIAM SCOTT once said to Johnson, 'What a pity it is, Sir, that you did not follow the profession of the Law, You might have been Lord Chancellor.' Johnson, with agitation, replied, 'Why will you vex me by suggesting this when it is too late?' If he had become a lawyer,[1] what was this profession in his time, and what was the Law which it administered?

In the first place the profession was, by comparison with to-day, a very small one. The Lord Chancellor and the Master of the Rolls were the only two Chancery judges; there were twelve Common Law judges; there was one judge at Doctors' Commons. Against these fifteen our modern system provides about forty, together with some sixty County Court judges.[2] The earliest Law List I have seen is of the year 1783. Including twelve Serjeants and seventeen King's Counsel, there were then less than 350 men at the Bar. There were also some Conveyancers, who were not called to the Bar. These were mostly Roman Catholics who adopted this line because they were incapable of being called.

In the Law List of 1932 there are 288 King's Counsel, and over 10,000 members of the bar. The same disparity would appear in any contrast of the attorneys and solicitors[3] of the eighteenth and the solicitors of the twentieth centuries.

The four Inns of Court, though their bounds were as to-day,

[1] In 1739 he inquired as to the possibility of his becoming an Advocate at Doctors' Commons, but his lack of a degree was a fatal obstacle. Hunter, who was his Master at Lichfield school, is said to have flogged seven boys, who afterwards sat as judges at Westminster. They included Sir John Eardley Wilmot, who was Johnson's schoolfellow; Lord Northington; Sir Thomas Clarke, Master of the Rolls; Sir John Willes; and Chief Baron Parker.

[2] There were a few ancient local courts, e.g. at Bristol and Norwich. In the latter half of the century a number of Acts were passed for erecting Small Debt Courts, e.g. 1753 at Boston, 1757 at Yarmouth, 1764 at Chippenham, 1773 at Exeter.

[3] The Officers of the Common Law Courts were attorneys, and those of the Court of Chancery solicitors. A man could hold both qualifications.

were small communities; the more so because two other institutions, Serjeants' Inn and Doctors' Commons, served a similar purpose. All the Common Law judges, who are now Benchers of one of the four Inns, would then have removed to Serjeants' Inn. They were chosen from the serjeants, but very often a man was formally made a serjeant and a judge at the same time. The majority of benchers and barristers lived in their Inn, and the majority also were bachelors, though a good many had mistresses.[1] The proportion of Oxford or Cambridge men at the Bar was much lower than it is now, though Blackstone in his lectures was pleased to recall that at that date the four highest judicial offices were filled by gentlemen, two of whom had been Fellows of All Souls, another a Student of Christ Church, and the fourth a Fellow of Trinity, Cambridge. For an attorney to be an Oxford man, as was Oliver Edwards, the hero of the immortal remark about 'cheerfulness breaking in', was rare indeed. On the whole, I think the level of education among lawyers was much lower than to-day: Sir William Garrow, who rose to be Attorney-General and a baron of the Exchequer, was said to be almost illiterate.

The social life of an Inn of Court was much less vigorous than in earlier times, but much more so than now. The festivities of Christmas continued, but declined throughout the century. But most judges and barristers lived, if not in their Inn, at least within a walk of it, and the Inn was to them what his college is to an Oxford or Cambridge resident.

The student had to spend seven years from his admission until his call to the Bar. This period was diminished, about 1760, to five years, and even to three for a graduate of Oxford or Cambridge. The old Exercises of Learning—Readings, Moots, Imparlances—had entirely ceased in the latter part of the seventeenth century. A semblance of them survived, in the form of certain Latin sentences, which were supplied by the butler, and recited by the student,[2]

[1] When a man was made a judge he was expected to marry the lady. But Lord Thurlow, even as Lord Chancellor, went openly into society with his natural daughters. Sir James Mansfield, Chief Justice of the Common Pleas, declined a peerage in 1804 on the ground that all his children were illegitimate (though he had married their mother), and he did not wish to emphasize that fact by accepting an hereditary title.

[2] *Life of Lord Campbell* (1881), vol. i, p. 134.

very much in the fashion of the examination for his degree at Oxford which Lord Eldon recorded.[1] Many students for the Bar appear to have begun by attending in an attorney's office. The modern system of 'reading in chambers' with a barrister only appears about 1770; Erskine as pupil in 1777 of Buller, afterwards a judge of the King's Bench and of the Common Pleas, is the earliest instance I know. When the student had kept his necessary terms he had no examination to pass for his call, but he had to take an oath in denunciation of the Pope. When a barrister was advanced to be of His Majesty's Counsel, he had again to forswear transubstantiation, and also to produce a certificate that he had received the Sacrament according to the rites of the Church of England. The recognized venue for this performance was St. Martin-in-the-Fields, where the churchwardens had a settled fee of a guinea for their certificate of its having taken place.

If the student, in the earlier part of the eighteenth century, had little opportunity to learn the practice of the profession except by hanging about the Courts,[2] the books available to him were equally unsatisfactory. Traditionally he was recommended to read *Coke upon Littleton*, and he could also apply himself to Rolle's *Abridgement*, and Sheppard's *Touchstone*. The only two books regarded as students' text-books were *Doctor and Student*, by Christopher Saint-German (first edition in Latin, 1523, and in English, 1530, but often reprinted), and Thomas Wood's *Institute of the Laws of England* (1720). I defy any one to read them through to-day.

But the path of the student was made easier by an event which in some ways is the most notable in the history of the Law—the publication of Blackstone's *Commentaries*. William Blackstone was a Pembroke man (who even qualified as one of the 'nest of singing birds'), and Johnson might well have approved his style; but I know of no record of their ever being acquaintances. Under the advice of Lord Mans-

[1] He was examined in Hebrew and History. He was asked by the Examiner what was the Hebrew for 'the place of a skull', and who founded University College. He answered 'Golgotha', and 'King Alfred', and was accorded his *testamur*.

[2] When Boswell consulted Johnson in 1784 about his project of joining the English Bar, he replied: 'You must be careful to attend constantly at Westminster Hall; both to mind your business, as it is almost all learned there (for nobody reads now); and to show that you want business.' Boswell's *Life*, vol. iv, p. 309.

field, then Solicitor-General, he began lecturing on English Law at Oxford in 1753, and continued when appointed the first Vinerian Professor in 1758. These lectures he published as his great work, in four handsome quartos, from 1765 to 1769, and thereby became the founder of English legal education. Bentham, who has many hard things to say of him for other reasons, with justice calls him 'the first of all institutional writers, who has taught Jurisprudence to speak the language of the Scholar and the Gentleman'.

Blackstone's four volumes contain about 2,000 pages. Of these about 500 are concerned with Real Property and its amazingly complicated incidents. This is significant of the fact that the land was still the chief source of wealth and the most important kind of property. Some 400 pages deal with Crime and its punishment: some 300 with the procedure of various Courts. Only about 30 pages deal with the Law of Contract, 20 with the Law of Corporations, and there cannot be above 50 pages that condescend to notice any part of what is now called Commercial Law. But it remained for his patron, Lord Mansfield, to create Commercial Law, as Blackstone was creating legal education.

If Blackstone used the language of the scholar and the gentleman, unhappily he also used that of the incurable optimist.[1] Throughout his pages the existing fabric of the law is belauded as the last achievement of human wisdom, beyond the possibility of criticism or improvement. His book, as it deserved, became immensely popular: every scholar, and almost every gentleman, had it in his library, even if he did not read it. Its authority was overpowering; its value for the student, and even for the experienced lawyer, was great. But Blackstone's optimism may well have been the most potent cause of the total stagnation of legal reform in the second half of the eighteenth century, and of the continuance into the nineteenth of many absurdities and abuses.

At no time until the nineteenth century did Parliament do much for legal reform. Anything that was achieved was the work of judges and lawyers by the invention of new forms of procedure. For example it was actually the law

[1] That is surely a mild description of the writer who could speak of the House of Commons in 1765 as 'freely chosen by the people from among themselves'.

until the reign of William IV that to a Writ of Debt or Detinue a defendant could 'wage his law', i.e. swear that he did not owe the money, or detain the thing claimed, and produce eleven 'Compurgators' to swear that they believed him. If he achieved this—and there were no doubt as many people as in Pickwick's time, ready 'to perjure themselves before the judges of the land, at the rate of half a crown a crime'—he went free. Such a thing actually happened in 1824. Parliament did not abolish this medieval absurdity until 1833, but the lawyers had long rendered it innocuous by inventing the writs of *Indebitatus Assumpsit* and of *Trover*, which were actions on the case, and were not liable to this form of defence. Similarly the old real actions[1] to recover land were subject to many archaic technicalities: so the lawyers invented the action of Ejectment, in which the claimant alleged that he had leased his land to John Doe, who had entered but had been ousted by Richard Roe. Richard Roe was then supposed to hand on this complaint to the defendant, who was thus made to fight the plaintiff. In a claim for the freehold one of the old real actions must be brought; but in a claim for the disturbance of a leasehold interest it need not: hence the invention of John Doe as the fictitious lessee of the plaintiff, and of Richard Roe as 'the casual ejector'.

In their origins the three Common Law Courts had different functions. The King's Bench was concerned with *Placita Coronae*, Pleas of the Crown, crimes or other wrongs, like trespass or assault, that savoured of a breach of the King's peace. The Common Pleas was concerned with *Communia Placita*, ordinary litigation between subjects. The Exchequer dealt with the rights of the Crown to its revenue, or other debts owing to the Crown. Long before the eighteenth century each of the three Courts, by the devices of *Ac etiam* and *Quominus*, had enlarged its jurisdiction so that each of them dealt with all sorts of common law actions in very much the same way. Thus, a writ in the King's Bench would begin with a fictitious allegation of Trespass, and go on to allege (*Ac etiam*) a breach of contract &c. In the Exchequer the plaintiff fictitiously alleged that by the wrong done to him by the defendant he was less able to pay a debt

[1] The extraordinary names of about 60 of these Writs are given in the section of the Act of 1833 (3 and 4 Will. IV, cap. 27, sect. 36) that abolished them.

to the King (*Quominus sufficiens existit*, &c.). The survival of so many Latin tags in English law is due to the fact that until 1730 all pleadings and indictments were in Latin. The reform substituting English had been made in 1650 under the Commonwealth, but Latin was reintroduced at the Restoration. Blackstone, of course, deplores the abandonment of Latin in 1730, on the ground that the change had impaired the culture of attorneys and their clerks.

The two Chief Justices of the King's Bench and the Common Pleas and the Chief Baron of the Exchequer were partly paid by fees collected in their courts, which was perhaps the reason why their jurisdictions came to be enlarged; the three puisne judges of the King's Bench and of the Common Pleas, and three puisne barons of the Exchequer were paid fixed salaries out of the King's Civil list. Of the Chiefs he of the King's Bench got most (Lord Mansfield had a princely income), while the Chief Baron was the worst paid. Until 1760 all judges ceased to hold office on the demise of the Crown, and they were not necessarily reappointed by the new sovereign. An Act passed on the accession of George III altered this, and continued them in office for the future. Another section of that Statute lays down 'that such Salaries as are settled upon Judges for the Time being by Act of Parliament shall in all Time coming be paid and payable to every such Judge so long as his Patent or Commission shall continue and remain in force'.[1]

Neither the Lord Chancellor,[2] nor any of the judges had a retiring pension. The Lord Chancellor and the Chief Justice of the King's Bench commonly stipulated on his appointment for a sinecure for himself or for his son, usually a Tellership of the Exchequer.[3]

In the three Common Law courts every issue of fact was

[1] Parliament paid scant attention to this in the autumn of 1931.

[2] Lord Loughborough, in 1801, was the first to be granted a pension of £4,000 a year.

[3] This system caused some gross scandals when the increase of business made such offices enormously valuable. Lord Camden's son was appointed to a Tellership when he was twenty-one, and it was worth £2,500 a year. But in 1807 its value had risen to £23,000, and it went even higher. Eventually he agreed to accept £3,683 a year, and did so until 1840. One of Lord Thurlow's nephews, who was never more than a Suffolk rector, had three sinecure offices in the Courts given him by his uncle. He lived until 1874, and was then receiving over £11,000 a year as compensation for the abolition of these offices! How much he made in his most profitable year would be unbelievable.

always decided by the verdict of a jury, and never until 1854 by a judge alone. In order to arrive at the question to be submitted to the jury a most elaborate series of written pleadings was exchanged between the parties. The plaintiff began with his Declaration, to which the defendant put in his Plea; the plaintiff might then deliver a Replication, the defendant a Rejoinder, the plaintiff a Surrejoinder, the defendant a Rebutter, and the plaintiff a Surrebutter, in that order; but the whole of the series were not used in every case. The object was to arrive at a single issue of fact upon which a jury could be asked a decisive question. At any stage either party could put in a Demurrer, i.e. a contention by the plaintiff that on the facts so far alleged the defendant must be wrong in law, or by the defendant that the plaintiff had disclosed no case in law to be answered. Such a question would be heard and decided as a matter of law by the Court *in banc* sitting at Westminster. Other questions of law to be decided by the full Court would arise when a jury found a special verdict (which was really a statement of agreed facts settled by Counsel for the parties with the assistance of the presiding judge, and formally assented to by the jury as *their* verdict), or on a motion after a verdict to set it aside, or for a new trial, or for the entry of judgement, on legal grounds, *non obstante veredicto*.

For the hearing of these questions of law each of the three Courts sat *in banc* in the full term time, i.e. about three weeks four times a year. Hilary term was January 23 to February 12, Michaelmas November 6 to 28; Easter and Trinity terms varied according to the date of Easter. After term the trial of issues of fact took place before each of the Chief Justices and a jury, usually at the Guildhall,[1] while the puisne judges went off to hear civil cases on circuit, or to try prisoners there or at the Old Bailey. So much were the three Courts really part of one Common Law system that two judges of assize might be from different Courts, e.g. a judge of the King's Bench and a baron of the Exchequer.

There were six circuits in England—the Home (Hertford, Essex, Kent, Surrey), the Norfolk (Bucks., Beds., Hunts., Cambs., Suffolk, and Norfolk), the Midland, the Oxford,

[1] It will be remembered that in an action in the Common Pleas on February 14, 1828, in the 'settens after term', at the Guildhall, Mr. Justice Stareleigh sat 'in the absence of the Chief Justice, occasioned by indisposition'.

the Western (all three as at present), and the Northern (York, Durham, Northumberland, Cumberland, Westmorland, and Lancashire). On the Northern Circuit[1] the Judges went only once a year, in the summer: until well into the nineteenth century, a prisoner committed for trial in any of these six northern counties might be eleven months in gaol awaiting his trial, and few prisoners were ever granted bail. On the other five circuits there were two assizes a year,[2] in the winter and summer, after Hilary and Trinity terms.

The judges from Westminster did not go on circuit in Wales. An Act of Henry VIII in 1543 created special 'Judges of the Great Sessions' in Wales and Chester. These offices were filled by members of the Bar who could still practise, and, until an Act of 1773 forbade it, they were allowed to appoint deputies to sit for them. Indeed a Law Officer could be one of the Welsh judges: Sir John Willes, Sir William Garrow, and Sir John Copley were each Chief Justice of Chester and Attorney-General at the same time. The Great Sessions of Wales were abolished in 1830.

The procedure which provided so many of the legal questions decided by the full Court is now intelligible only to the antiquary. If you take down a volume of reports you may find two head-notes such as these within a few pages: 'On a joinder in demurrer without a Serjeant's hand, there may be a *non-pros.*, as a Serjeant must be met by a Serjeant' (*Brooker* v. *Simpson* (1800), 2 B and P. 336); 'Aid prayer is a dilatory plea within 4 Anne, Cap. 16, and must be verified by affidavit' (*Onslow* v. *Smith* (1801), *Ibid.* 384).

The rules of pleading and of procedure were applied with rigorous precision; there was no power to allow the amendment of the most venial error. If a plaintiff spelled the defendant's name incorrectly in his process, he was non-suited. If a plaintiff, suing a carrier, alleged in his declaration that the defendant had agreed to carry his goods from A. to B., and on the facts it appeared that the agreement was 'to carry them from A. to B. unless prevented by fire or robbery', this was a fatal variance, though there was no suggestion that there had been any fire or any robbery, and the plaintiff

[1] In Lancashire one assize a year, at Lancaster only, has to be contrasted with three a year at Lancaster, four at Liverpool, and four at Manchester to-day.

[2] There are now three assizes a year everywhere, except at Liverpool, Manchester, and Leeds, where there are four.

WESTMINSTER HALL: THE FIRST DAY OF TERM

After a drawing by H. Gravelot

was non-suited. It was even the rule that the plaintiff must be present to hear the verdict of the jury, and if he were not there to answer to his name he was non-suited: a plaintiff who was advised that his case was going badly would absent himself, and so avoid the probability of hearing a verdict for the defendant. For if the plaintiff was non-suited he could bring another action, and try again; but if he had a verdict against him he could not.

A trial, at *nisi prius* or at the assizes, before a jury would be similar to a trial to-day, but with some notable differences. No one who had any interest in the result was competent to give evidence. With persons who might be supposed to be so interested it was common form to get them to execute a deed disclaiming their rights, if any, and this would be produced if they were objected to. Obviously the plaintiff and defendant were incapable of executing such a deed, and thus the two people who in most cases knew more about what had happened than any one else were never allowed to inform the jury of what they knew.[1] It seems hardly credible that this disability was removed only in 1853, nor is it easy to understand how litigation could have been conducted at all when it was in force.

Another great difference from to-day was that in the Common Law Courts there was no power to order 'discovery', i.e. to make each side disclose to the other material documents in its possession. This could only be done in Chancery: sometimes a man had to start a Chancery suit for this purpose, in order that with the knowledge thus obtained he could then start an action at law.

When a man had got a judgement for a sum of money he could issue a writ of *Ca. Sa.* (*Capias ad satisfaciendum*) to the Sheriff to seize his debtor's body, or a writ of *Fi. Fa.* (*Fieri Facias*) to seize his goods. If he had his writ of *Ca. Sa.* he could not also have a writ of *Fi. Fa.*[2] But if on a writ of *Fi. Fa.* only part of his judgement was satisfied, he could

[1] This, of course, was the reason why in 1828 neither Mrs. Bardell nor Mr. Pickwick was called to give an account of the interview at which no one else was present. If the very loud voices had not forced themselves on the ear of Mrs. Cluppins Mrs. Bardell might have been unable to sue at all.

[2] Again *Bardell* v. *Pickwick* may be cited in illustration. Presumably the well-to-do defendant had property which might have been subjected to *Fi. Fa.* But as Dodson and Fogg elected to issue a writ of *Ca. Sa.* they disabled themselves from touching his property. But see Sir William Holdsworth's *Charles Dickens as a Legal Historian* (1929), p. 142.

have *Ca. Sa.* for the balance. Only a 'trader' had the privilege of becoming a bankrupt, and so being relieved of his debts. 'For the law,' says Blackstone, 'holds it to be an unjustifiable practice for any person but a trader to encumber himself with debts of any considerable value.'

In all the history of the Common Law Courts in the eighteenth century the brightest feature was the reign of Lord Mansfield, as Chief Justice of the King's Bench, from 1756 to 1788. In those thirty-two years the Court sitting *in banc* was only twice divided in opinion, and only two of its judgements were reversed in the House of Lords. Directly he took his seat Mansfield introduced various salutory reforms. It had previously been the practice to allow any number of counsel on the same side to address the Court, and also to let them re-argue a case on a later day as often as they pleased:[1] to all this otiose oratory he put an end. It had also been the practice for the Court to reserve judgement in almost every case: Mansfield introduced the better plan of delivering it forthwith whenever there was no real need for further consideration. But his greatest achievement was the creation of English commercial Law. Before his time commercial cases hardly ever came into the Courts, though at an earlier date a certain number were tried in the Court of Admiralty at Doctors' Commons. Mansfield gradually attracted to the King's Bench a great volume of business from the City. To assist him he had a panel of special jurymen, who were 'merchants'. They apparently served constantly, and the judge was intimate with them, not only conversing with them freely in Court, but consulting with them privately, and sometimes entertaining them at dinner. Lord Campbell says, 'Several of these gentlemen survived when I began to attend Guildhall as a student, and were designated and honoured as "Lord Mansfield's Jurymen". One in particular I remember, Mr. Edward Vaux, who always wore a cocked hat, and had almost as much authority as the Lord Chief Justice himself.'[2]

The only thing that can be said in praise of the Court of

[1] The judges would read newspapers ostentatiously while Counsel argued. According to Lord Campbell even Lord Mansfield would 'by looking at the *Daily Advertiser* give a hint that the public time was wasted by Counsel', but 'he never did so till the evidence was closed and he was complete master of the case'. (*Lives of the Chief Justices*, 3rd ed., vol. iv, p. 17.) Judicial manners, I think, have improved, as all manners have.

[2] Ibid., vol. iii, p. 280.

Chancery in 1750 is that it was not quite so monstrous an institution as it had become by 1820 under Lord Eldon. From the time of Edward I until 1813, when the first Vice-Chancellor was appointed, it had only two judges; its official machinery had been enlarged, but remained medieval in pattern. The Lord Chancellor sat at Westminster in term time, and in Lincoln's Inn Hall out of term: the Master of the Rolls sat in the Court at his official residence in Chancery Lane.

The plaintiff began by addressing to the Lord Chancellor a Bill by way of complaint against the defendant: this was engrossed on parchment, and was always an enormous document, as it set out the plaintiff's case three times over, the third time being in the form of interrogatories to the defendant which sought to establish the case against him. The defendant was then served with a *subpoena* calling upon him to answer, but nothing was told him of the nature of the claim. He had to appear and pay the officials for a copy of the Bill. There were hosts of underlings in the offices, who spent their lives in copying documents, which the litigants were compelled to take and pay for, however little they desired them and however useless to them they were. The defendant having got the copy of the Bill could either demur, by way of objection in law, or plead, i.e. assert other facts not stated in the Bill, or answer, i.e. reply to the interrogatories in the Bill. Of course he did so with as little assistance as possible to the plaintiff. Unless the defendant lived within twenty miles of London, a special commission issued, with more fees, to take his answers upon oath, or, if he were a peer, upon his honour. There might then be motions for the production of documents, or the plaintiff might get leave to amend his Bill, adding further interrogatories, upon which a further answer must be made by the defendant. This was called 'scraping the defendant's conscience'. Ultimately the pleadings would close with a replication by the plaintiff.

For the proof of the case, on either side, no witnesses were ever heard in Court. Elaborate interrogatories for the examination of witnesses were prepared by Counsel, who often had no idea who the witnesses were, or what they knew. Upon these the witnesses were examined in private by more officials, while none of the parties or their lawyers were allowed to be present, and the answers were put down in writing. Anything in the way of cross-examination was of course impossible, and there was no one to see whether, as often happened, a witness palpably misunderstood any of the questions. The answers were written down by the Commissioner, as he understood them, and in his own version; there was no verbatim record of what a witness said. When all the evidence had been thus obtained the parties could get official copies of it, paying more fees, and upon these materials the case was argued in court.

It was impossible to apply to the Court to determine, for example, the meaning and effect of some particular bequest in a will. If the Court was to decide one point as to the administration of an estate, it insisted on administering the whole estate. One perverse legatee could drag the whole of the others into chancery and waste the benefits of all, as well as his own, in costs; the story told to Sam Weller in the Fleet by the cobbler is not an impossible one. Every person in any way interested had to be made a party: if any party died, or by birth became interested, lengthy measures must be taken to add executors, or guardians. At every stage there were fees to the army of officials. Every officer of the Court, from the Lord Chancellor down to the door-keeper, was paid by fees, the higher ones being sinecurists, whose work was done by their ill-paid deputies. Lord Eldon's income from fees reached £22,730 in 1810.

At any stage of the proceedings there might be a case sent to a Master in Chancery to make inquiries or take accounts. If a question of Common Law arose (and the provinces of Common Law and Equity were kept rigidly distinct), the Lord Chancellor would not decide it, but would send a special case to the King's Bench or the Common Pleas for its opinion, or sometimes would require a plaintiff to bring a Common Law action in order to test his right. And if, upon the hopeless sort of evidence that its own procedure provided the Court was in doubt as to the facts, it would direct a 'feigned issue' to be tried before a jury.

If any matter of fact is strongly controverted, [says Blackstone] this court is so sensible of the deficiency of trial by written depositions, that it . . . usually directs the matter to be tried by jury; especially such important facts as . . . whether A is the heir at law to B . . . But, as no jury can be summoned to attend this court, the fact is usually directed to be tried at the bar of the court of king's bench

DOCTORS' COMMONS

From the drawing by T. Rowlandson and A. C. Pugin

or at the assises, upon a *feigned issue* . . . an action is feigned to be brought, wherein the pretended plaintiff declares, that he laid a wager of 5*l.* with the defendant, that A was heir at law to B . . . The defendant allows the wager, but avers that A is not the heir to B; and thereupon that issue is joined . . . and thus the verdict of the jurors at law determines the fact in the court of equity.

The Lord Chancellor, sitting as judge in Chancery, could call in any of the Common Law judges to advise him as to the Law, but they only delivered their opinions; he alone decided the case. In the great *Thellusson Will* case Lord Loughborough had the assistance of Mr. Justice Buller and Mr. Justice Lawrence, as well as that of the Master of the Rolls.

If, after many years, a final decree was pronounced, any party could present a petition for a rehearing 'signed by two counsel of character, usually such as have been concerned in the cause, certifying that they apprehend the cause is proper to be reheard', and thereon a rehearing was granted as of course. A decree of the Master of the Rolls was not effective until it was signed by the Lord Chancellor, 'for whoever may have heard the cause, it is the chancellor's decree'.[1] There was an appeal from the Master of the Rolls to the Chancellor. And there was, in addition to any rehearing, an appeal from the Chancellor to the House of Lords; but that was usually *ab eodem ad eundem,* since as a rule the Lord Chancellor was in effect the House of Lords.

Such was the Court of Chancery, and such were its methods. It is significant that Blackstone, though he does not venture on dispraise, abstains in regard to them from the encomiums he showers upon all other parts of the legal system.

In the eighteenth century there was, of course, no Divorce Court. The method by which a man[2] of means could get rid of an unfaithful wife may be illustrated by the story of Topham Beauclerk. In 1766 he had a liaison with the wife of Lord Bolingbroke, born Lady Diana Spencer. Lord Bolingbroke brought an action for *Crim. Con.* against Beauclerk in the King's Bench, and recovered £500 damages. Lord Boling-

[1] Blackstone, *Commentaries*, bk. iii, p. 452.

[2] No private Act dissolving a marriage in the interests of a wife because of her husband's adultery was passed until 1801. One was then strongly opposed in the House of Lords by, amongst others, the future King William IV, and of course by Lord Eldon, but was passed chiefly owing to a speech by Lord Thurlow in its favour.

broke then obtained in the Consistory Court of the Bishop of London a sentence of divorce from bed and board against his wife. Finally in 1768 a private Act of Parliament (8 Geo. III, cap. lxx) was passed: 'An Act to dissolve the marriage of Frederick Lord Viscount Bolingbroke with Lady Diana Spencer, his now Wife, and to enable him to marry again.' Two days after this Act received the Royal Assent, Beauclerk married Lady Diana at St. George's, Hanover Square.

Appeals from a decision as to law were by writ of error. The Court of Appeal from the King's Bench was either to the Exchequer Chamber, composed of the judges of the Common Pleas and the Exchequer, or to the House of Lords direct. Appeal from the Common Pleas was to the King's Bench. Appeal from the Exchequer was to the Exchequer Chamber composed of judges of the King's Bench and of the Common Pleas. A final appeal from any of these tribunals lay to the House of Lords. A writ of error could be brought at any time within twenty years of the date of the impugned judgement, so that a piece of Common Law litigation might last half a century; but in Chancery they could easily beat such a record.

There was theoretically no difference between the House of Lords as a Law Court and as a branch of the legislature.

> Lastly [writes Blackstone, in a characteristic outburst], there presides over all one great court of appeal . . . a court consisting of prelates selected for their piety, and of nobles advanced to that honour for their personal merit, or deriving both honour and merit from an illustrious train of ancestors; who are formed by their education, interested by their property, and bound upon their conscience and honour, to be skilled in the laws of their country.

In the great case *Bishop of London* v. *Fytche* in 1783, as to the legality of a resignation bond given to the patron of a living, Lord Thurlow was the only lawyer in the House: its decision was by 19 votes to 18, Lord Thurlow being in the majority, but the other 36 were lay peers or bishops. In the even greater *Douglas* case in 1769 the Duke of Newcastle spoke first, and Lord Sandwich followed him; but after Lord Camden and Lord Mansfield had delivered their opinions in favour of allowing the appeal the House agreed to that result without a division. In 1806 in an appeal as to whether Mrs. Fitzherbert should continue to be guardian of Miss Seymour the Prince Regent canvassed the peers to get their votes on the question in her favour.

But in most cases the House of Lords was practically the Lord Chancellor sitting alone. Throughout his nineteen years as Chancellor (1737 to 1756), Lord Hardwicke decided every case, including all appeals from the Court of Session in Scotland, alone. In Lord Northington's time (1757 to 1766) Lord Hardwicke and Lord Mansfield sometimes sat with him, and not infrequently outvoted him in appeals from his own decisions in Chancery. In Lord Camden's time (1766 to 1770) Lord Mansfield usually sat with him. The House of Lords could of course summon the judges to attend, and give their opinions by way of advice: Lord Thurlow, from 1778 to 1792, did this in every case.

If a lawyer of to-day could be transported back to the English Courts of the eighteenth century he would be best able to understand what was going on at a criminal trial at the Assizes, or at the Old Bailey. There, though he would be indignant at the unfair treatment of the accused, shocked by the indecent haste of the proceedings, and horrified by the sentence, the substance of the procedure would be that of to-day.

But an inferior criminal court might present as unfamiliar a spectacle as the Court of Common Pleas debating whether aid-prayer is a dilatory plea. The whole system of the preliminary investigation of a charge leading up to a committal for trial depended upon an Act of 1554. Under this the magistrate was a public prosecutor rather than a judge; he would examine and cross-examine the accused, very much as a *Juge d'Instruction* does now in France; he would go about, like a modern detective in charge of a case, making inquiries and finding witnesses; and he would often be called at the trial as the principal witness against the prisoner. This system lasted until Jervis's Act of 1848. The object of the Act of 1554 was to expose and detect a man assumed to be guilty; the object of that of 1848 and of the system it inaugurated is to make full inquiry into his guilt or innocence.[1]

There were a few magistrates in London who would now be called stipendiaries. The great Henry Fielding was the most distinguished of them, and no doubt the most efficient. Like

[1] Stephen, *History of the Criminal Law* (3 vols., 1883), vol. i, p. 221.

nearly all officials they were paid by fees.[1] Everywhere else the ordinary Justice of the Peace, too often of the type of Squire Inglewood, was alone available. And the Commission of the Peace was not filled with that excess of numbers which is its chief weakness to-day: his friends in Northumberland got Squire Inglewood put upon the Commission because the nearest acting justice was the Mayor of Newcastle; and an Act of 1767 was passed 'to obviate inconveniences in towns which have only one justice of the quorum'.

An Act of 1695 allowed a person indicted for high treason to be fully represented by counsel, and this was extended by an Act of 1747 to one impeached for high treason. But on a charge of felony counsel for the accused was not, until 1837, allowed to examine or cross-examine witnesses or address the jury; he could only speak on a point of law, and he could only do this when the accused had raised the point himself, and the Court had agreed that it was a point of law. It was not until 1839 that any prisoner was allowed to see the depositions, i.e. the written record of the evidence against him in the Court where he had been committed for trial, and only in 1849 was he allowed to have a copy of them. All this meant that in most trials the accused had to conduct his own defence, except so far as the judge helped him. I need hardly say that he could not himself give evidence for—strange as it seems to-day—no accused person was allowed to give evidence until 1898.

The property of a convicted felon was forfeited to the Crown. In a trial for felony, when the jury returned their verdict, after being asked whether they found the man guilty or not guilty, they were always further asked, if they said

[1] Fielding, in the Introduction to *A Voyage to Lisbon,* hints not obscurely that his predecessors enlarged their incomes by an abuse of their powers, e.g. by haling street-walkers to their courts and exacting fees for their release. A prisoner who was acquitted by the jury had to pay a fee to the Clerk of Assize, and further fees to the jailer of the prison where he had been awaiting his trial. Indeed, until an Act of 1774 made the County responsible for paying to a jailer a fee not exceeding 13*s.* 4*d.* for an acquitted prisoner, the man found innocent was often detained in prison from his inability to pay his dues to the jailer. Another Act of 1774 recites that poor persons may be kept for years in prison from inability to pay a debt under 40*s.*, and that after paying the debt they may still be kept in prison from inability to pay the jailer's fees. The first incentive to John Howard's campaign for the reform of prisons was his discovery, as High Sheriff of Bedfordshire in 1773, that the Keeper of Bedford Jail was wholly paid by fees.

'Guilty', what goods and chattels he had; to which they always answered formally, 'None to our knowledge.'[1]

As it was thought quite proper for lay peers to vote on an appeal to the House of Lords in a civil case, so the Aldermen, who were included in the Commission at the Old Bailey,[2] could have their say as to a sentence there. When the celebrated Elizabeth Canning was convicted of perjury in 1754 Chief Justice Willes proposed seven years' transportation as her sentence; an alderman moved an amended sentence of six months, and the proposal of the Chief Justice was only secured by the vote of six judges and five aldermen against eight aldermen.

A prisoner who upon his arraignment 'stood mute', i.e. refused to plead, in order by his silence to avoid conviction and the consequent forfeiture of goods, was pressed with heavy weights, and if he remained obstinate was so pressed until he died. This actually happened in 1726. An Act of 1772 provided that one who thus stood mute should be treated as convicted, but another Act of 1774 changed this and enacted that one who refused to plead should be deemed to say 'Not Guilty'. I think it is hardly too much to say that the only salutory reforms in the criminal law before 1780 were the Act of 1730 which substituted English for Latin as the language of Indictments, the Act of 1736 which abolished witchcraft as a crime,[3] the Act of 1747 which allowed Counsel to one impeached for high treason, and the above-mentioned Act of 1774.

Down to 1826 the penalty for all felonies, except petty larceny, was Death. But this was subject to the operation of the Benefit of Clergy. Originally this arose from the immunity of the cleric from the jurisdiction of the civil courts. And as clerics were alone literate, or were supposed to be so, the benefit of clergy came to be allowed to any one who upon

[1] Having read many trials I have never seen any other answer recorded. If a felon were a well-to-do man possibly evidence about it would have been adduced to the jury.

[2] The Lord Mayor and aldermen are still named in the Commission at the Central Criminal Court, and one of them has to be present as well as the judge. What would happen if two of them now tried to overrule the judge's sentence I really do not know.

[3] As to this Act Blackstone's comment is that 'to deny the possibility, nay, actual existence of witchcraft, is flatly to contradict the revealed word of God, in various passages both of the old and new testament'. The last conviction for witchcraft was in 1712, but the offender was reprieved.

conviction could display his power of reading in the dock. A woman, of course, could not, even by a fiction, be of the clergy; but by an Act of Philip and Mary she was allowed the like benefit without reading for it. In the seventeenth century the proof was always made by an ability to read or recite (even with the book open at the wrong place) the first verse of the 51st Psalm—'Have mercy upon me, O God, according to thy loving kindness: according unto the multitude of thy tender mercies blot out my transgressions'—which was known as 'the neck verse'. But by an Act of 5 Anne the claim was allowed, without the reading, to any one convicted of a clergyable felony.

Under this system there was a time when the most brutal murderer with sufficient wits, could go scot free. The natural result was the cutting down of the privilege. An Act of 1487 provided that any convict, who successfully claimed the benefit of clergy should be branded[1] on the thumb with M for murder, and with T for theft. A convict found to be thus branded, i.e. convicted a second time, was to be denied the benefit of clergy, unless he was actually in Holy Orders. In 1547 the benefit of clergy was taken away upon conviction for murder, highway robbery, horse-stealing, burglary, and other felonies. And throughout the eighteenth century successive Acts[2] declared various offences to be felonies punishable by death without benefit of clergy, so that by the end of the reign of George III there were 160 capital offences, including stealing in a dwelling-house to the value of 40*s.*, stealing in a shop to the value of 5*s.*, and stealing anything privily from the person. This was the bloody code that was eulogized by Lord Eldon and defended by him against the dangerous attacks of Romilly. And the fatuous optimism of Blackstone perhaps reached its zenith

[1] The branding was done in open court. In the fine Crown Court in Lancaster Castle there survive in the dock the brazier, the M branding iron, and the iron device into which the convict's hand was fixed for the operation. In a venial case the judge would sometimes recommend the warder to brand the man lightly. By an Act of 1717 transportation for seven years was substituted for the branding in the case of a clergyable larceny. And by one of 1779 a judge was authorized to substitute whipping, or a fine, in place of the branding.

[2] e.g. in 1741, stealing sheep or cattle; in 1767, destroying a turnpike gate; in 1768, being found anywhere in Great Britain before the expiration of a sentence of transportation; in 1769, demolishing or burning any mills; in 1773, making or possessing moulds for counterfeiting Bank of England notes. But manslaughter, however heinous, remained a clergyable felony until 1822. And an attempt to murder was merely a Common Law misdemeanour until 1803.

when he wrote, 'In this state does the benefit of clergy at present stand; very considerably different from its original institution: the wisdom of the English legislature having, in the course of a long and laborious process, extracted by a noble alchemy rich medecines out of poisonous ingredients.'

It was one of the privileges of peerage to be immune from any punishment upon a first conviction of felony. When the Duchess of Kingston was tried before the House of Lords for bigamy in 1776, every one knew that the proceedings were a farce, for even if convicted she could suffer no penalty. When she was found Guilty she prayed her privilege. Lord Bathurst, the Chancellor, as Lord Steward, had to say that this was allowed, and 'Madam, you are discharged, paying your fees.'

An Act of 1752 provided that the death penalty should be carried out on the day next but one after sentence, which must be pronounced immediately after conviction; that part of the sentence should direct the body, after hanging, to be delivered to Surgeons' Hall for dissection or else to be hung in chains; and that after sentence the convict be fed on bread and water only. But the same Act gave the judge power to stay execution, and this was often done by the more humane, while they sent a recommendation to the King in Council for a reprieve. Such reports, and the Recorder's report after every session at the Old Bailey, were considered at a Council at which, down to the end of the reign of William IV, the Sovereign was always present in person, and the Lord Chancellor attended to advise him.

But the opportunity for leniency thus provided was not everywhere applauded. In 1784 the Rev. Martin Madan published anonymously a pamphlet, *Thoughts on Executive Justice*, which created no little stir. It was an extravagant eulogy upon the benefits of capital punishment, and deplored the laxity with which many judges exercised their power under the Act of 1752. This amiable parson especially denounced 'the lenity exercised towards horse-stealers. The law says they *shall be hanged*; those who put this law in execution say—they shall *not*. In short the *sic volo* of the legislature is absolutely controuled by the *Sic nolo* of a Judge.' In his second edition of 1785 he says that he sent a copy of the first to each of the twelve judges, and goes on to take one of them to task, who, in a charge to a grand jury, had suggested that 'the author of a late publication must be a very cruel and blood-thirsty person.'

Unhappily his pamphlet had a considerable effect. It 'was followed by the useless sacrifice of many lives. Some of the judges and the Government for a time adopted his reasoning.'[1] In 1783, before the tract appeared, there were 51 executions in London; in 1785 there were 97, including 20 upon one day. During this period of increased savagery, upon June 23, 1784, Boswell visited Johnson, after being present in the morning at the execution of 15 prisoners at Newgate. Not one of them was a murderer; 12 were burglars, 2 had been guilty of street robbery, and 1 of personating another man to obtain his wages. Birkbeck Hill with reason makes the comment, 'There is something dreadful in the thought of the old man quietly going on with his daily life within a few hundred yards of this shocking scene of slaughter.' And it must be confessed that even the great mind of Johnson did not rise superior to the prejudices of the age. When, in 1783, Tyburn was abolished, and the new system of executions outside Newgate was begun, he exclaimed against the innovation. 'No, Sir, it is *not* an improvement . . . Sir, executions are intended to draw spectators. If they do not draw spectators, they do not answer their purpose. The old method was most satisfactory to all parties: the public was satisfied by a procession, the criminal was supported by it.'[2] If any one be inclined to think the worse of Johnson for such sentiments, let him remember that in 1810 Romilly's Bill for abolishing the death-penalty for stealing in a shop to the value of 5*s*. was thrown out in the Lords by a majority that included seven bishops.

'The punishment of High Treason,' says Blackstone, 'is very solemn and terrible.' The sentence began by ordering the culprit to be drawn to the place of execution, 'the humanity of modern times', as Blackstone observes, permitting him to have a hurdle to be drawn upon. He was then to be hanged, but cut down alive, his entrails taken out and cast upon a fire, his head cut off, and his body quartered. These horrors were enacted in many cases, e.g. upon Colonel Townley, for his participation in the '45. But the penalty was actually inflicted in 1719 in the case of John Matthews, a

[1] Romilly's *Memoirs* (1840), vol. i, p. 89.
[2] Birkbeck Hill's *Life of Johnson*, vol. iv, p. 188.

printer aged nineteen, because he had produced a stupid and quasi-jocular pamphlet which was said to favour the Old Pretender. Until the trial of Mure and Palmer in Edinburgh in 1794 there was no more monstrous case.

As a prisoner rarely knew how to cross-examine witnesses against him, and equally rarely had any witnesses of his own, trials were dispatched very speedily. The trial of Colonel Townley in 1746, which would now take at least a week, was all over in a few hours. The trial of Hardy for high treason in 1794 was the first that ever lasted more than one day, and the Court seriously considered whether it had any power to adjourn: though it decided that it could, it still sat daily from 8 a.m. until after midnight. Erskine's speech for Lord George Gordon, before Lord Mansfield in 1781, was begun after midnight, and the verdict given at 5.15 in the morning. Even in 1814, at the trial of Lord Cochrane, Lord Ellenborough refused to adjourn at 9 p.m. after sitting for twelve consecutive hours. A Scots trial in 1765 actually lasted for forty-three consecutive hours. And any jury which retired to consider their verdict, in a civil as well as in a criminal case, had to be kept without fire, food, drink, or candle.

The preliminary investigation and committal being sometimes equally speedy, sentence for a crime in London often followed very closely upon its commission, though in a northern county an untried prisoner might languish for eleven months in jail. Perhaps the record for dispatch was achieved in 1812 when Bellingham shot the Prime Minister on May 11. He was committed at once, he was tried and convicted on Friday, May 15, and he was hanged upon Monday, May 18: the time might have been bettered but for the intervening Sunday.

The severity of the criminal law was not wholly due to the greater brutality of the age. In the absence of any real system of police, society was as weak against the depredations of the malefactor as to-day it is strong.[1] Further, though there were innumerable prisons, lock-ups, and Houses of Correction all over the land, there was nowhere for a man to serve a long term of imprisonment, and to ship him to the American 'plantations' was an expensive business. One of the earliest attempts to provide for long-term

[1] When a particular crime grows rife, and threatens to be a general menace, there is even to-day an outcry for greater severity of punishment.

imprisonment in lieu of transportation was an Act of 1774, whereby convicts were to be set to hard labour 'in the raising of soil and gravel from and cleansing the river Thames'. One section of this directed that such prisoners should be 'fed with bread and any coarse and inferior food and water or small beer'.

But many in that age revolted against the full severity of the law, and in practice its horrors were mitigated, not only by the reprieves I have mentioned, but also by the operation of extreme technicalities[1] in procedure. If a man were indicted as John Smith and he could prove that his name was James Smith the indictment was quashed, and he went free, whatever his offence. If he were indicted in his proper name for stealing in the house of John Smith, and it was really James Smith's house, he escaped. If before 1730 his counsel could successfully impugn the Latinity[2] of the indictment, or if 'burglariter' (or, after 1730, 'burglariously') was by accident omitted from it, he was released. To the same end jurors, in defiance of their oaths, and with the encouragement of many judges (including Lord Mansfield) constantly found that a valuable article stolen in a shop was worth less than 5*s.*: the thief might then claim the benefit of clergy, and depart, after being burned in the hand with an iron that (again by the judge's connivance) was only luke warm.

Such was the English criminal law of the age of Johnson, and of it Blackstone wrote that it 'is with justice supposed to be more nearly advanced to perfection' than that of any other country.

[1] In 1818 Baron Garrow, travelling on circuit from Monmouth to Gloucester arrived an hour after midnight of the day fixed in his commission for the Gloucester Assize. He did not dare open the commission when the proper day was over, and the whole business of the Assize was postponed for three weeks, while a messenger went to London and got a new commission from Lord Eldon. *Life of Lord Campbell*, vol. i, p. 353.

[2] Counsel for John Matthews in 1719 tried to save him by a plea that the indictment was bad, as it said 'impressit', when it ought to have been 'impressit *anglice* printed'. And he argued with some reason, that printing was unknown to the Romans. Chief Justice King overruled the objection, holding that 'imprimere' had come to mean 'to print', and citing the precedent of 'imprimatur'. But if he had sustained the objection, and quashed the indictment, no one would have regarded it as an absurdity.

BIBLIOGRAPHY.—The best contemporary account of the English Law of the eighteenth century is obviously BLACKSTONE'S *Commentaries*. Even the general reader may find the book interesting. He will also find *The Statutes at Large* interesting, and even entertaining: the older an Act of Parliament is the less repulsive is it—and perhaps the more intelligible. *The State Trials* afford many illustrations of the course of criminal trials. And there are innumerable separate *Trials* published contemporaneously. A few have been reprinted and edited in modern times, e.g. *The Trial of Mary Blandy* (1914) edited by W. ROUGHEAD. Upon the very numerous contemporary volumes of *Reports* of civil cases the general reader cannot be advised to embark. But he might find some entertainment in SIR JAMES BURROW'S *Reports*, since they contain mostly cases tried by Lord Mansfield, and record his methods. (It is on a page of Burrow that he records Lord Mansfield's utterance, *Fiat justitia ruat coelum*, which Lord Mansfield perhaps invented, as no one seems to know another origin).

Of modern books the best is Professor Sir WILLIAM HOLDSWORTH'S monumental *History of the English Law* (9 vols., 1922–6). There is a valuable article by Sir William on 'Some Aspects of Blackstone and his Commentaries' in the *Cambridge Law Journal*, 1932. The best succinct account of the old procedure of the common law courts is *Personal Actions at Common Law*, by Mr. RALPH SUTTON (1929). Sir JAMES FITZJAMES STEPHEN'S *History of the Criminal Law* (3 vols., 1883) leaves little more to be said on that topic. For procedure in appeals and in writ of error and in Bills of Divorce see J. MACQUEEN, *The Appellate Jurisdiction of the House of Lords* (1842).

Of books that deal with legal personalities of the time, P. C. YORKE'S *Life of Lord Chancellor Hardwicke* (3 vols., Cambridge, 1813), and the biographies of LORD CAMPBELL—*Lives of the Lord Chancellors* (8 vols., 1845–69), *Lives of the Chief Justices* (3 vols., 1849–57), and his own autobiographical *Life* (1881) provide a mine of information. It is the fashion to say that Lord Campbell was inaccurate, and so he sometimes was, but in minor matters. Sir James Stephen, I think, was right when he said that he was 'a delightful writer' though 'as impressible by topics of prejudice as a common juryman'. ROMILLY'S *Memoirs* (3 vols., 1840), and H. TWISS'S *Life of Eldon* (3 vols., 1848), though of a rather later date, contain much of interest. Of anecdotes of the law and lawyers I would commend a collection called *Westminster Hall* (3 vols., 1825). Volume viii of EDWARD FOSS'S *The Judges of England* (9 vols., 1848–64) is also useful.

XXVI

AUTHORS AND BOOKSELLERS

By R. W. CHAPMAN

Thus, dear Sir, I have been incited by Dr. ——'s letter to give you a detail of the circulation of books, which, perhaps, every man has not had opportunity of knowing; and which those who know it, do not perhaps always distinctly consider.—*Letter to the Master of University College, Oxford* (12 March 1776).

IN any consideration of the book trade we may distinguish the producers—the author, who corresponds to the inventor or designer in other trades, and the physical producers, printer, paper-maker, and binder; the publisher, who furnishes the capital and normally shoulders the risks of enterprise; and the retail bookseller. The history of the book trade in the eighteenth century has been not a little obscured by an accident of terminology; the century had no name for what is now called a publisher. The verb *publish* is still unappropriated; an author, as well as a publisher, may *publish* a book. But the noun is now restricted to the professional venturer who makes it his business to multiply and distribute the author's unique exemplar. In the eighteenth century, on the other hand, the term *publisher*, when it is used, ordinarily means an author, or more commonly an editor or compiler.[1] Tonson and Dodsley were called booksellers.[2]

The significance of this nominal identity of the retail bookseller and the wholesale, capitalist, originating and venturing publisher (as we shall hereafter term him) has sometimes been exaggerated. But the confusion has a significance. In the early ages of printing, the printer was naturally foremost in publishing enterprise; for it was he who held the new secret of dissemination. The specialization of the publisher, with the consequent limitation of the printer to his technical art, was a later evolution. In Elizabethan and Jacobean England the relation between printer and

[1] There was no occasion to call an author publisher; but a term was wanted for the performer of those secondary tasks which fall short of authorship; and *publisher* was as good as another.

[2] Johnson's own definition of a bookseller is comprehensive. 'Old Gardner was a member of the Stationers' company, kept a shop in the face of mankind, purchased copyright, and was a *bibliopole* in every sense' (*Life*, vol. ii. p. 345).

author was still intimate; and though there were great publishers in England in the seventeenth century, it was not until the age of Anne that the publisher attained full stature. It is significant that the normal seventeenth-century imprint is 'Printed by A.B. for C.D.', and that the great majority of eighteenth-century books bear no printer's name. The legal and commercial importance of the printer had declined.

But before considering the arrangements of the book trade something must be said of the commodity in which it dealt. Unlike most commodities (not enjoying the protection of a patent) a book is a unique article, and one for which the demand is, as a rule, not large. It is therefore very important, for all concerned in its production, that its value should not be dissipated by competition. The protection enjoyed by author and publisher in England was, throughout our period, imperfect. It was especially precarious in the first decade of the century. Until 1695 the Licensing Act had afforded a measure of protection against piracy, for the Licenser would not license the same book twice, and to print without licence was dangerous. But in that year the Act, being due for renewal, was not renewed. It was not until 1710 that an Act was passed which secured literary property to its author or his assigns for a term of fourteen years, renewable for a second term of fourteen years if the author were still alive at the end of the first term. Under this provision *Rasselas* (1759) was protected till 1787, the *Lives of the Poets* (1781) only until 1795. The duration of copyright was a matter less important than it was often represented to be; for relatively few books were of sufficient value, twenty-eight or even fourteen years from publication, to tempt the pirate. It was, however, important, for the works of Shakespeare and Milton were held to be copyright. Throughout the period the issues are confused; the views and motives of the booksellers themselves are ambiguous and inconsistent, and legal pronouncements left the matter long in dispute. In general, booksellers maintained that literary property was in its nature like other property, therefore inalienable; and it was urged that the effect of the Act of 1710 was to impose statutory penalties for a limited period, but not to destroy any rights existing at common law. In this they had the support of many authors, and the countenance of some judges. In this faith, or hope,

BOOKS Printed for J. NEWBERY,
in *St. Paul's Church Yard.*

1. THE RAMBLER. In four Volumes in Twelves. The fifth Edition. Price Twelve Shillings bound.

2. The STUDENT; or the *Oxford* and *Cambridge* Monthly Miſcellany. Conſiſting of Original Eſſays, in Proſe and Verſe. In two Volumes Octavo. Price Twelve Shillings.

3. A familiar Explanation of the Poetical Works of MILTON. To which is prefixed Mr ADDISON's Criticiſm on *Paradiſe Loſt*. With a Preface by the Rev. Mr. *Dodd*. Price Three Shillings bound.

4. The Works of ANACREON, SAPPHO, BION, MOSCHUS, and MUSÆUS. Tranſlated from the original Greek, by *Francis Fawkes*, M. A. Price Three Shillings bound.

5. The SHRUBS of PARNASSUS: Conſiſting of a Variety of Poetical Eſſays, moral and comic. By *J. Copywell*, of Lincoln's Inn, Eſq; Price Three Shillings bound.

6. The NONPAREIL, or, The Quinteſſence of Wit and Humour: Being a choice Selection of thoſe Pieces that were moſt admired in the ever-to-be-remember'd *Midwife*, or *Old Woman's Magazine*; Pieces which, (as a celebrated Author obſerves) will ſtand the Teſt of all Ages, and live and be read till Time is no more. To which is added, an Index to Mankind; or Maxims ſelected from the Wits of all Nations, for the Benefit of the preſent Age, and of Poſterity. Interſperſed with ſome Axioms in Life, and ſeaſonable Reflections by the ſame Author. With a PREFACE by her good Friend the late Mr. POPE.

My

An Advertisement of New Publications, from *The Idler*, 1761.

they continued to assert their rights in Shakespeare, both by legal action and by various measures of boycott against pirates, and to deal afresh in copyrights no longer enjoying the protection of the Act. After a long series of litigation matters reached a head in the 'seventies, when an Edinburgh bookseller, Donaldson, invaded the supposed rights of the London publishers, set up a shop in London, and sold cheap editions of popular books. In 1774 the House of Lords, by a narrow majority, rejected the doctrine of perpetual copyright. Johnson perhaps expressed the prevailing moderate opinion when he declared that he would not have the right perpetual, but that a longer term would be equitable. The law was altered in this sense early in the next century. Even after 1774 booksellers continued to respect 'honorary copyright, preserved among them by mutual compact, notwithstanding the decision of the House of Lords'. This statement was made by Boswell, describing (in 1790) the great collection of the poets which was produced in 1779 by the London publishers in combination, and was vulgarly known as 'Johnson's Poets'.

The Act of 1710 was limited to the United Kingdom; and internal piracy was probably a less serious menace to the book trade than the production of competing editions in Ireland and Holland. These editions were imported into England; and the underselling, by a Dutch edition, of Pope's *Iliad* was so damaging that Lintot was obliged to produce a cheap edition in duodecimo to meet it; he was compelled, says Johnson, 'to contract his Folio at once to a Duodecimo, and lose the advantage of an intermediate gradation'. An Act of 1739 imposed penalties on the sale in England of editions printed abroad, and seems to have been tolerably efficacious. But no serious attempt was made to secure the Irish market for English editions. Throughout the period any book likely to be saleable was immediately, and as a matter of course, reprinted in Dublin. The practice was sometimes complained of, but was generally regarded as respectable. When Johnson in 1773 published a revised edition of his *Dictionary*, a reprint of it was issued in Dublin by subscription, and one of the subscribers was Johnson's friend, Edmond Malone.

Internal piracy was perhaps no very serious deduction from the profits of author or publisher, for the most constant offenders were the editors of periodicals, and the publication of extracts in this form had advertising value. But the editors sometimes went too far. It was doubtful whether there were copyright in abridgements; and under cover of this the magazines took liberties. Dodsley had to protect *Rasselas* by getting an injunction; and when the *Idler*, printed in the *Universal Chronicle*, was plundered by other magazines, Johnson threatened reprisals in a mock-heroic notice. The proprietors, he wrote, would issue cheap editions of popular books owned by the pirates, and sell them 'for the support of penitent prostitutes', who were more deserving support than 'prostitutes in whom there yet appears neither penitence nor shame'. We hear less of the piracy of whole books in book-form; but it was always rife. Unauthorized editions of *The Traveller* and *The Deserted Village* were common in Goldsmith's lifetime. The *Journey to the Western Islands* was pirated in London in the year of publication. An anonymous imprint, such as 'Printed for the Booksellers of London and Westminster', seems always to indicate piracy.

The course of trade in Johnson's time may be conveniently outlined from the famous letter which he addressed to the Master of University College in 1776, offering advice on the better management of the Clarendon Printing House. He there explains the necessity of more liberal discounts, to induce the booksellers 'to circulate academical publications', and traces the progress of a book of which the retail price is assumed to be twenty shillings.

We will call our primary agent in London Mr. Cadell, who receives our books from us, gives them room in his warehouse, and issues them on demand; by him they are sold to Mr. Dilly, a wholesale bookseller, who sends them into the country; and the last seller is the country bookseller. Here are three profits to be paid between the printer and the reader, or in the style of commerce, between the manufacturer and the consumer; and if any of these profits is too penuriously distributed, the process of commerce is interrupted. . . .

The deduction, I am afraid, will appear very great; but let it be considered before it is refused. We must allow, for profit, between thirty and thirty-five *per cent.*, between six and seven shillings on the pound; that is, for every book which costs the last buyer twenty shillings, we must charge Mr. Cadell with something less than fourteen. We must set the copies at fourteen shillings each, and superadd what is called the quarterly-book, or for every hundred books so charged we must deliver an hundred and four.

The profit will then stand thus:

Mr. Cadell, who runs no hazard, and gives no credit, will be paid for warehouse room and attendance by a shilling profit on each book, and his chance of the quarterly-book.

Mr. Dilly, who buys the book for fifteen shillings, and who will expect the quarterly-book if he takes five-and-twenty, will sell it to his country customer at sixteen and six-pence, by which at the hazard of loss, and the certainty of long credit, he gains the regular profit of ten *per cent.* which is expected in the wholesale trade.

The country bookseller, buying at sixteen and six-pence, and commonly trusting a considerable time, gains but three and six-pence, and, if he trusts a year, not much more than two and six-pence; otherwise than as he may, perhaps, take as long credit as he gives.

Boswell, who prints this letter, adds that the profits allowed by Johnson were more than the booksellers in fact usually demanded.

Johnson's concern is here with discounts; and he is dealing with the peculiar position of a University Press. But we can make out clearly enough what he regards as the normal process. 'Mr. Cadell' is evidently a publisher in the fullest sense, and 'Mr. Dilly' what we now call a wholesaler, whose function is to supply the retailer, who finds it convenient to give all his orders to a single London house. Johnson's account is, of course, simplified to his purpose. The real Cadell had a shop in the Strand, and sold his books over the counter. The real Dilly we know to have been a publisher, for he was Boswell's. The various functions doubtless overlapped; at no time have they been precisely delimited. It is worth while to recall that in our own day, or within living memory, retail booksellers have become publishers on a large scale; printers have been tempted to secure regularity of employment by engaging in publishing enterprise; publishers have sought to serve their convenience and increase their profits by printing on their own account; and in America at least publishers have invaded the retail trade. Some of these complexities can be paralleled in the eighteenth century; but they were no doubt exceptional. The ordinary course of trade is what Johnson had in mind. Even so his account of the matter is incomplete. He makes no mention of the retailer in London, and leaves us wondering whether Dodsley sold only his own books from his shop in Pall Mall, and, if not, whether he obtained other stock direct from the publishers or through a 'Dilly'. What, again, is the significance of such an imprint as 'Printed for R. Dodsley in Pall Mall and sold by M. Cooper in Pater Noster Row', which is found in many of Dodsley's books? Mrs. Cooper must have been in a position of privilege; was perhaps the normal source of supply to the trade in general. It seems unlikely that a bookseller in Pall Mall had much warehouse accommodation in the shop. Printers and binders may have held some of the stock; but that is not contemplated in Johnson's description; and it is natural to suppose that the main warehouses were in the City, as Dilly's was. The evidence hitherto available does not seem to provide certain answers to such questions. But it is clear that the trade was well organized, and that literature flowed through easy channels. It may be added that magazines with wide circulations, like the *Gentleman's*, gave useful accounts of new publications, and that the country bookseller was probably often, like Michael Johnson, a man of some cultivation, who could advise his customers what was worth reading.

Valuable information on the publisher's trade may be derived from the exceptional career of William Strahan, for which we have ample documentary evidence. It is well known that Strahan was a successful printer, who set up his carriage and became a member of parliament. But we know from himself that his affluence did not come from his printing. In a letter of 1771 he wrote:

> I quickly saw that if I confined myself to mere printing for Booksellers I might be able to live, but very little more than live. I therefore soon determined to launch out into other Branches. In which I have happily succeeded to the astonishment of the rest of the Trade here, who never dreamed of going out of the old beaten Track.

Strahan, being a printer, had no bookshop, and that no doubt is why his name is not very familiar on title-pages. But in the letter quoted he states that he had a 'multiplicity of concerns in the property of Books, about 200 in number'. The kind of partnership here indicated was a feature of the period, and was much commoner than the imprints show, though they reveal the co-operative nature of many enterprises. Thus the title-page of Johnson's *Dictionary* (1755) bears the names of five publishers; and 'Johnson's Poets' was the joint undertaking of thirty-six publishers.

The motive to such co-operation is readily understood.

The number of publishers was large, and the total volume of their trade not very great. There was no means of raising capital by calling the general public into partnership; and the shortage of capital must always have been acute. The difficulty was met in various ways; by fixing prices which allowed a liberal margin of gross profit; by restricting editions to such number of copies as could probably be sold within a few years; by some degree of understanding between the members of what was called 'the Trade', tending to discourage the competition of outsiders; but above all by the method of partnership in books, which reduced the capital required from any individual and 'spread' the risk of loss.

Publishers have at all times been a much abused class. We hear a great deal, both from contemporary writers and from modern commentators, of their monopolistic practices, of their inordinate wealth, of their oppression and contempt of genius, and of the worthless trash manufactured to their order in Grub Street, both by worthless scribblers and by men who deserved better work and better pay. There is justice in all these charges; but they have been made and echoed by authors, and the other side has hardly been heard. The facts, however, show that the 'monopoly' of the 'Trade' was no very close ring. New publishers frequently made their appearance and achieved success; authors were free to offer their wares in the highest market, and publishers to compete for the best authors. Much cant was talked, then as in later times, about the dignity of letters. Lord Camden, though a judge, was so foolish as to declare that, 'Glory is the reward of science; and those who deserve it scorn all meaner view.' The same people who spoke in this strain would abuse publishers for cheating authors, and complain because they managed their business as men of business and not as learned academies. That publishers pandered to the baser tastes of a growing public by worthless or tedious compilations was true, and it is true to-day; 'publishers' books' has been used as a term of contempt in the twentieth century.[1] But this is common frailty. On the whole we need not refuse to accept Johnson's verdict in favour of the booksellers, that they were 'generous, liberal-minded men', and that their enterprise 'raised the price of

[1] By Professor Trevelyan in *Clio, a Muse*.

literature'.[1] With the scale of their payments to authors we shall deal later.

In one respect the booksellers have received scant justice. Literary historians have naturally focused their attention on the famous writers, and nearly all they tell us of publishers is in relation to these writers' work. But most of the largest undertakings of the period were not the work of a Johnson or a Gibbon, but of lesser, often of nameless men. These works are for the most part now obsolete, but their importance was once great. They were made possible by the system of partnership; but no system could have availed if courage and public spirit had been lacking. It was largely to the initiative of publishers that the age owed such compilations as the *Biographia Britannica* (1747–66), our first dictionary of national biography; the *Cyclopaedia Britannica* (1728) of Ephraim Chambers, our first national encyclopaedia; the *Universal History* (1747–66); or the *Harleian Miscellany* (1744–6). These books are in many large volumes, containing an enormous number of words. Their usefulness must have been great. The achievement does credit both to the promoters and to the public which gave them support.

It is notoriously difficult to compare the prices of one period with those of another. In an age when readers were few, and the total population of Britain not very great, we should expect books to bear the prices of luxuries; and if we consider the prices of commodities in general, or recall Johnson's own economy,[2] with its travelling expenses and its charities, supported by an income little exceeding £300 a year, it is clear that books were not cheap. Pamphlets were sometimes sold as low as sixpence, but a shilling or even eighteenpence was a common price for pieces of 50 or 100 pages, and plays, which seldom reached 100 pages, were regularly 1*s*. 6*d*. For essays and novels the ordinary price was 2*s*. 6*d*. or 3*s*., 'sewed', for a volume in small octavo or duodecimo containing about 300 pages with not more than 200 words to a page. Larger octavos fetched a higher price; Johnson's *Journey* was 5*s*. for nearly 400 pages (of very large type), and Boswell's *Corsica*, a larger book, 6*s*. Johnson's

[1] This he said of Andrew Millar, one of the publishers of his *Dictionary*.

[2] He declared in 1744 that £50 a year 'was undoubtedly more than the necessities of life require'—that is, more than would feed a literary bachelor, like Savage or himself.

Samuel Harding
Bookseller & Stationer
at the Bible &
Anchor on the
Pave- ment in
St. Martin's Lane.

Selleth, Books in all Languages,
& Faculties; Imperial, and other large
Papers for Drawing, & all Smaller
Sorts, Gilt; or Plain, Pens, Quills, Ink, Wax,
Wafers; Alſo most Excellent Black-Ink, call'd
Amſterdam-Ink, of his own Making, at Six-
pence ℘ Bottle, Account Books of all Sorts,
either for Shops, or Memorandums; Bibles,
& Com. Prayers of all Sizes, in Turkey, or Calves-
Leather, wth great Variety of Books of Devotion.

Where may be had, Money for any Library, or
Parcell of Book's; Likewise for Prints, & Books of
Sculpture; & Books neatly bound in all kinds of Binding.

A BOOKSELLER'S TRADE CARD

Shakespeare was two guineas for eight volumes, or about 5*s*. for nearly 600 pages. But this was competitive publishing, and the sale was steady. For a substantial quarto a guinea could be asked. Boswell's *Life* was two guineas for two volumes. But when it came to the second edition, the three fat octavos were sold at 8*s*. each. A closer analysis seems to show that for polite literature, in cheap editions in the smaller sizes, the price varied between sixpence or a shilling for 10,000 words; it might be less for a long book. The average price for similar books to-day (not novels, or other books calculated for a very large sale) is perhaps between a shilling and 1*s*. 6*d*. for 10,000 words. A shilling to-day has, in general, a far lower purchasing power than sixpence had in 1750. But prices of books were lower than in the early decades of the nineteenth century, when a guinea was asked for the three slim volumes of *Emma*, and a guinea and a half for a quarto *Marmion*.

On the profits of the trade, or the share of them secured by authors, it would be vain to generalize. We know that a few publishers made large fortunes, and that some authors made decent incomes. But we hear something of ruined publishers, and much more of the penury of Grub Street. The weakness of the author's position arose from his poverty —he could not afford to wait—and from the rudimentary nature of the method of payment—for the royalty system had not yet been devised. Usually, therefore, the author sold his copyright; and though he might be reasonably paid in the ordinary way, the ripest plums fell into the publisher's mouth. A further payment was sometimes made as an act of grace; but the author had no hold on his work, unless he could persuade a publisher that a corrected edition was worth paying for. Thomson's correction and recorrection of his *Seasons* may have had an economic as well as a poetic motive. The authors of books which from their nature required or invited correction to bring them up to date were in a stronger position. Johnson was paid £300 for revising his Dictionary, Baretti a somewhat larger sum for his work on the second and third editions of the Italian Dictionary. Sometimes, indeed, publishers contracted to pay for every new edition, without limit of time. Evasion of this undertaking was sometimes prevented by a stipulation that an edition should not exceed a stated number of copies.

The path of the publisher is often represented as easier than it was. A story was told of the publisher Flexney, that he was ruined by publishing every quarto poem he was offered, in the hope of a second *Rosciad*. The records show that *The Vicar of Wakefield* went through three editions without paying its expenses; and this has led a recent writer to call it 'almost a unique loss', which consideration shows that it cannot have been. Johnson was paid 10 guineas for *London*: *London* had a quite incalculable success, and the payment is spoken of as paltry. But the publisher's profit, doubtless disproportionate, can easily be exaggerated. If Dodsley sold 5,000 copies of *London* at a shilling he was lucky, and 5,000 eightpences (allowing a third for discount) is about £150, from which the cost of printing five editions is to be deducted.[1]

When an author was able to wait, and in a position to bargain, he could do much better. The account between Johnson and Newbery for the collected *Idler* is instructive. The *Idler*, unlike the *Rambler*, had been popular in its periodical publication. It was reprinted in 1761 in two volumes duodecimo at 5*s*. 'sewed'. 1,500 were printed, and the costs were for printing £41, for paper £52, for advertising £20 (doubtless an exceptionally high proportion); in all £114. The 1,500 copies were sold at £16 per 100 (that is, at a discount closely approximating to the 35 per cent. mentioned by Johnson), or £240, leaving a profit of £126. It will be seen that the account includes no allowances for warehousing, interest on capital, or other 'hidden' costs. Of the profit shown, the author received two-thirds. The *Idler* was not reprinted for six years, so we may presume it was some years before the publisher and author received their full return.

Even when an author wanted money down, he need not part with all his rights; the purchase was often limited in various ways. Thus in the negotiation with Dodsley for *Rasselas* it was a question whether Johnson should receive £60 for the first edition, the property then to revert to him, or £40 'and share the profit, that is retain half the copy'. It is interesting to find that, in the former alternative, the

[1] Johnson in the *Life of Savage* describes as matter for indignation the payment of 10 guineas for *The Wanderer* (1729). But that poem is some eight times the length of *London*, and was sold at twice its price.

publisher was 'himself to fix the number' printed; for this, in principle, approaches the modern system of royalties. In the end he was paid £100 for the first edition and a further £25 for the second, in which he made a few trifling corrections. That is at the rate of £3 for a thousand words. No doubt Dodsley did well, for *Rasselas* became a classic. But the payment was not penurious. There was, however, a feeling that an author had a moral claim on the profits of an unexpectedly successful book; in 1737 it was even proposed in Parliament that no author should have power to alienate his copyright (otherwise than by will) for more than ten years. The publishers no doubt urged on their side that ten years' purchase of many properties was less than was paid for them in the first year and that it was intolerable that the author should have power to sell the copyright a second time to a rival publisher. Where success was certain, a limit of time was not impracticable; Pope actually gave Gilliver one year's lease of the *Essay on Man*, receiving £50 for each of the four parts.

The remuneration of Goldsmith's later compositions was on average rather more than £100 for an octavo volume, which may be reckoned as £4 or £5 a sheet. It will be remembered that Johnson declined to believe that a reviewer was paid 6 guineas *communibus sheetibus*. A volume of the *Roman History* was sold for 6*s*., and therefore the fee of £125 was equivalent to a 10 per cent. royalty on more than 8,000 copies. The publisher made a good bargain. These payments have been regarded as much higher than those made for Goldsmith's works of original genius—£150 for *The Good-Natur'd Man* and £21 for *The Traveller*. It should be remembered that most plays, unlike many Roman Histories, were ephemeral; and that this play is only 80 pages and sold for 1*s*. 6*d*. *The Traveller* happens to have lived, but Newbery could not be sure of that, and it has only 438 lines. The price was 1*s*. 6*d*., so that £21 is equal to a royalty of 10 per cent. on 3,000 copies; and it is possible there were further payments.

A good illustration of the defects of the system is afforded by a work which suffered the extremes of fortune. When Noon the publisher in 1737 undertook the risk of Hume's *Treatise of Human Nature* he did a very rash thing. It was a total failure; and since it is a substantial work in three volumes, Noon cannot have lost much less than £500. Hume was very lucky to get his book published without expense to himself; absurdly lucky to be paid £50 for it. Yet £50 has no relation to the value of the most famous philosophical book of its century and country. If the *Treatise* had had the success of his later essays, Hume might have nursed a grievance. *Evelina*, for which Miss Burney was paid £30, is a similar case in its own field.

One hundred guineas was the price paid by Dodsley in 1765 for Percy's *Reliques*. This was a laborious work, and Johnson had certified its merit and importance. But its popularity must have been doubtful; and in fact there were only four editions in half a century.

When the risk was negligible and the prospect of profit good, much higher prices were paid. Johnson named his own price, 200 guineas, for the 'little lives and little prefaces' which he undertook to write for the collection of the poets. We cannot but admire the shrewdness of the associated booksellers in asking Johnson to name his own terms; they knew he would ask less than they could in decency offer. In the end they paid him 300; it must be remembered that he wrote much more than he had intended, and that he gravely embarrassed them by being two years late. But Malone declared that if he had asked 1,000 or even 1,500 guineas, the publishers would have paid it. A thousand guineas would have been 250 for an octavo volume.

If £100 be taken as standard for an octavo volume, perhaps £200 is the corresponding figure for a quarto. But Hume in the 'fifties, and Robert Henry in the 'seventies, got more than £500 a volume for their Histories of England. Adam Smith in 1776 had £500 for the first edition of *The Wealth of Nations*. Gibbon, whose independence enabled him to claim two-thirds of the profits, got over £300 for 1,000 copies of one volume. The account for the third edition of the first volume has survived. It shows a cost of £310 (the chief items being printing £117, paper £171) and a return of £800, '1,000 books at 16*s*.' The price was a guinea, so the discount was about 24 per cent.; not so high a rate as we have hitherto noticed, but the risk was negligible. Then as now the bookseller paid the cost of carriage. Of the profit of £490 Gibbon had two-thirds, Strahan and Cadell dividing the remaining third.

STERNE TOUTING HIS BOOKS AT RANELAGH

From a print in the British Museum

Pure literature, unsupported by other emolument, has never afforded much more than competence to other than a very small proportion of writers by profession. It is clear from the figures, and from their own statements, that the writers of George III's reign could not be regarded as ill used by the world. Conditions were harder in the previous reign, when patronage was rare and fitful, and the publishers were less prosperous. But even Johnson in his first ten years in London, though often in dire poverty, was yet able to live by his pen, and to do so without either achieving popularity or stooping to do work beneath his powers. His work on the Parliamentary Debates, or on the *Harleian Catalogue*, or for the *Gentleman's Magazine*, though much of it was drudgery, ought not to be called hack-work. The story of Goldsmith's youth is painful, and has roused just indignation against his taskmaster. But whatever Goldsmith had, he spent more; and in the days of his freedom and prosperity he was content to give most of his time to compilations not very different in kind from those he had ground out in bondage.

We have hitherto considered authors as working in co-operation with booksellers; and this was, then as later, normally the best if not the only way to make money by writing. What other expedients were open to the writers of the time? Little need be said here of patronage; for Johnson and his contemporaries made it plain that they regarded patronage as a servitude which, with the help of publishers and the support of the public, they had for ever shaken off. The system which made a writer the pensioner of a great nobleman, or gave him a sinecure under government by that nobleman's interest, had conferred benefits on literature in the age of Anne, though benefits seldom unmixed with the evils of dependence. Political and other reasons have been given for its decline under Walpole's administration. But a system which, even in its best days, had been practised by only a small number of noblemen or gentlemen, exceptionally gifted or exceptionally generous, and had always been open to grave abuse, might well fail from accident or change of fashion. Its decline was hastened by the growth of the reading public and the activity of publishers, which offered authors better, and perhaps not more precarious, rewards. But patronage lasted long enough, in Johnson's experience, to give reality to his denunciation. Men of letters who were famous in his youth—Young, Thomson, and Savage—had all lived by patronage; Young and Savage, at least, had known its disappointments and humiliations. Though he was too proud to solicit patronage in his early poverty, or even to dedicate a poem, yet when he embarked on his *Dictionary* he was persuaded by his publisher to address his *Plan* to the Earl of Chesterfield, a great nobleman who was himself a man of letters. The sequel is familiar. Whatever indignities Johnson suffered, or conceived himself to have suffered, they were sufficient to confirm him in independence. But his celebrated Letter to Lord Chesterfield, though it may be called the epitaph of patronage, was not its death-blow; for it was not printed in Johnson's lifetime; and in fact patronage, though long since moribund, did not come to an end in 1755. It had indeed a measure of revival after the accession of George III, who was acclaimed as a patron of learning and the arts. The pensions granted by the King or his Ministers to Johnson in 1762, and later to Beattie, were in the nature of patronage, though there was no private patron, and no obligation of service.

Political patronage continued to exist, for political purposes, its importance varying with political exigences. Preferment in the Church or in the Universities was sometimes partly the reward of literature; Young, Warburton, and Percy were clergymen; Gray, Blair, and Beattie became professors. Otherwise the avenues to direct and permanent patronage were virtually closed. But honorary patronage, the published countenance of the great, retained its efficacy. The price of a dedication was no longer so many guineas; but the continued practice of dedication shows that it had a value. Johnson, though Boswell tells us that 'the loftiness of his mind prevented him from ever dedicating in his own person', did not impose this austerity on his brother and sister authors. 'The known style of dedication is flattery', he said; but he wrote a great many dedications, and was a master in that style. The incomparable tact of his phrasing made his dedications ingratiating, while it kept them free of servility. The dedication of Percy's *Reliques* to the heiress of the Percies was in itself an appropriate and graceful act; but it was written by Johnson, and doubtless its courtly strain promoted the author's advancement.

Authors have commonly regarded publishers as an evil, and have sometimes asked if they were a necessary evil. In the eighteenth century it was a frequent complaint of authors that the publishers denied them direct access to the public ear. There is some evidence of discreditable boycotting by the trade of books 'printed for the author'; but authors were perhaps unreasonable in their expectations. It was not reasonable to expect any publisher to take much trouble to promote a book in the sale of which he had no interest beyond a meagre commission. In general, at all events, the advice of Johnson and others was sound—that an author should go to the booksellers and make the best bargain he could. But there was one famous way in which an author could make his own appeal to the public; he might publish by subscription. The enormous success of Pope's *Iliad* was a golden example, followed successfully by Gay, by Thomson, and by Prior for collected editions of their poems. In the succeeding age subscription was not much used in the ordinary way; but it was useful in special cases. Sometimes the motive was purely charitable, as when Johnson helped his dependant, Miss Anna Williams, to produce a volume of *Miscellanies*. Sometimes an unknown author, who had no chance with the booksellers, was able to bring out a volume by appealing to private friendship and local patriotism. But the most important function of subscription was to finance an enterprise which required years of labour, or of which the commercial success was impossible or doubtful. The rule was that the subscriber paid half the purchase money in advance and half on delivery of his copy. In this way Johnson was able to start work on his *Shakespeare* in 1756, and to complete it (his pension intervening to retard its progress) in 1765.

The success of this device was sometimes surprising. In 1741 Conyers Middleton, the Cambridge University librarian, published his *Life of Cicero*. It was an ambitious work in two quarto volumes, and was backed by powerful Whig support. There were nearly 2,000 subscribers, of whom over 200 were resident in Cambridge and over 50 in Oxford. A similar if humbler success was achieved in 1776 by William Mickle, a 'corrector' at the Oxford University Press, with his translation of the *Lusiad*. There were nearly 600 subscribers, of whom 200 were resident in Oxford. The book was a guinea

LONDON, *June* 1. 1756.

PROPOSALS

For PRINTING, by SUBSCRIPTION,

THE

DRAMATICK WORKS

OF

WILLIAM SHAKESPEARE,

CORRECTED AND ILLUSTRATED

BY

SAMUEL JOHNSON.

SUBSCRIPTIONS are taken in by

J and R. TONSON, in the Strand; J. KNAPTON, in Ludgate-Street; C. HITCH and L. HAWES, and M and T. LONGMAN, in Pater-noster Row.

quarto, and its success was held to justify what was not very common, a second edition in the same form.

These lists contain the names of very few booksellers. This does not mean that the trade was excluded; for many of the subscribers would be secured by booksellers, at a recognized commission, from among their customers. But it means that an author was able to appeal directly, if he chose, to the friendship or generosity, the public spirit or vanity, of eminent persons throughout the country. It means, too, that the London publisher was not omnipotent.

The lists exhibit the remarkable accessibility, to such appeals, of the royal family, the great nobles, and the wealthy clergy. They show the readiness of authors to help one another. They show, further, unexpected public spirit in the Fellows of Oxford and Cambridge colleges, of whose poverty and intellectual sloth, in this period, we have heard too much.

An example of a successful subscription is Cowper's *Homer*, the particulars of which he gives in a letter of 1791. He secured 700 subscribers at 3 guineas, for which Johnson, the publisher, was to pay him £1,000. He puts the printing at £600, and Johnson's commission at £100. This means that the return from 700 copies was £1,700, or 48*s*. 7*d*. a copy (which means a discount of 23 per cent. to the booksellers who collected the subscriptions, if all copies were on the same terms).

Subscription was not, however, a necessary element in publication by an author on his own account. Many books were 'printed for the Author' which there is no reason to believe were subscribed. It is true that the evidence for subscription might be suppressed. Johnson's *Shakespeare* ignores the subscribers, and his reasons for ignoring them are famous—he had lost all the names and spent all the money. But this seems to have been very exceptional procedure. Johnson himself, when told that Young had made a large sum by subscriptions for his *Universal Passion*, doubted the story, because he had never seen a 'subscription-book', that is a subscriber's copy. We must in general assume that if a book was 'printed for the author' the author found the money somehow. Famous examples of such enterprise are Cibber's *Apology* and Sterne's *Tristram Shandy*. A very profitable example is Robert Henry's *History of England* in six volumes quarto. Henry, employing Cadell as his agent, produced five volumes between 1771 and 1785, and soon after this sold the property to Cadell for over £1,400. It was still a standard work when Jane Austen read, or proposed to read, it in 1800.

The physical aspect of the books which Johnson and Goldsmith read is still happily familiar. It is not unworthy of a great age. The printers of the century have been unjustly neglected by students of the art of printing. Their work lacks the exuberant fancy of the Elizabethans, and the mechanical excellence of the nineteenth century; but artistically it is superior to both. The finest performances of the early decades, such as Clarendon's *History*, Pope's *Homer*, or the folio poems of Pope and Young, attain a severe nobility of design. The best work of later years is not greatly inferior; the 'fifties and 'sixties are remarkable for the great charm of their small octavos and duodecimos. Some time before Johnson's death a decline in taste is apparent in ordinary books. The age saw little self-conscious effort at fine art in printing. Horace Walpole's privately printed books, though amateurish, have a sober elegance of their own; and Baskerville was a pioneer, though he showed the way to the excesses of his later followers. The books of the time owed, and owe, much to their binding, which is almost uniformly good. Books were often sold in a temporary casing of boards, lettered by hand; but before they found their permanent home on a library shelf they were almost always bound, in calf if not in morocco, and lettered in gold. A wall covered with eighteenth-century books in contemporary bindings has the same solid elegance as Augustan silver and mahogany.

The folio, which in the seventeenth century was the natural form of dignified literature, began in the reign of Anne to give place to the large quarto.[1] Folio was reserved for very lengthy works of reference. Similarly the large folio pamphlet in verse, so characteristic of the age of Pope, gave way, about 1740, to a more modest quarto size;[2] just

[1] When Boswell, who had large ideas, talked in 1790 of printing his *magnum opus* in folio, Malone told him he 'might as well throw it into the Thames, for a folio would not now be read'.

[2] Gray's 'Eton Ode' (1747) was a late survival of the folio. Gray's 'Elegy' (1751) and his 'Odes' (1757), Johnson's 'Vanity' (1749), Churchill's 'Rosciad' (1761) and its successors, Goldsmith's 'Traveller' (1765) and 'Deserted Village' (1770), Crabbe's 'Library' (1781) and 'Village' (1783) are all quarto.

as, about 1815, the quarto poem declined to octavo. There is doubtless an economic reason for the supersession of folio by quarto, but it is not known. Works of bulk and importance in prose[1] were first printed, and often reprinted, in substantial quarto; but if they became popular, a cheaper octavo edition soon followed. Shorter books, if esteemed important, sermons, controversial pamphlets, and (for obvious reasons of convenience) plays in prose or verse, were in octavo, rather larger than the modern novel. Cheap books, such as essays or novels, were either in a small octavo or in duodecimo. The economic advantage of duodecimo is plain. The smaller page made it possible to use a smaller type without the appearance of meanness; and a sheet of paper in the standard size made 16 pages of octavo, 24 of duodecimo. The size of type, it may be noted, was a more important economic factor than it is to-day, because the cost of setting type was very low, and the cost of paper relatively very high. Cheap mass production by means of stereotype plates had not become possible; and the practice of printing two or more editions from the same type was hardly known. Human labour was cheap, and it was not worth while to lock up capital either by keeping type standing or by printing large editions requiring a heavy outlay on paper.

It remains to consider how far the trade was organized to meet the demand for books and to stimulate it. There is no doubt that, relative to the population, the production of books was high; and the promotion of literature in the age of Johnson must be held largely accountable for the growth of the 'reading public', and the 'march of mind', which were acclaimed in the age that followed. Then, as now, books were sold by reviews and lists, by the efforts of retail booksellers, and by the talk of the town. In spite of difficulties of transport and communication, the activities of the metropolitan publishers were well supported throughout the country. The Bibliographical Society's *Dictionary* for 1726–75 shows about 150 'booksellers' for England and Wales outside London, and a rather larger number for London. In the course of the half-century there were some twenty-five booksellers in York, and one or more in a dozen other

[1] For example, Hume's and Gibbon's Histories, Blackstone's Commentaries, Warton's History of Poetry, Mason's Life of Gray and Boswell's of Johnson, Chesterfield's *Letters*.

Yorkshire towns. A remarkable number of country gentlemen fulfilled a duty, or indulged an inclination, by forming libraries of solid books, protected by durable bindings and dignified by armorial bookplates. Those who could not afford to buy such books, or wanted more ephemeral literature, might have recourse to the 'evergreen tree of diabolical knowledge'—so Sir Anthony Absolute describes the circulating library—or to membership of the private reading clubs which served the needs of small towns or country districts. It is recorded that the first circulating library in London was set up in 1740, and had successful imitators. Their stock-in-trade cannot have been confined to the kind of literature indicated by Sir Anthony's phrase; by the end of the century the library in Southampton boasted nearly 7,000 volumes, 'a more general assemblage of polite literature than is usually found'; and the library at Dawlish, which Jane Austen about the same time found 'particularly pitiful', must have been contrasted in her mind with that richer collection in Bath from which Lady Russell drew 'all the new poems and states of the nation' which bored Miss Elliott. These examples are outside our period; but the growth must have been gradual. The same is doubtless true of the reading societies, such as that of 'Clergy and Gentlemen at Pembroke', which subscribed for Middleton's *Life of Cicero* in 1741. Such associations doubtless had a long and useful history. James Lackington, writing in 1791 and surveying his career as a bookseller, stated that there were book-clubs all over England. The books, after going the round, were put up to auction and bought by individual subscribers. Lackington believed that the sale of books had been increased—not as booksellers had feared, diminished—by the book-clubs and by the circulating libraries.

BIBLIOGRAPHY.—NICHOLS'S *Literary Anecdotes of the Eighteenth Century* (9 vols., 1812–15) and *Illustrations of Literary History* (8 vols., 1817–58) contain valuable material. Agreements, accounts, and other documents are printed in monographs on individual authors or publishers, e.g. FORSTER'S *Life of Goldsmith* (3rd. ed., 1862), CHARLES WELSH, *A Bookseller of the Last Century*, i.e. John Newbery (1885), RALPH STRAUS, *Robert Dodsley* (1910), and in the publications of the Bibliographical Society; R. A. AUSTEN-LEIGH, 'William Strahan and his Ledgers', in *Library*, March 1923, is of exceptional importance. Information on prices, derived from advertisements, is to be found in special bibliographies, and the arrangements for publication by subscription may be studied in the printed *proposals*, many of which have survived. A. S. COLLINS, *Authorship in the Days of Johnson* (1928), is a very useful survey of the whole subject, and is strong on the history of copyright.

A YOUNG LADY LEAVING A CIRCULATING LIBRARY

From a mezzotint by J. R. Smith

XXVII
THE NEWSPAPER

By D. NICHOL SMITH

To us, who are regaled every morning and evening with intelligence, and are supplied from day to day with materials for conversation, it is difficult to conceive how man can subsist without a News-paper, or to what entertainment companies can assemble, in those wide regions of the earth that have neither *Chronicles* nor *Magazines*, neither *Gazettes* nor *Advertisers*, neither *Journals* nor *Evening-Posts*.—*The Idler*, No. 7.

Now we have not only in the metropolis papers for every morning and every evening, but almost every large town has its weekly historian.—*The Idler*, No. 30.

The trade of advertising is now so near to perfection, that it is not easy to propose any improvement.— *The Idler*, No. 40.

THE newspaper grew steadily in range and power in the time of Johnson, but it grew slowly. It changed little in character, and, while continuing to meet the needs of an increasing public, it changed as little in the methods of its management and production. To a greater degree than any other member of the literary profession, the journalist has always been subject to the printer—to what the printer can perform in a stated time; and the printer has become increasingly dependent on the engineer, who is mainly responsible for the growth of the newspaper in our day. What we can now circulate in millions could throughout the whole of the eighteenth century be circulated only in thousands. The articles of Defoe and the letters of Junius were printed on a press which in design and method was still the press of Caxton. The first steam-press was not installed in this country till 1814, and stereotyping was not adapted to the economic needs of the newspaper-office till many years later. With the conditions of production such as they were in the eighteenth century, the progress of journalism could at no stage be revolutionary or spectacular; but within the limits of these conditions English journalism maintained and enhanced its acknowledged pre-eminence in vigour and independence.

The size of the newspapers increased steadily but slowly. In the days of Queen Anne the normal form was still double columns on a single half-sheet, with a printed area on each side of eleven or twelve inches by six; and this was the form also of *The Tatler* and *The Spectator*. Three columns a page, on a larger sheet folded to make four pages, were adopted in *Mist's Weekly Journal* and *The London Journal* in 1725, and—whether on four quarto pages or two folio pages—were more or less regular from about 1730. *The London Chronicle*, for which Johnson wrote the 'preliminary discourse' in 1757, was printed in three columns on eight quarto pages. *The Public Ledger* began in 1760 with four pages, but they were of full folio size, and each had four columns; and when in 1761 *The St. James's Chronicle* adopted the same form the standard was fixed for all the leading newspapers till the end of the century. Cowper in his *Task* speaks of a newspaper as a 'folio of four pages'; Crabbe, about the same time, described it as 'a single sheet' with a fixed number of 'rows' or columns. When *The Times* started from unpromising beginnings as *The Daily Universal Register* on January 1, 1785—within three weeks of Johnson's death—it followed the fashion in containing sixteen columns on a folded sheet measuring nineteen inches by twenty-four. The English newspaper had worked its way steadily from the simple model in the reign of Queen Anne to another model which was as generally accepted. It presented a printed area which was more than five times greater, and it had grown almost to the limits of what the old hand-press would allow.

The circulation of the newspaper likewise reflected the conditions of the printing-house, and grew little throughout the century. The available evidence is scanty, but it shows that the sale of a successful paper was normally under three thousand copies and could very rarely have reached five thousand. From the portions of the office ledger of *The Public Advertiser* now in the British Museum we learn that the daily sale of that paper in the months preceding the publication of the Letters of Junius was about 2,800 or 2,900 copies, and that during their publication, from January 1769 to December 1771, the numbers rose during the winter months to an average of about 3,400, but only thrice exceeded 4,100; the highest number is 4,800 (for the issue of December 19, 1769, containing the letter to the King), and the number which comes next is 4,250 (February 14, 1770). A page of the same ledger now in the Bodleian Library shows that in December 1775, a time of no unusual excitement, the numbers ranged from 2,700 to 2,800; and this may be taken to have been a satisfactory circulation for a newspaper in the third quarter of the eighteenth century. By the end of the century there was no great increase. *The Times* is said to have sold between 4,700 and 4,800 copies in 1795, but *The Morning Chronicle*—an older and well established paper—did not then sell a third of that number, and *The Morning Post* had fallen to 350. The editor who took over the charge of *The Morning Post* at this juncture has left us his recollections of its circulation, and though he writes of a later age than Johnson's he may be called in evidence as he describes the fortunes of a paper which was printed under the conditions that prevailed in Johnson's day:

I began (says Daniel Stuart) the management of the Morning Post in the autumn of 1795, when its sale was only 350 per day. In the Spring of 1797 it was 1,000 per day; before Coleridge returned from Germany [July 1799] it was upwards of 2,000 per day. The Morning Herald and the Times had been the leading papers: they were then much neglected, and The Morning Post, by vigilance and activity, threw them both into the back ground. It took a strong part against Bonaparte during the Peace of Amiens: that was popular, and raised the paper rapidly, till its permanent circulation was, in August 1803, 4,500.[1]

Daniel Stuart was an old man when he wrote these recollections, but his figures will not be questioned. They may be taken to be roughly representative of the three degrees of a paper's popularity at that time, and earlier. Much larger circulations have sometimes been assumed. *The Spectator* was said by a contemporary to have risen 'above 14,000',[2] and by a later writer to over 20,000;[3] and *The Craftsman* at the height of its power was supposed to have frequently reached between 10,000 and 12,000.[4] Such figures are out of relation to the later figures which can be verified.

But how could even 2,000 copies of a paper of four pages

[1] *Gentleman's Magazine*, New Series, vol. ix, June 1838, p. 579.

[2] Letter of William Fleetwood, Bishop of St. Asaph, to the Bishop of Salisbury, dated June 17, 1712, printed in *Mr. Pope's Literary Correspondence* (E. Curll, 1736), vol. iv, p. 83.

[3] *Addisoniana* (1803), vol. ii, p. 52.

[4] *Essays illustrative of The Rambler*, etc. by Nathan Drake, 1809, vol. i, p. 60. We shall more readily accept the figure given in the 'Narrative of the Sufferings of Mr. Henry Haines, late Printer of the *Craftsman*', as published in *The Daily Gazetteer* for September 27, 1740; Haines is there reported to have said that 'he printed 4500'.

be printed daily on the hand-press? The question will not so readily arise with the evening papers, which appeared generally thrice a week; but *The Public Advertiser* and other morning papers appeared daily. We know the rate of working. The older hands in a printing-house to-day can confirm what we read in such a book as Timperley's *Printers' Manual.*[1] A 'token' consists of 250 sheets, and 'each token, in ordinary work, is reckoned an hour'. This allows only about fifteen seconds for inking and pulling. It was a rate which could not easily be long maintained, but relays of experienced pressmen could print 2,000 sheets in eight hours—on one side; and as the printing of the other side could be carried on concurrently, the rate for the completed paper would be much the same. If the circulation rose to 3,000, twelve hours' printing at top speed would be required. These figures have only to be stated to show that in the printing-house of a popular paper at least four presses had to be used—two for each side of the sheet, and that, in these days before stereotyping, the whole paper had therefore to be set at least twice.

This we may sometimes prove by comparing copies of the same date. They will agree in contents and in arrangement, but they may not agree typographically. Even periodical essays, which did not appear daily, sometimes show differences of this kind. The most notable example is *The Tatler*, which came out thrice a week. In two of the complete series of its original numbers in the Bodleian Library, 82 of the 271 have been found to differ in the setting; and some of the 189 which agree differ from the copies in other series. Probably every number appeared in at least two settings, one of them being as much the 'original issue' as the other. In the list of Errata in No. 255 it is admitted that this paper had been 'worked off in different Presses', and the list in No. 155 is introduced thus: 'Several of the last Papers not having been printed from the corrected Copy, the Reader is desired to mark the following Errata in those of the faulty Impression'. Similar differences are, of necessity, found in *The Spectator*, which had a larger circulation and appeared daily. As it was customary to bind up sets of periodical essays—back numbers of *The Spectator* were advertised by the month—an essay that had sold well might have to be reprinted; and we

[1] 1838, p. 104.

therefore run some risk of confusing reprints with simultaneous prints. But there was not the same reason for a reprint of a newspaper. We have always to be careful in assuming that two copies of the same number of a newspaper are duplicates; though they are identical in contents they may not have been printed from the same setting of type.[1]

When Johnson made his way to London in 1737 to become by necessity an author, party politics were raging in the Press as they had not raged since the reign of Queen Anne. It is significant that the one paper which he should mention in his poem *London* is the 'Gazetteer'. This was *The Daily Gazetteer*, the chief organ of Walpole's ministry, founded in 1735 and tenacious in its defensive fight against cleverer opponents. From 1731 to 1741 Walpole spent £5,000 a year in subsidies to his papers, and, like grateful Ministers at all times, distributed appointments as rewards. His journalists did not all live in Grub Street; one of them, Henry Bland, an old school-fellow, was at the same time Provost of Eton and Dean of Durham. Fielding, when writing for the other side, applied to them these lines in *The Dunciad*, with a slight adjustment to make the satire more pointed:

> A motley Mixture! in long Wigs, in Bags,
> In Silks, in Crapes, in Garters, and in Rags,
> From Drawing-Rooms, from Colleges, from Garrets,
> On Horse, on Foot, in Hacks, and gilded Chariots,
> All who true Dunces in his Cause appear'd,
> And well he knew those Dunces to reward.[2]

Pope had not described any one set of writers in these lines, nor is there much about 'the Weekly Journals' in *The Dunciad* as it first appeared; but on recasting the poem after the long domination of Walpole he admitted the claims of the journalists to fuller recognition, and added them to the list of competitors in the diving match:

> Next plung'd a feeble, but a desp'rate pack,
> With each a sickly brother at his back:

[1] Two rare examples of 'conjugate' printing of consecutive numbers of a daily paper are found in the copies of *The Daily Gazetteer* for September 26 and 27, 1740, and October 3 and 4, 1740, in the Rawlinson Collection in the Bodleian Library. These may be classed as reprints, from standing type. Probably they were intended for country circulation. On the other hand, the early numbers of *The True Briton*, 1723, were reset when reprinted in groups of four (twelve pages).

[2] *The Champion*, No. 128, Sept. 6, 1740.

> Sons of a Day! just buoyant on the flood,
> Then number'd with the puppies in the mud.
> Ask ye their names? I could as soon disclose
> The names of these blind puppies as of those . . .
> 'These are,—ah no! these were, the Gazetteers'.

This passage appeared in *The Dunciad* of 1743, when Walpole was out of office. In the compromise which followed with the ministry of Carteret, newspaper controversy lost something of its violence; and it remained on the whole less violent under the Broad Bottom Administration.

The ablest of the papers which attacked Walpole, and represented the Country Party as opposed to the Court Party, was *The Country Journal, or The Craftsman* 'by Caleb D'Anvers, of Gray's-Inn', conducted and largely written by Nicholas Amhurst, and published weekly. William Pulteney, afterwards Earl of Bath, the leader of the Opposition, had some share in its direction, but his cousin Daniel Pulteney played a bigger part in bringing it to power. 'A certain accuracy and shew of reasoning easily distinguished his papers from all others', says an anonymous writer whose sympathies were with the other side, 'and his death, which happened soon after this paper was set on foot, was an irretrievable loss to the party, who lost in him the clearest head, as well as the best heard speaker they could boast'.[1] The best known of its writers now is Bolingbroke, who contributed in a series of letters his *Dissertation upon Parties*. During Johnson's early years in London, *The Craftsman* was the paper which attracted most talent, and had the largest circulation. After it, as an organ of the Country Party, came *Common Sense, or The Englishman's Journal*, which was founded in 1737 on the demise of *Fog's Weekly Journal*, itself the successor of *Mist's Weekly Journal*. It was not so much a rival as an ally of *The Craftsman*. As was stated in the preface to the collected edition, 'it was necessary to take off from the shoulders of *The Craftsman* some part of the burthen which every man labours under who is struggling against corruption'. Chesterfield wrote the first number, and several others.

Though Walpole acknowledged the power of the Press by his subsidies and rewards—and in giving them he continued an established practice—he spoke of the Press with the

[1] *Historical View of the Political Writers* (1740), p. 24.

cynicism in which he habitually masked his earnest purpose. In a debate in the House of Commons in 1740, Pulteney is reported to have fulminated against 'the contemptible scribblers of the ministerial vindications: a herd of wretches whom neither information can enlighten, nor affluence elevate; low drudges of scurrility, whose scandal is harmless for want of wit, and whose opposition is only troublesome from the pertinaciousness of stupidity'. These were not the days of verbatim reports, and this speech was written up from notes in a garret. We are probably no nearer the actual words of Walpole's reply, but what we read will be accepted as at least in character. He would not, he said, show the same earnestness in defending the writers whom Pulteney had attacked; 'nor', he continued, 'do I often read the papers of either party, except when I am informed by some that have more inclination to such studies than myself, that they have risen by some accident above their common level. . . . I have never, from these accidental inspections of their performances, discovered any reason to exalt the authors who write against the administration to a higher degree of reputation than their opponents. That any of them deserve loud applauses, I cannot assert, and am afraid that all which deserves to be preserved of the writings on either side may be contracted to a very few volumes.' This is from the speech as it is given in the *Parliamentary History*; and the whole speech is admirable in its satirical examination of political journalism. But it was written by Samuel Johnson, and for this once, at least, he could not prevent the Whig dogs having the best of it.

There is no better account of political journalism in the year 1740 than is to be found in a short pamphlet entitled *An Historical View of the Principles, Characters, Persons, &c. of the Political Writers in Great-Britain*. The anonymous writer has a bias in favour of Walpole's party, but he can be impartial (as in the passage about Daniel Pulteney which has been quoted), and he gives information which will not easily be obtained elsewhere. He is particularly hard on Fielding, in whom he finds a good stock of abuse and scurrility. 'It is generally thought that his flashy wit must be soon exhausted',[1] he says, thinking only of *The Champion*, 'by Captain Hercules Vinegar.' Fielding's heart was never long

[1] *Historical View*, p. 37.

possessed by politics, and though *The Champion* was a political paper its main articles are mostly on the manners of the times; some of them are on new books and the theatre.[1] One is an enthusiastic review of Dyer's *Ruins of Rome*,[2] and others deal with Cibber's *Apology*. Captain Vinegar desired his correspondents to ask him 'Questions concerning Virtue, Wit, Gallantry, Love, Poetry, and such like, and to consult others in Politicks'.[3] But Fielding had his own views in politics; and in this paper he had the assistance of James Ralph, one of Pope's dunces, but a skilful journalist, who is understood to have written most of the political articles, and claims to have been responsible for the novel arrangement of the news. The following brief letter professedly written by a keeper of a coffee-house, but possibly by Fielding himself, indicates the politics of *The Champion*, and is interesting for its short catalogue:

> It is very hard upon me to be obliged by my Customers to take in your Paper, having before been at the constant Expence (beside the *Craftsman* and *Common Sense*; for which a Man does not grudge his Money) of the *Universal Spectator*, the *Weekly Miscellany*, the *London Evening Post*, the St. *James's Evening Post*, the *Whitehall Evening Post*, the *Daily Advertiser*, the *London Daily Post*, *Daily Post*, &c., &c. I therefore desire you would either write no more, or write away all the rest.[4]

Fielding began *The Champion* in November 1739 and controlled it till June 1741, but it continued till 1744, apparently under the direction of Ralph, who edited the collected edition published in 1741. At the time of the Jacobite troubles Fielding returned to journalism, and as a man 'of no party'—a word which he hoped 'to eradicate out of our Constitution'—conducted *The True Patriot* (1745–6) till the troubles were ended at Culloden; and he followed it up with *The Jacobite's Journal* 'by John Trottplaid Esq.' (1748–9), written with the less serious purpose of turning the remains of Jacobite sentiment to ridicule. He was then finishing *Tom Jones*; and no sooner had he published *Amelia* than he returned to journalism once more, and,

[1] 'Notwithstanding the frequent Hints and Petitions I have receiv'd to take the Theatre under my Protection, I have hitherto declined it.' No. 129, Sept. 9, 1740.

[2] *The Champion*, No. 50, March 8, 1740. Dyer's poem was published three days later.

[3] Ibid., No. 40, Feb. 14, 1740.

[4] Ibid., No. 8, Dec. 4, 1739.

in failing health, from January to November 1752, brought out *The Covent Garden Journal* 'by Sir Alexander Drawcansir, Knight, Censor of Great Britain'. In this he disclaimed any dealing in party politics and concerned himself as a censor with social conditions and contemporary literature and drama. Written at a time when as a justice of the peace he was concerned with 'the late increase of robbers' and similar problems, *The Covent Garden Journal* had a practical moral purpose, but it did not keep the peace in its critical articles, and these would seem, on the evidence of the rejoinders which they invited, to have attracted most attention. His satire is always high spirited, and it never fails. He is the most gifted journalist of the middle of the century; but he was a restless journalist who reserved his strength for his greater works. Of all his four papers, only one ran for more than a year. *The Westminster Journal* (1741), which survived in various forms till the nineteenth century, and *Old England, or the Constitutional Journal* (1743), were the most important of the other journals founded at this time. The chief writer on *Old England* was William Guthrie, the friend of Johnson, and among the occasional contributors were Chesterfield and Horace Walpole.

As a rule a 'journal', then as now, came out once a week. In England the name has seldom been given to a daily paper. The 'perfect diurnals' of the seventeenth century may have recorded what passed day by day, but they appeared weekly; and our first periodical to be called a journal, *The Gentleman's Journal* of 1692–4, an anticipation of the magazine, came out monthly and latterly once in two months. With more thought of the derivation than of English usage, Johnson, in a heedless moment, defined a journal in his *Dictionary* as 'any paper published daily', and this definition is still repeated; but the only English newspaper which he could have cited was *The Daily Journal* (1720–37). The word came into regular use in titles between 1713 and 1720 and was defined in Bailey's *Dictionary* in 1736 as 'a common name of several news-papers who detail the particular transactions of Europe'. But by that time, as *The Dunciad* will suggest, it had gained a more definite meaning. A 'journal' had come to be a weekly paper containing an article—whether political, literary, or social, and whether in the form of an essay or letter—as well as general news, and advertisements. It was larger and more miscellaneous in its contents than either the newspaper or the essay-paper. But the distinctions cannot be rigidly drawn, for it was to affect the development of the newspaper, in which it ultimately merged.

The journal and the newspaper were to take the place of the pamphlet as the normal medium of political controversy. The pamphlet had predominated in the days of Defoe and Swift and to the days of Burke it remained the best means of expressing deliberate opinion, but under Walpole the needs of party were found to be better served by the rapid succession of attack and counter-attack on stated days. His son, Horace Walpole, was to remark on the change in 1763. 'The paper-war', he wrote, 'is rekindled with violence, but produces no wit; nay, scarce produces the bulk of a pamphlet, for the fashionable warfare at present is carried on by anonymous letters in the daily newspapers'; and he afterwards added in a note that 'it is certain that from this time, when anonymous writers could get their letters printed in the daily newspapers, pamphlets grew exceedingly more rare'.[1] But the beginning of the change may be dated roughly from *The Craftsman* and *The Daily Gazetteer*—from the early days of Johnson's England.

Of more importance ultimately in the development of journalism than the controversies of these days was the success of a paper devoted to business and commerce. The foundation of *The Daily Advertiser* on February 3, 1730/1 proved to be one of the great events in the history of the periodical press. It started from modest beginnings, consisting at first only of advertisements, and smaller sections giving the prices of stocks, the rates of exchange, and lists of exports and imports; and many numbers were to be issued before it surpassed earlier trade papers. John Houghton's *Collection for Improvement of Husbandry and Trade* is invaluable as a record of English industry in the reign of William III, but it was a one-man venture devoted primarily to the description of industrial conditions, though with a view to their improvement. Advertisements had been inserted in periodicals from about the middle of the seventeenth century, and from Marchamont Needham's *Publick Adviser* of 1657 to *The Generous Advertiser, or Weekly Information of Trade and*

[1] Letter to Sir Horace Mann, Sept. 13, 1763; ed. Mrs. Paget Toynbee, vol. v, p. 372.

Business of 1707 and *The Useful Intelligencer for Promoting of Trade and Commerce* of 1711, there had been several papers designed for 'persons that are any way concerned in matter of Buying and Selling'. Other papers about trade were mainly political: Defoe's *Mercator* and *The British Merchant* (1713) supported and attacked the proposed commercial treaty with France at the time of the Peace of Utrecht, and *The Manufacturer* and *The British Merchant* (1719) were led by the condition of the woollen industry to fight over the question of protection or free trade. But the immediate needs of business men had been best met by the popular papers. In the later numbers of *The Tatler*, advertisements occupy more than one of the four columns, and in the very last number almost two. Addison wrote a paper on them (No. 224). 'It is my custom in a dearth of news', he begins, 'to entertain my self with those Collections of Advertisements that appear at the end of all our publick prints', and he went on to write our best treatise on publicity in the reign of Queen Anne. The novelty of *The Daily Advertiser* was that it was planned to collect to itself every day the advertisements which would have been dispersed in several papers.

The idea of a paper of this kind had been suggested in a pamphlet issued by the keepers of the coffee-houses about the end of 1728—*The Case of the Coffee-Men of London and Westminster; or, an Account of the Impositions and Abuses put upon them and the whole Town, by the present Set of News-Writers.* They complained that they were used as tools in the business of advertisement. 'The *Coffee-Men*', they said, 'are the Persons who do the Business of the *Advertisers*. The Coffee-Men are They who *circulate* Advertisements, and direct them to their proper Ends. The *Coffee-Men* pass them from Hand to Hand, and make them known to the whole Town. And if the Coffee-Houses were to be shut up . . . what would become of *Advertisements*?' They therefore argued, inconclusively, that they were the only persons who deserved to reap the profits of the advertisements, and they proposed to set up two daily papers of their own, giving advertisements and the news of the town, of which they regarded themselves as a central agency; and these two papers, to be published in the morning and evening, would be the only papers to be seen in the coffee-houses. Even if the scheme had been workable, it could easily have been countered; but what the coffee-men said stands in obvious relation to what *The Daily Advertiser* was to say in its early numbers:

> And whereas by reason of the great Number of News-Papers daily Printed, and that few Persons Advertise in more than some one of them, and that none except the most eminent Coffee-Houses take in all the Daily Printed Papers, and that few Gentlemen or Others who frequent those Houses, read every Paper there taken in, the Advertisement remains unknown to great Numbers of Persons, to the Prejudice and Inconvenience of the Advertiser. It is apprehended that the Publication made by this Paper will be very general and useful, all the Advertisements being collected together, every Person may readily find out whatever can properly fall under the Denomination of an Advertisement, without having recourse to any other Paper.

This is the idea of the coffee-men made to work.

The Daily Advertiser at an early stage added 'the best and freshest accounts of all occurrences foreign and domestic', and occasionally included letters. It printed, for instance, some of George Whitefield's letters from America. At a later date it is said to have had 'the best Foreign Intelligence before the French Revolution'.[1] But it always remained true to its title. As a rule at least three-quarters of the paper consisted of advertisements; in the number for January 5, 1756, and in many other numbers, they occupy eleven of the twelve columns. It was the definitely commercial paper of Johnson's time, circulating in business houses and clubs and taverns, but little in private households. John Nichols speaks of it as 'a paper which for many years stood at the head of all the diurnal publications', and adds that property in it 'was considered to be as permanent as a freehold estate, shares having been frequently sold by public auction as regularly as those of the New River Company'.[2]

With the success of *The Daily Advertiser* there came a steady increase of advertisements in the papers in general. A good illustration is given by *The Champion*. It had begun as a folio of two pages or six columns, but with its sixty-fourth number (April 10, 1740) it became a quarto of twelve columns, appeared in the evening instead of the morning, and altered its sub-title from 'British Mercury' to 'Evening Advertiser'. The only reason given for these changes was

[1] Daniel Stuart, in *The Gentleman's Magazine*, New Series, vol. x, July 1838, p. 25.

[2] *Literary Anecdotes*, vol. i, p. 290.

IF NEWS-PAPERS, are only calculated to *kill Time*, the present Set will answer that End very effectually. But, if to *inform*, or even to *entertain* is the Tenure of their Charter, a *new One* is absolutely necessary to save it from being forfeited beyond Redemption.

On this Presumption, this Paper was, a few Months ago, set up; which had, at least, something of Novelty, if no more, to recommend it. But, having a vigorous *Opposition* on all Hands to struggle with: (*Booksellers*, who were Sharers in the Profit of other News-Papers; *Coffee-men*, who thought they were encumbred with too many already; *Place-men*, because it made War on their Patron; *Patriot-writers*, because it might possibly interfere with their own; and *Hawkers* in Fee with them all) it made its Way but slowly, nay was actually given out for *Dead*, long ago.

And no sooner was it received with Approbation by some, and Indulgence by all unprejudiced Readers, but the * *Craftsman*, LONDON EVENING POST, &c. and many of the *Country Papers* began to enrich themselves with its Spoils; which (tho' their Sanction may be no Proof of its Merit) argued, at least, that it was not *unacceptable* to the Publick.

Rather, therefore, than give Way to such *Piracies* any longer, it has been thought expedient to alter the *Time* of publishing this Paper, called the CHAMPION, from *Tuesday*, *Thursday* and *Saturday* Mornings, to the EVENINGS of the same Days, when it will be punctually sent to such publick or private Houses, as shall order it in, by

J. GRAHAM, under the *Inner Temple-Gate*, opposite *Chancery Lane*, in *Fleet street*, where Advertisements and Letters for the AUTHOR are taken in.

It will contain, as before,

I An ESSAY on the *Manners* or *Politicks* of the Times

II. Frequently, new Articles of Intelligence.

III. The News of Two Days, Foreign and Domestick, stated and digested in a peculiar Manner.

IV Extracts from, or Remarks upon such Books, Poems, Pamphlets, &c. as are worthy the Notice of the Publick.

* *In the* Craftsman *of last* Saturday, *no less than ten Paragraphs were taken* verbatim *from the* Champion; *besides the* remarkable *one in* Mourning.

From *The Champion*, April 10, 1740.

that other papers—*The Craftsman, The London Evening Post,* and many of the country papers—had been taking too much from it, and that the later hour of publication would prevent such piracies. The writer of the *Historical View of the Political Writers* had another explanation: it was not able, he said, to 'hold up its head' as a morning paper and so 'was changed into an evening paper, in which shape it has had some success, and gained over some of the lower class of readers'. Both explanations may be sound, so far as they go; but the fortunes of the paper were probably more affected by the change indicated in the new sub-title. Whereas in the original form advertisements were few, in the new form they occupied generally more than five columns.

Other 'advertisers' followed, and appealed to more than the business community. *The London Daily Post and General Advertiser,* which came from the press of Henry Woodfall from November 4, 1734, and shortened its name to *The General Advertiser* in March 1744, gave a large portion of its advertisements to the theatre. One of its columns was regularly occupied during the London season by the play-bills of Drury Lane and Covent Garden and other places of entertainment, and, with the loss of the original play-bills, has become invaluable as a record for the dramatic history of the time. There we learn how Garrick, when he decided to prolong the run of Johnson's *Irene* to the ninth performance, provided on the seventh and eighth nights 'entertainments of dancing, particularly the Scotch dance', and on the ninth 'the Savoyard dance'. A long letter about *Irene,* though it reads suspiciously like an advertisement by Garrick, gives us our earliest criticism of the play. *The General Advertiser* was an important paper when it took over the goodwill of *The Covent Garden Journal* and became on December 1, 1752, *The Public Advertiser.* On taking leave of his readers, Fielding recommended the new paper as one which he had 'some reasons to think will deserve their encouragement better than any which hath yet been published'. Under Henry Woodfall's elder son, Henry Sampson Woodfall, who assumed the editorship in 1758 at the age of nineteen, *The Public Advertiser* was to become one of the great papers of the century. In it were published the Letters of Junius—and 'John Gilpin'.

Another 'advertiser' which appeared daily was *The*

Gazetteer. It developed out of Walpole's *Gazetteer*, becoming in turn *The Daily Gazetteer or London Advertiser*, *The London Gazetteer* (1748), *The Gazetteer and London Daily Advertiser* (1755), and finally *The Gazetteer and New Daily Advertiser* (1764). Its first column was likewise reserved for the play-bills, and in other ways it resembled *The Public Advertiser*, of which it was a serious rival. It is said to have had a steady circulation in the city. Johnson contributed to it in 1759 three letters on the design for Blackfriars Bridge.

These were the chief daily papers of the 'fifties, and they all survived to the 'nineties, when others had arisen to outdo and incorporate them. Each was an 'advertiser'. The word was admitted to Johnson's *Dictionary* in 1755 and defined as 'the paper in which advertisements are published'. It had been brought into fashion by *The Daily Advertiser*, and was used in the titles of more papers than were successful. With only unimportant exceptions, an 'advertiser' was a morning paper.[1]

In addition to these three morning papers there were in London at the beginning of 1757 several evening papers (notably *The Whitehall Evening Post*, *The London Evening Post*, and *The General Evening Post*), as well as several weekly papers and the official *London Gazette*, when Robert Dodsley took a main part in setting up *The London Chronicle, or Universal Evening Post*. Like the other evening papers it came out thrice a week, but it was a paper of a new kind. It was novel in form with its eight quarto pages, and novel in title, for it is the first of our 'chronicles'. No less notable is the absence of advertisements, and, though they gradually crept in, they seldom occupied as much as five of its twenty-four columns. *The London Chronicle* set out to succeed by giving trustworthy news and reasonable comments with little or no political bias, and including nothing that was exceptionable in tone. It was, as a recent writer has called it, 'a family paper', and the first newspaper that deserves the name; and to the end, among papers of greater brilliance, it preserved its reputation of being safe, if sometimes dull. Its

[1] Another 'advertiser' which, on the evidence of the advertisement duty, succeeded beyond what we should have thought possible was *The Penny London Post*. Larger sums are entered as paid by it than by any other two papers together in 1757, 1758, 1759, and 1760. What is equally suspicious is that the same sum is entered to it for each of these years. We surmise that these entries cover payments from several sources.

policy must have been discussed by Johnson before he undertook, on behalf of Dodsley and the other partners, to write the opening article describing 'the importance of their design, the extent of their plan, and the accuracy of the method which they intend to prosecute'. This article was Johnson's earliest acknowledged contribution to a London newspaper, and the earliest that has been identified. He justified the new venture by the faults which he found in contemporary journalism—its stubborn adherence to statement and opinion whether right or wrong, its falsehood and slander, its alliance of faction and fiction.

> We pretend to no peculiar Power of disentangling Contradiction, or denuding Forgery. We have no settled Correspondence with the Antipodes, nor maintain any Spies in the Cabinets of Princes. But as we shall always be conscious that our Mistakes are involuntary, we shall watch the gradual Discoveries of Time, and retract whatever we have hastily and erroneously advanced.

Of more interest to the ordinary man were the ordinary affairs of daily life, and to these the new paper would give due attention:

> The Accounts of Prices of Corn and Stocks are to most of our Readers of more Importance than Narratives of greater Sound, and as Exactness is here within the reach of Diligence, our Readers may justly require it from us.

Likewise there would be notices of Deaths, Marriages, and Preferments. And thus far Johnson had said nothing that might not have served equally well as the introduction of many another paper. The section of *The London Chronicle* which was to distinguish it from all other newspapers was 'the Literary Journal, or Account of the Labours and Productions of the Learned'. Reviews of books were to be regularly included, impartial reviews, avoiding petulance and the cruelties of criticism, and telling 'rather what our authors have attempted than what they have performed'. Another distinction was that attention would be paid to style. In the narratives of the daily writers every reader 'perceives somewhat of neatness and purity wanting', an unavoidable fault so long as the journalist must write in haste; 'some improvements however we hope to make'.

Taken as a whole, and with allowance for its introductory purpose, the article gives us a clear view of English journalism

No 1

The London Chronicle:

OR,

UNIVERSAL EVENING POST.

To be continued every TUESDAY, THURSDAY, and SATURDAY.

SATURDAY, JANUARY 1, 1757.

I T has been always lamented, that of the little Time allotted to Man, much muſt be ſpent upon Superfluities. Every Proſpect has its Obſtructions, which we muſt break to enlarge our View: Every Step of our Progreſs finds Impediments, which, however eager to go forward, we muſt ſtop to remove. Even thoſe who profeſs to teach the Way to Happineſs have multiplied our Incumbrances, and the Author of almoſt every Book retards his Inſtructions by a Preface.

The Writers of the *Chronicle* hope to be eaſily forgiven, though they ſhould not be free from an Infection that has ſeized the whole Fraternity; and, inſtead of falling immediately to their Subjects, ſhould detain the Reader for a Time with an Account of the Importance of their Deſign, the Extent of their Plan, and the Accuracy of the Method which they intend to proſecute. Such Premonitions, though not always neceſſary when the Reader has the Book complete in his Hand, and may find by his own Eyes whatever can be found in it, yet may be more eaſily allowed to Works publiſhed gradually in ſucceſſive Parts; of which the Scheme can only be ſo far known as the Author ſhall think fit to diſcover it.

The Paper which we now invite the Publick to add to the Papers with which it is already rather wearied than ſatisfied, conſiſts of many Parts; ſome of which it has in common with other periodical Sheets, and ſome peculiar to itſelf.

The firſt Demand made by the Reader of a Journal is, that he ſhould find an accurate Account of foreign Tranſactions and domeſtick Incidents. This is always expected; but this is very rarely performed. Of thoſe Writers who have taken upon themſelves the Taſk of Intelligence, ſome have given, and others have ſold their Abilities, whether ſmall or great, to one or other of the Parties that divide us; and without a Wiſh for Truth, or Thought of Decency, without Care of any other Reputation than that of a ſtubborn Adherence to their Abettors, carry on the ſame Tenor of Repreſentation through all the Viciſſitudes of Right and Wrong, neither depreſſed by Detection, nor abaſhed by Confutation; proud of the hourly Encreaſe of Infamy, and ready to boaſt of all the Contumelies that Falſehood and Slander may bring upon them, as new Proofs of their Zeal and Fidelity.

With theſe Heroes we have no Ambition to be numbered; we leave to the Confeſſors of Faction the Merit of their Sufferings, and are deſirous to ſhelter ourſelves under the Protection of Truth. That all our Facts will be authentick, or all our Remarks juſt, we dare not venture to promiſe: We can relate but what we hear, we can point out but what we ſee. Of remote Tranſactions the firſt Accounts are always confuſed, and commonly exaggerated; and in domeſtick Affairs, if the Power to conceal is leſs, the Intereſt to miſrepreſent is often greater; and what is ſufficiently vexatious, Truth ſeems to fly from Curioſity; and as many Enquirers produce many Narratives, whatever engages the publick Attention is immediately diſguiſed by the Embelliſhments of Fiction. We pretend to no peculiar Power of diſentangling Contradiction, or denuding Forgery. We have no ſettled Correſpondence with the Antipodes, nor maintain any Spies in the Cabinets of Princes. But as we ſhall always be conſcious that our Miſtakes are involuntary, we ſhall watch the gradual Diſcoveries of Time, and retract whatever we have haſtily and erroneouſly advanced.

In the Narratives of the daily Writers every Reader perceives ſomewhat of Neatneſs and Purity wanting, which at the firſt View it ſeems eaſy to ſupply: But it muſt be conſidered, that thoſe Paſſages muſt be written in Haſte, and that there is often no other Choice, but that they muſt want either Novelty or Accuracy; and that as Life is very uniform, the Affairs of one Week are ſo like thoſe of another, that, by any Attempt after Variety of Expreſſion, Invention would ſoon be wearied, and Language exhauſted. Some Improvements however we hope to make; and for the reſt we think, that when we commit only common Faults, we ſhall not be excluded from common Indulgence.

The Accounts of Prices of Corn and Stocks, are to moſt of our Readers of more Importance than Narratives of greater Sound, and as Exactneſs is here within the Reach of Diligence, our Readers may juſtly require it from us.

Memorials of a private and perſonal Kind, which relate Deaths, Marriages, and Preferments, muſt always be imperfect by Omiſſion, and often erroneous by Miſinformation; but, even in theſe, there ſhall not be wanting Care to avoid Miſtakes, or to rectify them whenever they ſhall be found.

That Part of our Work by which it is diſtinguiſhed from all others, is the *Literary Journal*, or Account of the Labours and Productions of the *Learned*. This was, for a long Time, among the Deficiencies of Engliſh Literature, but as the Caprice of Man is always ſtarting from too little to too much, we have now, amongſt other Diſturbers of human Quiet, a numerous Body of *Reviewers* and *Remarkers*.

Every Art is improved by the Emulation of Competitors; thoſe who make no Advances towards Excellence, may ſtand as Warnings againſt Faults. We ſhall endeavour to avoid that Petulance which treats with Contempt whatever has hitherto been reputed ſacred. We ſhall repreſs that Elation of Malignity, which wantons in the Cruelties of Criticiſm, and not only murders Reputation, but murders it by Torture. Whenever we feel ourſelves ignorant, we ſhall, at leaſt, be modeſt. Our Intention is not to preoccupy Judgment by Praiſe or Cenſure, but to gratify Curioſity by early Intelligence, and to tell rather what our Authors have attempted, than what they have performed. The Titles of Books are neceſſarily ſhort, and therefore diſcloſe but imperfectly the Contents; they are ſometimes fraudulent, and intended to raiſe falſe Expectations. In our Account this Brevity will be extended, and theſe Frauds, whenever they are detected, will be expoſed; for though we write without Intention to injure, we ſhall not ſuffer ourſelves to be made Parties to Deceit.

If any Author ſhall tranſmit a Summary of his Work, we ſhall willingly receive it; if any literary Anecdote, or curious Obſervation, ſhall be communicated to us, we will carefully inſert it. Many Facts are known and forgotten; many Obſervations are made and ſuppreſſed; and Entertainment and Inſtruction are frequently loſt, for Want of a Repoſitory in which they may be conveniently preſerved.

No Man can modeſtly promiſe what he cannot aſcertain. We hope for the Praiſe of Knowledge and Diſcernment, but we claim only that of Diligence and Candour.

[Price Two Pence.]

The first number of *The London Chronicle*, with Johnson's introductory article.

as Johnson saw it. He returned to its deficiencies in two essays in *The Idler* (Nos. 7 and 30), and they and the article complete and illustrate each other. In his account of the proposed 'Literary Journal' he repeated at greater length what he had said in the previous year in his introduction to *The Literary Magazine*, and wrote with expectant satisfaction. He was pursuing his consistent policy of spreading the knowledge of letters and raising the status of the literary profession. It was no novelty for a periodical to give accounts of books; but it was a novelty that they should form a regular section of a popular newspaper. In all probability Johnson suggested this section; at the least he sponsored it.

In neglect of the promise to avoid invective and personal abuse *The London Chronicle* reprinted passages of violent controversy from *The Test* and *The Con-Test*, and Robert Dodsley felt compelled to withdraw, still believing that this family paper would 'succeed prodigiously' if the plan, which was 'universally approved of', were strictly followed. But before the editor and publisher of the *Collection of Old Plays* resigned his partnership, a new section had been introduced called 'The Theatre', with accounts of the performances at Drury Lane and Covent Garden. It was a novelty of the same kind as the accounts of books; there had been much about the drama in the periodicals, and there had been a periodical devoted mainly to the drama—*The Prompter* (1734–6)—but now a newspaper provided a regular and numbered series of dramatic criticisms. At a time when there was little to say of theatrical matters 'The Theatre' (No. 33) consisted of Johnson's Proposals for his edition of Shakespeare. 'I once printed them at length in the Chronicle', he said, so showing, not that he had any control in the paper, but that his interest in it remained active. He called it familiarly 'The Chronicle'. According to Boswell, it was the only newspaper he constantly saw; according to Percy, the proprietors always sent it to him gratis as long as he lived. It contains his few known contributions to the newspapers after 1760, the last of them being the character of the Rev. Zachariah Mudge in 1769.

Boswell tells us that *The London Chronicle* had a more extensive circulation on the Continent than any other English paper, and ascribes to it the qualities at which it had always aimed when he adds that 'it has all along been distinguished for good sense, accuracy, moderation, and delicacy'. It was losing ground when Boswell wrote these words. But its success had been so immediate that *Lloyd's Evening Post and British Chronicle* was started in imitation of it in July 1757, and the two papers came out on alternate evenings in friendly rivalry.

'Chronicles' became the fashion as 'advertisers' had been. *The Universal Chronicle or Weekly Gazette* (afterwards called *Payne's Universal Chronicle*) and the *New Weekly Chronicle or Universal Journal* (afterwards called *Owen's Weekly Chronicle*), both weekly papers, started on the same day in April 1758, and, as if by arrangement, adopted their more distinctive titles before the end of the month; and *The St. James's Chronicle or British Evening Post,* which came out thrice a week, followed in March 1761. The first of these is best known now as the newspaper to which Johnson contributed *The Idler,* thereby providing the most notable instance—but by no means the first—of the attempt to establish a newspaper by including in it a periodical essay. *The Idler* began in the second number and was printed in spaced type on the front page every Saturday for two years. When it ceased in April 1760 *The Universal Chronicle* had been merged with the old *Westminster Journal.* To use Johnson's words when concluding *The Rambler,* he had supported the anxious employment of a periodical writer till he had multiplied his essays to make two volumes when reprinted by themselves; and they had not stayed the decline of the newspaper. By contrast, *The St. James's Chronicle*—the first of the 'chronicles' to be published as a 'folio of four pages'—was soon to be established as one of the leading newspapers of its time.

None of these 'chronicles' was a daily paper. The only daily paper founded at this time was *The Public Ledger,* and it at once became important. As the title suggested, and as the sub-title stated, it was a 'Register of Commerce and Intelligence'—and of Commerce first. An early correspondent called it 'the new mercantile daily paper'. In its origin it had some resemblance to *The Daily Advertiser.* Besides printing its own advertisements it gave abstracts of advertisements in other papers:

Experience, therefore, has long shewn, that there is yet wanting a Paper which may serve as an *Index* to all other Papers and

Publications, and which will supply the Deficiencies of each from all the rest, yet not render any of them useless; as, instead of giving the full Account required, it will only shew the Paper or Place in which the Advertisement or Public Notice may be found.

All advertisements were to be seen at 'the Register-Office next the Great Toy-Shop in St. Paul's Church-Yard', and there 'every Enquirer, on paying *Three-pence* for searching the Office, may find whatever he can require, or be convinced that he requires what is no where to be found'. Further information was also to be obtained there about advertisements inserted directly in this paper; 'every Advertisement inserted in the Public Ledger shall be also registered in the Office . . . so that by advertising in this paper he that desires to conceal any part of his proposal from the public eye may insert a short hint in the paper'. It was thus primarily a commercial organ; but it undertook to be as good as any other paper in foreign and domestic news, and not to reject any political essays that appeared to be calculated for the public good. Nor would it exclude 'criticism or literature'. Goldsmith was employed regularly on it in 1760 and 1761, and wrote for it more than his Chinese Letters. To most students of English literature *The Public Ledger* calls up a picture of Goldsmith's early struggles, but it won its place by its appeal to the world of business; and as a paper devoted exclusively to trade it survives to this day.

With the accession of George III and the administration of Bute, politics regained the prominence which they had lost with the fall of Walpole. As if with a premonition of the coming troubles, *The Monitor, or British Freeholder* had begun in 1755 with the purpose of emancipating the King from an arbitrary administration and exposing the arts by which Ministers encroach on the power of the people; and it continued to pursue its purpose so energetically when George was on the throne that a paper was set up by the Court, on May 29, 1762, 'to pluck the mask of patriotism from the front of faction'. The King had said in his first speech to Parliament that he gloried 'in the name of Briton',[1] and the

[1] 'I glory in the Name of Briton' in the official version of the King's Speech as printed in the *Journals of the House of Lords*; but what George III had written with his own hand, in the paragraph which he inserted in this speech, was: 'I glory in the Name of Britain.' For a reproduction of this passage, now in the British Museum, see Turberville, *English Men and Manners in the Eighteenth Century*, p. 42.

new paper was therefore called *The Briton*. It was written by Smollett, and in turn called forth, on June 5, 1762, *The North Briton* by John Wilkes, who had the support of his friend Churchill the satirist. 'I will exert', said Wilkes, 'the undoubted privilege of every North Briton, that of speaking my opinion freely on every subject that concerns the community, of which I am a member. One thing I mean to be very careful in, and that is to write *good English*, both the language and the sentiments. Though I am a North Briton, I will endeavour to avoid the numerous *Scoticisms* the Briton abounds with; and then, as the world is apt to mistake, he may be taken for a *Scotchman*, and I for an *Englishman*.' *The Auditor*, written by Arthur Murphy in defence of the Government, followed on June 10. None of these four papers—which all appeared weekly—was a newspaper. They are better described as periodical essays devoted to politics. But by the feelings which they aroused, and in particular by the prosecution of Wilkes for the famous 45th number of *The North Briton* of April 23, 1763, they were to advance the cause of the liberty of the Press.

The North Briton was carried on for some years after Wilkes's imprisonment. *The Monitor* lived longest of the other papers of this group, and when it ceased in 1765 politics found adequate room in the newspapers. But nothing of outstanding importance happened till 1769, when two new newspapers were founded, *The Middlesex Journal* and *The Morning Chronicle*, and when the first of the Letters of Junius appeared in *The Public Advertiser*. There is no convincing evidence that the writer of these Letters had written under other names before he assumed the name of Junius, though he cannot be mistaken for a novice. Who he was remains the best preserved secret in the history of English journalism. The strongest candidate for an honour which every one refused is still Sir Philip Francis. That the secret should have been so well preserved is the more remarkable as the Letters were spread over three years (from January 1769 to January 1772), and in their invective and general mastery of rhetorical device were the most effective political contributions to any newspaper of the century.

The Middlesex Journal was the direct outcome of these 'present discontents'. It began on April 4, 1769, at the height of the trouble over the Middlesex election, when

Wilkes having been chosen thrice by the county, and as often either expelled from the House or declared incapable of sitting, was about to be elected a fourth time, and it took its name with an obvious purpose. It called itself in the sub-title the 'Chronicle of Liberty', and was the most definitely partisan of the newspapers at this time. Designed for an occasion, it widened its interests as the occasion passed and assumed the simpler sub-title of 'Evening Advertiser' about the same time as it professed to be a 'singularly entertaining paper'. The most obvious advance which it made in journalism was to include once a week 'a Piece of Music consisting either of a Song, Catch, Glee, or Minuet'. Music had for many years been printed in *The Gentleman's Magazine*, and as early as 1692 had been one of the striking features of *The Gentleman's Journal*, but it had never before been 'attempted in a newspaper'. In the more bellicose days of *The Middlesex Journal*, Chatterton, while still at Bristol, sent up two letters in crude imitation of Junius, and continued to write for it when he came to London, hoping to make a livelihood by occasional essays for the Press.

The Morning Chronicle began more quietly, but of all the papers founded before 1770 it was in after years to attain to the greatest eminence, and for a great part of the nineteenth century to be the chief rival of *The Times* when its more noisy or more prosperous contemporaries of Johnson's day had ceased. Its first great editor was William Woodfall, younger brother of Henry Sampson Woodfall of *The Public Advertiser*. He was one of the proprietors, as well as printer and publisher, when it was founded in June 1769; but he did not settle down to journalism till his return from a dramatic tour in Scotland, when he was engaged as editor of *The London Packet, or New Lloyd's Evening Post*.[1] Of this paper—which began as *The London Packet* (simply) in October 1769[2] —he became also the publisher about the beginning of May 1773, so that he was at once the editor and publisher of this evening paper and printer and publisher of *The Morning Chronicle*. But he was soon thereafter called to the editorship of *The Morning Chronicle*, and to it he gave the best of his

[1] See Nichols, *Literary Anecdotes*, vol. i, p. 303.

[2] It was *The London Packet* from Oct. 1769 to Feb. 1771; then *The London Packet, or New Evening Post*; and then *The London Packet, or New Lloyd's Evening Post* from April 17, 1772. It was 'printed for T. Evans' till April 1773.

energies till 1789, when the interference of the other proprietors caused him to resign and to found a new paper under the name of *The Diary*. He had made the reputation of *The Morning Chronicle* by its parliamentary reports and its dramatic criticisms, both of which he contributed. An editor in those days depended largely on correspondents for the political articles, which were usually sent in as letters 'To the Printer'. The Letters of Junius need not be taken to have expressed the views of the editor of *The Public Advertiser*; but the political colour of any paper was given by the opinions which were stated, sometimes with considerable variety, in the letters which were accepted, as much as by editorial paragraphs. *The Morning Chronicle* did not go to extremes, and had the reputation of avoiding 'that daring scandal, scurrility, and frivolous levity too characteristic of the public prints'. William Woodfall did not forget that it was a 'chronicle', and set store by the fullness and accuracy of his parliamentary reports. He was the greatest reporter of his day.

The fight for the liberty of reporting had gone on intermittently throughout the whole century, and only towards the end of the century can we be certain about the actual words of any speaker—unless we know that the speaker himself provided the printer with them, and even then what he wrote may not be what he uttered. In the reign of Queen Anne, reports began to appear in Abel Boyer's *Political State of Great Britain* (1711–37), but though they may be trusted for the general lines of the debate, and the tenor of the chief speeches, they sometimes combine two, if not more, speeches into one; and this is true also of the reports in *The Historical Register* (1716–38). Parliament would grant no facilities. In 1722 the House of Commons resolved 'that no newswriters do presume . . . to intermeddle with the debates or other proceedings of the House'. The intermeddling continued, and in 1738 the Speaker, Arthur Onslow, declared that newspaper reports 'a little reflected on the dignity of the House', and opened a discussion in which all agreed with him. One speaker said—but we cannot be sure of his words—that 'you will have every word that is spoken here by gentlemen misrepresented by fellows who thrust themselves into our gallery; you will have the speeches of this House printed every day, and we shall be looked upon as the most contemptible assembly on the face of the earth'. To the same effect Pulteney argued that 'to print and publish the speeches of gentlemen in this House, even though they were not misrepresented, looks very like making them accountable without doors for what they say within'. Thereupon the Commons resolved that 'it is a high indignity to and a notorious breach of the Privilege of this House, for any News-Writer, in Letters, or other Papers (as Minutes, or under any other denomination), or for any Printer or Publisher of any printed News-paper of any denomination, to presume to insert in the said Letters or Papers, or to give therein any account of the Debates or other Proceedings, of this House, or any Committee thereof, as well during the Recess, as the Sitting of Parliament; and that this House will proceeed with the utmost severity against such offenders'. This comprehensive resolution of April 13, 1738, put the printers and publishers to their shifts to continue their reports. *The London Magazine* at once, in its May number, had recourse to a Political Club purporting to be composed of young nobles and gentlemen who agreed to speak and argue as much as possible in the style and manner of Parliament on questions before Parliament, and who, though they were given Roman names, were understood, or even stated, to speak 'in the character' of members of either House. In June, *The Gentleman's Magazine* adopted the disguise of 'Debates in the Senate of Magna Lilliputia', with this explanation: 'we doubt not but our Readers will be much pleased with an Appendix to Capt. Gulliver's Account, which we received last Month, and which the late Resolution of the House of Commons, whereby we are forbidden to insert any Account of the Proceedings of the *British Parliament*, gives us an opportunity of communicating in their Room.' The names were transmuted to the Gulliverian fashion, Walpole becoming 'Walelop' and Pulteney 'Pulnub', while the Lords were 'Hurgoes' and the Commons 'Clinabs'—as was fully explained in the magazine by way of advertisements of a book of anagrams. Both devices succeeded in so far as the Houses took no action. From the first *The Gentleman's Magazine* had the advantage in enjoying the services of Johnson, whose hand is evident in the explanation of the Lilliputian disguise. He began by editing what William Guthrie supplied, but he wrote the speeches from November 1740 to February

1743. He is better described as their composer than their reporter, for he was only once in the gallery of the House. He wrote up the speeches from notes which had been brought to him, and he said that he never again wrote 'with equal velocity'. Some of the debates he admitted to be 'the mere coinage of his imagination'. The British Senate never maintained a higher standard of eloquence. But he can be checked by the less elevated accounts in *The London Magazine*, which were generally much more punctual in their appearance. On the evidence of *The Gentleman's Magazine*, the interest in parliamentary reports slowly dwindled. Lilliput disappeared in 1746, and thereafter such reports as were given were only occasional.[1] But *The London Magazine* continued its Political Club till August 1757, and then gave monthly a 'History of the last Session of Parliament'. It is our chief authority for the debates in the latter half of the reign of George II.

Meantime little had appeared in the newspapers about the proceedings of Parliament, nor was much to appear for the next ten years. In the political troubles of the early reign of George III, the Government was more concerned with letters than with reports, with libels than with breaches of privilege, and as the troubles became more acute the newspapers took courage. The crisis came in 1771, and the credit of forcing it belongs in the main to John Almon. Believing that the country ought to know what Parliament was doing, he secured notes of each day's debate, and worked them into one or two paragraphs for his paper, *The London Evening Post*. His example was at once followed, and in February and March 1771 the House of Commons took action against the printers of eight papers—*The Gazetteer, The Middlesex Journal, The Morning Chronicle, The London Packet, The St. James's Journal, The Whitehall Evening Post, The London Evening Post*, and *The General Evening Post*. Their prosecution, which makes a complicated story, ended in failure. The right of printing parliamentary reports was silently conceded. No express leave was given, nor has ever been given; nor has

[1] The methods of procuring their Parliamentary reports were described by Edward Cave of *The Gentleman's Magazine* and Thomas Astley of *The London Magazine* when they were examined by the House of Commons on April 10, 1747, for reporting the trial of Lord Lovat. See *Parliamentary History*, vol. xiv. 57–61.

the resolution which declared them to be a breach of privilege ever been rescinded.

In the consequent advance of reporting, the lead was taken by *The Morning Chronicle* under William Woodfall, who employed his remarkable memory in work which a great editor would be expected to depute to junior members of his staff. How big his staff was we do not know, and of the inside of any newspaper-office in those days we have still much to learn; but his assistants must have been far outnumbered by his printers, and the foremen printers may have had editorial duties. While controlling his paper in all its departments—he was at once editor, printer, and publisher—he appears to have written more for it than any one else. The parliamentary reports were wholly his own. 'Without taking a note to assist his memory, without the use of an amanuensis to ease his labour, he has been known to write sixteen columns after having sat in a crowded gallery for as many hours without an interval of rest': so says his friend John Nichols in the obituary notice written for *The Gentleman's Magazine* for August 1803 and reprinted in *Literary Anecdotes*. Another friend, John Taylor, tells us that 'his practice in the House of Commons during a debate was to close his eyes, and to lean with both hands on his stick', and that 'he was so well acquainted with the tone and manner of the several speakers that he only deviated from his customary posture when a new member addressed the house, and having heard his name, he had no subsequent occasion for further enquiry'.[1] He gave his *Morning Chronicle* a pre-eminence which the other newspapers could challenge only by resorting to relays of reporters. The strain told in time and he had to yield, but not before he had abandoned *The Morning Chronicle* for *The Diary*, and that was after Johnson's day. His fame spread beyond London as a prodigy of memory, and he has a strong claim to be considered the most gifted reporter in the whole history of the English Press. When Boswell wrote about the reports of Johnson's friend, William Guthrie, and qualified his praise by adding that Guthrie had been 'surpassed by others who have since followed him in the same department', he was thinking of 'Memory Woodfall'.

But 'Memory Woodfall', who had acted on the Scottish stage, never willingly lost a first night at Drury Lane or

[1] *Records of my Life* (1832), vol. ii, p. 245.

Covent Garden, and *The Morning Chronicle* under his editorship is a good hunting-ground for information about the drama in these days. His accounts of new plays and entertainments preserve many details that would have been forgotten. It is *The Morning Chronicle,* for instance, which tells us that 'The British Grenadiers' was sung in 'the new pantomime of "Harlequin Everywhere"' at Covent Garden on January 17, 1780, and received as a novelty.[1]

The Morning Post began with less interest in Parliament and politics than in commerce, and had at first the sub-title 'And Daily Advertising Pamphlet', which after the thirteenth number was changed to 'or Cheap Daily Advertiser'. Founded on November 2, 1772, it appears to have been designed by a group of business men to include their own advertisements. But its first editor, Henry Bate,[2] the fighting parson, conducted it with a 'sportive severity' in keeping with his reputation in private life, and in marked contrast to the somewhat staid and responsible manner of *The Morning Chronicle.* Johnson condemned him, despite his politics. When Boswell praised this 'clergyman of extraordinary character' for 'exerting his talents in writing on temporary topics and displaying uncommon intrepidity', and maintained that merit of any sort was entitled to reward, the great moralist while admitting his courage would not allow him to have merit. Bate had to give up his editorship in 1780, and by that time *The Morning Post* was well established. It had begun with an abnormally large circulation. The earliest number now known, that of November 5, 1772,[3] tells us that the demand had exceeded the ordinary capacity of the printing-house, and that special arrangements had been made for an impression of 6,000. For reasons already stated, this figure must be regarded as exceptional; we have also seen that the sale was to fall seriously before it was raised again by a greater editor, Daniel Stuart.

In opposition to *The Morning Post* Bate started on November 1, 1780, *The Morning Herald, and Daily Advertiser,* and conducted it more seriously. It was to become the organ of the Carlton House circle, and was the last important daily paper to be founded in Johnson's lifetime.

[1] The words are older. [2] Afterwards Sir Henry Bate Dudley.

[3] The front-page of this number (No. 4) is reproduced in *The Morning Post* for March 14, 1933.

The Morning Chronicle had set a new fashion by including the word 'Morning' in the title. These three morning papers were all to have distinguished careers in the nineteenth century. *The Morning Chronicle* survived till 1862, and *The Morning Herald* (our first 'Herald') till 1869. *The General Advertiser and Morning Intelligencer*, founded in 1776, was very successful for some years as an 'advertiser', but appears not to have been otherwise distinguished during its brief career. Of all the London newspapers known to Johnson, only *The Public Ledger* and *The Morning Post* have come down to us, and only *The Morning Post* remains a newspaper.

These, then, were the chief London papers which were published daily towards the close of Johnson's life—*The Daily Advertiser* (a business paper with good foreign news, and an excellent property); *The Public Advertiser* (for long the leading Whig paper); *The Gazetteer* (a favourite in the city); *The Public Ledger* (by this time circulating chiefly 'below bridge, among the shipping'); *The Morning Chronicle* (a moderate Whig paper, with the best parliamentary reports and good dramatic news); *The Morning Post* (high-spirited and Tory); and *The Morning Herald*. The evening papers are conveniently set out in a news-agent's advertisement in *The London Chronicle* of June 3–5, 1777 (here reproduced), as *The St. James's Chronicle, The London Chronicle, The Middlesex Journal, The London Packet, The London Evening Post, The General Evening Post, The Whitehall Evening Post,* and *Lloyd's Evening Post*; and when to this list is added a ninth, *The English Chronicle,* founded in January 1779, we have the names of all the important evening papers of the later years of Johnson's London.

All these evening papers came out thrice a week. The first successful evening papers to appear daily were *The Star* (1788) and *The Sun* (1792).[1] As the older morning papers declined, others arose to take their place or to unite with them; neither *The Daily Advertiser*, nor *The Public Advertiser*, nor *The Gazetteer* outlived the century independently. *The Times* began modestly in 1785 and competed with *The World* (1787), *The Diary* (1789), and *The Oracle* (1789). These were years of steady rather than striking development in English journalism, and the general impression to be now derived

[1] *Robinson Crusoe's London Daily Evening Post* had a short run towards the end of 1742.

from the newspapers of this time is one of increasing vigour and liveliness acting competently within a somewhat narrow range. There were notable typographical improvements, but, as has been seen, far-reaching changes were to depend on new

LONDON NEWS-PAPERS, ſent to perſons reſiding in the country; free of poſtage, and in the neateſt and moſt punctual manner, at the under-mentioned fair price, viz.

EVENING PAPERS,
Three Times a Week.

St. James's Chronicle	London Evening Poſt
London ditto	General ditto
Middleſex Journal	Whitehall ditto
London Packet	Lloyd's ditto

Thirty-nine Shillings per Annum.

Daily Advertiſer, 3 l. 5 s. The other Daily Papers, 3 l. 18 s. (3 d. per Number, and the Daily Advertiſer only 2 ½ d.)

By JOHN WHORWOOD, No. 13, Bull and Mouth-ſtreet.

At the above eaſy rate, ready money to be paid for the year.

On credit, my terms are, per annum.

	l.	s.	d.	
The Daily Advertiſer	3	15	0	Payment to be made in London.
The other Daily Papers	4	8	0	
Evening Papers each	2	4	0	
London Journal, weekly	0.	16	0	
London Gazette	2	10	0	

☞ I charge no more when ſent to any part of North Britain or Ireland.

Votes of the Houſe of Commons, &c. &c. very moderately charged.

Letters to be poſt-paid.

*** Permit me to return my beſt thanks for the generous and diſtinguiſhed encouragement I have experienced.

A newsagent's advertisement from *The London Chronicle*, June 3–5, 1777.

mechanical devices. To a less extent they were to depend on better means of communication. The success of *The Star* is said to have been made possible by Palmer's Improved Mail Coach Plan, which was first tried in 1784.[1]

The evening papers had a larger circulation in the country than the morning papers,[2] and were published at 4 or 5

[1] *The Star* was set up by Peter Stuart, brother of Daniel Stuart: 'My elder brother Peter, who started the first daily evening newspaper, the Star, now exactly half a century ago, in consequence of the increased facilities of communication by Palmer's mail-coach plan, then just begun, had written to Burns, offering him terms for communications to the paper, a small salary, quite as large as his Excise-office emoluments', Daniel Stuart, *The Gentleman's Magazine*, New Series, vol. x, July 1838, p. 24.

[2] Trusler, *The London Adviser and Guide* (1786), p. 126, says that the evening papers 'circulated chiefly in the country'.

o'clock,[1] in time to catch the evening posts to places outside the London area. The imprint of *The London Packet* concludes with this note: 'Persons who chuse to be served with This Paper are desired to send their address to the Publisher, W. Woodfall, or to the Clerks of the respective Roads at the Post-Office.' This country circulation helps to account for the comparatively small space given to announcements of entertainments in London. Brief advertisements, or statements, of what was to be seen at the theatres were usually included, and several of the evening papers contained a section of 'theatrical intelligence'; but for a full advertisement of the coming performance at Drury Lane or Covent Garden, the Londoner had to go to a morning daily paper. If he had a copy of *The Public Advertiser* or *The Gazetteer* he had the play-bill—and we can imagine how these papers must have rustled in the theatres. In these days of short theatrical runs, the play for the following day was announced at the close of a performance, and just enough time was left to include the new bill in next morning's paper.

The larger country towns had their own papers, which as a rule appeared once a week. The English provincial Press was the creation of the eighteenth century. Apart from the 'mercuries' which were published in Oxford in the troubles of the previous century, and *The Oxford Gazette*, which began at Oxford in the year of the great plague and was soon to become *The London Gazette*, no paper is known to have been produced outside London till the end of the reign of William III. By the end of the reign of Queen Anne, papers had been started at Norwich (1701), Bristol (1702), Exeter (1707), Worcester (1709), Newcastle (1710), Nottingham (1710), Liverpool (1712), and Stamford (1712). The reign of George I shows a steady development with new papers at Salisbury (1715), Bury St. Edmunds (1716), St. Ives, Hunts. (1716), Canterbury (1717), Cirencester (1718), Plymouth (1718), Leeds (1718), York (1719), Ludlow (1719), Derby (1719), Manchester (1719), Northampton (1720), Ipswich (1720), Chester (1721), Gloucester (1722), Reading (1723), and Maidstone (1725).

Some recognition of the importance of the country papers is to be found in the title-pages of *The Gentleman's Magazine*,

[1] Trusler gives 4 o'clock, and this may be accepted as the earliest time in 1786; the hour had been later, and was still sometimes later.

but the lists there given could not be complete. Birmingham first appears in these lists in the number for November 1742, but the *Magazine*'s most famous contributor had written for *The Birmingham Journal* in 1733. As far as is known, this was Johnson's only direct connexion with the provincial Press.

Though only one of our London newspapers goes back to the last years of Johnson's life, there are several country newspapers now in active circulation which date from his early youth. *The Northampton Mercury* of 1720, *The Gloucester Journal* of 1722, *The Reading Mercury* of 1723, *The Norwich Mercury* so called in 1725, and *The Salisbury Journal* of 1729 have all celebrated their bicentenaries, and, whether or not they have incorporated earlier or later papers, have continued without interruption under the same titles. The only English periodical that can boast a longer life is the official *London Gazette*, the oldest of all existing newspapers. The country newspapers founded in Johnson's middle life were equally numerous. As was to be expected, Bath, Oxford, and Cambridge had their Journal or Chronicle, or their Journal and their Chronicle. Newspapers seem to have sprung up in every town where there was an active printer. Complete runs are seldom found. The office files of *The Northampton Mercury* from 1720 were deposited in 1860 in the Northampton Public Library, which has thus an unbroken set of this local newspaper for over two hundred years. The best run of *Aris's Birmingham Gazette* is, properly, in the Birmingham Reference Library. Many newspapers guard their early numbers in their offices with obstinate piety. But we have often to lament that our knowledge of old papers is derived from odd numbers, or even from lists or descriptions. There were marked differences in the quality of the printing. *Jackson's Oxford Journal* (May, 1753) compares not unfavourably in this respect with any London contemporary—and it offers good hunting to the student of the eighteenth century.

Sunday papers began in March 1780 with *E. Johnson's British Gazette and Sunday Monitor* (commonly called *The Sunday Monitor*), though no number is known of earlier date than July 14, 1782 (No. 121). It was distinguished from other papers only in its first column, which was devoted to a religious or moral article. Within a few years it rose to a circulation of 4,000—'which circumstance', said Mrs. Elizabeth Johnson, 'must give a most pleasing sensation to all Advertising Customers'. Crabbe, who grouped the 'Ledgers, Chronicles, and Posts' in his general satire on the Press, gave it special attention:

> No changing season makes their number less,
> Nor Sunday shines a sabbath on the press!
> Then lo! the sainted MONITOR is born,
> Whose pious face some sacred texts adorn:
> As artful sinners cloak the secret sin,
> To veil with seeming grace the guile within;
> So Moral Essays on his front appear,
> But all is carnal business in the rear;
> The fresh-coin'd lie, the secret whisper'd last,
> And all the gleanings of the six days past.

Two other papers followed during Johnson's lifetime, *The London Recorder, or Sunday Gazette* (sometimes called *The Sunday Recorder*), and *Ayre's Sunday London Gazette* (sometimes called *The Sunday Gazette*); and several more followed before the end of the century. Of all these *The Observer* (1791) alone survives. Johnson is not known to have said anything about Sunday papers, but he probably thought much as Crabbe did.

The usual price of a paper in the reign of Queen Anne had been one penny till August 1, 1712, when a tax of one halfpenny was put on every paper 'contained in half a sheet or any lesser piece of paper', and a tax of one penny on every paper 'larger than half a sheet and not exceeding one whole sheet' (10 Anne, c. 18, § 113).[1] *The Spectator* immediately doubled its price to twopence, and other papers of the same size, such as *The Examiner* and *The Flying Post,* added only the amount of the tax, and sold for 'three halfpence'; and from this time prices were to rise, with new legislation, for the next hundred years, and more. The circulation would appear to have been less affected by the tax than was expected. The weaker papers fulfilled *The Spectator*'s prediction of 'the fall of the leaf', and *The Spectator* itself sold fewer copies; but there is no evidence that English journalism suffered more than a brief check. The impression to be derived from a general

[1] So numbered in *The Statutes of the Realm* (1822), vol. ix; c. 19, § 101 in *The Statutes at Large* (1786), vol. iv.

survey—such as may be obtained from the great collection formed and arranged chronologically by John Nichols, and now in the Bodleian Library—is that the Press was more vigorous under George I than it had been under Anne.

The Act of 1712, which was the basis of newspaper legislation throughout the century, required that the sheets of paper should be stamped at the Head Office while they were still blank. We may be apt to suppose that the stamp was put on the completed newspapers, and not on the unprinted sheets, but the Act leaves no room for doubt; nor does Addison's statement that 'a sheet of Blank Paper . . . must have this Imprimatur clapt upon it, before it is qualified to communicate any thing to the Publick'.[1] Ocular proof is provided by the numerous newspapers in which the stamp is not wholly in the margin: the black print is on the red stamp, and not the stamp on the print. It was a well designed and finely cut stamp. 'Have you seen the red stamp the papers are marked with? Methinks,' said Swift to Stella, 'it is worth a halfpenny, the stamping it.'[2]

The Act took into account only papers of a half-sheet (2 pages) and of a whole sheet (4 pages), and left a loop-hole for a new class of paper consisting of a sheet and a half (6 pages). This was the weekly Journal, which—as has been seen—became common between 1714 and 1720, and was to all appearances so secure in its evasion of the tax that a halfpenny paper was tried for at least ten numbers from November 1724—*The Half-Penny London Journal, or the British Apollo.* New legislation was called for:

And whereas the Authors or Printers of several Journals, Mercuries, and other News-Papers, do, with an Intent to defeat the aforesaid Payments, and in Defraud of the Crown, so contrive as to print their said Journals and News-Papers on one Sheet and Half-Sheet of Paper each, and by that Means they neither pay the aforesaid Duties of one Penny for each Sheet, nor a Half-penny for the Half-Sheet, as by Law they ought to do, but enter them as Pamphlets, and pay only three Shillings for each Impression thereof, whereby his Majesty hath been much injured in his Revenue, and the Printers of other News-Papers, who do regularly pay the said Duties, are great Sufferers thereby: For Remedy whereof, it is hereby enacted and declared, That such Journals, Mercuries, and News-Papers, so printed on one

[1] *The Spectator*, No. 445, July 31, 1712.
[2] *Journal to Stella*, August 7, 1712.

Sheet and Half-Sheet of Paper, shall not for the Future be deemed or taken as Pamphlets to be entred and to pay only three Shillings for each Impression thereof. (11 George I, c. 8, § 13.)

This Act came into force on April 25, 1725, and the Journals of six pages at once ceased. In May they became papers of four pages bearing the stamp, and either remained at their old price of three halfpence or raised it to twopence. In its effort to contain as much as hitherto *Mist's Weekly Journal* won the distinction of being the first paper to give three columns a page (No. 3, May 15, 1725).

Under the Act of 1712 *The Spectator* and *The Examiner* had both been taxed, but the Act of 1725 made it clear that no tax was required on papers which did not contain news. There are no stamps on Johnson's *Rambler*. But it has yet to be explained why *The Rambler* should have been printed in large and well spaced type so as to extend to six pages. A sheet and a half is not the most convenient form for the printer, and we have to ask if he had only the dignity of the publication in view and its suitability to collection in a bound folio. *The Rambler* set a new fashion not only for the essay on moral and social topics, but for the political diatribe. *The Monitor*, *The Briton*, and *The North Briton* all filled six pages. But they are not newspapers, and they are not stamped.

An additional tax of one halfpenny over and above the rate fixed in 1712 was imposed during the Seven Years War on 'every News Paper or Paper containing publick News, Intelligence or Occurrences' (30 George II, c. 19, § 1),[1] and came into force on July 5, 1757, when the leading newspapers raised their price from twopence to twopence halfpenny. A further tax of a halfpenny was made during the American War (16 George III, c. 34, § 7), and from July 5, 1776, to the end of Johnson's life the regular price was threepence. In 1792 it was fourpence, and in 1800 sixpence.

Advertisements in newspapers were taxed by the Act of 1712 at the rate of one shilling each, without regard to their length. The ordinary charge had been twopence a line, or one shilling for eight lines,[2] with a reduction for a larger number,

[1] Since the Act of 1725 was drafted the Magazine had arisen (*The Gentleman's Magazine*, 1731; *The London Magazine*, 1732, &c.). It had escaped the tax though it contained news, and it continued to escape under the Act of 1757.

[2] See Nichols, *Literary Anecdotes*, vol. iv, pp. 80 and 82. *The Generous*

but the charge had to be increased to include the new duty. *The Daily Advertiser* and *The General Advertiser* printed 'advertisements of a moderate length' at two shillings each. From the office file of *The General Advertiser* preserved in the Burney Collection in the British Museum we learn that a moderate length was taken to extend to about 2½ inches of a column. The total receipts for the fifty-one advertisements in the number of this newspaper for March 6, 1744/5, amounted to £5 16*s*., of which £2 11*s*. had to be handed over as duty. By the Act of 1757 the duty was raised to two shillings. Thereafter *The Public Advertiser* (as *The General Advertiser* had then become) announced that 'Advertisements of a moderate Length are taken in at Three Shillings each'. An additional duty of sixpence had to be paid on June 1, 1780 (20 George III, c. 28, § 1), and the price was again advanced. In 1786, according to Trusler's *London Adviser and Guide*, 'advertisements in the front of the morning papers are inserted, if not above 18 lines in length, for 5*s*. 6*d*., in other parts of the paper for 3*s*. 6*d*. In the evening papers the price is 4*s*. each time.'

For the years ending August 2, 1779, 1780, and 1781 the eight leading morning papers paid the following sums in advertisement duty:[1]

	1779			1780			1781		
	£	s.	d.	£	s.	d.	£	s.	d.
Daily Advertiser									
Jossia Jenour .	482	12	0	510	15	0	538	7	6
Daily Gazetteer									
George Redmayne	356	4	0	626	13	6	354	5	6
Public Advertiser									
Henry Woodfall .	833	14	0	666	3	0	564	2	6
Public Ledger									
Thomas Brewman	645	2	0	343	16	0	343	16	0
F. Blith . .	112	0	0	254	14	0	509	17	6[2]
Morning Chronicle									
William Woodfall	595	6	0	710	11	0	555	5	0

Advertiser, 1707, took advertisements 'very cheap, *viz*. after the Rate of 3d. for every Fifty Letters'.

[1] Public Record Office, A.O. 3, 972–4.—The writer is indebted to Mr. J. R. Sutherland.

[2] The double entry for these three years needs explanation, and the second payment of £343 16*s* is suspicious.

	1779			1780			1781		
	£	s.	d.	£	s.	d.	£	s.	d.
Morning Post									
Robert Haswell .	900	8	0	990	9	6	..		
Macleish . .	..			222	15	0	944	17	6[1]
Morning Intelligencer									
William Parker .	476	6	0	721	7	0	159	5	0
Morning Herald									
T. Barr . .	..			..			1,083	10	0

Taken as a whole, the newspapers show a steady increase in the number of their advertisements, but to the end of the century the main profit was expected from sales. Even *The London Chronicle* had advertisements only of books, and very few of these, during its first months. In December 1775 the receipts of *The Public Advertiser* from advertisements varied from £13 14*s.* 6*d.* to £18 9*s.* a day and amounted in the whole month (twenty-six days) to £387 15*s.* 6*d.*; and as £190 8*s.* had to deducted as duty on 1,904 advertisements the sum taken worked out roughly at £197. The sale of 69,975 copies during the month brought in £559 16*s.*, but as £285 14*s.* 8*d.* was paid for the stamps, the surplus from this source was about £274. Of the total income of about £947 quite one-half went to the Exchequer. Little more than £470 remained to meet the costs of production and management for one month.

These were not the days in which great fortunes could be made by the Press. But there can be no doubting the vigour and ability shown in its service, or the range of its interests. Of the four forms of the periodical in Johnson's England—the Newspaper, the Essay-paper, the Magazine, and the Review—four forms which do not always remain distinct, we have been concerned in this chapter only with the first, and with that only as it developed in England. The Scottish Press and the Irish Press fall outside the scope of these volumes. The Essay-paper—which was the creation of the century and hardly survived it—the Magazine, and the Review have all their own history; but all affected the Newspaper, which might combine its 'foreign and domestic intelligence' with essays, serials, notices of books and plays,

[1] The double entry is explained by change of publisher in 1780, when there was also a change of editor.

poetry, music, woodcuts, acrostics. There are few features or habits of modern English journalism which are not discoverable in its direct ancestor in the eighteenth century. The more obvious distinctions are not in spirit or character, but have been induced by scientific discovery and mechanical contrivance.

BIBLIOGRAPHY.—'MARFORIO', *An Historical View of the Principles, Characters, Persons, &c. of the Political Writers in Great-Britain* (1740). JOHN TRUSLER, *The London Adviser and Guide* (1786), pp. 124–6 (2nd ed. 1790). JOHN NICHOLS, *Literary Anecdotes of the Eighteenth Century*, vol. iv (1812), pp. 33–97. C. H. TIMPERLEY, *A Dictionary of Printers and Printing* (1839, revised as *Encyclopaedia of Literary and Typographical Anecdote*, 1842). F. KNIGHT HUNT, *The Fourth Estate* (2 vols., 1750). A. A. ANDREWS, *A History of British Journalism* (2 vols., 1859). CHARLES WENTWORTH DILKE, *The Papers of a Critic* (1875), vol. ii. H. R. FOX BOURNE, *English Newspapers* (2 vols., 1887). MASON JACKSON, *The Pictorial Press* (1885). [J. G. MUDDIMAN], 'Tercentenary Handlist of English and Welsh Newspapers, Magazines and Reviews', *The Times*, 1920. R. S. CRANE and F. B. KAYE, *A Census of British Newspapers and Periodicals, 1620–1800*. (University of North Carolina Press, 1927.) STANLEY MORISON, *The English Newspaper, Some Account of the Physical Development of Journals Printed in London between 1622 and the present day* (Cambridge, 1932).

Other authorities are mentioned in the footnotes.

The writer desires to express his special obligation to the last three books in the above list, and also to the Bibliography (still in type-script) which Mr. Graham Pollard is preparing for the *Cambridge Bibliography of English Literature*.

INDEX

PRINTED IN GREAT BRITAIN AT THE UNIVERSITY PRESS, OXFORD
BY JOHN JOHNSON, PRINTER TO THE UNIVERSITY